In the Vortex of Violence

VIOLENCE IN LATIN AMERICAN HISTORY

Edited by Pablo Piccato, Federico Finchelstein, and Paul Gillingham

1. *Uruguay, 1968: Student Activism from Global Counterculture to Molotov Cocktails*, by Vania Markarian
2. *While the City Sleeps: A History of Pistoleros, Policemen, and the Crime Beat in Buenos Aires before Perón*, by Lila Caimari
3. *Forgotten Peace: Reform, Violence, and the Making of Contemporary Colombia*, by Robert A. Karl
4. *A History of Infamy: Crime, Truth, and Justice in Mexico*, by Pablo Piccato
5. *Death in the City: Suicide and the Social Imaginary in Modern Mexico*, by Kathryn A. Sloan
6. *Argentina's Missing Bones: Revisiting the History of the Dirty War*, by James P. Brennan
7. *In the Vortex of Violence: Lynching, Extralegal Justice, and the State in Post-Revolutionary Mexico*, by Gema Kloppe-Santamaría

In the Vortex of Violence

*Lynching, Extralegal Justice, and the State
in Post-Revolutionary Mexico*

Gema Kloppe-Santamaría

UNIVERSITY OF CALIFORNIA PRESS

University of California Press
Oakland, California

© 2020 by Gema Kloppe-Santamaría

Library of Congress Cataloging-in-Publication Data

Names: Kloppe-Santamaría, Gema, 1979– author.
Title: In the vortex of violence : lynching, extralegal justice, and
   the state in post-revolutionary Mexico / Gema Kloppe-Santamaría.
Other titles: Violence in Latin American history ; 7.
Description: Oakland : University of California Press, [2020] | Series:
   Violence in Latin American history ; 7 | Includes bibliographical
   references and index.
Identifiers: LCCN 2020006463 (print) | LCCN 2020006464 (ebook) |
   ISBN 9780520344020 (cloth) | ISBN 9780520344037 (paperback) |
   ISBN 9780520975323 (ebook)
Subjects: LCSH: Lynching—Mexico—History—20th century.
Classification: LCC HV6471.M6 K56 2020 (print) |
   LCC HV6471.M6 (ebook) | DDC 364.1/34—dc23
LC record available at https://lccn.loc.gov/2020006463
LC ebook record available at https://lccn.loc.gov/2020006464

28 27 26 25 24 23 22 21 20
10 9 8 7 6 5 4 3 2 1

To my mom, Yelbita Balmaceda Vivas

q.e.p.d.

CONTENTS

List of Illustrations   ix
Acknowledgments   xi
Abbreviations   xv

    Introduction   1
    In the Name of Justice: Lynch Mobs and the State in Post-Revolutionary Mexico

1. Between Civilization and Barbarity   15
    Lynching and State Formation in Post-Revolutionary Mexico

2. In the Name of Christ   40
    Lynching and Religion in Post-Revolutionary Mexico

3. The Lynching of Atrocious Criminals   63
    Justice, Crime News, and Extralegal Violence

4. The Lynching of the Wicked   89
    Fat Stealers, Bloodsuckers, and Witches in Post-Revolutionary Mexico

    Conclusion   109
    Lynching Past and Present: Notes on Mexico and Latin America's Trajectory of Violence

    Appendix   117

Notes   121
Bibliography   177
Index   195

ILLUSTRATIONS

MAP

Mexico, with states of Central Mexico highlighted (Puebla, Mexico City, Estado de México)   xvi

FIGURES

1. "El policía asesino, a punto de ser linchado por indignada multitud" (The Murderous Policeman, about to Be Lynched by the Outraged Crowd), *La Prensa*, August 17, 1943   30
2. ¡Muerte al chacal! La multitud pidió al monstruo para lincharlo" (Death to the Jackal! The Crowd Asks for the Monster in Order to Lynch Him), *La Prensa*, April 22, 1943   64
3. "Una multitud quiso linchar a los descuartizadores" (A Crowd Wanted to Lynch the Slaughterers), *La Prensa*, July 30, 1950   76
4. "Hombre fiera que intentó matar a su madre, iba a morir linchado" (Beast-Man Who Tried to Kill His Mother Was Going to Die Lynched), *La Prensa*, June 30, 1941   80
5. "Mujeres indignadas iban a linchar al chacal Santín" (Outraged Women Were Going to Lynch the Jackal Santín), *La Prensa*, January 25, 1944   84

ACKNOWLEDGMENTS

This book was made possible thanks to the support, guidance, and collegiality of many individuals and institutions. I am indebted first and foremost to my husband, Andrew Kloppe-Santamaría, whose love, solidarity, and companionship allowed me to write this book with the energy, focus, and intellectual commitment it demanded. Not only did he read several drafts of the manuscript, but he also discussed with me at length the subject of this book and took care of our baby daughter, Emma, so that I could bring this book to fruition. Without him, this book would not have been possible.

This book began as a doctoral dissertation during my graduate years at the New School for Social Research in New York City. Throughout my doctoral studies I had the support of several institutions. I was a recipient of the Fulbright–García Robles Fellowship and received support from Mexico's National Council of Science and Technology (CONACYT) and Secretariat of Public Education (SEP). At the New School, I was awarded a Dean's Fellowship, a Janey Rothenberg Fellowship, and a Dissertation Fellowship. Archival and on-site research was conducted thanks to the financial support provided by the Janey Program in Latin American Studies at the New School. A pre-doctoral fellowship granted by the Center for U.S.- Mexican Studies at the University of California, San Diego (UCSD), allowed me to complete the writing of the dissertation.

In addition to this institutional support, during my doctoral studies I was fortunate to find inspiration and intellectual guidance from several scholars, many of whom continue to be close colleagues and friends. Pablo Piccato was from the very beginning a mentor, a source of inspiration, and a friend. Our conversations on the nature and character of violence have stayed with me over the years. At the

New School, Federico Finchelstein, Eiko Ikegami, Robin Wagner-Pacifici, Andrew Arato, and Jeremy Varon encouraged me to think of the phenomenon of lynching and its reverberations from a critical, theoretical, and global perspective. My conversations with Michael Pfeifer on the history of lynching in the United States and beyond provided valuable insights and kept reminding me of the importance of bringing to the fore the history of lynching in Mexico and Latin America. At the New School, my colleagues and friends Hadas Cohen and Luis Herrán enriched my time in New York both personally and intellectually. On completion of the dissertation, I was awarded the Charles A. Hale Fellowship by the Latin American Studies Association (LASA) as well as the Albert Salomon Memorial Award in Sociology for best PhD dissertation by the New School.

The transformation of the dissertation into a book manuscript required substantial time, revisions, and original research, as I decided to widen the geographic scope of my dissertation—originally focused on Puebla—and write a history of lynching in post-revolutionary Mexico as a whole. The resources needed for this endeavor were made possible by a 2016 Women in the Humanities Fellowship granted by the Mexican Academy of Sciences. With the support of this award, I was able to work with Fabiola Peinado, an insightful young historian who provided valuable research assistance throughout the development of the book.

The research needed to write this book was carried out during my time as an assistant professor at the Instituto Tecnológico Autónomo de México (ITAM). I am grateful to my colleagues as well as to my former students there, who allowed me to share my work at research seminars and interdisciplinary venues. Special thanks to Rafael Fernández de Castro, Stephan Sberro, Vidal Romero, Catheryn Camacho, Rodrigo Chacón, Isabel Flores, and Juana Gómez. In Mexico City, I also found a wonderful network of scholars whose work on issues of security, violence, and democracy more broadly allowed me to revisit some of my original ideas. These include Andreas Schedler, Luis de la Calle, and Sandra Ley at the Centro de Investigación y Docencia Económica (CIDE); Celia Toro, Mónica Serrano, and Erika Pani at the Colegio de México; and Elisa Speckman, Susana Sosenski, and Martha Santillán at the Instituto de Investigaciones Históricas at the Universidad Nacional Autónoma de México (UNAM).

The writing of this book was made possible by a Visiting Fellowship at the Kellogg Institute for International Scholars at the University of Notre Dame in 2017–18. It provided the space, time, and intellectual environment that was required. I am especially grateful to Jaime Pensado for his friendship and generosity during my time at the Kellogg Institute. Special thanks are also due to Ted Beatty, Karen Graubart, Guillermo Trejo, and Lucía Tascornia for their feedback and suggestions, as well as to Denise Wright and Therese Hanlon, who welcomed me to the Kellogg family. I also want to thank the members of the Mexico

Working Group and of the Kroc-Kellogg Peace, Conflict, Crime and Violence Workshop for providing me with a venue to present and discuss early drafts of this work.

I had the privilege of finishing the writing and editing of this book during my first two years as an assistant professor of Latin American history at Loyola University Chicago. I found in Loyola an incredible group of scholars whose collegiality and support have made me feel at home in Chicago. I am most thankful to Stephen Schloesser who as chair of the history department made sure I had the time to complete this book. I am also thankful for the guidance and friendship I received from my colleagues at Loyola: Alice Weinreb, Edin Hajdarpasic, Suzanne Kaufman, Benjamin Johnson, Michelle Nickerson, Héctor García and especially Timothy Gilfoyle, who has been a wonderful and invaluable mentor.

Throughout the completion of this book and throughout my academic career, I have had the opportunity to be part of a rich network of scholars from a variety of disciplines. Among the community of historians, many of which are "violentólogos" or "criminólogos," I am indebted to Paul Gillingham, Wil Pansters, David Carey Jr., Gladys McCormick, Ben Smith, Ben Fallaw, Mathew Butler, and Andrew Paxman for many conversations, coffees, and conferences. I have benefited also from the stimulating dialogue and exchange with fellow sociologists, anthropologists, and political scientists working on Latin America and beyond, including Desmond Arias, Angelica Durán-Martínez, Cecilia Farfán-Méndez, Nicholas Smith, Javier Auyero, José Miguel Cruz, Jenny Pearce, and Alexandra Abello-Colak.

Outside academia, my friends and family continued to remind me there are greater things in life than the wonders of archival work or studying violence past and present. I am especially thankful to my dear friends Coyolxauhqui Anhder, Adriana Alfaro, Angélica Morales, Jocelyn Pantoja, Aleister Montfort, Héctor Velarde, Alma Luz Beltrán, and Ana Pamanes. I am also grateful for the love and care of my father, Noel Santamaría; my sister, Taryn Santamaría; my nieces, Taryn Lopez Santamaría and Anna-Sophie Kloppe; and my sister-in-law, Alexandra Kloppe. My mother-in-law, Emma Kloppe, allowed me to enjoy the marvels of her love, guidance, and unique wisdom. Her memory will always live among us.

At the University of California Press, I would like to thank Kate Marshall, acquisitions editor, for believing in this project from the beginning, as well as Enrique Ochoa, acting editor, for his careful and dedicated work. My deepest appreciation goes also to the three anonymous reviewers and to Margaret Chowning for their valuable comments and suggestions on the book manuscript. I would also like to thank Marina Vázquez Ramos and Irina Escartín at *La Prensa* for granting me permission to reprint images from the newspaper. Thanks are also due to Joel Rendón, who generously agreed to let me use his beautiful and strong artwork to illustrate the cover of the book.

In the process of writing this book, life kept unfolding with its gifts and losses, its lights and shadows. My daughter, Emma, was born, and with her my life began a new chapter of joy and self-discovery. My mom, Yelbita Balmaceda Vivas, whose unconditional love, dedication, and passion for life will forever shape who I am, left this world. To her, I dedicate this book. Tu bendición estará siempre conmigo mamita linda.

ABBREVIATIONS

ACM   Acción Católica Mexicana (Mexican Catholic Action)
INEGI   Instituto Nacional de Estadística y Geografía (National Institute of Statistics and Geography)
LEAR   Liga de Escritores y Artistas Revolucionarios (League of Revolutionary Writers and Artists)
LNDLR   Liga Nacional Defensora de la Libertad Religiosa (National Defense League for Religious Liberty)
PNR   Partido Nacional Revolucionario (National Revolutionary Party)
PRI   Partido Revolucionario Institucional (Institutional Revolutionary Party)
SEP   Secretaría de Educación Pública (Secretariat of Public Education)
UNS   Unión Nacional Sinarquista (National Synarchist Union)

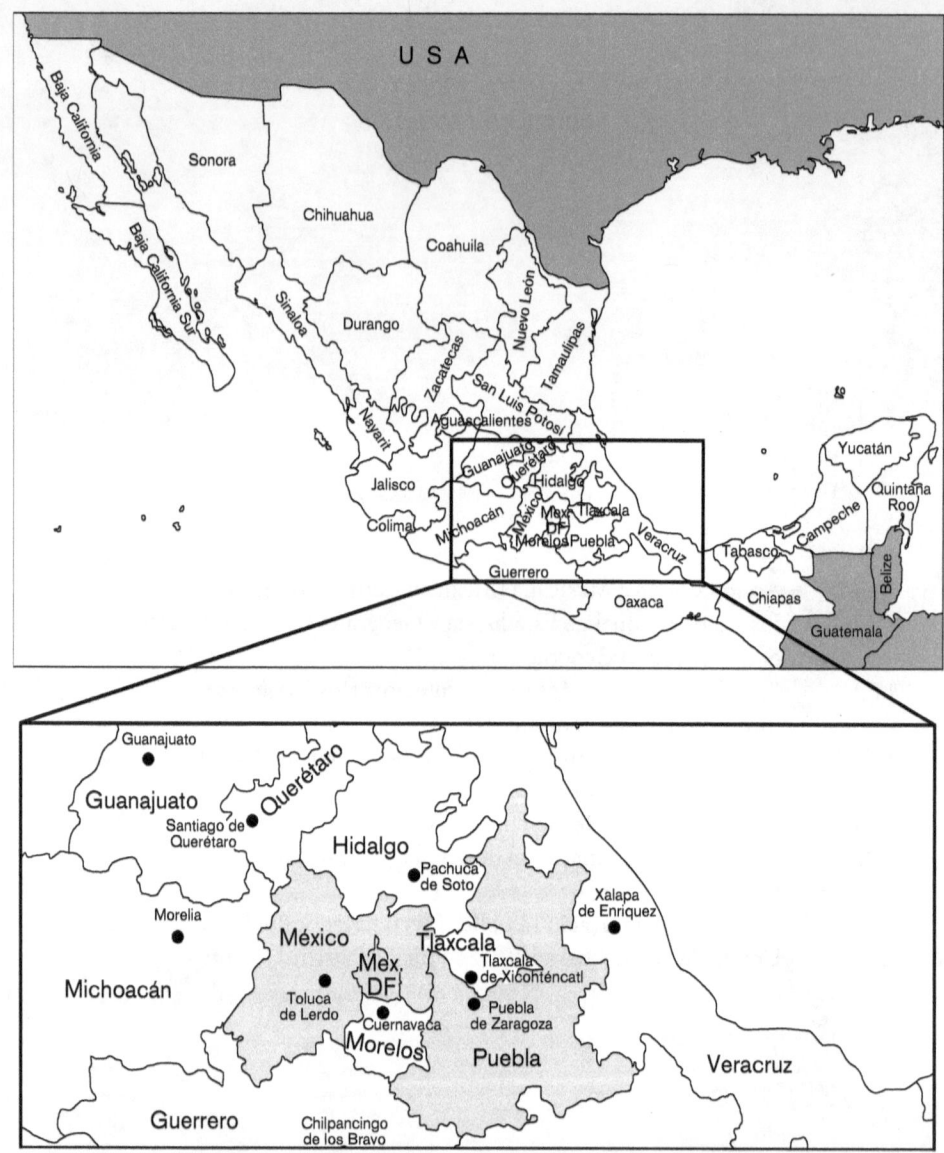

Map of Mexico, with states of Central Mexico highlighted (Puebla, Mexico City, Estado de México). Credit: Original map created by alaznegonzalez, licensed under Creative Commons Attribution-Share Alike 2.0 Unported. This is a reconfigured and redrawn version of the original map. https://commons.wikimedia.org/wiki/File:Mapa_pol%C3%ADtico_de_M%C3%A9xico_a_color_(nombres_de_estados_y_capitales).png.

Introduction

In the Name of Justice: Lynch Mobs and the State in Post-Revolutionary Mexico

On October 19, 2015, a mob of hundreds of people lynched José Abraham and Rey David Copado Molina in the main square of Ajalpan, a town located in the state of Puebla. The municipal police had apprehended the brothers hours earlier, after neighbors accused them of trying to kidnap a little girl. Rumors had been circulating in the town for days about cases of child theft linked to the trafficking of human organs, none of which had been substantiated by police investigations. The brothers, both in their thirties at the time of their death, had allegedly been seen talking to the girl. Questioned by the police, they denied the allegations against them and stated they were pollsters doing a survey on tortilla consumption. Their employer in Mexico City corroborated their claim when contacted by the police, and the alleged victim, joined by her parents at the police station, stated she had never seen the brothers before. Despite evidence of their innocence, a group of neighbors began ringing the church bells, announcing that a collective killing was about to take place. The twenty policemen who were protecting José Abraham and Rey David were quickly outnumbered by the mob, which broke into the police station and then the municipal offices carrying machetes, chains, and metal clubs. The mob dragged the men into the streets and proceeded to beat and torture them and finally burned their already inert bodies in a bonfire made of paper and wood. After the lynching, the mob vandalized the municipal offices and set fire to them and adjacent buildings.

Covered extensively by national and international newspapers, the lynching of José Abraham and Rey David became a symbol of the insecurity and sense of distrust of state authorities that continues to permeate neighborhoods and communities in contemporary Mexico.[1] In a country where 98 percent of murders go unpunished, the case was referred to as an example of the type of violence that citizens were willing to carry out and tolerate in the name of justice. Reflecting on the motivations of the perpetrators and the context that made this lynching possible, a *New York Times* article stated, "Tired of government corruption and indifference, the mob fashioned its own justice, part of a longstanding problem that Mexican officials say is on the rise."[2]

Notwithstanding the attention it received at the time,[3] the lynching of the two men in Ajalpan was not very different from the hundreds of cases that have been reported in the country over the past several decades. Furthermore, the case has important similarities with several instances of mob violence that took place in the first half of the twentieth century, during Mexico's post-revolutionary period. Characterized by an analogous sequence of events, lynchings that took place from the 1930s to the 1950s began with a rumor or accusation transmitted by neighbors or passersby. The tolling of church bells often followed, allowing neighbors to congregate and possibly participate—either as perpetrators or witnesses—in the lynching. After a mob seized the suspect, people gathered in a public space, whether a plaza, a public school, or a church, wherein dozens or even hundreds of individuals beat, hanged, stoned, or burned the victim. The police or local authorities were sometimes present but were not always able or willing to save the victims. If the wrongdoing pertained to an attack against the church or against the Catholic religion, the overt or covert presence of religious authorities during the incident was not uncommon. Although lynchings were by and large local events, journalists contributed to making them known to a wider public.

The attempt to lynch Valentín Moyetón Flores on April 11, 1957, shows how extralegal justice has endured across different periods in Mexico, according to a recognizable script.[4] On that day thousands of people—women, men, and children—gathered in the main square of the neighborhood of Xochimilco in Mexico City with the intention of lynching Valentín. The incident unfolded after a group of neighbors saw Valentín forcing three boys—around eleven or twelve years old—into his automobile. Believing he wanted to kidnap the children, they began to toll the church bells in order to warn others of the presence of the alleged criminal. A large crowd surrounded the man, who escaped the mob and took refuge in the police station. Once there, the crowd demanded that authorities hand over the so-called criminal so they could lynch him. Angered and frustrated, some men started to throw stones into the police station while others vandalized Valentín's automobile. A man who tried to appease the crowd was beaten and stoned. Despite the presence of more than sixty police officers, the police station was severely damaged. Like the two brothers in Ajalpan, Puebla, Valentín Moyetón Flores turned out to be innocent. In an interview with the newspaper *Excélsior*, Valentín stated he was a police officer whose intentions were not to kidnap the children but to take them to the police station after a woman named Carmen López had accused them of robbery.[5]

Despite their sensational character, lynchings are not isolated or anomalous events. Rather, they are recognizable sociological and historical phenomena that can be studied in terms of their motivations, organization, and cultural and political significance. Over the past forty years scholars have documented an increase in the incidence of lynching,[6] with attempted or actual cases reported with greater intensity in the states of central and southern Mexico: Puebla, Estado de México, Mexico City, Oaxaca, Morelos, and Chiapas.[7] In the vast majority of cases, accusations brought against the victims were based on an account provided by a few witnesses, with rumors circulating before or during the event, adding to the frustration and anger that makes the collectivization of violence possible. Although there are considerable variations in these cases, with some involving as many as three hundred or four hundred perpetrators and others fewer than a dozen, all are characterized by the use of collective, brutal, and overt forms of violence.

The occurrence of these acts of violence is at odds with a narrative that celebrates the consolidation of Mexico's democratic institutions as well as its claim to be one of the most thriving global economies.[8] At the same time, incidents of mob violence reflect a darker side of the country's contemporary context, one that involves a pervasively corrupt justice system, high rates of economic inequality, and homicide rates that by most accounts surpass the number of deaths associated with civil war and traditional political conflict.[9]

Mexico is not alone in this seemingly paradoxical path. Most Latin American countries are considered fully functional electoral democracies that are well integrated into the global economy and that possess a vibrant civil society and active citizenry. Nevertheless, most countries continue to struggle with high levels of violence, weak justice systems, and, increasingly, the emergence and proliferation of various forms of vigilante justice.[10] Lynching, in particular, has been on the rise in countries as different as Brazil, Bolivia, Argentina, Ecuador, Guatemala, Venezuela, and Mexico, just to mention some of the most visible and most frequently analyzed cases.[11]

This book defines lynching as a collective, extralegal, public, and particularly cruel form of violence aimed at punishing individuals considered offensive or threatening by a given group or community. In the Latin American context, lynchings are characterized by different levels of ritualization and premeditation and do not necessarily lead to the victim's death.[12] Nonetheless, most of them involve an unusual and excessive use of violence, such as the torture, mutilation, burning, or hanging of the victim in prominent public spaces. In spite of their illegality, lynchings are not considered criminal or unlawful by the perpetrators. Rather they regard their recourse to violence as a legitimate means to attain justice.

In Mexico and other Latin American countries, lynchings are part of broader range of extralegal and collective forms of justice perpetrated by both state and non-state actors, including self-defense forces, death squads, and vigilante groups or organizations.[13] Although new technologies of communication, including the use of cell phones and social media, have transformed the ways in which lynchings are publicized, the tactics of violence used by perpetrators have not undergone any discernible change. These tactics include hanging by a noose—the most identifiable form of lynching in the United States—as well as beating, maiming, stoning, burning, and killing by gunfire.

The occurrence of lynching across different countries in the region reflects the deep-rooted challenges posed by the state's incapacity to uphold the rule of law and citizens' proclivity to endorse undemocratic or uncivil attitudes and values.[14] This book originated in an interest to elucidate Mexico's and Latin America's present-day challenges of violence and insecurity through the lens of lynching. Despite their short-lived character, lynchings are grounded in intracommunity conflicts and historical dynamics that precede and inform their occurrence. As collective responses to an alleged wrongdoing or threat, lynchings also express people's shared notions of deviancy and danger, as well as communities' perceptions of the legitimacy of the state and its capacity to provide citizens with security and justice.

The analysis of lynching allows us to illuminate some of the most pressing questions regarding Latin America's trajectory of violence and state formation: How does the state establish its authority and legitimacy over a given population? How is violence sanctioned, normalized, or contested by the state and by civil society? How are conceptions of crime and danger constructed, and through which mechanisms are they controlled, punished, or disciplined?

Scholarly literature on lynching in Latin America has by and large interpreted this practice as a recent reaction to increasing perceptions of crime, in a context characterized by unequal access to justice and by corrupt or unresponsive state institutions.[15] This book acknowledges the contributions made by this literature but argues also that prevailing interpretations of lynching have fallen short of elucidating the political, cultural, and long-term underpinnings of the practice. By construing lynching as a recent phenomenon, this literature has explained mob violence as an expression of the region's contemporary levels of insecurity and criminality. This has, perhaps inadvertently, precluded scholars from analyzing alternative interpretations concerning the political and cultural motivations of this practice as well as its relation to citizens' understanding of justice.

In the case of Mexico, in particular, scholars have construed lynching as a novel phenomenon whose occurrence and apparent proliferation during the past four decades can be explained by looking at the increase in insecurity and crime, on the one hand, and at the state's incapacity to respond to crime, on the other.[16] All these factors—insecurity, crime, and lack of state response—are often examined against the backdrop of an unfinished process of democratization that, coupled with neoliberal reforms, has allegedly led to the weakening of the state's capacity to control and govern local communities. According to these perspectives, lynching occurs in a context in which state authority is assumed to be absent, weak, or in crisis,[17] or where corporatist relations that belonged to the hegemonic Partido Revolucionario Institucional (PRI; Institutional Revolutionary Party) have been replaced by unruly social spaces and by self-help forms of justice.[18]

By examining Mexico's uncharted history of lynching during the post-revolutionary years (1930s–1950s), a period that laid the foundation for the dynamics of coercion and resistance that followed the establishment of the PRI,[19] *In the Vortex of Violence* brings to the fore a number of alternative political and cultural factors that have shaped the history of this practice in the country and that have been largely underexamined or unexplored.

Through an examination of more than three hundred cases of lynching and attempted lynching,[20] I trace how this practice, instead of signaling state absence, was triggered by the presence of state authorities that were nonetheless perceived by communities as insufficient or incapable of providing the type of justice people deemed appropriate or necessary to punish transgressions.[21] I suggest that lynching reflected the dynamics of coercion, resistance, and negotiation that characterized citizens' encounters with state authorities at the local level. In this respect, lynching constituted a means to resist the encroachment of the state in given communities, but it also echoed the use of coercive and extralegal forms of social control perpetrated with the consent and overt participation of public authorities— from mayors to police officers and military personnel. In addition, lynching reflected the dynamics of negotiation and accommodation between citizens and state authorities (in particular, police officers) in regard to the provision of security and the administration of justice.

In addition to examining the ways in which lynching was shaped and contributed to shaping citizens' interactions with the state, this book traces the manifold behaviors, practices, and beliefs that precipitated lynching. It shows that instances of mob violence were triggered by perceptions and representations of wrongdoers as individuals who deserved to be punished by physical, swift, and extralegal means. In this sense, rather than crime levels per se, it was discourses and representations surrounding crimes and suspected wrongdoers that drove support for this practice.[22] The book also points to the importance of religion in the collectivization of violence. Folk or popular strands of Catholicism, in particular, provided the ideological grounds to justify collective assaults against socialists, communists, Protestants, and impious individuals whose conduct was considered offensive or threatening to the spiritual and political order of communities. Mythical beliefs and accusations made against individuals associated with figures such as fat suckers and witches further contributed to the collectivization of violence in post-revolutionary Mexico. Taken together, these elements illuminate the deeper political, cultural, and sociological factors that shaped the trajectory of mob violence in Mexico.

LYNCHING IN MEXICO'S POST-REVOLUTIONARY PERIOD

Violence is a historical rather than static or predetermined phenomenon. As such, a central question informing this work is why lynching continued to occur with considerable frequency during a period otherwise characterized by greater political stability and lower levels of violence. The period from the 1930s through the 1950s signaled a distinct moment in Mexico's process of state formation and consolidation. By 1930, the country had formally transitioned from civil war to peace, leaving behind two armed conflicts, the 1910 Revolution[23] and the Cristero War (1926–29),[24] and attaining a greater level of institutionalization, centralization, and socioeconomic development. Especially after the mid-1940s, the country experienced an overall decline in levels of homicide, with state-sponsored forms of violence becoming more covert, selective, and institutionalized.[25] In such a context, why did people resort to this form of overt violence? And in a period that witnessed the abolishment of the death penalty, why did citizens support a practice that entailed cruel, extralegal, and often deadly forms of punishment?[26]

The answer to these questions is far from obvious. The continuity of this practice seems paradoxical when examined against Mexico's own trajectory of violence during this period, as well as when it is put into comparative perspective. Mexico's northern neighbor, the United States, had witnessed the occurrence of close to four thousand cases of lynching during the second half of the nineteenth century and the first decades of the twentieth century.[27] By the 1930s, however, the number of lynchings in the United States—most of them driven by racial prejudice as well as by "rough" conceptions of justice—had significantly decreased and were counted in the dozens.[28] Shifting public attitudes toward extralegal violence, greater state capacity and willingness to prosecute these acts, and compromise among political elites that held opposing views on lynching have all been offered as viable explanations for this decline.[29] Why did Mexico follow such a different path, a path that translated into the persistence of this practice throughout the post-revolutionary period and beyond?

In the Vortex of Violence does not aim to offer a comparative analysis of lynching in Mexico and the United States. It does, however, seek to underscore the manifold beliefs, ideologies, and practices that contributed to Mexico's particular path of mob violence during the formative years of the post-revolutionary period. In so doing, the book contributes to advancing an understanding of lynching as a global phenomenon rather than as an American exception at the same time that it recognizes that place and time matter as variables that shape the meanings, practices, and dynamics of power linked to lynching.[30]

Centered on the different sources of legitimation that contributed to rendering lynching an acceptable, necessary, and even moral response to conduct considered threatening or offensive by given communities,³¹ *In the Vortex of Violence* covers three decades that were instrumental in the formation and consolidation of Mexico's post-revolutionary state. During the 1930s Mexican elites tried to provide cohesion and stability to a country that had been torn by civil war and political conflict during the 1910 Revolution and the Cristero War. Under Lázaro Cárdenas's presidency (1934–40), in particular, central elites promoted a capitalist model of development that incorporated land redistribution programs, cultural policies, and the mobilization and integration of teachers, workers, and peasants into a network tightly controlled by the recently founded Partido Nacional Revolucionario (PNR; National Revolutionary Party). Despite these official efforts to modernize and unify the nation, communities' opposition and resistance to the state's sponsored programs undermined the regime's stability and forced elites to reconsider their policies, particularly in regard to religion and the advancement of socialist ideas. The Second Cristiada, also known as La Segunda (ca. 1934–38), considered a sequel to the Cristero War, crystallized the opposition generated by the cultural and social transformations promoted by the post-revolutionary state.³²

The 1940s and 1950s signaled a moment of greater political and economic stability in the country, at least at the national level and from a macroeconomic perspective. Under the presidencies of Manuel Ávila Camacho (1940–46) and Miguel Alemán Valdés (1946–52), the country deepened its model of capitalist development by fostering foreign investment, industrialization via import substitution, and the creation of monopolistic businesses.³³ These policies, facilitated by the advent of World War II and the opportunities opened for Mexico in the global market, resulted in Mexico's "economic miracle": a steady GDP growth at low inflation rates across the two decades.³⁴ Politically, the regime moved away from the more radical and social promises of the Mexican Revolution and promoted instead a message of unity, reconciliation, and discipline based on an anticommunist, nationalistic, and conservative ideology.

This narrative of macroeconomic growth and social unity was, however, contradicted by the realities of economic inequality, social unrest, and political protest that affected most people during these decades. Macroeconomic growth primarily benefited a small economic elite composed of foreign investors, domestic bankers, and industrialists who enjoyed the protection and support of the government. In contrast, the real incomes of both rural and urban workers declined, the peasantry was economically and politically marginalized, and urban workers were continuously repressed.³⁵ Teachers, students, electricians, railway workers, and rioters actively protested against food shortages, price increases, political repression, and corruption. In the countryside, resistance to the government gave rise to peasant movements, popular protests, and even armed rebellion.³⁶ Thus, in spite of the overall decline in homicide rates at the national level that began in the 1940s, these decades were far from representing the idealized "pax priísta" that has traditionally been associated with these years.³⁷

Lynchings in post-revolutionary Mexico both reflected and contributed to the manifold transformations the country experienced during these decades. They articulated the discontent and distrust generated by the modernization policies promoted by the state, including secularization, land distribution, sanitation programs, and conscription campaigns. Lynchings also reflected the anxieties and fears provoked by the rapid process of urbanization that went hand in hand with demographic growth, the introduction of modern machinery and infrastructure, and increasing perceptions of crime in a context in which *nota rota* (crime news) stories took on a central role in shaping people's sense of security.[38]

The fact that the history of lynching is intimately connected to the processes of modernization and urbanization the country experienced during these years hints at the fact that mob violence was not an expression of some atavistic custom or tradition. Lynchings did not take place in communities that were isolated, backward, or freed from the interventions and changes promoted by the central state and the advent of capitalism. Even when lynching expressed a rejection of the modernization project promoted by the state, it was not "premodern" but the result of communities' exposure to modernity. The surge in lynching in the American South at the turn of the century followed a similar logic: mob violence against African Americans during this period did not signal southern communities' isolation from modern institutions but their "uncertain and troubled transformation into modern, urban societies."[39]

In Mexico's post-revolutionary period, lynching did not simply express a rejection of the state's modernization project; it also called into question the character and reach of the project itself. The state's capacity or incapacity to provide justice and security to citizens was central to the organization and legitimation of lynching. The endemic corruption that characterized the judicial system, the systematic abuse of force by the police, and the high levels of impunity that persisted across this period all contributed to citizens' understanding of lynching as a legitimate form of justice. Although evidence suggests the weakness of the justice system emanated from budgetary limits, poor training and equipment, and problems of institutional design, lack of institutional capacity alone does not explain the state's failure to deliver justice.[40] Instead, the elites' interest in pursuing and maintaining political power by legal and illegal means determined the high levels of impunity characterizing the country.

Political elites actively promoted and benefited from politicized forms of policing, selective law enforcement, and the use of repression and torture against suspected criminals and political dissidents. Furthermore, even if they originated in economic or institutional limitations, the practices of judges and police officers became over time an integral part of how these bureaucracies functioned and of how citizens expected them to work.[41] In other words, corruption and abuse of force became structural and systemic rather than exceptional or abnormal.

Citizens' perception of the police as corrupt, abusive, and prone to bend the law translated into people's understanding of swift and extralegal forms of violence as an acceptable and preferable means to attain justice. This belief materialized in citizens' support of lynching but also in people's approval of the so-called *ley fuga,* or law of flight. Defined as the killing of suspected criminals upon their alleged attempt to escape the law, the ley fuga was neither a law nor a legal practice despite its name.[42] It was an extrajudicial form of violence perpetrated by state actors. That people's support of lynching intersected with citizens' approval of the ley fuga suggests these two practices were perceived by citizens as part of a continuum of methods to punish criminals outside the law.[43] Moreover, that some attempted lynchings ended up in the ley fuga and vice versa points to the fact that authorities and citizens could be complicit in their support of extralegal forms of punishment.

MAIN ARGUMENTS

My main arguments center on the sources of legitimation, the logics of power, and the patterns of continuity and change that characterized lynching during the 1930s through 1950s. The term "sources of legitimation" refers to the set of beliefs that rendered lynching an acceptable or even preferable form of punishment in the eyes of perpetrators, witnesses, and citizens at large. "Logics of power" refers to the ways in which lynching intersected with ideologies and practices that served to exclude and control people who were at the margins of society or who were considered external or threatening to the dominant values observed by given communities. Rather than situate lynching unequivocally on the spectrum of bottom-up or top-down expressions of violence, the notion of logics of power allows us to illuminate the different and at times contradictory dynamics of exclusion and domination that gave rise to and were produced by lynching.

Regarding its sources of legitimation, I argue that lynching was grounded on people's view of state authorities as abusive, intrusive, and ultimately incapable of providing the type of punishment they deemed appropriate to attain justice. It was furthermore driven by religious beliefs and practices, perceptions of crime and criminals, and the fear and scapegoating generated by accusations of witchcraft and mythical beliefs.

Theoretically, the book advances the notion that public attitudes and publicly articulated sentiments in support of collective forms of violence ought to be taken seriously if we aim to understand the persistence of this practice. Even if such public attitudes cannot be equated, in any linear or simple way, with the occurrence of lynching, they provided the *conditions of possibility* of lynching. Inasmuch as these beliefs and ideologies were held to be true or valid by perpetrators and by the public at large, they provided the grounds to distinguish lynching from plain murder, thus adding to its tenacity and overall impunity.[44]

In addition to examining the sources of legitimation of lynching, the book offers an analysis of the contentious politics and power dynamics that surrounded the organization of lynching. In spite of their ephemeral character, lynchings were informed by and contributed to political vendettas and intracommunity conflicts that existed in the towns or localities where these events took place.

In contrast to the literature on lynching in contemporary Latin America that has described lynching as a "weapon of the weak,"[45] the historical evidence presented by this book shows that most lynch mobs targeted people considered at the fringes of society, individuals whose beliefs and practices placed them outside the boundaries of what communities deemed acceptable or tolerable.[46] Moreover, among those who supported lynching we can identify figures of authority—from local priests to mayors and police officers.[47] Still, lynchings were also perpetrated against some of these very same figures of authority. Police officers, mayors, caciques, and even a few military men were, at different points in time and with different degrees of intensity, targeted by lynch mobs.

Lynchings also defied traditional gendered notions of victimization centered on representations of women as passive victims. With the exception of lynchings driven by accusations of witchcraft, mob violence involved by and large the victimization of men.[48] Women who were accused of witchcraft and attacked by lynch mobs did not embody an ideal of female docility but rather defied notions of submissiveness, domesticity, and motherly care. Perpetrators, in turn, involved both men and women, with a few cases actually being organized either exclusively or primarily by women.[49] In light of these examples, it can be argued that lynchings were as much a weapon of the oppressed as they were of the powerful.

To make sense of the paradoxes of lynching, I focus on the politics and logics of power that shaped and were shaped by lynching within communities themselves. In this sense, I argue that lynchings were, overall, defensive in character and aimed at preserving communities' dominant values, beliefs, and practices.[50] Whether in the form of communities' resistance to the encroachment of the state into local affairs, people's rejection of communist ideologies and practices, or citizens' violent responses to crimes, lynchings reflected people's attempts to safeguard the political, economic, and religious status quo of their communities. As such, despite lacking the strong racial connotations of lynching in the United States, mob violence in Mexico, as in the United States, was a tool of social control.[51]

In terms of the historical trajectory of lynching, I identify patterns of both continuity and change during the period under study. The most significant pattern of change has to do with the decline during the last years of the 1940s in the occurrence of lynchings perpetrated against those state actors that represented the so-called modernizing forces of the state. Such state actors included socialist teachers but also alcohol inspectors, tax collectors, health officials, and engineers in charge of developing public works or promoting agrarian reform. This shift was the result of a process of resistance and accommodation that contributed to both modulating the state's encroachment into local affairs and rendering that presence more acceptable or desirable in the eyes of the governed.

In terms of continuities, I document the persistence of lynchings motivated by religious beliefs, perceptions of crime, and mythlike fears, as well as feelings of animosity and distrust toward individuals who were, either de jure or de facto, responsible for enforcing social control at the local level. In other words, I show how, despite the changes experienced by the country throughout these years, lynchings continued to be seen as a legitimate means to punish individuals considered threatening or offensive by neighbors and townsfolk.

By going beyond a "state-centered" and "center-centered" understanding of power and state making, the history of lynching in post-revolutionary Mexico reveals how changes observed at the national level followed a different path and pace at the local level and "in arenas outside of formal politics."[52] The persistence of lynchings of mayors, police officers, and caciques beyond the 1940s and well into the 1950s shows that violence was far from being centralized, institutionalized, or subdued in any stable way. Along the same lines, the continuation of lynchings motivated by perceptions of crime reveals that, despite the formal abolition of the death penalty, communities continued to support the use of extralegal violence in order to punish individuals perceived as dangerous or immoral.

The tenacity of lynchings driven by Catholic beliefs during the 1940s and 1950s further illuminates how, despite the so-called détente that emerged between the state and the Catholic Church during these years, people on the ground continued to view mob violence as a necessary means to defend the spiritual and moral integrity of their communities. The lynching of witches and other so-called mythical beings throughout the period under study suggests that despite, or rather *because* of, the rapid economic and technological changes brought about by the federal state, communities found in mythical narratives a means to resolve communal anxieties and ward off large-scale social transformations.

Geographically, the book provides evidence of lynching as a national phenomenon rather than a regional rarity. Despite the press's tendency to represent lynching as a practice carried out by backward, ignorant, and geographically isolated communities, evidence suggests that lynching occurred both in rural and remote communities and in politically and economically integrated urban neighborhoods and localities.[53] Contrary to some newspaper journalists and public officials who suggested an implicit relation between lynching and indigenous communities, lynching was not an expression of indigenous "traditions" but a reaction to conduct that was considered offensive by indigenous and nonindigenous populations alike.[54]

Historical sources do suggest a specific regional pattern, however, with states located in central Mexico occupying a prominent place in the history of this practice. According to this "geography of lynching," most cases of lynching and attempts at lynching in post-revolutionary Mexico are concentrated in Mexico City, Puebla, and Estado de México.[55] As these localities were among the most populated in the country at the time, it is not necessarily surprising that the occurrence of lynching was concentrated in them.[56]

On the other hand, the geographic distribution of lynching and its concentration in these places might reflect the dynamics of representation that characterized some of the historical sources used by this study.[57] National newspapers were a key source for tracing the historical trajectory of lynching in post-revolutionary Mexico. Printed for the most part in Mexico City, these newspapers tended to report on cases taking place in the capital, either because of the greater availability of reporters or correspondents there or because of the greater attention given to violent crimes taking place in the "core" areas of the country rather than in the periphery.[58] Lynchings chronicled in security reports, letters, and telegrams produced or received by government agencies were also characterized by these dynamics of representation. That is to say, lynchings presented by these sources were also, for the most part, connected to political conflicts or disputes that had to do with federal policies or programs. The geography of lynching identified in this book is thus inevitably framed, and limited, by the sources consulted, in very much the same way that past and present studies on crime and violence in Latin America have been.[59]

THE ORGANIZATION OF THIS BOOK

The book is organized thematically, drawing on the different sources of legitimation—politics, religion, crime constructs, and mythical beliefs—that made lynching an acceptable and legitimate form of violence. Each chapter covers cases that took place from the 1930s through the 1950s. Chapters 1 and 2 follow a more traditional chronological order, and chapters 3 and 4 privilege a more thematic narrative or structure.

Chapter 1 examines the impact of Mexico's post-revolutionary process of state formation on the persistence and legitimacy of lynching. It analyzes lynching as an expression of the discontent and divisions produced by the modernization and centralization projects promoted by central elites. In addition, it situates lynching against the backdrop of the multiple forms of illegal, public, and overt violence that were either tolerated or promoted by public officials at the local level. The chapter demonstrates that the encroachment of the post-revolutionary state into communal life, together with the abusive behavior of public officials, contributed to the occurrence of lynching. It further calls into question a narrative that portrayed the Mexican state as a "civilizing force" that was meant to incorporate "barbaric" or "uncivilized" communities.

Chapter 2 analyzes the impact that religion had on the organization and legitimacy of lynching. It looks at the importance of religious images, artifacts, and spaces for Catholics' spiritual and ritualistic experience of religion. The defense of these religious symbols by laypeople and clergy alike acquired a particularly belligerent character during the second half of the 1930s, particularly in the face of state-sponsored anticlerical and iconoclast campaigns. The chapter also examines the Catholic Church's promotion of a conservative and reactionary worldview that rejected the influence of other religious creeds as well as progressive ideologies. This worldview, which became particularly dominant during the 1940s and 1950s, provided the basis for rationalizing the lynching of communists, socialists, and Protestants in the name of the community and the motherland. The chapter furthermore shows that antigovernment parish priests were central in shaping Catholics' predisposition to violence.

Chapter 3 analyzes how public understandings of crime and justice contributed to shaping the acceptability of lynching so-called criminals. Based primarily on the examination of crime news, the chapter shows how the use of swift and extralegal forms of justice, such as lynching, was justified based on the purported gravity of the crime and the perceived ineffectiveness of the country's justice system. In this sense, even when public opinion acknowledged the brutal and uncivil character of lynching, it nevertheless portrayed this practice as a reasonable means to deal with crimes and criminals considered immoral, barbaric, and inhumane. Crimes that prompted lynchings were not limited to murder or to offenses that threatened a person's physical well-being such as rape, battery, and assault. Rather, they included more inconsequential crimes such as robberies of small items. Despite this, the press for the most part presented lynching as a justifiable way to deal with criminals.

Chapter 4 explores the role that mythical beliefs played in the collectivization of violence. In particular, it looks at how lynching was justified as a means to get rid of otherworldly powers and danger posed by witches and other wicked beings. Although victims of these lynchings were linked to supernatural doings and events, accusations made against them reflected rather earthly preoccupations. The lynching of so-called bloodsuckers and fat stealers, for instance, revealed anxieties regarding modernization processes that often entailed the presence of people who were external to the community and who were perceived as exploitative and deceitful. The collective killing of witches, on the other hand, was informed by envy, personal vendettas, and intracommunal conflicts, including political differences. Women who occupied positions of power were particularly susceptible to witchcraft accusations, reflecting the importance of gender in the dynamics of social control characterizing these cases.

The conclusion brings to the fore the ways in which the history of lynching in post-revolutionary Mexico contributes to our understanding of the political, cultural, and social motivations behind this practice. It furthermore situates this work within Mexico's growing historiography on violence and state formation as well as within a broader literature dealing with Latin America's history of violence and crime.

1

Between Civilization and Barbarity

Lynching and State Formation in Post-Revolutionary Mexico

In the last scene of Emilio Fernández's film *Maclovia* (1948), the two protagonists, José María and Maclovia, are chased by a mob of enraged villagers carrying torches. Encircled and with nowhere to go, José María and Maclovia embrace each other as the mob, including women and the elderly, throw stones with the clear intention of lynching them. As the dramatic music rises, the leading characters, who like the rest of villagers are presented as Tarascan Indians, are saved by a group of soldiers from the Federal Army headed by Cabo Mendoza. In perfect synchrony, the soldiers raise their bayonets and fire shots into the air. Cabo Mendoza, standing between the mob and the terrified couple, admonishes the crowd, "Your traditions, or whatever those are, have made you commit a great injustice! But the troops will give protection to these two innocents so they can leave Janitzio. There is a canoe there. Let's get out of here!" The camera then shows the couple leaving the town, dark and full of flaming torches, behind and navigating into a clear horizon.

As suggested by this closing scene, *Maclovia* juxtaposes the unruly, communal, and savage violence of the Indian crowd to the disciplined, bureaucratic, and modern Mexican state.[1] Representative of the *indigenista* films directed by Fernández,[2] *Maclovia* offers a window into the visual and discursive repertoire that shaped the portrayal of the post-revolutionary state during the Golden Age of Mexican cinema.[3] In particular, it sheds light on the ways in which the state came to be imagined as a civilizing force that, through its cultural and economic policies as well as its legal use of force, had the mission to incorporate and modernize communities that would otherwise be trapped in ignorance, poverty, and religious fanaticism.[4]

The reference to lynching in this and other influential films of the period is not accidental.[5] As a collective, public, and communal form of violence, lynching fitted nicely into a narrative that opposed the modernizing impetus of the state to the backwardness and so-called barbarity of communities that were, for the most part, rural.[6] An yet an analysis of lynching set against the background of the many expressions of violence perpetrated by state authorities and public officials during the post-revolutionary years reveals that such a dichotomous narrative of state formation—one that construes the state as modern and communities as unruly and backward—is problematic and, ultimately, wrong.

The aim of this chapter is to examine the impact that Mexico's process of state formation had on the organization and legitimation of lynching in the 1930s through 1950s. "State formation" refers to the ongoing process of negotiation and institutionalization that allows the state to be recognized by citizens as the ultimate source of authority, sovereignty, and legitimate use of violence.[7] It refers to the interplay between an emerging authority and communities of people that are incorporated into a larger political association. Understood as a historical process, rather than as a fait accompli, the process of state formation involves both the development of the state's institutional and material capacities and the creation of a cultural and symbolic repertoire that serves to render the state's authority both legitimate and desirable in the eyes of the governed.[8] In this sense, the process of state making is neither unilateral nor entirely coercive. Rather, it is relational, negotiated, and evolving in light of communities' attitudes of compliance or resistance vis-à-vis the encroachment of the state.[9]

To understand the impact of Mexico's process of state building in the organization and legitimation of lynching, I look at several modalities of lynching that involved state actors and local authorities, either as victims or as perpetrators. Although not all cases of lynching involved public officials or figures of authority in post-revolutionary Mexico, the cases that relate to such actors allow me to elucidate with greater clarity the linkages between state formation and lynching. In particular, they allow me to bring to the fore the dynamics of negotiation, resistance, and coercion characterizing the country's process of state building.

The lynchings analyzed in this chapter involved officials and powerful figures who represented the federal state and its projects (e.g., soldiers, rural teachers, and health inspectors), as well as officials or strongmen who embodied localized forms of authority (e.g., mayors, municipal police officers, and town caciques).[10] The chapter thus captures two manifestations of authority (federal and local) that, although seemingly distant in terms of their functions and manifestations, had a significant impact on the makings of the post-revolutionary state.[11]

In general terms, there are three modalities of lynching that can be identified: lynching as resistance, lynching as corrective justice, and state-sanctioned lynching. Each one of these modalities reveals particular patterns of resistance and negotiation between communities and the state, as well as specific patterns of hegemony and coercion on behalf of state actors.[12]

The first modality—lynching as resistance—entails the lynching of state actors who represented the state's efforts to modernize and secularize local communities. In this case, lynching emerges as a means to resist the encroachment of the post-revolutionary state into communal life as well as a means to assert communities' right to decide matters such as education, religion, sanitation, and land distribution. Under this modality, lynching resembles the type of defensive politics that informed the pre-revolutionary riots of eighteenth- and nineteenth-century Mexico.[13] Similarly, this modality of lynching includes instances of mob violence precipitated by people's attempt to defend communities' status quo as well as to reaffirm the legitimacy of local traditions over the norms and practices promoted by the central state.

The second modality—lynching as corrective justice—corresponds to lynchings that targeted officials and power figures that were either de jure or de facto responsible for enforcing social control within communities and neighborhoods.[14] These include attacks against soldiers, police officials, mayors, and caciques either because they had abused their authority or because, in the eyes of the community, they had unjustly punished a wrongdoer. Inasmuch as they reflected communities' propensity to assert their right to enforce social control through their own means and according to their own criteria, these lynchings share some of the defensive elements of the first modality. However, they are distinct in that they did not reflect communities' rejection of the authority of these officials per se. Rather, they signaled people's discontent with the behavior of specific officials who had, in their view, abused their power or somehow violated the unwritten rules of acceptable behavior.[15] In this sense, rather than being purely defensive, these lynchings were meant as a "corrective" to the behavior of these actors.

The third modality—state-sanctioned lynching—refers to lynchings perpetrated by, or in conjunction with, state authorities, mainly mayors but also soldiers and police officers. These cases entailed the killing of so-called criminals or political enemies through the use of visible and cruel forms of torment; or, in other cases, the collaboration of public officials and citizens who, in the face of an alleged criminal or wrongdoer, considered lynching an appropriate and legitimate form of punishment. The involvement of public officials and representatives of "law and order" in the organization and execution of these lynchings shows that state officials were far from being the purveyors of a "civilization process,"[16] as they themselves sanctioned the use of mob violence to punish suspected criminals. As I discuss in greater depth in chapter 3, the police were at times able or willing to save criminals from the lynch mob. However, their selective support of mob violence, together with their regular use of other extralegal means of punishment—such as the ley fuga—demonstrate that they were not foreign to the use of "barbarous" and "uncivilized" forms of violence.

Taken together, these three modalities of lynching allow me to make two general arguments about the impact of Mexico's process of state building on lynching.

First, they show that the encroachment of the post-revolutionary state into communal life, together with the behavior of public officials that was considered abusive or intrusive, contributed to the incidence of lynching. In this sense, counter to what classic sociological theories would predict, the greater presence of state authorities at the local level did not bring about a decrease in extralegal, overt, and public forms of violence such as lynching. Rather, it was conducive to its occurrence as well as to its legitimation in the eyes of perpetrators who perceived state authorities as intrusive or unfair. Second, these modalities of lynching, particularly the third one, highlight the fact that mob violence was not averted by public officials but was actually promoted as a form of governance and social control. Surely, central elites were quick to dismiss the violence promoted by mayors and municipal police officers as another sign of the backwardness of rural communities.[17] However, rather than reflect communities' so-called atavistic traditions, these instances of mob violence were symptomatic of the ways in which state authority was forged at the local level with the acquiescence of state and federal elites.[18]

The chapter is divided into three sections, each discussing in turn the three modalities of lynching. The analysis of cases of lynching across these decades allows me to identify patterns of continuity and change in this practice during two periods (the 1930s and the 1940s–1950s) that signaled two distinct moments in Mexico's process of state making.[19] In my concluding remarks, I reflect on how the occurrence of mob violence across these years might challenge or confirm some of the assumptions underpinning the characterization of these periods.

LYNCHING AS RESISTANCE

In March 1935, the press reported the lynching of a teacher, David Moreno Herrera, in Aguascalientes, by an "infuriated populace." The lynch mob dragged him out of his house and set fire to his furniture and books. It then beat him with clubs and gun butts, leaving his dead body hanging from a tree.[20] In 1936, a similar incident took place, this time in the town of Tzintzuntzan, Michoacán. Provoked by a fight between the school's director and a resident of the town, a group of villagers rang the church bells and proceeded to surround the school armed with pistols and stones. The villagers torched the school's doors and then shot its director. The teachers were saved by the arrival of federal troops from Pátzcuaro.[21] In July the same year, another violent attack on a teacher took place.[22] On the road from Chilchotla to Tecamachalco, in Puebla, more than fifteen men armed with clubs and pistols lynched Manuel Hurtado de Mendoza. Although the man survived, he was left seriously injured. The press lamented the victimization of yet another teacher despite the strong campaign promoted by the government to make people understand the "high mission" of the socialist school at which he worked.

From 1934 to 1940, armed vigilantes and lynch mobs assailed dozens of female and male teachers throughout Mexico, including Puebla, Michoacán, Jalisco, Querétaro, Veracruz, Aguascalientes, Guanajuato, Morelos, and Chiapas.[23] Considered an expression of the Second Cristiada (1934–38), these attacks were precipitated by the enactment of a new educational policy promoted by the federal government that, based on article 3 of the constitution, mandated that education would be socialist and conducive to the "defanaticization" of religious believers. Socialist education was central to Mexico's process of state making during the 1930s. Through its implementation, central elites sought to modernize rural and indigenous communities and integrate them into the national economy. They furthermore aimed to promote a new type of citizen, one who was productive, rational, sober, and patriotic.[24]

The creation of the Secretaría de Educación Pública (SEP; Secretariat of Public Education) in 1921 had established the basis for a nationwide educational policy that involved the development of public schools in rural communities.[25] However, the goals of socialist education proved to be more ambitious and contentious. The federal government intended to undermine the influence of the Catholic Church at the local level by implementing cultural missions and revolutionary festivals that were overtly anticlerical and even iconoclastic.[26] Moreover, through this model of education and with the support of socialist teachers, the central elites sought to implement agrarian reform as well as to promote hygiene and health care programs, including the government's antialcohol campaigns,[27] which were perceived as highly politicized by local communities and were thus often met with overt and covert forms of resistance.[28]

As I discuss at greater length in chapter 2, socialist education threatened both the spiritual and the material dimensions of Catholics' exercise of religion, including the observance of religious rituals, the authority of parish priests within the community, and parents' "natural" right to educate their children. The anticlerical and iconoclastic actions carried out in the name of socialist education, which included the burning of religious images as well as the use of churches as stables, left a deep mark on communities that regarded the profanation of sacred images and spaces as an assault on their spiritual integrity.[29] Moreover, through its defense of the government's agrarian reform, socialist education upset the interests of political and economic elites, which were often in tune with those of the Catholic Church. Accordingly, it was teachers' meddling in both political and religious affairs that prompted violent forms of resistance.[30]

Aware of the centrality of educational policies in expanding and legitimating the state's presence at the local level, the federal government tried to publicize and support the work of teachers as well as to honor their sacrifice. The dissemination of public art centered on the various assaults perpetrated against teachers was one way to do this. In 1939, for instance, the SEP supported the publication of a collection of lithographs created by the graphic artist Leopoldo Méndez.[31] Under the title

In the Name of Christ... they have murdered 200 teachers, each lithograph depicted vividly the murder of a rural teacher at the hands of people who opposed socialist education.³² Informed by newspaper reports published at the time and letters of complaint that workers and teachers sent to federal authorities, Méndez portrayed the various forms of torment endured by teachers.³³ One of the prints, for instance, depicts the killing of Ramón Orta del Río in the town of Barranca del Oro, Nayarit, on June 4, 1938. The image shows the teacher with his hands tied and his face against the floor while flames embrace his body, which lies next to pieces of paper and books.³⁴ Another print depicts a group of men with machetes attacking Arnulfo Sosa, who died on April 6, 1937, in San Andrés Xochimilco, Puebla. Adding realism to his work, Méndez reproduced the newspaper account of the event, which stated, "A party of armed men ... set fire to the school and murdered the rural teacher Arnulfo Sosa Portillo with machetes."³⁵

The title of Méndez's collection of lithographs, *In the Name of Christ...*, openly denounced the use of religion to justify murder.³⁶ It furthermore appropriated the notion of religious martyrdom to imagine teachers as martyrs of the new civil religion brought about by the revolution.³⁷ The collection was preceded by two pieces of graphic art that, like Méndez's lithographs, were representative of the "aesthetics of nation building"³⁸ promoted by the post-revolutionary state.³⁹ The first refers to the 1936 mural painted by Aurora Reyes titled *Attack against the Female Rural Teachers (Atentado contra las maestras rurales)*, which was exhibited at the Centro Escolar Revolución.⁴⁰ Although the mural makes no reference to a specific incident, Reyes probably had in mind one of the many attacks against female teachers perpetrated at the time.⁴¹ The second piece is an illustration produced by Méndez in 1938. Printed in the form of a flyer and meant to be used by teachers to defend their cause, the illustration depicted a defenseless and badly injured teacher surrounded by four attackers: a woman and a man who point at the teacher in an accusatory manner and two men wearing masks, one holding a knife and the other a pistol. The flyer had an accompanying text that read, "Teacher, you are alone against: the murderous *guardias blancas*,⁴² the ignorant provoked by the rich, the slander that poisons and breaks your relations with the pueblo." The text and the image denounced the different sources of violence that threatened teachers, namely, armed groups of men supported by landowners or local caciques (guardias blancas) and "ignorant" villagers who were provoked or manipulated by the rich.⁴³

Méndez's reference to villagers' opposition to socialist education as an expression of their ignorance rather than their own political inclinations was in tune with media and official representations prevalent at the time. An editorial published by the newspaper *Excélsior*, for instance, lamented the "sacrifice of teachers" and condemned the "barbarity" and "savage mutilations" committed against these "promoters of civilization."⁴⁴ It added that in order for the teachers' mission to succeed, educators had to "defeat the disbelief created by ignorance" and "destroy the superstitions that prevent the Indian to progress and develop." Similarly, in the context of the 1935 Scientific Congress, Jenaro Vázquez from the Department of Labor lamented that Indians "did not understand the spirit of the constitutional reform."[45] (Vázquez was referring to the revision of article 3 of the constitution, which, as mentioned before, stated public education would "fight fanaticism and prejudices.")[46] Vázquez reasoned that this lack of understanding was due to the fact that Indians, and really much of the pueblo, had for too long lived under the influence of the Catholic Church. The challenge, he said, was that the state had "displaced" but not "replaced" religion.

The emphasis on people's so-called ignorance and religious fanaticism concealed the political, material, and practical reasons that led people to oppose socialist education, including their rejection of agrarian reform and the central state's interference in local affairs.[47] It also obscured the entanglement of material and spiritual concerns that informed the exercise of religion in post-revolutionary Mexico. Furthermore, by equating villagers' violent opposition to teachers to the "barbarity" and "fanaticism" of local communities,[48] the government was able to promote an image of the state as a civilizing force that needed to transform backward and superstitious people into modern and rational citizens "mobilized for development."[49] As will become evident when discussing cases of lynching sanctioned by state authorities, this image did not correspond to reality, yet it provided a powerful narrative to legitimate the central elites' state-making project.[50]

Despite the publicity that opposition to socialist education received at the time, teachers were not the only representatives of the state whose presence was challenged by communities. The perceived or actual hostility of public officials to Catholic practices and symbols also provoked the anger of villagers. In March 1931, for instance, a crowd of Catholic villagers threatened to lynch the municipal authorities of Actopan, Veracruz.[51] A newspaper reported that the mayor and his subordinates had "committed some acts of hostility against the Catholics of this town" and that, in retaliation, these villagers sought to lynch him along with other municipal employees and police officers. The mayor had ordered the police to open fire on the crowd. This action, which resulted in the killing of one Catholic, further inflamed the mob, forcing the mayor to call in federal troops. Similarly, a few months later, the villagers in Cholula, Puebla, attempted to lynch two engineers who were sent by the SEP to restore an important archeological site located in the town so that it could be "admired in all its architectural beauty by tourists."[52] The site lay underneath a Catholic church that was a place of pilgrimage for Catholics. When Catholic villagers heard rumors about the engineers' intention to destroy the church, they surrounded the place armed with machetes and pistols. Although local authorities were able to save the engineers, the latter were forced to suspend their activities, thus demonstrating that these acts of resistance could effectively put the work of federal authorities on hold.

As suggested by the cases discussed thus far, lynchings committed against the so-called modernizing forces of the state were often informed by communities' rejection of the anticlerical measures implemented by the state during the 1930s. Nonetheless, collective attacks were also perpetrated against other state actors who had no relation to the religious question.[53] Although evidence for these cases is more scattered, the occurrence of these instances of mob violence illustrates the existence of a pattern of opposition and resistance to the state's meddling in affairs that people believed went beyond its purview. In October 1931, for instance, Porfirio Mendoza González, an inspector from Mexico City's Central Department who was commissioned to review the pipelines of various neighborhoods in the city, was attacked by a group of twenty men who beat him with clubs and left his face completely disfigured.[54] The press stated that the attack, which took place in a *pulquería* (pulque bar), had been driven by a "false supposition." Although the press did not offer any further details regarding the exact causes of this attempted lynching, the response that the inspector's presence generated, together with similar cases reported at the time, suggests the assailants might have thought he was there to close down the pulquería, as it was not uncommon for people to react violently to such situations.[55]

Post-revolutionary politicians considered alcohol an obstacle to the formation of the sober, rational, and productive citizen they envisioned. They regarded inebriation as directly linked to laziness, poverty, mental and physical illnesses, and aggression, particularly domestic violence. Reformers promoted several measures—from laws to antialcohol parades—to convince people of the dangers of alcohol and the benefits of sobriety.[56] For various individuals and communities, however, the consumption and production of alcohol was intimately connected to local economies and religious rituals, as well as political interests.[57] In the countryside, in particular, local authorities and caciques were often involved in the business of producing and selling alcohol and were thus complicit or even responsible for resisting the state's efforts to control or criminalize its production.

In August 1939, alcohol inspectors sent by the federal government were nearly lynched in the town of Nopalucan, Puebla.[58] The press, which noted that similar incidents had occurred days before in Chalchicomula, stated that the inspectors had orders to close down an illegal distillery that operated in the town. When they tried to shut the distillery, however, a group of more than thirty armed villagers instigated by the mayor rang the church bells and thereafter surrounded the inspectors with the intention of lynching them. A military detachment from Tehuacán was sent to the town to ensure that the distillery was shut down, a business, the press asserted, that belonged to a local congressman.

Agrarian reform was an equally contentious policy. Although the distribution of land was certainly welcomed by individuals, families, and communities that saw in it the fulfillment of one of the revolution's most valuable promises, agrarian reform also generated and deepened political and religious conflicts and contributed to weakening and disrupting traditional forms of authority in indigenous and rural communities.[59] Land disputes thus led to lynchings carried out by contending factions,[60] as well as to lynchings of public officials who promoted agrarian reform. For instance, in November 1936, close to one hundred peasants lynched the military engineer Guillermo Pérez Silva and four other men who were in charge of parceling the *ejidos* (common lands) of the towns of Santo Tomás and Alpuyecac in the municipality of Tecali, Puebla.[61] According to a local newspaper, the engineer, who represented the Agrarian Department, was shot and then hacked with machetes. The article explained that the attack was organized by local caciques and lamented the villagers' misjudgment of "the benefits of the Revolution."[62] As this case illustrates, and as documented by other scholars, in Puebla (as well as in states like Sonora and Veracruz) lynching and vigilante killings occurred with the acquiescence—if not full support—of landowners, caciques, and even political elites who opposed the implementation of the agrarian reform.[63]

Opposition to socialist education forced central elites to revise and eventually abandon altogether the anticlerical undertones of the state's approach to the religious question. As a result, lynchings of socialist teachers and other officials linked to the government's cultural policies significantly decreased at the end of the 1930s. Lynchings organized in opposition to the state's modernization and centralization efforts, however, continued during the 1940s. Although the scale of these incidents of mob violence does not match the series of collective killings directed at socialist teachers during the 1930s, they reveal the continuing challenges the state faced in making its policies legitimate and desirable in the eyes of the governed.

Two policies that stood out in terms of the degree of discomfort and animosity they generated among local communities during this period were military conscription and the campaign to eradicate foot-and-mouth disease.[64] Military conscription came into effect under Ávila Camacho's presidency. Mexico's entry into World War II together with central elites' view of conscription as an instrument that would allow them to discipline the masses and create a sense of national unity became powerful arguments to draw political support for the new measure.[65] Military conscription was enthusiastically embraced by central elites but was highly unpopular among the rural poor. Several issues contributed to its unpopularity, among them, the abusive, corrupt, and intransigent practices of the recruitment committees and the municipal authorities that presided over them and people's fear and reluctance about Mexican young men being sent overseas to fight a war perceived as foreign and alongside an unpopular ally, the United States.[66]

It is in the context of these various grievances that we need to understand the attempt to lynch military inspectors and all the members of the recruitment committee in Tuxtepec, Oaxaca.[67] The incident, which took place in December 1942, is mentioned in a brief message sent out to the chief of the 29th Military Zone,

Antonio Gómez Velasco, on behalf of Ezequiel Navarro of the Regional Peasant's Committee.[68] In the message, Navarro stated that a group of women, incited by a man named Manuel I. Juárez, rioted against the military inspector and the municipal recruitment committee and thereafter attempted to lynch them. Although Navarro asserted that Juárez had manipulated the women, letters of complaint written by mothers of young recruits to federal authorities reveal these women might have had their own reasons to oppose conscription. For instance, Rosenda A. de Méndez and Saturnina R. de Miller asked the president to punish a lieutenant who had taken their children by force and dragged them "as if they were animals" to comply with the mandatory military service.[69] Also, in a letter addressed to the Ministry of Defense, Agustina Gutiérrez opposed the recruitment of her eldest son given that, as a single mother of three younger children, she depended on him for her economic subsistence.[70] Similarly, Luisa García wrote to the president to denounce the fact that her son had been seized and forcibly recruited by a group of police officers only because the family had not had enough money to buy off the recruitment committee.[71] She asked the president to correct this wrong as she and her mother depended on her son's labor to survive.[72]

On September 1, 1947, another incident concerning members of the military and female villagers took place in the town of Senguio, Michoacán, this time with fatal consequences. The incident involved hundreds of female and male peasants who, armed with machetes, stones, knives, clubs, and various sharp objects, lynched the veterinarian Augusto Juárez Medina and all members of the military escort, including the commander, Julián Gómez Macías, and six other soldiers. Dr. Juárez Medina, together with American doctors, who were not present at the time of the incident, were members of a "sanitary brigade" in charge of eradicating the foot-and-mouth disease that had infected Mexican cattle in 1946.[73] Inspired by the Americans' "efficient" and "swift" methods to deal with the virus, Mexico's campaign privileged the killing of cattle over the application of vaccines that, according to American experts, had shown either mixed or poor results.[74] This method was violently opposed by Mexican peasants who depended on cattle for their economic subsistence. Aware of the popular discontent that the campaign generated, the Mexican government sent soldiers to escort and protect the Mexican and American doctors in charge of identifying potentially infected animals and ordering their slaughter. If necessary, the soldiers enforced the killing of infected animals at gunpoint.

The lynching in Senguio, Michoacán, involved great brutality. An investigation following the incident described the event as a massacre and stated that one of the female participants and main instigators of the lynching, Teodora Medina Guijosa, stabbed and gouged the eyes out of one of the soldiers and the commander, Gómez Macías.[75] Furthermore, according to the testimony of witnesses and perpetrators, women and men stabbed the soldiers and the doctor, threw stones at them, shot their already dead bodies, and took away their weapons and possessions.[76] The number of people who participated in the lynching—close to five hundred—suggests the attack was premeditated. Among the perpetrators were men and women from neighboring communities, some arriving by foot and others riding horses and waving machetes.[77] Simón López Venegas, who was found guilty of having participated in the lynching, asserted the incident was provoked by the "unconsidered" behavior of the military commander who dismissed women's grievances and told them to go away, as well as by the "irresponsible" conduct of female villagers who started rioting against the soldiers.[78]

Echoing the description of other witnesses, one suspect, Clemente Santos de la Rosa, asserted that they had agreed to attend a meeting with the sanitary brigade after municipal authorities assured them no cattle would be sacrificed.[79] Although he denied that they intended to kill any soldiers, various witnesses declared that on the days leading up to the attack several of the men and women involved held meetings in the house of Benito Malagón Arroyo, a known Sinarquista, or member of the Unión Nacional Sinarquista (UNS; National Synarchist Union), who incited villagers to take direct action against authorities in order to save their cattle.[80] The investigation by federal inspectors Clodomiro Morales Camacho and Ríos Tivol reached the same conclusion. In their report, they stated that Teodora Medina Guijosa was a "fanatic of the Sinarquista creed" and that Malagón Arroyo was the "autor intelectual" (mastermind) behind the attack.[81]

Mexican public officials considered the UNS responsible for mobilizing peasants and farmers against the foot-and-mouth disease eradication campaign.[82] An ultranationalist organization that professed a Catholic, conservative, and anticommunist ideology, the UNS also promoted the defense of communities' autonomy and traditions vis-à-vis the encroachment of central authorities.[83] In this sense, similar to the role of Cristeros and armed vigilantes in the organization of lynchings against socialist teachers, Sinarquistas reflected and amplified the sentiments of locals who deemed the presence of the central state intrusive and disruptive.[84]

Far from being driven by "fanaticism," however, popular opposition to the government's campaign was grounded in pragmatic considerations, such as peasants' reliance on their cattle for food (milk and meat) and for working their land.[85] It was furthermore grounded on the government's failure to take into account villagers' voices in the design and implementation of the foot-and-mouth eradication campaign.[86] The following excerpt from José Guadalupe López's testimony illustrates this point, and it allows me to bring to the fore the contested legitimacy of the central government's response to the virus:

> You, mister ministers, that have never worked in the arduous tasks of the field, receiving the meager daily wage that for that work we get, [you] that do not know about not eating in order to collect a small amount everyday ... you cannot estimate the immense value that cattle has for us.... When an ox gets sick, you can rest assured that the most instrumental member of our family has gotten sick, the tireless

and enduring source of our support, the only treasure we possess, and do not alarm yourselves that I call an ox part of the family because I can assure you that it is equally or more valuable than each member of [the family]. . . . Be certain then mister ministers, that we will look after it carefully and we will attempt to save it, because we are saving our selves. . . . [I]t is a mistake to think that we will abandon a sick animal to its illness. Since immemorial times the foot-and-mouth disease has existed and we have fought it with the rudimentary procedures acquired with experience, but that have always proven to be effective, less costly, unassuming in their application, and that never entailed, neither here nor in Europe, nor in any other part of the world, the sacrifice of cattle.

As the above quotation makes clear, peasants contested the scientific and elite-based expertise promoted by the post-revolutionary state with their practical and communal knowledge.[87] Their demands for a more moderate approach to dealing with the infected animals—one that entailed vaccination instead of massive slaughter—eventually forced Mexican officials to change its policy, even if this prompted the skepticism and discontent of their American counterparts.[88] In the meantime, however, distrust in the government abounded and violent forms of resistance continued to unfold in other states of central Mexico, even when federal inspectors assured villagers they would vaccinate, rather than kill, their animals.

In January 1949, for instance, in the municipality of Temascalcingo, Estado de México, a mob of six hundred peasants lynched the American doctor Robert L. Proctor. Proctor was a livestock inspector from Tucson, Arizona, who was part of the Mexican-American Commission for the Eradication of Foot-and-Mouth Disease that had been established in 1947.[89] According to newspaper accounts, Proctor was accompanied by the Mexican inspector Raúl Sánchez as well as by two soldiers, all of whom managed to survive the attack. A group of women led the lynch mob and attacked Proctor armed with fists and stones while male villagers stabbed him to death.[90]

As in the lynching in Senguio, Michoacán, evidence suggests the collective killing of Proctor was not entirely spontaneous. In this case, villagers had been summoned by the *comisario municipal* (municipal commissioner) and by the leader of the peasants' union, Unión Nacional de Campesinos, Luciano Gómez Nieto.[91] According to the press, Gómez Nieto had told villagers the vaccine made animals sick and had encouraged them to oppose its implementation through all means possible, including killing those in charge of promoting it. American newspapers were quick to attribute the incident to the ignorance of locals. The *New York Times,* for instance, lamented the loss of "another victim of the ignorance in rural communities where the aims and methods of a scientific campaign are misunderstood."[92]

In August the same year, this time in the town of Jolalpan, in the municipality of Izúcar de Matamoros, Puebla, another group of peasants threatened to lynch a group of health inspectors who were rumored to be members of a foot-and-mouth disease vaccination brigade.⁹³ In fact, the inspectors had arrived in the town to vaccinate people against typhoid. In the event, the inspectors were forced to seek refuge in the municipal offices. A local newspaper reported that peasants of Jolalpan were prejudiced against the foot-and-mouth disease vaccination brigade because they believed the vaccine itself, rather than the disease, had killed their cattle. It further reported that villagers distrusted vaccines used to cure human diseases and noted sarcastically that locals' recalcitrance was such that they preferred to see their people die before being inoculated by the government.⁹⁴

Villagers continued to resist the central state's encroachment into communal life during the 1940s. Although smaller in scale compared to the collective attacks endured by socialist teachers and anticlerical officials during the 1930s, its occurrence suggests that the post-revolutionary project of state making was far from uncontested or willingly accepted. In this sense, these lynchings contribute to problematizing an official narrative that claimed that by the 1940s the different factions that made up Mexico's political landscape had joined together under the umbrella of a big "revolutionary family."⁹⁵

Lynchings organized as a reaction to the encroachment of the central state did recede in the 1950s,⁹⁶ reflecting the cumulative effect of the dynamics of resistance and accommodation that characterized the previous decades. Similar to the federal government's shift in its policies on the religious question during the 1930s, central elites' approach to foot-and-mouth disease and to other health and hygiene matters was modified during the 1940s as a result of the resistance encountered at the local level. After the lynching of soldiers and veterinarians in Senguio, Michoacán, and other towns in central Mexico, public officials began increasingly to vaccinate animals rather than kill them.⁹⁷ Likewise, state officials started to incorporate communal practices and local forms of knowledge in their public health programs.⁹⁸ In the case of military conscription, the resistance the campaign encountered eventually led to the adoption of a more modest program that no longer considered avoidance of military service a crime.⁹⁹

The decrease in this modality of lynching thus reflects a process of accommodation and resistance that resulted in the moderation or even complete transformation of elites' centralization and modernization efforts. Nevertheless, the lynching of public officials did not wither away.

LYNCHING AS CORRECTIVE JUSTICE

In July 1932, in the neighborhood of El Carmen, in Puebla City, a policeman was nearly lynched by a group of people who witnessed how the "guardian of law and order" had shot José García, a newspaper salesman.¹⁰⁰ The incident took place during the celebration of El Carmen's festival and, according to a local newspaper, was preceded by a fight between García and the policeman, who was apparently drunk when he shot the salesman. After García was shot, a group of bystanders who felt "understandably" outraged by the behavior of the policeman attempted to lynch him. The newspaper article stated the incident confirmed the persistence of the type of police misconduct people denounced time and again and asserted "the police should neither go beyond its functions nor be the instigator of punishable abuses that it, itself, should admonish more than anyone else."

The attempted lynching of this Puebla City policeman was not isolated. It represents a larger practice in post-revolutionary Mexico that entailed the punishment of state officials and powerful figures who were seen as responsible for enforcing social control within communities and neighborhoods. Triggered by a variety of situations, these lynchings involved individuals who, in the eyes of perpetrators, had abused their power or applied the law in ways that people deemed unjust or illegitimate. Although these cases were most commonly directed against police officers, evidence suggests they were also triggered by the behavior of soldiers, mayors, and caciques. Even when the military and military policing were, overall, seen in a more positive light than police actions and civilian policing,[101] soldiers were not exempt from this practice.

Perhaps one of the best-documented cases involving a member of the military corresponds to the attempted lynching of a twenty-four-year-old soldier, Juan Castillo Morales, in the northern city of Tijuana on February 15, 1938.[102] A mob tried to break into the prison where Castillo Morales was being held and interrogated by the police. The young soldier, who would become popularly known as "Juan Soldado," was accused of having murdered and raped an eight-year-old girl, Olga Camacho.[103] Outraged by the cruelty of his alleged actions—the girl had been beaten in the head, strangled, and her throat slashed open with what appeared to be glass or a sharp knife—a mob of hundreds of people rioted outside the prison and demanded that authorities hand them Castillo Morales so they could lynch him. Distrustful of state authorities and convinced that the military would protect one of their own, they attacked the prison and the municipal building with stones, rifles, and pistols.[104] Despite the military's forceful response, the crowd did not dissipate and continued hurling rocks and yelling insults at the soldiers who were safeguarding the buildings and the alleged killer.[105] Although the military averted the lynching of Castillo Morales, he was thereafter executed under the state-sanctioned "ley fuga" with the approval of President Cárdenas himself.[106] In the eyes of Tijuanenses, justice was served.

The press reported at least two more cases during the same decade. In December 1936, a group of men lynched two soldiers in the town of Huejotzingo, Puebla.[107] One of them was mutilated with machetes; the other was stoned and then hanged from a tree. Although in this case the press offered no explanation for what led to the incident, three years later, this time in the neighborhood of La Resurección, in Puebla City, two soldiers accused of stealing firewood were lynched and sent to the hospital with serious injuries.[108] The neighbors lynched the soldiers with machetes, fracturing their arms and ribs. Similar cases were reported during the 1940s and 1950s, directed against soldiers who engaged in criminal conduct, including battery, child theft, and murder.[109]

As stated before, lynching was more commonly directed against police officers than against military officials. The fact that members of the army were in general better armed and perceived as less politicized than the police made them less vulnerable to lynching.[110] Moreover, collective attacks against the police signaled people's disapproval of their abusive practices as well as their handling of certain criminal or illicit conduct.[111] The latter is illustrated by the above-mentioned incident when two policemen were nearly lynched after they tried to close an illicit pulque distillery in Mexico City in 1934. The case reveals how the attempt to control a practice—in this case, the illicit production of alcohol—that was regarded as legitimate by certain neighborhoods and communities led to clashes with the police. A similar incident was triggered by a policeman's attempt to arrest a drunkard who was creating a public disturbance in Puebla City in September 1937.[112] Although the policeman shot twice into the air to disperse the gathered crowd, his assailants—numbering close to one hundred men—managed to seize his weapon and then beat him.[113] A few years later, also in Puebla, a group of neighbors attempted to lynch another policeman who was trying to reprimand a local vendor for selling illegal products in the streets.[114]

These cases were informed by people's disagreement with police responses to criminal conduct. Other examples were a reaction to police officers' violent behavior. In August 1944, for instance, neighbors from the town of Tecuala, Nayarit, attempted to lynch three policemen, including the police inspector, Juan Pérez, in retaliation for the murder of two traveling salesmen.[115] Although the policemen had been imprisoned for their crime, people tried to break into the jail to take and lynch the culprits, as they had grown wary of the municipal authorities and their potential involvement in this type of criminal activity. The press reported that the police inspector managed to run away and that the other two policemen were saved thanks to the intervention of federal forces.

A different fate awaited the police commander Adolfo Jiménez, who could not escape the anger of people despite the presence of federal forces in the small town of Estación Carrillo, Chihuahua.[116] Jiménez had shot a schoolteacher, Guillermo Hernández, on March 1, 1943, apparently in relation to some local labor conflict. "Beloved" by locals, the schoolteacher was avenged by a group of men and women who lynched Jiménez armed with stones and sticks. The press reported that although federal forces were sent to the town to ease the situation, no arrests could be made because "in this bloody event all the pueblo was involved."[117]

Similar events were reported elsewhere. They occurred not only in small towns but also in urban settings. In the latter, bystanders and curious witnesses felt compelled to act even if they barely knew the victims of police abuse. A case in point was the

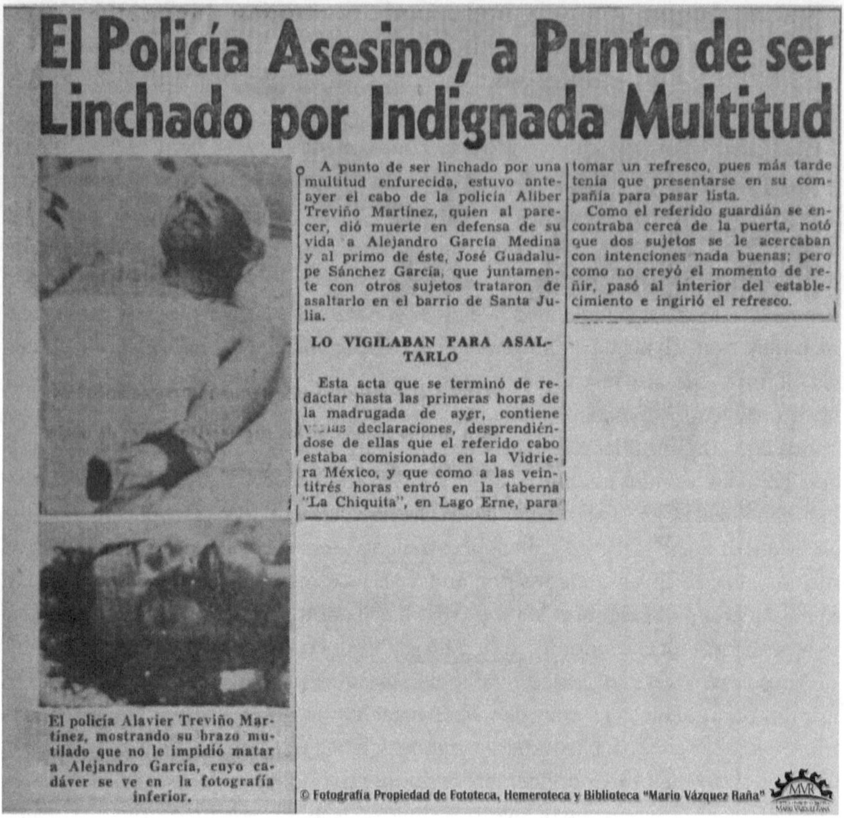

El Policía Asesino, a Punto de ser Linchado por Indignada Multitud

A punto de ser linchado por una multitud enfurecida, estuvo anteayer el cabo de la policía Aliber Treviño Martínez, quien al parecer, dió muerte en defensa de su vida a Alejandro García Medina y al primo de éste, José Guadalupe Sánchez García, que juntamente con otros sujetos trataron de asaltarlo en el barrio de Santa Julia.

LO VIGILABAN PARA ASALTARLO

Esta acta que se terminó de redactar hasta las primeras horas de la madrugada de ayer, contiene varias declaraciones, desprendiéndose de ellas que el referido cabo estaba comisionado en la Vidriera México, y que como a las veintitrés horas entró en la taberna "La Chiquita", en Lago Erne, para tomar un refresco, pues más tarde tenía que presentarse en su compañía para pasar lista.

Como el referido guardián se encontraba cerca de la puerta, notó que dos sujetos se le acercaban con intenciones nada buenas; pero como no creyó el momento de reñir, pasó al interior del establecimiento e ingirió el refresco.

El policía Alavier Treviño Martínez, mostrando su brazo mutilado que no le impidió matar a Alejandro García, cuyo cadáver se ve en la fotografía inferior.

FIGURE 1. "El policía asesino, a punto de ser linchado por indignada multitud" (The Murderous Policeman, about to Be Lynched by the Outraged Crowd), *La Prensa*, August 17, 1943. Credit: Fototeca, Hemeroteca y Biblioteca Mario Vázquez Raña, Organización Editorial Mexicana S.A. de C.V. © Fotografía Propiedad de Fototeca, Hemeroteca y Biblioteca "Mario Vázquez Rana."

attempted lynching of a policeman, Aliber Treviño Martínez, on August 15, 1943, in the Santa Julia neighborhood of Mexico City.[118] (See figure 1.) Treviño Martínez had shot two men, allegedly in self-defense. According to his declaration, the two men had attacked him with a machete, severing his left hand. It was only after seeing that his life was in danger, or so he claimed, that he decided to shoot the two men. Distrustful of his version of the incident and convinced that he was the aggressor, a group of neighbors severely beat Treviño Martínez in retaliation for the double murder.

Two years later, in the Peralvillo neighborhood of Mexico City, the policeman Agustín Fierro Gómez suffered a similar fate.[119] According to witnesses, including the owner of a local café, a jeweler, and another police officer, Fierro Gómez shot a man named Jorge Burey for no reason except that he was very drunk. The outrage generated by Burey's assassination was such that a group of bystanders tried to lynch Fierro Gómez, who only escaped with the aid of fellow policemen.

That citizens could retaliate against police officers' transgressions by using violence against them sheds light on the complex nature of police-society relations. Citizens were not merely passive observers of police abuse, even when the police had the upper hand in this relationship. After all, as representatives of the state, police officers had the right to use violence and also enjoyed the benefits of a political system that enabled their discretionary use of force.[120] And yet the use of lynching against police officers shows how citizens managed to circumvent these power dynamics, even if their tactics ended up reproducing the excessive use of violence they allegedly sought to correct in the first place.[121] Lynchings of police officers were not part of the everyday interactions between police officers and citizens. However, their occurrence, even if exceptional, is indicative of the underlying tensions that characterized the relationship between the two groups.

A parallel argument can be made in the case of lynchings perpetrated against mayors and caciques. These cases suggest people's interactions with these authority figures could turn explosive and that citizens were willing and able to challenge these actors' violent and corrupt practices. The lynching of mayors and caciques signaled villagers' feelings of anger provoked by years of political abuse, manipulation, and exploitation. Cases included self-proclaimed mayors, former or current mayors involved in assassinations or political vendettas, and authorities who sought to limit people's exercise of Catholicism.[122] Reminiscent of Luis Estrada's film, *La ley de Herodes* (1999), which opens with the lynching of the mayor of the fictionalized town San Pedro de los Saguaros, these types of lynchings continued well into the 1950s, in a context characterized by rigged elections as well as by the participation of police and the military in acts of political repression. These incidents of mob violence offer a window into the ongoing tensions and disagreements between citizens and authorities during a period that has traditionally been associated with greater levels of political stability.

One of the most salient cases that took place during the 1950s involved the attempted lynching of the mayor of Izúcar de Matamoros, Puebla, in October 1950. The mayor was Salvador Martínez Cairo, an infamous colonel who was placed by Governor Carlos Betancourt as head of the municipal council in 1948. The case is revealing of the abuses perpetrated by the military under the auspices of political elites who aimed to control political opponents and social protesters.[123]

Martínez Cairo was known for his crude use of violence, which included multiple political assassinations, extortion, and the illegal appropriation of public funds.[124] Before starting his tenure, Martínez Cairo had already been involved in disputed affairs such as the "León massacre" of 1946 in which dozens of unarmed demonstrators—including Sinarquistas—were shot by federal troops.[125] According to the press, his prior behavior together with his constant aggression against and exploitation of the inhabitants of Izúcar de Matamoros provoked the anger of villagers who marched to the municipal palace with the intention of ousting him and the rest of the municipal authorities.[126] The lynching of Martínez Cairo was only prevented by an official sent by Governor Betancourt who assured villagers the colonel had ran away and that a new municipal council, one truly supported by the people, would be put in place.[127]

Similar episodes involving political abuse and candidates imposed by the official party, PRI, were reported in the following years.[128] On December 31, 1955, for instance, a mob comprising both men and women assaulted the municipal offices of the town of Tecomán, Colima. In a telegram sent to the president, Colima's governor explained that a mob had attempted to take over the municipal offices and hang the town's police commander. Among those participating in the assault, he argued, were female members of the organization Acción Católica.[129] He further stated that, acting in self-defense, members of the police and of the federal troops had killed three and injured eleven of the rioters. Referring to the same incident, Luis Aguilar Gutiérrez, on behalf of the Comité Nacional Campesino "Emiliano Zapata," condemned the killings perpetrated by the police as well as the abuses committed by the governor and members of the PRI who constantly imposed their own candidates. Addressing the president directly, he denounced the authorities (including the president himself) for not fulfilling their obligation to protect and respect the rights of citizens as established in the constitution. He further demanded adequate punishment for the "criminal murderers" who had shot at "the defenseless pueblo."[130]

These cases reveal how citizens called into question authorities' abuses of power. Although people's strategies to hold authorities accountable for their actions were certainly not always violent, lynching was nonetheless part of the language of protest, negotiation, and resistance available to citizens in post-revolutionary Mexico. This language included marches and demonstrations, letters of petition written to federal or state authorities, the organization of strikes and armed forms of opposition, as well as collective forms of violence including rioting and lynching.

Perhaps no other figures of authority represented the types of political abuses that were characteristic of the period as did caciques. Caciques were local political bosses who without necessarily holding formal positions of power exerted, in practice, a great deal of influence over the economic and political dynamics of local communities. Due to their knowledge of local politics and the control they had over local means of coercion and co-optation, they could either facilitate or obstruct the central state's intervention in given communities.[131] Caciques also exercised social control at the local level either within or outside the margins of the law, just as did mayors, police officers, and military personnel. Hence the lynching of these influential figures confirmed that abuses perpetrated by those in power did not go unchallenged.

A case of particular significance because of the visibility it acquired at the time it occurred and in its aftermath is the lynching of Aquiles de la Peña,[132] cacique of Ciudad Hidalgo, Michoacán, in April 1959.[133] Former president Cárdenas himself traveled to the town immediately after the lynching and attended the funeral of De la Peña, who was a political ally and a close friend. The case was documented and later fictionalized by the journalist Fernando Benitez in his novel, *El agua envenenada* (1961). In the novel, the cacique appears under the name Don Ulises Roca and the town is referred to as Tajimaora, which corresponds to the old name of Ciudad Hidalgo. Benitez tells the story of the lynching in the voice of the parish priest who, unable to avert the killing of the cacique, writes to the archbishop to explain what precipitated such tragic events.[134]

As indicated by Benitez's novel's title, the lynching was provoked by a rumor claiming that the cacique had poisoned the water of Ciudad Hidalgo. The rumor was false, but it was credible enough to ignite the anger of villagers who had accumulated years of hatred and resentment against the cacique and his pistoleros. The context was ripe for a violent incident such as this. Just a few weeks before the lynching and in the midst of a series of protests and public meetings, villagers managed to overthrow the mayor imposed by De la Peña, Rosendo Bucio.[135] Furthermore, elections for local congressmen were about to take place and people were convinced that De la Peña was set to manipulate the process in order to secure the appointment of his own candidates. In this context, the rumor was nothing but the tipping point in a longer history of tensions.

The rumor started just hours before the incident. After a villager died from food poisoning, a few men claimed that one of the cacique's pistoleros, Avelino Pérez Estrada, had poisoned the water. When people learned about the alleged death of other villagers the rumor spread like wildfire.[136] People started to gather and headed to the cacique's house armed with stones, knives, pistols, and petrol bombs. The cacique responded to the angered villagers by firing his machine gun, killing two of his assailants. People's anger escalated. The assailants—a multitude of men, women, and even children—continued to advance toward the cacique with the intention of lynching him.[137] Although some versions claimed that De la Peña killed himself by accident with his own machine gun, the several gunshots he received suggest that, even if one of his injuries was self-inflicted, villagers completed the assassination. At least two of his pistoleros were shot, and one of them, Avelino, was tied to a tree and stoned to death. In the frenzy of the events, people shot the cacique's horses, plucked and killed his peacocks, and set fire to his house and sawmill. People demanded to lynch members of his family too and the rest of his pistoleros, but the parish priest together with the arrival of federal troops from Zitácuaro finally eased the crowd.

Investigations carried out by the state police as well as by newspaper inquiries suggested the lynching was organized and premeditated by De la Peña's political opponents.[138] Independently of who the actual instigators were, the lynching was clearly regarded by villagers as an act of justice. Nidia Marin, a journalist who was born in Ciudad Hidalgo and whose mother played an active role in defending some of the perpetrators of the lynching, asserted that seemingly everyone participated in the attack: "In the assault, all the people from the pueblo participated: the woman who sold tomatoes, the fish vendor, the mechanic, the taquero of carnitas.... [W]hen the cadaver was put on the stretcher, people screamed, 'We killed the deer!' The house was in flames."[139]

The killing of Aquiles de la Peña makes clear that people regarded lynching as a form of justice that allowed them to redress the wrongs committed by those in positions of power. Citizens were not alone, however, in embracing this form of violence. Public officials, particularly mayors and police officers, also organized and perpetrated lynchings.

STATE-SANCTIONED LYNCHING

On May 11, 1930, the press reported a "triple lynching" perpetrated in the town of Tepetzala, Puebla.[140] Three men, merchants from a neighboring town, were wrongly accused of having participated in the theft of a few chickens that belonged to the local cacique. After a woman identified them as the wrongdoers, a group of men and women surrounded the three men and, after beating them badly, dragged them to the municipal offices. Once there, the town's mayor together with the local judge ordered some men to ring the town's church bells in order to summon villagers in front of the municipal offices.[141] Then, while in the presence of a growing crowd, the mayor and the judge gave the order to hang the men from a tree. The crowd completed the lynching armed with pistols, stones, and knives.[142]

The lynching of these merchants in Tepetzala illustrates the ways in which local authorities, who were in principle responsible for upholding the rule of law, could themselves act as instigators of mob violence.[143] The participation of the authorities in the organization of lynchings reveals these actors' approval and reliance on extralegal forms of violence to punish alleged criminals and political enemies. Lynchings were in fact part of a broader repertoire of extralegal forms of violence used by mayors, police officers, and the military in post-revolutionary Mexico. This repertoire included the use of torture to fabricate suspects and repress political dissidents, as well as the killing of suspected criminals on their alleged attempt to escape the law (the so-called ley fuga).[144]

In contrast to torture and the ley fuga, however, lynching offered the possibility of making an extrajudicial killing look like an act of communal justice. Lynching also offered the anonymity and seeming impunity for incidents of mob violence that, based on their collective nature, were often attributed to the "pueblo" rather than to individuals.[145] These "convenient" attributes of lynching might explain why, in September 1931, the mayor of San Aparicio, Puebla, attempted to stage the assassination of two men as a lynching.[146] According to a local newspaper, the mayor wrongly accused the men, Felipe León and Ramón Mora, of having participated in the rape of María Antonia Flores, a local villager who was sexually assaulted by six men a few weeks before. After taking the men to the police station, the mayor dragged them out in the middle of the night and took them to the town's church. Once there, and with the intention of staging their killing as a lynching, the mayor rang the town's church bells in order to summon the townspeople. A group of villagers who believed the two men were innocent prevented the lynching, however, and helped the intended victims escape.

Another attempt to stage a lynching was reported in May 1937, this time in Huitzilan in the municipality of Tetela, Puebla.[147] The case involved the hanging of four men who were accused of breaking into the property of some local landlords. The men were hanged in the patio of the town's school in the middle of the night. The press explained that after the municipal authorities caught the men, they turned them over to the mob so that villagers could take justice into their own hands. The same article suggested another, and equally convincing, explanation. In order to avoid being implicated in the men's assassination, authorities hired some individuals to execute the crime and then blamed the "pueblo en masa" for the killing. By staging the incident as a lynching, authorities presented their violent actions as representing the people's demand for justice.

As mentioned previously, lynching was part of a broader repertoire of extralegal forms of violence used by authorities. Although some of these other expressions of violence were not necessarily supported by neighbors and communities and thus lacked the communal dimension of a lynching, their level of cruelty and visibility suggests that authorities were far from being purveyors of a "civilizing process." The following examples make clear that the line between state-sanctioned violence and the lynch mob was rather blurry. In March 1933, for instance, widow Martina Vázquez and a group of *agrarista* peasants (supporters of land reform) from Villa Lerdo de Tejada, Veracruz, addressed the local judge, the public prosecutor, and the state governor to demand justice for the assassination of Zenón Bolaina.[148] They explained that on March 18, 1933, five policemen, including the police commander, had killed Zenón after forcing him out of a town's fiesta (*fandango*) in the middle of the night. The policemen beat Zenón with clubs and then shot him in the back when he was already disarmed. Martina asked local authorities to punish the policemen, who not only remained free and in the same job but also kept "bragging about their cowardly [acts]."

Another incident bearing the hallmarks of a lynching took place in the town of Axocopan, Puebla, in May 1938. In this case, a group of police officers, including the police commander himself, attacked the house of Aaron Tufiño armed with machetes, axes, and pistols.[149] Tufiño was shot multiple times, and his wife was severely injured by machetes. The policemen then paraded Tufiño's corpse through the streets of the town. Pablo Castillo, the brother of a local congressman, orchestrated the attack.[150]

Suggesting a feature of state-society relations predicated on the tolerance of extrajudicial forms of retribution, the assassination of Tufiño was followed by an attack perpetrated by a group of neighbors who, armed with machetes and pistols, injured six of the policemen. A local newspaper stated that the policemen's behavior had "all the tragic and bloody characteristics of past times when, motivated by the Mexican Revolution, there were gangs who organized themselves in order to assault, rob, and carry out personal vengeance."[151]

Despite the press's portrayal of this type of behavior as anachronistic, the use of extralegal violence was in fact a central feature of authorities' coercive practices in post-revolutionary Mexico. The assassination of Pedro Ortega in June 1940 by elements of the municipal police of Ahuatempan, Puebla, shows that extralegal violence was not confined to "village" politics but was connected and in many ways instrumental to the national political machinery.[152] In a letter addressed to the representative of the pro-Almazán committee in the state of Puebla, villagers from Ahuatempan explained that Ortega was shot more than forty times in the public square, leaving his body "essentially destroyed."[153] Ortega was killed in retaliation for supporting the presidential candidate Juan Andreu Almazán, who was running against Manuel Ávila Camacho, the brother and favored candidate of Puebla's governor, Maximino.[154] They demanded that the pro-Almazán committee "reach out to the President of the Republic so that justice can be done, otherwise we believe our protections will disappear and our town will be abandoned and only the assassins will remain . . . as we know without a doubt that the police and the mayor will continue with their soulless attacks."

Lynchings organized or perpetrated with the clear acquiescence of public officials continued during the 1940s. The continuity of this practice demonstrates authorities' failure to protect citizens and to uphold, through their own behavior, the observance of so-called civilized conduct. The lynching of Simón García in February 1940 in the town of Quecholac, Puebla, was particularly telling of the vulnerability of those who not only lacked protection from authorities but also were handed over to the lynch mob by authorities themselves. In a letter addressed to President Lázaro Cárdenas, Albina Hernández and Francisca García, Simón's widow and sister, denounced the mayor for having instigated the lynching.[155] After calling him into his office, the mayor, together with a group of men, unarmed Simón and then proceeded to turn him over to a mob of close to thirty people who were waiting for him outside the municipal offices armed with clubs, machetes, and daggers. The mob, shouting, "This one returned the lands to the owner of the ranch El Carmen," stabbed and beat Simón to death. They then paraded his body through the streets of the town. In the letter, the women asserted the mayor had no right to have "sentenced Simón García to be lynched by the pueblo" and cited article 17 of the constitution, which established that no person could take justice into their own hands.

In his testimonial book, *Mi palabra (A la vera de Tlacuilo)*, Filadelfo Gayosso Ríos refers to another lynching perpetrated with the assent of authorities during the same decade.[156] The case took place only a few years after Simón García's lynching, in the town of Tlacuilotepec in the Sierra Norte of Puebla. The victim was an infamous criminal, Vicente Nepomuceno, who due to the several robberies and murders he had committed in the town, was despised by the residents. Tired of his abuses, villagers decided to take justice into their own hands and headed toward Vicente's house with the intention of lynching him. Although the mayor initially averted the lynching and took Vicente to the town's jail, he later gave the villagers access to the jail so that they could kill him. When the criminal survived after being shot twice in his jail cell, the villagers started thinking Vicente had a "pact with the devil." Badly injured, the "devilish" criminal was taken into military custody. Attending to the clamor of the villagers, a sergeant shot him in the chest and then left the doors of the jail open so they could finalize the lynching.[157]

A case reported by the press in October 1949 revealed that lynchings sanctioned by authorities not only involved political opponents and infamous criminals, as in the two cases described above, but also representatives of the government. The case pertained to the attempted lynching of Antonio Rodarte Díaz, a representative of the federal tax office, who had orders to confiscate a truck that belonged to Julio Carrillo, a villager from Huitzizingo, Estado de México.[158] Rodarte Díaz asked a local policeman to help him seize Carrillo's truck, but the man tried to escape, forcing the tax official, who was apparently well armed, to shoot Carrillo. Rodarte Díaz was next taken to the town's jail for the murder of Carrillo. Once there, the police commander together with a group of villagers dragged him out of the jail and brutally beat him. Although Rodarte Díaz survived the lynching, villagers killed José Cruz, a man who had accompanied him to the town.

The attempted lynching of Rodarte Díaz resembles the cases discussed in the first section of this chapter, which involved the lynching of federal officials by local communities that considered their presence offensive or threatening. Although it would be tempting to see this and other cases involving municipal authorities as expressions of those "powerful traditions of atavistic feud and petty authoritarianism"[159] that belonged to a distant rural world rather than to the political maneuvering of central elites, the pervasiveness of these abusive practices suggests that, at the very least, central elites took a conscious decision to overlook them.

The state's incapacity to control and punish these types of conduct could very well be seen as one reason for central elites' negligence regarding them. After all, the reach of the central state in the countryside remained limited and unevenly distributed, even during the 1940s and 1950s. However, the fact that several cacique-like individuals built their political careers precisely based on their use of coercion suggests this type of behavior was not only passively accepted as a "necessity" but also actively sought as a means to give the regime a level of cohesiveness and stability.[160] Powerful figures such as Salvador Martínez Cairo and Aquiles de la Peña, for instance, developed their authority based on coercive practices and the exchange of political favors with regional and federal authorities who guaranteed their impunity.[161] So long as they remained loyal to the regime and so long as their abuses did not attract unnecessary publicity, central elites tolerated and even rewarded strongmen's use of extralegal forms of violence.

The overt participation of public officials in the organization of lynchings receded during the 1950s.[162] Although this shift might suggest a transition to less overt or more "civil" (as in legal) forms of violence, evidence indicates that public officials' sanctioning of extralegal forms of violence was far from over. Newspapers, official documents, and letters of complaint continued to refer to incidents that entailed a level of cruelty that resembled the lynch mob. Examples abound. One case involved the brutal assassination of two brothers on the orders of the chief of the state police of Guerrero, Colonel Carlos Arango de la Torre, in July 1957. The brothers, Agapito and Heliodoro Pita, had the palms of their feet and hands lacerated (*despalmadas*) and their testicles cut off.[163] The same year, a group of police officers, acting with the support of the town's mayor, tortured Miguel Prieto Mora.[164] The man was suspected of having stolen a typewriter in the town of Otatitlán, Veracruz. The policemen tortured him in order to force a confession. Prieto Mora was hanged and beaten and had his tongued pulled out. His son found him dead in his prison cell.

State-sanctioned violence during the 1950s might have become more covert, perpetrated behind doors and in the "privacy" of the prison cell, or through the use of pistoleros acting on behalf of post-revolutionary politicians.[165] Even if hidden, however, this violence was as brutal and uncivilized as the lynch mob in its expressions and methods. Construing the state as a civilizing force that had the mission to tame the violence of unruly and backward communities is problematic at best. Rather than being symptomatic of the so-called backwardness of communities, lynching was very much in tune with the ways in which state authority was forged at the local level with the acquiescence of state and federal elites in post-revolutionary Mexico.

CONCLUSION

This chapter has sought to analyze the impact of Mexico's process of state building in the organization and legitimation of lynching. It examined three modalities of lynching that involved state actors and local authorities, either as victims or as perpetrators of mob violence. The first modality, lynching as resistance, signaled the contested legitimacy of the projects of modernization and centralization promoted by the post-revolutionary state. The state's efforts to secularize communities by attacking their religious symbols and practices were met with particularly violent expressions of resistance, including lynching. Although during the 1930s lynchings perpetrated against socialist teachers were the most prominent in terms of their frequency and public visibility, lynchings were also directed against state representatives that had no connection to the religious question. This included alcohol inspectors, tax collectors, health officials, and engineers in charge of promoting agrarian reform. During the 1940s, military conscription and the campaign to eradicate foot-and-mouth disease also provoked the frustration and anger of villagers who perceived both measures as intrusive and unjust. Even though lynchings organized as a reaction to the encroachment of the central state into local affairs declined at the end of the 1940s, lynchings against public officials did not disappear.

Cases of mob violence against powerful figures who were de jure or de facto responsible for enforcing social control within communities and neighborhoods continued well into the 1940s and 1950s. Perpetrated against police officers, soldiers, mayors, and caciques, this second modality of lynching reflected people's disapproval of these actors' handling of criminal conduct, as well as citizens' outright rejection of their abusive and violent practices. An examination of these lynchings suggests citizens were not merely passive observers of the abusive practices of these figures of authority. Instead, citizens both challenged and retaliated against their "uncivil" behavior, even though their responses ended up reproducing the excessive use of violence they allegedly sought to correct in the first place.

The last modality of lynching, state-sanctioned lynching, demonstrates clearly that public officials—including mayors and police officers—did not avert the use of mob violence but actually promoted it as a form of governance and social control. Although state-sanctioned lynchings receded during the 1950s, reflecting a shift toward more covert forms of violence, the use of extralegal forms of violence involving high levels of cruelty persisted as a means to deal with so-called criminals and political opponents. Cases of torture and extralegal killings perpetrated by public officials, bearing the hallmarks of lynchings, demonstrate clearly that the behavior of state actors did little to minimize violence through legitimate and legal practices.

Together, these three modalities of lynching challenge the narrative of state making that claims that the centralization of authority, together with the greater presence of the state at the local level, entails a decrease in extralegal, overt, and public forms of violence such as lynching. Furthermore, these modalities of lynching suggest that mob violence was not an expression of atavistic traditions but was actually part of a broader repertoire of extralegal forms of violence used by public officials and citizens in post-revolutionary Mexico.

2

In the Name of Christ

Lynching and Religion in Post-Revolutionary Mexico

On the night of November 11, 1934, dozens of villagers lynched the widow Micaela Ortega in the town of Acajete, in Puebla.[1] A fifty-eight-year-old woman, Micaela was known for her socialist ideas as well as for being a spiritist. According to testimonies collected by an inspector, Fernando A. Rodríguez, villagers resented Micaela's politics and anticlericalism. She had threatened neighbors with turning the church into a library as well as with burning the image of Jesus the Father. She was also known as a close friend of Moisés Juárez, an agrarista peasant who had allegedly stolen the harvest on indigenous communal lands and whose house was set on fire just moments before Micaela's lynching.

The autopsy revealed perpetrators used conspicuous cruelty against Micaela. Clad in a white dress with red flowers, a necklace made of coral, and white underwear that was now torn and burned, her body showed clear signs of torture. Her face presented several bruises and cuts made close to her ears with knives and machetes, her thorax and gluteus had been burned with pieces of hot iron, and her left leg had been broken with clubs. In their testimony, Micaela's children, Rafael and Enedina Castillo, recounted that just minutes before the lynching they heard the town's church bells ringing and people shouting, "¡Viva Cristo Rey!," "Death to socialism," and "Death to the spiritist Doña Micaela." Enedina, who was also attacked that night, stated that among those who participated in the lynching was the mayor, Pedro Loranca Rosas, an alleged Cristero who was sent to the Islas Marías prison after the incident.

Despite its overt cruelty, the lynching of Micaela Ortega was not an isolated event. As discussed in chapter 1, from 1934 to 1940, dozens of socialist teachers were hanged, mutilated, and tortured, all in context of the so-called Second Cristiada.² The attacks were perpetrated by armed groups of vigilantes as well as by lynch mobs,³ which proliferated throughout different rural communities, mainly in west and central Mexico. The violence used against socialist teachers constituted a reaction to the anticlerical and pro-agrarian undertones of the government's official campaign to secularize and modernize the countryside by means of schooling.

Conversely, during the 1940s and into the 1950s, dozens of Protestants were expelled from their communities,⁴ had their homes and churches burned, and were either threatened or actually lynched by groups of Catholics in the states of Puebla, Estado de México, Guanajuato, Oaxaca, Veracruz, Guerrero, and Chiapas.⁵ Informed by religious differences and intracommunity conflicts, these events were precipitated by local enactments of the "Crusade for the Defense of the Catholic Faith" launched by Archbishop Luis María Martínez in 1944 against Protestantism.

In addition to violence perpetrated against socialist teachers and Protestants, throughout these decades, rioters and lynch mobs attacked dozens of individuals who were accused of desecrating Catholic churches and religious symbols in several cities and towns in Puebla, Michoacán, Estado de México, Veracruz, Guanajuato, and Mexico City. Victims included people who were allegedly caught stealing religious images, as well as heretical men and women thought to have defiled the sacredness of churches or undermined the authority of local priests.

This chapter analyzes the impact of religion on the organization and legitimation of lynching during the period.⁶ I discuss the three expressions of violence mentioned above: the lynching of impious individuals accused of stealing religious images or desecrating religious spaces, collective attacks against socialist teachers, and assaults on Protestants.

All the cases analyzed here took place after Mexico's armed conflict over the religious question, the Cristero War, had formally ended. As such, these violent episodes bring into question whether a modus vivendi was truly reached between the state and the church after the conflict.⁷ In light of the church's growing rejection of armed resistance, these expressions of violence bring to the fore the importance of popular or folk strands of Catholicism in legitimating violence.⁸

For the purpose of this chapter, I define religion, particularly Catholicism,⁹ as a set of practices, beliefs, and institutions that are connected to spiritual as well as material and political concerns.¹⁰ In other words, I understand religion as a field that involves both otherworldly and mundane questions.¹¹ The spiritual realm includes the belief in the holy and transcendental, the observation of religious rites, and the reverence of images associated with the sacred. Conversely, the realm of the material and political involves the power and influence of local priests in given communities,¹² the intricate connections between priests and public officials (mayors in particular), and the relationship between lay members of the Catholic Church and the interests of economic and political elites at the local level.

An understanding of religion that accounts for the spiritual and material dimensions of the religious experience is especially pertinent for the period under study. The Cristero War revealed the contentious character of the secular and anticlerical undercurrents of the post-revolutionary project. It further revealed the deep influence of Catholicism in the social and political makeup of communities throughout Mexico, as well as the extent to which attacks on religion could result in political mobilization, organized dissent, and even armed resistance. The decades following the Cristero War further illuminated the extent to which the Catholic religion was deeply embedded in the sociopolitical structure of communities. The galvanizing effect that anticlericalism had at the local level was connected not only to the defense of the spiritual and symbolic dimensions of religion but also to the power structures promoted by the clergy and by lay members of the Catholic church.[13]

In addition to the material and symbolic dimensions of religion, it is important to recognize the fault lines between popular and institutional strands of Catholicism as well as between different members of the clergy. As argued by the historian Ben Fallaw, behind its monolithic facade, Mexico's Catholic Church was traversed by multiple divisions, including different approaches to the ways in which the church ought to relate to the state and to those who opposed the influence of Catholicism.[14] These divisions involved bitter disagreements between the clergy and lay groups and organizations,[15] as well as significant friction among members of the Catholic hierarchy itself, including prelates and diocesan priests. The 1929 accords that put an end to the Cristero War were themselves a source of discord among the clergy. Radical members of the clergy and the laity felt betrayed by the episcopate's willingness to negotiate with authorities who had consistently attacked their faith and disrespected their worldviews.[16]

Divisions within the Catholic Church became more evident in the following decades. Higher-ranking officials in the church distanced themselves—at least officially—from the actions of those who opted to take up arms or use violent means in the name of religion.[17] However, in clear contrast to the church's official position, many lay Catholics endorsed the use of violence, including lynching, as a means to defend the moral and material integrity of their communities. Parish priests played a particularly relevant role in legitimating lynching through their actions and omissions, all in light of the spiritual and moral weight they had in communal life. This is not to say that the higher ranks of the church were entirely opposed to the violence that was being waged in the name of religion. Despite condemning the use of violence, bishops' use of belligerent and intransigent language, as when referring to the threat posed by socialism and Protestantism, did little to stop the violence against so-called infidels and instead provided ideological grounds for its legitimation.[18] The influence of their words and opinions was, however, ultimately mediated by the role of local priests as well as by laymen and laywomen who appropriated and deployed the church's official position according to their own views and religious beliefs.[19]

Rather than present a linear cause-and-effect relationship between lynching and religion, I am interested in understanding the ways in which the religious experience contributed to shaping both the legitimacy and the occurrence of lynching. Several interrelated dynamics characterized the exercise of Catholicism in postrevolutionary Mexico. The first involved the importance of religious images, artifacts, and spaces for Catholics' spiritual and ritualistic experience of religion, at both the individual and community levels.[20] The defense of these religious symbols by laypeople and clergy alike acquired a particularly belligerent character, as representatives of the government and anticlerical groups sponsored by postrevolutionary politicians openly engaged in acts of iconoclasm.

The second dynamic was the Catholic Church's promotion—on behalf of both official and folk members—of a conservative and reactionary ideology that rejected the influence of religious creeds and progressive ideologies considered foreign and a threat to the stability and internal cohesion of the community and the nation.[21] This ideology provided the basis for rationalizing the lynching of communists, socialists, and Protestants.[22]

The third relevant aspect of the religious experience in relation to lynching was the role of parish priests in the spiritual, social, and political makeup of communities. Local priests blessed the newborn and the dead, organized the towns' festivals, formed alliances with the economic and political elites, and delineated the moral contours of the community by establishing what were considered acceptable or unacceptable forms of behavior. As such, their actions and omissions were central to shaping Catholics' predisposition to violence.

Finally, Catholic religion, particularly its folk strands, contributed to the formation of a sacrificial ethos that regarded the use of violence as redemptive and purifying in the face of dangerous and polluting elements.[23] This sacrificial ethos, which had its most immediate manifestations in the Cristero War and in the stories of martyrdom and sacrifice that developed in its aftermath,[24] rendered the use of violence a necessary, even moral, response to maintain the unity and integrity of a community.[25]

I develop my argument in three sections, each focusing on one of the three different manifestations of mob violence mentioned earlier: lynchings of heretical individuals, of socialist teachers, and of Protestants.[26]

A WAR OF SYMBOLS: THE LYNCHING OF THE BLASPHEMOUS

On June 16, 1931, a group of worshippers lynched León J. Muste outside a small church in the town of Santa Ana Maya, Michoacán. Muste, a Dutch national who was initially described by the press as either Russian or German, had ignited the sentiments of churchgoers when he started shouting offenses against the Catholic religion and defending communism.[27] The worshippers, who were praying inside the church, asked Muste to stop his antireligious diatribe. The town's priest, Agustín Parra, joined his congregation and reprimanded the man for his provocative actions. Instead of discontinuing his incendiary speech, Muste threatened the priest with what appeared to be a gun. In that moment, a crowd of worshippers, including a group of young women, surrounded Muste and started beating him severely. The man died at the hands of the lynch mob before the police could intervene. Parra and four young women were taken to the Morelia penitentiary while an investigation established who was responsible for the lynching. Interviewed by the press, the priest stated that he had been taken inside the church by members of the congregation who were trying to defend him against Muste and that he was "absolutely unaware" of what his flock had done afterward.

The lynching of Muste in a town located in the state of Michoacán, hometown of Lázaro Cárdenas and one of the hotbeds of the Cristero War, illustrates the violent reactions that impious individuals and their deeds precipitated among Catholic devotees. Although press accounts portrayed these and other incidents as sudden and irrational, an analysis of several cases that took place under similar circumstances in post-revolutionary Mexico allows me to situate them in a context characterized by revolutionary anticlericalism and by Catholics' fierce defense of their religious beliefs and practices.

Anticlericalism was a key aspect of nineteenth-century liberalism and its efforts to modernize society.[28] Although it receded temporarily under the dictatorship of Porfirio Díaz (1884–1911), it returned in full force during the revolutionary years. During the first three decades of the twentieth century, hundreds of churches were closed down, occupied, damaged, or destroyed by government officials as part of the defanaticization and secularization campaigns promoted by the elites.[29] President Plutarco Elías Calles (1924–28), in particular, promoted the use of anticlerical measures in order to undermine the influence exercised by the Catholic Church and establish a new civil religion based on reason, individual autonomy, and socialist values.[30]

The *ley de cultos* (law of religious worship) promulgated in 1926, for instance, limited the number of priests and churches that towns could have and prohibited the public exercise of religion.[31] Moreover, some political elites incorporated the adoption of iconoclastic actions as part of their mission to defanaticize. Iconoclasm was common among military commanders during the Mexican Revolution and continued to be performed during the 1920s and 1930s as a means to weaken the influence of Catholicism in given communities. By burning and destroying religious symbols and desecrating churches,[32] post-revolutionary leaders not only sought to assault the political and economic power of religion, but also to "strike at the heart of religion's symbolic structure."[33]

The enduring authority of the Catholic Church and the strong presence of popular religiosity in rural and urban communities alike meant that these policies faced substantial opposition and resistance. Throughout the 1930s and 1940s, and with less frequency during the 1950s, rumors and accusations regarding the potential expulsion of priests, the closing of churches, and the robbery or destruction of religious images prompted riots, lynchings, and other forms of collective violence in different localities of central Mexico.[34]

Cárdenas's presidency (1934–40) promoted a more conciliatory approach to the religious question. This eventually led to the abandonment of anticlericalism and especially iconoclasm as hallmarks of the revolution.[35] However, the persistence of anticlericalism at the regional level, together with Catholics' past encounters with revolutionary Jacobins, contributed to the perpetuation of religiously motivated violence. This is not to suggest that all those who engaged in acts of blasphemy were Jacobins or anticlerical ideologues. People accused of stealing religious images, in particular, acted more like small-time thieves than anticlerical revolutionaries,[36] yet their activities were seen as equally offensive. For instance, in contrast to Muste, whose verbal attacks on religion were informed by communism, the motivations of Fructuoso Concha, a man who stole several religious images from a church in Tlaxcala, east of Mexico City, were economic in nature.[37] Concha had stolen religious images made of gold and precious stones in April 1933 and was taken to prison after confessing to his crimes. Considering the punishment insufficient, a mob broke into the prison a month later, dragged him out of the building, and lynched him. On the morning of May 12, the town's church bells were rung to announce to villagers that something had happened the night before. When they walked out of their homes, people saw Concha's corpse, showing signs of torture, hanging from a tree in the middle of the town's plaza.[38]

The lynching of Fructuoso Concha demonstrates that sacrilegious robberies, even when not overtly political in intent, could inflame Catholic mobs.[39] Reported a few years earlier, the story of Jacinto B. Saldaña, a man accused of trying to steal an icon from the church of San Miguel Nonoalco, in Mexico City, resembles that of Concha.[40] In this case, however, the victim turned out to be innocent. After spending an unusually long time inside the church, Saldaña became the object of a rumor that claimed he was there to commit a robbery. Although they had no evidence to confirm that this was the case, a group of worshippers dragged Saldaña out of the church with the intention of lynching him. Later on, they decided to throw him into a nearby river from which he was rescued by the Red Cross.

The circulation of rumors regarding alleged assaults on religious images, spaces, and authorities played a key role in the occurrence of lynchings. Rumors constitute collective and unverified interpretations that serve to make sense of uncertain events as well as stressful situations.[41] They enable people to create a plausible narrative regarding situations that would otherwise seem too overpowering. In the case of Saldaña's lynching, the plausibility of a robbery was based on the fact that the church had indeed been robbed many times before. A more basic source of anxiety, however, had to do with the continuing assault on religious symbols that Catholics experienced during this period. This context, together with the centrality of religious images and spaces in Catholics' experience of the sacred, contributed to the veracity of these rumors as well as to the violent reactions that ensued. Several cases of rioting in Mexico City illustrate the entanglement of rumors and the government's policies.

On November 13, 1935, a riot broke out outside Espíritu Santo Church in the Santa Maria neighborhood of Mexico City.[42] The riot was provoked by the arrival of public officials from the education and interior ministries who were trying to close a Catholic school located next to the church. Their presence prompted the rumor that they were actually planning to close the church and detain the priest. After ringing the church bells, a group of Catholic neighbors defiantly stood outside the church to guard it. The officials called on the police to ease the crowd, but people became even more infuriated and started to gather stones and throw them at the police officers. The disturbances lasted until the middle of the night. Rioters retreated only after authorities reassured them that the church would not be closed and the priest would not be taken prisoner. In May 1936, another riot took place in the church of San Miguel Nonoalco, the same church in which Saldaña was nearly lynched.[43] This time, rioters surrounded the church after learning by word of mouth that the government was planning to remove the church's religious images and burn them. The crowd threatened Alfaro Vázquez, a public official who was commissioned to collect the images. Vázquez tried in vain to assuage the crowd by explaining the images were indeed being removed but not to be burned as Catholics feared; rather, they were being taken to the Museum of Religious Arts to be preserved and exhibited. The police had to intervene to disband the rioters.[44]

Despite newspapers' references to some of these incidents as an expression of the ignorance or "religious fanaticism" of people, assaults on religious symbols were in fact part of a systematic attack on the Catholic faith. The arrest and expulsion of Catholic priests who did not comply with the ley de cultos, the closing of churches, and the burning of religious images were all part of an official campaign that sought to create a new model of citizenry, freed from the "backward" influence of Catholicism.[45] The defilement and destruction of Catholic symbols was particularly crucial to fulfill the aims of revolutionary anticlericalism. Although not all post-revolutionary politicos embraced iconoclasm,[46] the visibility and impact of those who did made iconoclasm a salient feature of the post-revolutionary period.

Among those revolutionaries who embraced iconoclasm, and this with particular ferocity, was the Tabasco governor and strongman Tomás Garrido Canabal (1919–34).[47] Convinced of the need to create a new society based on reason and science, Garrido Canabal promoted an aggressive strand of anticlericalism that involved the profanation of religious rites and spaces, the harassment and killing of priests, and the systematic use of iconoclasm as a means to "educate" and "defanaticize" people. An integral part of his strategy to create an "enlightened" citizenry was the formation of Bloques Juveniles Revolucionarios (Young Revolutionary Blocs), also known as Camisas Rojas (Red Shirts). The Red Shirts operated like a paramilitary organization. Its members, young male anticlericals, orchestrated acts of provocation and religious defilement, including the destruction and burning of religious images and statues. When Garrido Canabal was appointed minister of agriculture during the first year of Cárdenas's presidency, the Red Shirts started a campaign aimed at bringing Tabasco's "exemplar model" of anticlericalism to the capital and eventually to the whole country.[48]

It was in the context of this so-called campaign to step up the presence of anticlericalism that the riot in Coyoacán and the ensuing lynching of Ernesto Malda took place. On Sunday morning, December 30, 1934, about sixty Red Shirts gathered in front of the San Juan Bautista church, located in the Coyoacán neighborhood in Mexico City.[49] The young radicals had arrived from Tabasco a few weeks before and every Sunday had been organizing antireligious demonstrations where they manifested their rejection of the church's authority and called into question the existence of God. That Sunday was no different. While worshippers listened to the morning Mass, the Red Shirts gathered outside, planted a red and black flag in the soil,[50] and started their vociferous attack on religion. Official newspapers reported that it was the worshippers who first confronted the Red Shirts as they came out of Mass, incited by the priest and enraged by the inflammatory speech of the young iconoclasts.[51] Regardless of who started the clash, the fact that five Catholics, including one woman and four men, were shot and killed as the confrontation unfolded makes clear that the Red Shirts were certainly not passive agents.[52]

Following the deaths of the five Catholics, tensions escalated. The young radicals rushed to the Coyoacán delegation, just across from the church, while a large group of Catholics rioted outside the building and demanded authorities turn in the Red Shirts. Ernesto Malda arrived at the scene in the midst of this mayhem. A young man in his early twenties, Malda had joined the Red Shirts as one of a number of Mexico City residents who were persuaded by the organization's mission.[53] He was late to the Red Shirts' gathering and was immediately spotted by the infuriated crowd, as he was wearing the typical uniform of the group, red shirt and black pants. After being dragged by the mob in the direction of the church, Mazda was beaten to death with fists, knives, and stones. His skull showed two large injuries, pieces of his scalp were ripped off, his thorax was crushed, and one of his eyes was gouged out.[54] The police arrested sixty-two Red Shirts in connection with the killing of the five Catholics, and three men were held in connection with the lynching of Malda.[55]

Demonstrations ensued on both sides of the conflict. The Red Shirts organized a funeral for the young Malda. They carried his coffin through the streets of Mexico City and promised to intensify their campaign against religious fanatics.[56] Catholics, for their part, formed the Club of the Assassinated of Coyoacán and demanded, among other things, the resignation of Garrido Canabal as well as the prosecution of the Red Shirts.[57] While supporters of anticlericalism came to see Malda as a martyr, Catholics highlighted the martyrdom of the five believers who died at the hands of the intransigent Red Shirts.[58] These conflicting stories of martyrdom reflect the use of narratives and symbols by both Catholics and revolutionaries to capture the hearts and minds of people.[59]

The lynching of Malda drew the condemnation of official newspapers and government supporters.[60] A representative article published by the government's mouthpiece, *El Nacional,* on January 3, 1935, explained the lynching as part of a systematic campaign promoted by the highest ranks of the Catholic Church to "oppose in a violent way the implementation of socialist education, the economic liberation of the worker, and the defanaticization of the masses." It was, the article editorialized, not an exceptional and entirely spontaneous attack but rather the manifestation of a careful strategy directed against "our institutions, against our advanced laws, and against the modernizing labor of the government."[61] A related article reinforced the notion that the clergy was responsible for a systematic campaign against the government, which included the tactical use of lynching on the part of the "ignorant multitude" against the socialist and collectivist ideas promoted by the state.[62]

These and other newspaper articles framed these lynchings as expressions of the backwardness and religious fanaticism of people,[63] as well as the result of a master plan orchestrated by the higher ranks of the clergy. In other words, they presented lynching perpetrators as individuals who, blinded by their religious fanaticism and ignorance, fell prey to the astute manipulation of priests.[64] The influence of the clergy in the organization of lynching was, however, more nuanced and was certainly not part of a top-down strategy carefully crafted by the higher ranks of the Catholic Church.

Although the antagonism promoted by bishops provided an important source of legitimation of the use of violence in the name of religion, the influence of the church was most clearly manifested in the behavior of local priests who adopted a belligerent stance against the government's anticlerical policies and who, through their discourse and actions, ignited the sentiments of churchgoers. Furthermore, the influence of the clergy in the legitimation of lynching was mediated by ordinary Catholics whose folk or popular reinterpretations of Catholic beliefs sanctioned the rightfulness of violence as a means to defend religion.[65] In other words, Catholic laity who approved the use of lynching did so on their own terms and were not, as the press hinted, instruments of an orchestrated and top-down strategy.[66]

The lynching of Micaela Ortega in November 1934 described at the beginning of this chapter illuminates the complexities of the clergy's influence in the organization of mob violence. The lynching had prompted an investigation by the federal government in order to elucidate to what degree the local priest, Federico Osorio y Corona, bore responsibility for the killing of Micaela.[67] According to neighbors interviewed by the federal inspector Fernando A. Rodríguez, the priest had warned his flock about the laws promoted by the government and about the possibility of the church being closed as a result of these laws. The priest had also made reference to Micaela's political inclinations and repeatedly told churchgoers that if they were not happy with him he would leave the town.

Despite this, the inspector did not believe the priest was responsible for the lynching of Micaela. This is remarkable considering that the inspector was a government official who had explicitly been asked to investigate the possible responsibility of the priest in the lynching. Instead, the inspector echoed the opinion of most villagers, including family members of the deceased, who reportedly identified Moisés Juárez as the person who had stirred the sentiments of villagers. Moisés was an agrarista who had allegedly stolen communal lands' harvest and who was a close friend of Micaela. The day of Micaela's lynching, Moisés had called a group of villagers "indios cristeros" (Cristero Indians) and while in the company of two soldiers had threatened them with closing the church. The villagers, who already resented Moisés, decided to punish him for these offenses and walked over to his house with the intention of lynching him. When they did not find Moisés, they set his house on fire. While some villagers watched Moisés's house burn, others started to walk toward Micaela's home. It was thus her close relationship with a loathed agrarista such as Moisés and the fact that she had also threatened villagers with closing the church and even with burning the image of Jesus the Father that made Micaela a target.[68]

As this account of the event suggests, the influence of the priest alone cannot explain the lynching of Micaela. Villagers' defense of religious symbols as well as intracommunity conflicts over land and resources were also crucial. Even if the priest's opinions about Micaela's socialist ideas or the government's anticlerical polices influenced the temper of the crowd, we cannot rule out the genuinely affective experience of distress and anger that threats against religion provoked among Catholics. The same statement can be made in regard to the lynching of Ernesto Malda. In that case, churchgoers were not merely incited by the priest, as the press accounts seemed to suggest. Rather, they were reacting to what they regarded as an open assault on their beliefs and those who shared their faith.

The press and public officials, however, privileged a narrative that put the onus on priests' ability and propensity to *azuzar* (incite) their flock. For instance, in March 1936, in relation to a riot that took place in Ciudad González, Guanajuato, the press pointed to the priest's responsibility for having incited churchgoers to attack a group of teachers participating in a cultural brigade outside the church.[69] The article went so far as to suggest that the priest had carefully planned the attack, as the churchgoers came out of the church armed with pistols, stones, and knives. The attack was met with violence by the other side, teachers and a group of armed agraristas, and resulted in fifteen deaths and more than twenty injured. President Cárdenas himself visited Ciudad González to show his support for the teachers. The day of the incident, an official statement on behalf of the president's office proclaimed that "the responsibility of the bloody events" in Ciudad González was precipitated in its entirety by "fanatic elements that, stirred up [azuzados] by the local priest, had attacked for no reason the teachers of the Cultural Mission." What the official statement and the newspaper account of the event failed to acknowledge was the possibility that churchgoers felt themselves offended by the organization of a cultural activity sponsored by the government on a Sunday, right outside the church precisely at the time of the Mass.[70]

To acknowledge that the influence of the clergy in the organization of lynchings was more nuanced does not mean, however, that such influence was not relevant.[71] Parish priests, in particular, were considered a central source of local authority, and their presence was regarded as an essential component of the spiritual well-being of communities.[72] They acted as a moral compass that helped delineate the boundaries between acceptable and unacceptable behaviors, norms, and ideologies. Their religious authority, particularly in small towns, often mixed with politics as priests developed close relationships with landed elites and were able to exercise their influence over local secular authorities.[73] The adherence to or rejection of certain political ideologies, the appropriate upbringing of children, and the expected participation in communal festivals and rituals all fell under the purview of the priest. This authority did not escape the notice of teachers, workers, and agrarista peasants who time and again complained about the priests' ability to agitate worshippers.

IMPIOUS EDUCATION: THE LYNCHING OF SOCIALIST TEACHERS

In July 1934, the *jefe máximo* (supreme leader) Plutarco Elías Calles announced the beginning of a new era of the revolution in which revolutionary ideas would be inculcated in children and youth in order to fight the detrimental influence of conservative and clerical elements.[74] The main battlefield for this new front of radical transformation would be education. Within months of this announcement and only a couple of weeks into Cárdenas's presidency, federal authorities established that the content of public education would be socialist. The amended article 3 of the constitution stated, "The education provided by the State will be socialist and, in addition to excluding all religious doctrines, it will fight fanaticism and prejudices; to such an end, the school will organize its [model of] education and activities in a way that will inculcate in the youth a rational and exact concept of the Universe and of social life."[75]

The dangers presented to the Catholic Church by this new model of education were evident. Socialist education was informed by an overt anticlerical and antireligious ideology and entailed the state's interference in a realm that the church considered central for the promotion of its religious doctrine. Furthermore, socialist education threatened two of the church's most valued natural rights: the right of parents to provide a religious education to their children and the natural right to private property.[76] Agrarian reform and the mobilization of workers and peasants were both endeavors entrusted to rural teachers that directly challenged the right to private property.[77] Equally problematic in the eyes of Catholics was the role that socialist teachers played in the defanaticization campaigns promoted by the government. Teachers denounced the "seditious" activities of priests, petitioned for their removal or expulsion, and contributed to the closing of churches and the organization of patriotic festivals and cultural activities intended to eclipse religious celebrations.[78] Although not all teachers embraced radical forms of anticlericalism and many actually preferred to avoid an all-out confrontation with the church,[79] their image as official representatives of an anticlerical state, together with the iconoclastic actions of a few Jacobin teachers, made them vulnerable to the hostility of Catholic mobs.

Acts of iconoclasm, such as teachers and young pupils destroying crosses, setting fire to images of the Virgin, mutilating images of patron saints, and vandalizing churches, left a deep impression on Catholics.[80] In San Juan de Gracia, Michoacán, for instance, the *maestro rural* (rural teacher) used the church as a kitchen, a toilet, and even a chicken coop. Ildefonso Vega, in charge of the parish, reported that the church was vandalized, with damage that included "two virgins without head, a Christ without head, a sacred heart without head, and the body of the local patron saint, San Jose, with only his feet [left]."[81] He added that these abuses could "result in great disorders" among villagers. Indeed, in some cases, these impious acts did carry great consequences. In a small town in the Sierra Madre Occidental, in the northwestern state of Durango, two teachers who asked their students to deny the existence of God and to make other heretical pronouncements in the classroom were found dead in the town's main plaza.[82] The female teacher asked students to greet her by saying, "There is no God," while the male teacher told students that he "urinated on God." Sometime later, the woman was found naked, raped, and with her breasts mutilated; the man was found castrated, with the urinary meatus cut. On his body the perpetrators left a note that, in poor spelling, said, "So you do not go around peeing on God."[83]

The maiming of socialist teachers as a means to retaliate for their assault on Catholic symbols and practices deserves attention. Catholic mobs and groups of vigilantes responded to teachers' defilement of religious symbols and practices not only by threatening them with violence or by physically assaulting them but also by mutilating and marking their bodies.[84] On November 15, 1935, for instance, three teachers were killed in different towns of the municipality of Teziultlán, in the Sierra Norte of Puebla, by a group of vigilantes under the command of Clemente Mendoza.[85] One of the teachers, Carlos Pastrana, had his head practically decapitated with a machete blow. The other two, Carlos Sayago and Librado Labastida, were shot and their bodies left outside the school where they had imparted socialist education. Days later, a group of armed men assaulted two sisters, Micaela and Enriqueta Palacios, for imparting socialist education in San Martín Hidalgo, Jalisco. The group cut the teachers' ears off and also assaulted their father, who was with them at the time of the attack.[86] The same month, another female teacher was mutilated using machetes, this time in Jalancigo, Veracruz.[87] The suspected killers were Mendoza's vigilantes. In April 1936, in Tlapacoyan, also in Veracruz, around seventy armed men carrying a flag with the motto, "¡Viva Cristo Rey!," burned one teacher, Carlos Toledano, alive and cut off the ears of another teacher, Pablo Jimenez. The men set the school on fire for being a center of heresy.[88]

The mutilation of ears was a common form of violence against teachers,[89] as were hanging and, to a lesser extent, burning. One of the most famous vigilantes who participated in the Segunda Cristiada, Odilón Vega, was known as "el desorejador de maestros" (roughly, the teachers' ear cropper).[90] The maiming of opponents, including the cutting off of ears, was common during the Mexican Revolution. The use of this technique of torture against teachers was probably a direct reference to this experience.[91] At a more symbolic level, the cutting off of ears can be interpreted as a way to denounce the government's deafness to those who opposed socialist education or as a means to mark the teachers' bodies in order to send a message to a broader audience. For instance, a picture of Micaela and Enriqueta Palacios published in November 1935 in *Excélsior*, showing them wearing heavy bandages around their heads, sent a powerful message to others regarding the potential costs of imparting socialist education.[92]

Although the cutting off of ears was more closely linked to groups of vigilantes than to lynch mobs, lynchings of teachers also involved the use of torture as well as the exposure of teachers' bodies or corpses in visible public spaces. For instance, in March 1935, the nineteen-year-old teacher David Moreno Herrera was lynched in Aguascalientes. After being forced out of his house, the lynch mob proceeded to torture him and then hanged him from a tree.[93] A few months later, a teacher was tortured and tied to a rock in the municipality of Zacatlán, Puebla; the perpetrators had also hanged the mayor and the president of the agrarian committee in protest against socialist education.[94] In September 1935, the teacher León Fernández and his wife were severely beaten with clubs by a group of men and women in the town of Atoyac, Jalisco.[95] And in Tlaltenango, Zacatecas, the teachers Saúl Maldonado and Guillermo Suro were hanged from a tree after being brutally attacked and forced to pray by their assailants.[96]

As implied by these cases, teachers were victimized by both armed groups of vigilantes and more spontaneous lynch mobs. Reflecting on this dynamic, Fallaw has suggested that attacks against teachers can be categorized under the rubrics of offensive and defensive attacks, with the former consisting of well-planned attacks perpetrated by vigilantes and the second involving more impulsive, bottom-up, communal reactions to teachers' anticlericalism.[97] According to Fallaw, whereas in the case of offensive violence it is difficult to distinguish between political and religious aims, as vigilantes received the support of landowners, clergy, and Catholic activists, defensive attacks reflected more clearly people's attempts to protect "their community's moral core from godless government agents."[98] In his earlier work on socialist education and the violence against teachers, the historian David L. Raby reached a similar conclusion.[99] In his view, discerning between the purely religious motivations and the material interests driving violence against socialist teachers is particularly challenging, as the political and economic interests of caciques, landed elites, and the clergy could influence people's violent responses to socialist education. Akin to Fallaw's interpretation, Raby suggests further, "It was just in the cases of lynching and tumultuous violence against teachers, where the religious motives straightforwardly prevailed."[100]

The analytical distinction between lynch mobs and vigilantes is an important one. It helps us elucidate the different degrees of premeditation and organization that characterized violence against teachers, as well as illuminate the extent to which La Segunda was a more or less cohesive armed conflict. However, particularly in those cases in which the violence perpetrated by vigilantes reflected the sentiments of villagers, the line between "top-down" and "bottom-up" attacks is not easy to draw. Furthermore, the suggestion that in contrast to vigilantes, lynch mobs were more transparently motivated by religious beliefs seems problematic. In spite of their apparent impulsiveness, lynchings were far from reflecting pure religious frenzy. Instead, political and material interests, together with symbolic and spiritual concerns, informed their occurrence. Conversely, what we know about the motivations of vigilantes suggests that at least some of them genuinely embraced Catholic beliefs or were moved by both material and spiritual interests.[101] Several examples illustrate the blurred lines between vigilante killings and the lynch mob.

On March 2, 1938, newspapers reported that a group of vigilantes under the command of Enrique Rodríguez aka El Tallarín had assassinated a teacher, José Ramírez Martínez, and two local officials in the town of Cuautomatitla in the municipality of Tochimilco, Puebla.[102] Maximino Ávila Camacho, then governor of Puebla, sent a letter to the minister of the interior explaining that an investigation conducted by local authorities had established that El Tallarín had indeed provoked the attack.[103] He explained further that, contrary to rumors, villagers had not participated in the killing of the teacher as they had consistently demonstrated their willingness to cooperate with federal authorities. However, a letter addressed to the president on behalf of the local teachers' union provided an alternative explanation.[104] In that letter, Jesús A. Ceja explained that although El Tallarín had allegedly shot the teacher and then demanded that villagers hang his corpse from a tree only after he was killed, the autopsy revealed the victim had died from asphyxia and not from gunshot wounds. This, together with villagers' contradictory accounts of the events, made Ceja conclude that villagers had played a more active and complicit role in the teacher's killing.[105] The local newspaper *La Opinión* was even more suggestive. In an article published on March 3, 1938, it stated that El Tallarín was not to be blamed for the death of Ramírez Martínez, and that the people of Cuautomatitla, who had previous conflicts with the teacher, had provoked his assassination.[106]

The popular support that vigilantes enjoyed in certain communities also complicates the distinction between vigilantes and lynch mobs. The case of the three teachers who were assassinated in Teziutlán, Puebla, in November 1935 exemplifies this. As stated above, the three teachers—Carlos Sayago, Carlos Pastrana, and Librado Labastida—were killed by a group of vigilantes under the command of Clemente Mendoza. The investigation that followed the attack revealed, however, that while it was true that the vigilantes were responsible for the murder of the three teachers, it was also true that villagers did not welcome the teachers and that the community thus probably approved of their assassination.[107] According to the report sent to the federal government, children's attendance at school had decreased in the last months. Moreover, parents had started a campaign with the support of the clergy and the Liga Nacional Defensora de la Libertad Religiosa (LNDLR; National Defense League for Religious Liberty) to denounce the immoral character of socialist education. Carlos Sayago's sister declared that the parish priest of Teziutlán had warned her days before the assassination that teachers had become "too anticlerical." Carlos Pastrana, for his part, had organized a dance in August that year to boycott a Catholic celebration in the town of Ixtecpan. As a result, one of the villagers had come to his house and, armed with a machete, threatened to kill him. Similarly, Librado Labastida had received various death threats from villagers who shouted "¡Viva Cristo Rey!" every time they saw him passing by. In sum, the actions of Mendoza coincided with the animosity of villagers toward anticlerical teachers.[108]

As this and other cases reveal, local priests contributed to shaping villagers' perceptions of socialist education. They were thus instrumental in the moral legitimization of those who decided to resist by violent means.[109] Aware of their influence, teachers, workers, and education inspectors denounced the activities of parish priests, sending letters and examples of "religious propaganda" to federal authorities. In reference to the context surrounding the killing of the three teachers in Puebla, the Unión Nacional de Maestros Federales (National Union of Federal Teachers) denounced the antisocialist propaganda promoted by "the fanatical clergy that tries through all means to stop the rising and continuous progress of the Mexican pueblo."[110] Included as an example of such propaganda was a copy of the publication *Rayo de Sol,* which referred to socialist education as an ideology that undermined Catholic morality and as a "plague" that promoted perverse and irreligious ideas. Similarly, in a letter to President Cárdenas, a socialist worker named José Parra denounced the seditious activities of a local priest in Guadalajara, Jalisco.[111] According to him, in a meeting that had taken place in February 1935 inside the church of San Sebastián de Analco, the priest had told the congregation that it was their duty to defend the integrity of their faith, even if this meant sacrificing their lives. In July 1936, in the town of Cuatlancingo, Puebla, a group of villagers tried to burn the school and attempted to kill the education inspector after the priest had urged them to get rid of the dangers of socialist education.[112] In reference to the precarious situation faced by teachers in Tonalá, Jalisco, a teacher named Luis N. Rodríguez asserted that priests threatened parents with excommunication if they sent their children to school. He complained about "una chusma de viejas beatas" (a rabble of pious old women) who had stoned a group of female teachers in front of the school.[113]

Violence against socialist teachers, including lynchings, declined considerably after 1938.[114] The resistance that socialist education encountered at the local level contributed to the government's decision to moderate its antireligious and anticlerical aspects.[115] As a result of this shift, the vulnerability of teachers as well as communities' perception of them as individuals who threatened their exercise of religion declined significantly.

The following years would witness a significant change in the relationship between state and church. Although this change began under the Cárdenas presidency,[116] it would be with the arrival of President Manuel Ávila Camacho (1940–46) that the state's relations with the Catholic Church would not only become less antagonistic, but would in fact become increasingly harmonious, even collaborative. However, this détente did not put an end to lynchings driven by Catholicism. Although lynchings of teachers declined, Protestants would become the target of attacks organized in the name of religion, morality, and the nation. Furthermore, lynchings of sacrilegious thieves continued throughout the 1940s and 1950s, reflecting the persistence of Catholics' belligerent attitudes to those who profaned religious symbols.[117]

FIGHTING THE INFERNAL SERPENT: THE LYNCHING OF PROTESTANTS

On April 16, 1944, in the town of Santa María Techachalco, Puebla, a crowd of approximately fifty people attacked a group of Evangelical worshipers armed with clubs, stones, and pistols. Shouting "Death to the Protestants" and "Arriba el

Sinarquismo" (Hail to Sinarquismo), the crowd injured several worshippers, who were taken to the municipal hospital. Reporting on the incident, a newspaper described that days before this attack a group of Sinarquistas had taken a national flag to the town's Catholic priest to bless it.[118] The federal deputy, Salvador Ochoa Rentería, declared that this was yet another case that illustrated the abuses of the Unión Nacional Sinarquista.[119] The following month, in Guadalupe Victoria and La Gloria, towns located at the border of the states of Puebla and Veracruz, a group of Catholics burned down the houses of twelve Evangelical families.[120] The attack was perpetrated in retaliation for the iconoclasm of Evangelicals who, after burying a member of their congregation, destroyed the crosses at the municipal cemetery.[121] In November the same year a group of Catholics burned down the houses of nine Evangelical families and blew up their temple after learning Evangelicals were planning to bring more pastors to the town.[122] The attack led to the exodus of seventy families.

From 1944 to the end of the 1950s, dozens of Protestants fell victim to Catholic rioters and lynch mobs in a number of states in central and southern Mexico. Echoing the dynamics of violence against socialist teachers during the 1930s, attacks against Protestants were perpetrated by both spontaneous mobs and armed groups of vigilantes, in this case, members of the Unión Nacional Sinarquista. Attacks against Protestants, together with the seeming impunity that followed them, need to be understood against the backdrop of the conservative politics introduced by the Ávila Camacho presidency and the new relationship that was forged between state and church during this period.[123]

From the moment he was elected president, Ávila Camacho made clear that the days of anticlericalism and state-sponsored socialism were over. He openly expressed his Catholic faith and eliminated the constitutional clause that characterized the content of Mexico's public education as socialist.[124] He also distanced himself from the progressive politics promoted in the 1930s, including agrarian reform and the promotion of peasants' and workers' rights.[125] Instead, he promoted a message of unity, reconciliation, and discipline based on an anticommunist, nationalistic, and conservative ideology. Furthermore, Ávila Camacho, together with a new generation of post-revolutionary politicians, laid the foundation for what became a mutually beneficial alliance between the state and the Catholic Church.

The Catholic Church had also changed during these years. From the mid-1930s on, the higher ranks of the clergy decided to distance themselves from those who sought to defend religion through the use of arms. Conversely, the church had opted for the pacific and civil mobilization of Catholic lay members through organizations that operated under the umbrella of the Acción Católica Mexicana (Mexican Catholic Action). This shift would become even more pronounced at the end of the 1930s and the beginning of the 1940s, as the church found new common ground with the Mexican state: the battle against communism and the defense of the motherland against foreign influences. A letter published by the archbishop of Mexico, Luis María Martínez, in 1943 is illustrative of this new relationship between church and state. In the letter, published in national newspapers, the archbishop asserted that the church was willing to collaborate effectively with the government for "the good of the country" as well as support enthusiastically the president's call for national unity.[126]

In addition to the battle against communism, the church engaged in a parallel struggle against Protestantism. In his pastoral letter of October 1944, the archbishop launched a crusade in defense of the Catholic faith and against the "infernal serpent of Protestantism."[127] In the letter he wrote that through their resources and propaganda, "Protestant sects" intended to take away Mexicans' "most valuable treasure, the Catholic faith that four centuries ago was brought to us by the Holy Virgin of Guadalupe."[128] This so-called crusade singled out both Protestantism and communism as foreign and dangerous ideologies that needed to be eliminated to secure the moral integrity of Catholic communities, all while reiterating that Catholicism was the only authentic national religion.[129] Representative of the verbal attacks against Protestants enabled by this crusade, a document that circulated at the time read, "Let the most vile of deaths fall upon them [Protestants] and let them descend alive into the abyss. . . . Let their burial be with wolves and asses. Let voracious dogs devour their cadavers. Let the devil and its angels be their perpetual companions. Amen, amen."[130] In time, this type of discursive incitement to violence became actualized at the local level through lynchings and collective attacks against Protestants.[131]

Catholics took into their own hands Archbishop Luis María Martínez's call to repel Protestants and their "dangerous" propaganda. In December 1944, for instance, a crowd attacked a group of Lutherans who were distributing flyers with information about their religious doctrine in a town close to Irapuato in the state of Guanajuato. In addition to destroying the Lutherans' flyers, the crowd attempted to lynch a member of their congregation.[132] Similarly, in May 1945, in the neighborhood of Coyoacán in Mexico City, the same place where the Red Shirt Ernesto Malda was lynched, three young men were threatened by a mob of Catholics in the neighborhood's main plaza. The young men were distributing religious leaflets and putting up posters in the streets urging the Mexican people to renounce Catholicism. Pressed by a group of Catholic women, five policemen approached the young men and asked them to stop their religious agitation and leave the neighborhood. When the young Protestants refused to comply, a crowd surrounded them and attempted to lynch them. The press reported that the police were able to save them, thereby preventing a massacre similar to the one that occurred "a few years ago when the Red Shirts reigned."[133] The following year, a policeman who was wrongly identified as a Protestant pastor was brutally lynched in Jiquipilco, Estado de México. The policeman was visiting the town to carry out an investigation pertaining to conflicts provoked in the locality by the conversion of some neighbors to Protestantism and the presence of a few "evangelizing brigades." After a rumor circulated claiming that he and another policeman were Protestant pastors who planned to seize the Catholic church, a mob of Catholics lynched him with stones, knives, and clubs. The man had his face and skull skinned.[134]

As these cases make clear, Catholics considered Protestants' dissemination of their religious beliefs offensive and threatening. Although Catholicism continued to be Mexico's dominant religion, the marginal increase of non-Catholic faiths,[135] together with the church's official discourse regarding the increasing presence of Protestants in the country,[136] heightened Catholics' animosity to this religious minority. Protestants had historically sided with political ideologies that were condemned by Catholicism, such as liberalism and socialism, both of which encouraged social change, the emancipation of the individual, and the elimination of the Catholic Church's corporate privileges.[137]

During the post-revolutionary period, in particular, Protestants supported socialist education and sympathized with the agrarian reform.[138] They also approved of the state's sanitation and antialcohol campaigns, which echoed Protestants' pursuit of moral regeneration.[139] Equally important, Protestants refused to participate in Catholic festivals and rituals that were contrary to their beliefs.[140] Grounded in folk expressions of Catholicism that prevailed in indigenous communities, these festivities were considered an integral part of communities' religious experience and played a key role in the socioeconomic integration and political order of communal life.[141] As such, Protestants' refusal to participate in these festivities was seen not only as an affront to Catholics' exercise of religion but also as a source of danger to the unity and stability of the community.

Although not all these attacks resulted in lynching, their occurrence demonstrates the climate of hostility that Protestants experienced during these years. Emulating the religious persecution that they themselves had endured in previous decades at the hands of anticlerical revolutionaries, Catholics intimidated and harassed Protestant ministers. They also directed their attacks against entire families of Protestant believers, breaking into their churches, vandalizing their houses, and forcing them into exodus. In March 1945, for instance, in Cuerámaro, Guanajuato, approximately two hundred Catholics broke into a Protestant church and assaulted a group of worshippers, including a pregnant woman.[142] The incident was triggered by an inflammatory sermon delivered by the town's Catholic priest against Protestants just moments before the attack. Similarly, on May 27, 1945, in Santiago Yeche, Estado de México, a group of Catholic neighbors raided the homes of nearly twenty Protestant families.[143] Among the victims was the pastor, Vicente Garita, who, together with his brother-in-law, died after his house was set on fire.

Proclaiming their rights as Mexican citizens, Protestants asked federal authorities to intervene to protect their lives and guarantee their right to exercise religion.

As socialist teachers did before them, Protestants denounced local authorities for their incapacity or unwillingness to act on their behalf. In May 1945, in a letter addressed to President Ávila Camacho, Evangelicals from the town of Acatzingo, Puebla, denounced an attack orchestrated by a group of Sinarquistas led by Esteban Mendez. The Sinarquistas had broken into their homes and attacked several members of their church.[144] Among the victims was their minister, Leonardo Tamariz, who was forced outside his house in the middle of the night and then shot in the town's plaza. The Sinarquistas had also forced their way into the house of Dr. Juan V. Montiel with the intention of killing him. When they did not find him, they decided to kill Enrique Aguilar, a young man who worked for Montiel. Aguilar was struck with machetes and clubs, and Montiel's wife was undressed and forced out of her house. The signees asked the president to intervene as local authorities supported the Sinarquistas and had done nothing to protect them.[145]

David Genaro Ruesga,[146] writing on behalf of the Comité Nacional de Defensa Evangélica (Evangelicals' National Defense Committee), echoed these demands. Addressing President Ávila Camacho, he claimed that the town's Catholic priest had incited the Sinarquistas and stated that this and several other attacks against his coreligionists demonstrated that Archbishop Luis María Martínez's pastoral letter against the Evangelicals was giving "óptimos frutos" (optimal results).[147]

The apparent complicity of local authorities, together with the influence of local priests, increased the vulnerability of Protestants. Moreover, similar to lynchings against socialist teachers, attacks against Protestants were precipitated by intra-community conflicts. In August 1945, for instance, a group of Evangelicals from the town of Esperanza in Puebla addressed the interior minister, urging him to condemn and investigate a number of assaults perpetrated against them during the previous month.[148] These assaults included the attempted lynching of Melquiades Lezama and three Evangelical women by a group of Catholics who had also threatened Evangelical families with burning down their homes. The signees complained about the disregard shown by local authorities toward these incidents, stating, "With a clear partial attitude, [authorities] have neither implemented measures to prevent such crimes nor proceeded against the wrongdoers." Following this petition, an investigation was carried out in the town of Esperanza in September. Although the federal inspector, Carlos Reyes Retana, concluded that local authorities had indeed protected Melquiades to the best of their ability, his description of the event deserves some attention as it brings into sharp focus the impact of intracommunity conflicts on religious violence.[149]

Based on several interviews with members of the community, Reyes Retana explained that over the previous few weeks Melquiades had been holding meetings inside his shop with some out-of-town Evangelicals who were distributing flyers with information about their religion. Melquiades wanted his children to convert to Protestantism, so he welcomed their presence. According to the parish priest, Odilón

Romero, the flyers were "insulting" to Catholicism because they contained images of the pope looking like Hitler and other fascist leaders. The day before the incident, a brawl took place in Melquiades's shop involving a group of Evangelical and Catholic men. As a result of this brawl, a Catholic man died. Although he was not involved in the fight, villagers blamed Melquiades for the death of the Catholic man and gathered outside his house with the intention of lynching him and burning down his house. Luz López, a Catholic woman who participated in the attack, claimed that she was summoned, together with dozens of women, by the president of Acción Católica, Josefina de Trujillo. The mayor prevented Melquiades's lynching by rushing him out of his house and taking him to the municipal offices. Meanwhile, three Evangelical women went to the local prison to visit one of the men involved in the brawl. At that moment another group of Catholics gathered to lynch these women. With the help of a military commander, the women were able to find refuge at the local school. The mayor asked Melquiades to leave town in order to prevent further problems. Melquiades left for a couple of weeks but then came back and "made peace" with Catholic villagers. Reflecting on this, Father Romero asserted that Melquiades had resumed activities at his shop "with all liberty" and that he had converted back to Catholicism. He ended his testimony by asking the inspector to let the Ministry of the Interior know that Evangelicals wanted to build a temple across from the Catholic church, which, he warned, could have fatal consequences.

Reyes Retana's report exposes Catholics' outright rejection of Protestantism. It also reveals the ways in which Catholic villagers reacted when a community member attempted to introduce a different faith into their town.[150] Although the lynching of Melquiades was averted, the resentment and antipathy built around him resembles the tensions that precipitated the lynching of Micaela Ortega, the spiritist and socialist who was killed in November 1934 in Acajete, Puebla. Although the priest did not participate in the organization of the lynching, his religious authority appears in the background of this incident as critical of Melquiades's Protestantism and of the religious propaganda being distributed at Melquiades's shop. Furthermore, that the leader of Acción Católica, an organization created by the Catholic Church to promote civil and pacific forms of resistance, summoned the potential lynchers demonstrates that it was ultimately ordinary Catholics, not the upper ranks of the church, who sanctioned lynching.

Protestants denounced several more incidents of violence in the coming years, pointing to the responsibility of local authorities and the seeming impunity that followed attacks organized against them.[151] Despite the various letters and telegrams sent to the office of the president and to the minister of the interior, the central government neither condemned these attacks publicly nor provided effective protection to these citizens. The Catholic Church was equally silent about violence against Protestants. Hence both civil and religious authorities implicitly tolerated the actions of perpetrators and contributed to their impunity.

Protestants tried to resist the narrative that claimed their religion was a symbol of foreign influence by reminding the government that it was Catholics who had tried to undermine both the country's independence and the revolutionary project by aligning themselves with reactionary forces.[152] Similar to teachers, Protestants appealed to the values of the revolution and urged authorities to live up to the promise of religious tolerance and secularism promoted by revolutionary elites. Their efforts, however, proved futile.[153] The détente between church and state did not bring an end to lynchings and other forms of collective violence motivated by the Catholic religion. In the case of Protestants, in particular, the new ideological proximity between the Catholic Church and post-revolutionary politicians, grounded in nationalism, morality, and the importance of the family, meant that violence against Protestants could go unpunished.

CONCLUSION

This chapter has analyzed the impact that Catholicism had in the organization and legitimation of lynching in post-revolutionary Mexico. Through the analysis of several cases of lynching perpetrated against iconoclasts, socialist teachers, and Protestant believers, I have shown the ways in which religious beliefs and practices contributed to rendering lynching a legitimate means to punish individuals perceived as threatening to the spiritual and political integrity of Catholic groups and communities.

To understand how mob violence came to be justified in the name of religion, I have looked at the ways in which the exercise of religion in post-revolutionary Mexico was shaped by both spiritual and material concerns. The rejection of agrarian reform and the defense of parents' right to decide how to educate their children were predicated on religious and moral considerations that were, nonetheless, deeply intertwined with material and political interests. By the same token, resistance to the presence of political ideologies or religious beliefs considered foreign or disruptive was informed by attempts to safeguard the moral integrity of Catholic communities as well as to maintain their economic and political status quo. Even the violent defense of religious images and spaces was as much driven by people's beliefs in their sacredness as by the political antagonism that the state's anticlerical measures had provoked among Catholics during the first decades of the post-revolutionary period.

The entwinement of worldly and otherworldly concerns thus played a crucial role in the collectivization of violence against the impious. Equally important was the influence of the higher and lower ranks of the Catholic Church. Through the promotion of a confrontational discourse that called on the defense of Catholics' values and traditions—from questions of land tenure to education, conservative politics, and the observance of religious rituals and festivals—Catholic authorities contributed to shaping the contentious politics that emerged among laymen and laywomen. The influence of Catholic authorities was, however, less straightforward than post-revolutionary politicians suggested. Public officials and pro-government newspapers tended to present lynchings motivated by religion as a result of priests' manipulation of the faithful and as part of a top-down plot planned by the higher ranks of the Catholic Church. In practice, however, it was the authority of parish priests, together with lay members' own appropriation and interpretation of what constituted proper "Catholic" behavior, that made mob violence tolerable and even moral in the eyes of perpetrators.

The cases presented in this chapter spanned two periods, the 1930s and the 1940s–1950s, which marked two distinct moments in the history of church-state relations. Whereas for the most part the 1930s were characterized by recurrent frictions between state and church, the 1940s and 1950s represent the pinnacle of the closer, even collaborative relationship that emerged between the upper ranks of the Catholic hierarchy and post-revolutionary politicians. The persistence of lynching across these periods demonstrates that the détente reached between state and church did not prevent the occurrence of lynchings driven by Catholicism. In fact, lynchings of religious minorities intensified in the 1940s precisely because the détente and the conservative politics it enshrined made Protestants increasingly susceptible to collective acts of violence enacted against "foreign" and "destabilizing" ideas. Furthermore, that religiously motivated lynchings continued even after the church officially abandoned its antagonistic stance toward the post-revolutionary state (and vice versa) highlights the importance of understanding Catholic practices and beliefs beyond the realm of church-state relations.

3

The Lynching of Atrocious Criminals
Justice, Crime News, and Extralegal Violence

On the morning of April 22, 1943, in the crime-ridden neighborhood of Santa Julia in Mexico City, dozens of people congregated in the streets to march in the funeral procession of Sofía Almanza de Mendoza and three of her children, Mario, Ventura, and María Margarita.[1] The bodies of the deceased were carried in coffins by groups of men that, together with women, children, and elderly, walked from the house of the now-widowed Ventura Mendoza to the cemetery. José Anguiano Armenta had brutally murdered Sofía and her children on April 19. An employee at Ventura Mendoza's foundry, José Anguiano Armenta, confessed to his crimes before a judge two days after the incident. In his declarations, he admitted to having hit Sofía more than twenty times with a sledgehammer and a club that weighed around fourteen pounds. He explained that he had killed Sofía because she had refused to give him money to continue drinking. After being denied the money for a second time, he became infuriated and decided to kill her. When the judge asked him why he had killed her children, he responded that he did it "because they were crying too much, and there was no remedy to it." Two more children of the Ventura family—the girls Violeta and Teresa—had survived the attack but remained at the Júarez Hospital recovering from serious injuries. Their father, Ventura Mendoza, was devastated.

Under the headline, "Death to the Jackal! The Crowd Asks for the Monster in Order to Lynch Him," the press described how the silence that characterized the procession was interrupted by the cry of women and men who demanded justice for the victims (see figure 2). Housewives, mothers, and even older women demanded the death penalty for Anguiano Armenta, stating that "if the government cannot kill him," then it should turn the criminal over to them so they could give him the proper

FIGURE 2. ¡Muerte al chacal! La multitud pidió al monstruo para lincharlo" (Death to the Jackal! The Crowd Asks for the Monster in Order to Lynch Him), *La Prensa*, April 22, 1943. Credit: Fototeca, Hemeroteca y Biblioteca Mario Vázquez Raña, Organización Editorial Mexicana S.A. de C.V. © Fotografía Propiedad de Fototeca, Hemeroteca y Biblioteca "Mario Vázquez Rana."

punishment. Although they acknowledged that human life was sacred, the women claimed that in this case "an animal in the shape of a man" had taken innocent lives and therefore deserved to die. A group of workers expressed similar sentiments. One of them stated that the *lex talionis*—the law of an eye for an eye—had to be applied to Anguiano Armenta because even if civilized societies promoted forgiveness, an "unprecedented butchery" had occurred that did not admit clemency. A street vendor, Enrique Sierra, echoed these sentiments. He told reporters that the Mexican people as a whole supported the reinstatement of the death penalty and that congressmen and authorities needed to respond to the unprecedented wave of crimes impacting the country.

Anguiano Armenta did not have to confront the outrage generated by his crime the day of the funeral. He was exposed to people's demands for justice a few weeks later, however, when taken to the Juárez Hospital by the police.[2] There, Violeta and Teresa were asked to meet Anguiano Armenta to confirm that he was indeed the man who had broken into their house and killed their mother and siblings. In front of a large group of people that included journalists, nurses, patients, medical students, and a few visitors, Anguiano Armenta stood in front of the two girls and their father. One of the girls recognized the murderer and while "widely opening her little eyes . . . screamed in desperation, 'Take him out of my sight, kill him, kill him.'" Fearing that the pueblo would lynch the killer, thirty police officers, along with members of the secret service and the judicial police, escorted Anguiano Armenta out of the hospital. Although the newspaper article did not provide any more details about the police investigation, the tone of the piece, together with the fact that people were willing to lynch him, suggested that in the view of journalists, readers, and witnesses, Anguiano Armenta was guilty and deserved to be swiftly punished.

Anguiano Armenta, known as "the Jackal of Santa Julia," was one of the many criminals who occupied crime news in post-revolutionary Mexico. The cruelty of his crime and the vulnerability of his victims merited comparisons with Gregorio Cárdenas Hernández, the famous murderer who strangled four young women in 1942, also in Mexico City.[3] In both cases, the indignation aroused by the murderers had prompted the public to demand summary retribution for their crimes, whether the death penalty or lynching.

This chapter analyzes how public understandings of crime and justice contributed to shaping the acceptability of the lynching of criminals in post-revolutionary Mexico. Based primarily on the examination of crime news, it shows that the use of swift and extralegal forms of justice such as lynching was justified on the basis of the purported gravity of the crime and the perceived ineffectiveness of the country's justice system.

Newspapers acquired increasing importance in shaping people's perceptions and understanding of politics, crime, violence, and justice in post-revolutionary Mexico. Rising literacy rates and higher levels of urbanization translated into a newspaper readership that went beyond the elites and incorporated the popular classes. This was particularly true of crime news, or nota roja, which appealed to a broader audience that included but was not limited to the urban middle classes.[4]

Crime news was the centerpiece of periodicals like *La Prensa*, but it was also found in mainstream newspapers such as *Excélsior, El Porvenir, El Universal*, and even the government's mouthpiece, *El Nacional*. The latter newspapers devoted entire articles or even sections to reports of crime and did so with no less sensationalistic undertones. In regard to the lynching of suspected criminals, newspapers—both tabloids and mainstream periodicals—concurred in representing mob violence as a legitimate form of justice.

Even when they acknowledged the brutal and uncivil character of lynching, journalists and editorial writers portrayed this practice as a reasonable means to deal with criminals who were considered immoral, barbaric, and inhumane. The perceived inability of the state to deliver justice and to respond to the different crimes that affected people's physical and material well-being added to the justification of lynching among crime news reporters and their readership.

This representation of lynching contrasted with that offered by news coverage on cases involving religion, mythical beliefs, or communities' opposition to the central state's modernizing projects. The press referred to lynchings motivated by Catholic beliefs—including cases against socialist teachers, Evangelicals, and "impious" elements—as an expression of people's fanaticism and irrationality. Lynchings motivated by mythical beliefs, including accusations of witchcraft, were also portrayed as a sign of the backwardness of communities that were thought of as living outside modernity. By the same token, cases of mob violence directed at health inspectors, tax collectors, and other federal representatives in charge of modernizing the countryside were described as the result of the ignorance and backwardness of people.

This differential treatment of lynching shows that mob violence was tolerated depending on the wrongdoing that elicited it and that there was no unequivocal condemnation of this practice. Lynchings against so-called criminals were more likely to produce a consensus between perpetrators and public opinion regarding the need to impose extralegal forms of justice. Although the press often justified these lynchings by referring to the need to apply a "proportional" punishment to hideous crimes, so as to punish murder with murder, lynching was far from being on a par with the gravity of the crime. The crimes that prompted lynchings were not limited to murder or to offenses that threatened a person's physical well-being, such as rape, battery, and assault. Rather, they included more inconsequential crimes such as robberies of small items. In addition, mob violence often was directed at individuals who were suspected of *wanting* to commit a crime but who had not actually committed it.

My main argument is that crime news and the narratives about crimes and criminals presented by the press were central in construing lynching as an acceptable, even moral, response to crime. Journalists, and by extension newspaper editors, were key actors in the portrayal of the lynching of criminals as an almost natural response to what was described as unnatural and immoral conduct.[5] Stories of monstrous killers who possessed animalistic instincts, aberrant mothers who were abusive to their children, duplicitous thieves and skillful cattle rustlers who deprived others of their possessions, or *robachicos* (child thieves) who would abduct boys and girls for the lowest purposes: these were all part of the narratives that contributed to rendering lynching as an adequate and necessary response to crime.

A favorite genre among a rapidly expanding readership,[6] crime news reflected and amplified the collective outrage generated by criminal conduct. It described in great detail the horrific and offensive nature of the crime as well as the indignation and anger leading up to the lynching. It narrated with dramatic undertones the torments endured by the suspected criminal at the hands of the lynch mob or in those cases prevented by the police the struggle between neighbors and the police over the fate of the criminal.

Despite the colorful and dramatized storytelling, crime news also reflected public debates on violence, justice, and the law.[7] As such, it allows us to reconstruct the indignation and fear that certain crimes generated among the readership and the ways in which swift and illegal forms of justice were tolerated for the greater good of securing the integrity and well-being of law-abiding citizens. Furthermore, crime news narratives were characterized by a pedagogical overtone that hinted both at the immorality of crimes and at the legitimacy of lynching.[8] Press coverage of crimes offered readers "lessons" on how to discern acceptable and unacceptable conduct. In this context, the actions of criminals—from bad mothers to abusive sons and petty thieves—were condemned as an expression of deviancy, vice, and immorality; those of the perpetrators of lynching were, in contrast, justified as an expected and acceptable consequence of citizens' exposure to horrific crimes and the lack of justice.

News coverage of lynchings of criminals also contained clear political messages directed at political elites and decision makers. By portraying lynching as a consequence of the inadequate and insufficient punishment administered by the state, the press urged politicians to toughen their responses to crime. Paradoxically, in the same pages, journalists revealed that citizens were not alone in embracing the use of extralegal forms of violence to punish criminals. News about suspected criminals being killed while allegedly trying to escape the law or about prisoners dying under mysterious circumstances while in police custody revealed the existence of a consensus between citizens and state authorities on the use of extralegal forms of punishment.[9]

The chapter is divided into two main sections. The first section focuses on cases of lynching perpetrated against so-called murderers and the public demands for lethal punishment—from the death penalty to the ley fuga and lynching—that they generated. It shows how stories of cold-blooded and "monstrous" murderers were the basis for people's demands for swift and rough forms of justice. It furthermore illustrates the manifestations and limits of the consensus between citizens and state authorities on extralegal forms of justice.

The second section brings to the fore a variety of criminal acts that, beyond murder, triggered the organization of lynching. It describes crime news narratives about "unnatural" mothers, abusive sons, and violent men who used violence against innocent victims, including the elderly and children. It also discusses narratives about "bloodless" crimes such as robberies and cattle rustling that led to lynching. Despite the nonviolent character of the latter crimes, lynching continued to be rationalized on the premise that robbers threatened people's means of subsistence and therefore deserved swift punishment.

Taken together, these cases demonstrate that the portrayal of criminals as individuals who had violated the norms of proper behavior was essential in the construction of lynching as justice. They further suggest the fate of these individuals was not decided by the law, or at least not only. Rather, a complex process that involved the vagaries of public opinion, citizens' perceptions of crime, and authorities' discretionary decisions determined the fate of criminals.

Despite the changes that the country experienced during the 1930s through the 1950s, particularly in regard to an overall decrease in homicide and crime rates,[10] support for lynching and other forms of extralegal punishment was consistent. Thus this chapter emphasizes a synchronic rather than diachronic analysis of the cases introduced in each section.

DEATH TO THE JACKALS! THE LYNCHING OF MURDERERS

On April 21, 1930, under the dramatic headline, "First Criminal Lynched in Mexico," *La Prensa* reported the lynching of Miguel Quiróz Martínez, a man who had killed a *taquero* (taco vendor), Pablo Cerrillo Durán, in the Juan José Baz Plaza in downtown Mexico City.[11] After ordering his tacos and enjoying his meal, Quiróz Martínez refused to pay the bill, saying he had no money. When he tried to leave, the taquero grabbed him by the arm and demanded payment. Instead, Quiróz Martínez pulled a knife out of his pocket and stabbed the taquero multiple times in front of a group of scandalized customers and bystanders. The outrage grew as more people learned about the cold-blooded murder. The press described how a *muchedumbre* (mob) of men and women surrounded Quirón Martínez, shouting all kinds of insults at him, slapping him in the face, and kicking him in the stomach while the man lay bleeding on the floor. When the police arrived the killer was practically unconscious and was taken to the Juárez Hospital.

Reporting on the same case, an editorial in *El Porvenir* also described the incident as the "first case of lynching" in the country and went on to reflect on the reasons for its occurrence.¹² The article lamented the insignificant reason for the murder: a quarrel over some 20-cent tacos. And yet it opined that most crimes in the country were just like that, involving the "most shameful degeneration imaginable." It argued that until authorities addressed the "horrifying crime wave that surrounds us as a curse," crimes like the one perpetrated against the taco vendor would continue to occur. The implication was that given these types of offenses and the authorities' inadequate response, lynching was understandable if not totally justified.

The reference to this case as Mexico's first lynching was inaccurate.¹³ In fact, just a few days before the lynching of Quiróz Martínez, Puebla's local newspaper, *La Opinión,* reported the lynching of a murderer in the town of Santa Úrsula. The case involved the killing of Antonio Rosario by his political rival, José María Sánchez, after the men got into a quarrel at the local pulquería. On learning about Rosario's murder, a group of villagers went after Sánchez to avenge the victim. They dragged him into the main plaza and there, in front of a growing number of spectators, clubbed and stoned the killer. The newspaper gave readers a detailed account of the lynching. It described how one of the stones had hit José María Sánchez with such force that it had virtually destroyed his skull and made his eyes come out of their orbits.¹⁴ Despite the gruesome violence involved in the narration of the lynching, the press's condemnation was directed at the actions of the murderer and not at the people's response.

Crime news emphasized the outrage that neighbors and witnesses felt toward murderers, thus bringing their readership closer to the feelings experienced by those who decided to take justice into their own hands. As illustrated by the attempted lynching of José Anguiano Armenta, cases of murder prompted public debates regarding the need to use lethal forms of punishment against the perpetrators. The death penalty was formally abolished in Mexico in the 1930s, after being removed from the country's 1929 Penal Code as well as from the penal codes of the different states.¹⁵

The systematic impunity surrounding cases of murder fueled Mexican citizens' demands for lethal forms of retribution.¹⁶ Because people suspected criminals would be released with the acquiescence of corrupt judges or crooked policemen, their killing was considered the only means to secure proper punishment. Thus, despite the de jure elimination of the death penalty, lethal punishment persisted in practice in the form of lynchings as well as in the extrajudicial killing of so-called criminals through the state-sanctioned ley fuga.

Although there were clear differences between lynching and the ley fuga—the latter was an extrajudicial form of violence perpetrated by authorities, whereas lynching was primarily carried out by citizens—both practices reflected an inclination, shared by citizens and authorities, to punish criminal conducts outside of the law. The extrajudicial killing of Manuel González and Ramón Fórtiz, who were presumed guilty of the rape and murder of a seven-year-old girl, María Juárez, in Cholula, Puebla, exemplifies the connections between these two practices.

On July 9, 1933, *La Opinión* reported that two "soulless criminals" had kidnapped María Juárez and, after sexually assaulting her, had thrown her into a well and dropped an 80-kilo stone on her body to kill her.[17] The suspected criminals, Manuel González and Ramón Fórtiz, were identified by María Juárez herself, who with her "last breath" uttered the names of her tormentors "as if wanting to recount what had happened to her." Outraged by the crime, a group of locals attempted to lynch González and Fórtiz. Although authorities were able to save them, a week after being taken into prison, the same newspaper reported that the two men had mysteriously "disappeared" while the police were taking them from Puebla's prison to the city of Cholula.

Although authorities denied knowing what happened to the prisoners, public awareness of cases of criminals being shot while being taken by the police into or from prison made their death plausible.[18] *La Opinión*'s statement suggested as much: "The murderers surely tried to escape and their guards were then forced to shoot at them, killing them in the act, and unwillingly executing the ley fuga."[19] Far from lamenting their apparent extrajudicial assassination, the tone of the article conveyed a clear message: no matter how the criminals were killed, justice had been served.

The murder of María Juárez in Puebla and the apparent extrajudicial killing of the perpetrators closely resemble the case of Olga Camacho and the attempted lynching of a soldier, Juan Castillo Morales. As discussed in chapter 1, Castillo Morales was accused of having brutally raped and murdered "la niña Olga" in Tijuana in 1938. While Castillo Morales was in military and police custody, a large group of people demanding justice for the girl broke into the prison and the city hall in an attempt to seize and lynch him. Although the crowd managed to set the buildings on fire, authorities were able to rescue the suspected killer. However, similar to the fate of the two murderers of María Juárez in Puebla, Castillo Morales was then killed by authorities, in this case, the military.

According to the press, there were two versions of the execution: "one that Morales fainted as the rifles were leveled and was killed as he lay on the ground; the other that he broke and ran, only to die under the traditional law of flight by which a prisoner is allowed the miniscule chance to escape but is overtaken by bullets."[20] Regardless of the circumstances surrounding Juan Soldado's slaying, Tijuana authorities considered his death an effective means to ease the "tense spirit" among the people by delivering them a swift form of justice.

The propensity shared by citizens and authorities to resort to extralegal forms of punishment did not mean that they were always in agreement regarding what crimes or which criminals deserved such retribution. The events following Castillo Morales's execution by the military illustrate this clearly. People started to doubt that the soldier was actually guilty of his purported crimes and became increasingly concerned about how the authorities had handled the case. Once regarded as a ruthless murderer and rapist, Castillo Morales soon came to be seen by Tijuana residents as a victim of the authorities' abuse of force. In a further twist of events, the alleged apparition of the deceased soldier at his grave and at the site of his murder turned him into a martyr and an object of popular devotion.[21]

Another suggestive example of the potential tensions and disagreements underlying citizens' and authorities' apparent consensus on extrajudicial justice was reported on December 5, 1941, in the town of San Andrés Tuxtla, Veracruz. *La Prensa* reported that the extrajudicial killing of Pedro Fomperosa prompted an attempted lynching of local authorities. Fomperosa, who was presumed guilty of a number of crimes, was dragged out of the prison by a group of police officers under the orders of Mayor Rogerio Rocha. After beating him and leaving his face disfigured, the policemen stripped Fomperosa of his clothes and hanged him with a noose.

Family members of Fomperosa recognized his body and, together with a group of neighbors who believed the man was innocent, rioted outside the municipal offices. The rioters demanded that Rocha and the policemen come out so they could lynch them in retribution for Fomperosa's assassination. The crowd dissipated only after the state governor promised proper punishment for the police officers and the mayor.[22]

The attempted lynching of local authorities prompted by Fomperosa's killing was not exceptional. Evidence discussed in chapter 1 showed that citizens were not mere passive observers of local authorities' abuse of force. Citizens expressed their discomfort by writing to local, state, or federal authorities, denouncing the criminal behavior of police officers, and demanding that the authorities remove abusive mayors from their towns. In other cases, however, citizens resorted to less than civil strategies, and they themselves became the perpetrators of extralegal forms of violence to punish the misconduct of police officers, local authorities, and even military personnel.

That authorities could embrace the use of extralegal forms of punishment against criminals does not negate the fact that they were sometimes opposed to it. Police officers, in particular, fulfilled their formal mandate as representatives of the law whenever they tried to prevent a lynching. Time and again, the press referred to the brave and opportune intervention of police officers who "against their own will" had to interfere in order to save so-called *chacales* (murderers), *rateros* (robbers), *sátiros* (rapists), and other wrongdoers from the wrath of the lynch mob. For instance, on August 27, 1942, the press published an article commending the "audacity and ability" of the police when they saved Alberto Ayala, a man accused of murdering Guillermo Garduño, a merchant, in the town of Ixtlahuaca, Estado de México.[23] After apprehending Ayala in the Tlalpan neighborhood of Mexico

City, three policemen were put in charge of transporting him to the Ixtlahuaca prison. On the road from Mexico City to the prison, the policemen encountered a "human roadblock" formed by family members of Garduño who, wanting to avenge the victim, offered a bribe to the policemen in exchange for Ayala. After turning down the bribe, the policemen continued their journey only to be once again confronted on the road, this time by dozens of men and women who, armed with stones and clubs, threatened to lynch Ayala. On both occasions, the policemen were able to protect Ayala from the lynch mob and take him safely to prison.

Another case of police "bravery" was reported on September 4, 1944, this time in relation to the lynching of two "jackals" from Papalotal, a small town in Estado de México.[24] The brothers Alberto and Felix Víctor Herrera had murdered their uncle Juan Ambriz Herrera after breaking into his house with the intention of robbing him. After spending a few months in prison and fearing that they could face the death penalty under the "emergency decree" declared by President Ávila Camacho,[25] the brothers escaped. With the help of a group of neighbors from Papalotal who knew the deceased uncle well and a member of the secret service from Mexico City, the local police located and apprehended the Herreras only a few days after their escape. Found hiding in an old house, the brothers resisted arrest and escaped once again, but a group of infuriated neighbors attacked them with stones, clubs, and fists. The press reported that the brothers would have been killed by the mob if it were not for the "energetic and opportune intervention" of the police. Fearing that neighbors would riot at night and try to break into the prison, the police relocated the criminals to Mexico City.

This and many more instances of police interference make evident that lynchings and attempted lynchings of alleged criminals did not happen in a vacuum of state authority.[26] Rather, they were often marked by the presence of state authorities, usually police officers, who were at times able (and willing) to save the suspected killers from the fury of the lynch mob. In this context, the press presented police officers as courageous defenders of the law who needed to "tame" the popular and irrational sentiments of citizens.

Policemen were reportedly confronted with a dual task: to resist the popular demand for swift punishment and, so the press hinted, to resist their inclination to let justice be served in a summary manner. And yet cases of the ley fuga as well as cases of lynching perpetrated or staged by the police—some reported by these same newspapers—suggest that they were far from being exemplars of tempered and law-abiding behavior. Instead, police officers were instrumental in the commission of collective killings that involved the use of visible and cruel forms of torment, often under the orders of mayors and police commanders. The many letters of complaint and telegrams sent by private citizens to the president or to other federal authorities provide further evidence of the violence of the police in both the city and the countryside. These letters also highlight the police's instrumental participation in the control and repression of agrarian, labor, and electoral conflicts.[27] For instance, Juana Inés González denounced the assassination of her husband by the mayor and a group of policemen in the town of Ameca, Jalisco, in February 1933. Explaining that her husband had been murdered for being considered a political enemy, Juana Inés stated she feared authorities would exhume and disappear her husband's body to hide their crime.[28] Similarly, the widow Delfina de Castro denounced the killing and hanging of her husband, José García Pinto, in July 1940 by a colonel and two policemen in Texmelucan, Puebla. A critic and opponent of presidential candidate Manuel Ávila Camacho, García Pinto was described as a bandit and his murder dismissed by state authorities.[29]

Coverage of these types of political murders was subject to more traditional forms of censorship, especially when it involved newspapers in the capital. Crime stories on lynchings of "common" criminals and even of infamous pistoleros, however, provided powerful occasions to question and critique the government's responses to crime. Because they were not directly occupied with traditional politics such as elections or party disputes, press reports of lynchings served as an opportunity to send a political message to political elites regarding the state's inability to provide justice. Such a message warned authorities that as long as the state was incapable of securing people's expected form of retribution against murderers, citizens would continue to take justice into their own hands.

This type of political message informed press coverage of the lynching of Rodolfo Nájera Guzmán in Mexico City in October 1940.[30] Nájera Guzmán allegedly stabbed Rafael Zavala Pérez in the middle of the night, when the latter was leaving a bar around 11 p.m. When they saw Rafael lying on the floor bleeding, a group of people passing by went after Nájera Guzmán and started to beat him with stones and clubs. The press reported that people shouted, "Let's lynch him, because there is no death penalty for the assassins!" The fact that there was only one witness to the stabbing and that the presumed culprit denied all accusations against him seemed to matter little, as the newspaper implicitly presented the lynching as an act of justice.

Similarly, the attempted lynching of the murderer of a fourteen-year-old boy in the neighborhood of Los Ángeles in Mexico City in January 1943 prompted reflection on the desirability of lethal forms of punishment: "A horrifying crime . . . that brings to mind the death penalty"; "The victim was a boy . . . and yet a brutal man, a real savage who does not deserve to live among humans, killed him with two gunshots."[31] The incident had taken place on the night of January 22, when Albino Mandujano Delgado, under the influence of alcohol and "blinded by jealousy," shot Ignacio Hernández Amezcua. Albino had for a long time believed the boy was having an affair with his lover, Margarita Laguna Guarduño. When he found Ignacio at his house with Margarita that night, he decided to kill him. A group of neighbors heard the gunshots and, seeing Albino running away, followed him with the intention of lynching him. Albino was saved by a police officer who arrived in time to prevent him from being killed by the mob.

Impunity was then, as it is today, at the center of citizens' distrust of the state's capacity to provide justice. In the face of a system of justice perceived and experienced as corrupt and riddled with impunity, people regarded prisons as spaces that could provide criminals with political protection or with the opportunity to escape and circumvent justice. Thus, similar to the case of Juan Castillo Morales, lynch mobs broke into prisons in order to apply the punishment they deemed appropriate for criminals. When reporting on these cases, the press echoed people's frustration with the law and with state institutions. The lynching of the well-known pistolero Raúl Castro, in the city of Torreón, Coahuila, exemplifies this.[32] Castro, the pistolero of some influential politicians in Coahuila and Durango, was considered responsible for killing at least ten people in Torreón alone. On February 20, 1940, the burial of one of Castro's latest victims, Ismael Rosales, turned into a riot and then into a lynching. Organizers of the funeral procession agreed to walk by the prison where the pistolero was being held on the way to the cemetery. Once there, a large group of people managed to break into the prison and take Castro out of his cell despite the guards' efforts to protect him. The mob shot and stabbed Castro multiple times. Rosales's widow, who had ten children and was described as "having lost her mind because of the tragedy," reportedly kicked Castro's already dead body.[33] The press stated that the lynch mob bitterly complained about authorities' corruption and a system of justice that "did not know how, or did not want, to punish criminals."

A similar case was reported in the town of Jilotepec, Estado de Mexico. In June 1943 a large group of people—according to the press, five hundred—tried to break into the local prison in order to lynch Dolores Alcántara, who was accused of multiple murders.[34] Juan Hernández, father of one of Alcántara's latest victims, led the crowd. Although the police were able to prevent the lynching, the press stated that local authorities asked the state government to transfer Alcántara to the Toluca prison, as it was clear that it would be difficult to stop the people from taking justice into its own hands, "given that none of the town's inhabitants believe in the judicial authorities."

Distrust of the police and in the authorities in general was also cited as the cause for the lynching of a policeman in the small town of Izamal, Yucatán, in May 1942.[35] The policeman had killed a man because of a personal vendetta days earlier and was being held at the local prison. The killing had stirred the outrage of locals, as the victim was a highly regarded man in the town. As the rumor spread that the policeman would be able to elude punishment, a group of people decided to drag the culprit out of the prison and lynch him. The author of the article, who reflected on the dangers that "crowd behavior" posed for individuals' self-restraint, stated that "not only in Yucatán, but in the whole Republic" it was necessary to reinstate the faith of the people in the judicial authorities: "There should be no more talk about revolting impunities, or of recidivism caused by the negative applications of the law. The seclusion of the criminal and his confinement in places appropriated for his integral betterment should not be empty words."

Distrust of the authorities, however, was not necessarily based on people's concern with the "integral betterment," or rehabilitation, of the criminal but rather on the application of a punishment commensurate with the gravity of his wrongdoing. This much shines through in the reporting of the lynching of two murderers who were serving time in the prison in the town of Tianguistengo, Hidalgo. When residents found out that the criminals were going to be transferred to the Pachuca prison, a large crowd rioted outside the prison "to protest against the humanitarian relocation of the criminals."[36] The press stated, "The police ... took precautions to defend them [from being lynched] and take them in peace to their destiny. But the policemen were [only] ten, and also they were not too convinced of having to defend the *chacalitos* [the little murderers]."[37]

Support for extralegal forms of punishment of murderers continued well into the 1950s. References to the ley fuga in parallel or almost conflated with people's support for lynching indicate citizens regarded these two practices as part of a continuum of methods to punish criminals outside the law. This becomes clear in the attempted lynching of Humberto Lara Montes and Francisco Durán Andrade, known as "the slaughterers" (*los descuartizadores*).[38] (See figure 3.) The two men were accused of having assassinated their boss, a dry cleaner, Urbano Maldonado Tejeda, on July 3, 1950, in Mexico City. After securing their confession, the police took the men to the site of the assassination, the Maclovia dry cleaners, to reconstruct the scene of the crime. There, in front of the police, the public prosecutor, journalists, and a growing group of curious bystanders, Humberto and Francisco described in great detail how they killed Mr. Urbano. As it was commonly done in criminal investigations at the time, the two men "staged" the scene of the murder with the help of a soldier who volunteered to play the role of the deceased.

The press, which did not spare its readers any details, reported that people's indignation intensified as the criminals revealed how they had carried out the assassination. Humberto and Francisco explained that they had first strangled Mr. Urbano and that when he was agonizing on the floor, they both knelt down to pray and to wish him a "good death." Once dead, Mr. Urbano's body was dismembered by Humberto and Francisco; they cut off his hands, broke his legs, and severed his head. With the exception of the head, which was left in the shop, the body parts were hidden in different places. As the slaughterers described their actions, the group of bystanders, now numbering dozens, shouted, "Lynch them. Burn them alive. Give them the ley fuga. Execute them!" The press described how people demanded that the descuartizadores be dismembered in the same way they had mutilated the dry cleaner: "Let us do justice. . . . [T]hese beasts do not deserve anything but dying like

FIGURE 3. "Una multitud quiso linchar a los descuartizadores" (A Crowd Wanted to Lynch the Slaughterers), *La Prensa*, July 30, 1950. Credit: Fototeca, Hemeroteca y Biblioteca Mario Vázquez Raña, Organización Editorial Mexicana S.A. de C.V. © Fotografía Propiedad de Fototeca, Hemeroteca y Biblioteca "Mario Vázquez Rana."

dogs, like animals."[39] At some point the crowd became so restless that the anti-riot police had to intervene to prevent the lynching of the men.[40]

In addition to the ongoing references to the ley fuga and lynching as desirable means to punish murderers, the popularity of the death penalty continued to loom large during the 1950s. Describing lynching as a practice that belonged to "the pueblo" but more aptly to "the plebe" (the common people), an editorial published in August 1950 explained that there were two reasons lynchings had increased in the country over the past years: because the death penalty was no longer applicable in the country's capital and because there had been an increase in the most "atrocious crimes."[41] Although the author never specified which crimes were to be characterized as atrocious, he probably had murder in mind, a crime that prompted discussions about the need to reinstate the death penalty. And yet evidence suggests that by 1950, at least at the national level, murder was not on the rise but was actually experiencing a downward trend, a trend that started in 1940 and that would continue in the following decades.[42] The press nevertheless referred to the need to punish murder with murder, under the logic of proportionality: an eye for an eye. Lynching was thus construed as a justifiable, proportionate, and swift form of justice to be used against those who, having taking the lives of others, did not deserve to be punished by procedural means.

Journalists and editorial writers went as far as to suggest that lynching and the ley fuga persisted *because* the state could no longer kill the culprits through legal means.[43] In reference to the lynching of a man who had killed his father, an editorial published in *Excélsior* in 1953 stated, "In such popular attitude, we must read an eloquent warning: . . . if those in charge of imposing severe punishments do not do it, or if laws continue to allow the impunity of criminals, the pueblo will look for a way to defend itself, of taking revenge, of putting itself at the margins of soft and flexible codes, to take justice into its own hands."[44]

Likewise, reporting on a triple murder committed by eight "jackals" who were nearly lynched, *La Prensa* stated, "The only punishment that the brutal instincts of these [murderers] can understand is death, the justice of the ignominious execution wall."[45] Echoing these opinions, an editorial published in 1956 in *El Informador* reflected on the need to punish "bloody crimes" by killing the culprit. The blunt tone used by the article merits quoting the piece at some length:

> In the state of Chihuahua, over the last days, horrendous crimes have been committed that have society under a state of alert; these are bloody crimes that have generated a great deal of indignation and that have led public opinion to ask for the application of the death penalty. . . . There have been conversations amongst the public about using lynching against the assassins if the death penalty is not applied in a legal way. . . .
>
> The death penalty must exist in the codes of countries where, like in ours, murder is used without spare. Here in Mexico the life of the peaceful is always at the mercy of the killer, of the *pistolero*, of the professional or amateur assassin who, for no reason, for any argument or disagreement . . . will harm or take the life of whoever is in front of him. Thus, in each inhabitant of this country, there is a potential criminal or a potential victim. Nobody is safe from anybody. But the advantage goes to the assassins and *pistoleros*, who are not punished with the same penalty that they apply to their victims.[46]

TRACING THE MORALITY OF LYNCHING BEYOND MURDER

Although the press often justified lynching by referring to the need to apply "proportional" punishment to hideous crimes, so that murder was to be punished by murder, evidence suggests that the types of crimes that provoked lynching went beyond murder and that lynching was far from being on a par with the gravity of the wrongdoing. Having focused thus far on cases of lynching perpetrated against infamous killers, I turn now to other criminal offenses that precipitated this form of violence. Such offenses included battery, violence against women, rape, and robbery.[47] Although these crimes were presented as involving a level of cruelty and violence that seemed "fit" for the equally brutal penalty of lynching, many of them were minor offenses or involved an individual's "intent" to commit a crime.

The fact that lynching could be precipitated by transgressions that differed greatly in terms of their gravity confirms what historians of crime have long established: conceptions of crime and deviancy are socially constructed and thus the severity of a crime lies in the eye of the beholder.[48] Lynching was driven less by the "objective" dimension of a crime—as in its frequency or level of harm—and more by perceptions of insecurity and dangerousness.[49] Most important, perhaps, the fact that lynching was directed at criminal conduct that involved various degrees of violence–or did not involve the use of violence—signals that lynching should not be understood as a "proportional" punishment.

Sociologically, lynching can be more aptly understood as a *disproportional* and *excessive* form of punishment.[50] Its aim is to apply public, overt, and corporeal punishment to a criminal who in the minds of perpetrators does not deserve to be punished by procedural means. Moreover, through its level of visibility, lynching is intended not only as a response to a single offender, but as a warning to other would-be offenders regarding what transgressions are not to be tolerated by a given neighborhood or community. This is not to say that lynchings were regarded as excessive in post-revolutionary Mexico. On the contrary, the narratives of lynching provided by the press reveal an understanding of this practice as a moral response to what was considered immoral and "unnatural" conduct. In spite of its illegality, then, lynching was not presented as a crime but as a legitimate means to attain justice.

News stories on lynching printed by both tabloids and mainstream newspapers were infused with didactic overtones that taught readers the boundaries between moral and immoral conduct. This didactic quality was expressed vividly in the narratives of lynchings perpetrated against "unnatural" mothers. The attempted lynching of Cleo Flores Hernández in the Tacuba neighborhood in Mexico City in June 1930 illustrates this point.[51] Cleo had left her eleven-month-old daughter at home alone in order to go drinking. Having witnessed Cleo's abusive behavior many times before, a group of neighbors decided to lynch her when she returned home that night after being away for more than eight hours. Although two policemen saved her from being killed, Cleo had to be sent to the Juárez Hospital because of injuries she suffered at the hands of her neighbors. Condemning her drinking habits, the press reported that Cleo's daughter was taken to a government institution in order to be "freed from the criminal neglect of her mother."

The same year, the press reported the attempted lynching of Lorenza Flores, also in Mexico City.[52] In this case, neighbors had caught Lorenza while she was trying to drown her eight-month-old son to "liberate him" from the pain caused by measles.

When the policemen arrived in the neighborhood, they saw a group of men and women kicking and beating Lorenza on the ground. She suffered a concussion and was left with several bruises. Calling Lorenza an "unnatural" and "cruel" mother, the press reported that the policemen could not establish who was responsible for the lynching as most neighbors claimed they had only witnessed the attack.

Under the headline, "A Mother Transformed into a Hyena Wanted to Kill with Clubs Her Own Daughter," *La Prensa* reported a parallel incident, this time in Jalapa, Veracruz.[53] The case involved a group of people who saw Juana Flores beating her nine-year-old daughter near a train station in March 1943. Hearing the screams of Juana's daughter and becoming outraged by the mother's abuse, bystanders seized the girl and tried to lynch the "bad woman," who escaped death thanks to the presence of the police. A decade later, *El Nacional* reported the attempted lynching of another "unnatural" mother in Mexico City. The case involved Domitila Domínguez Cruz, who had left her children unsupervised on several occasions in order to "go out with a man" despite knowing that one of her children, two-year-old José Arturo, was sick. As in the case of Juana Flores, the neighbors' attempt to lynch Domitila was frustrated by the police.[54]

In addition to confirming, again, that the police were not necessarily absent when a lynching took place, the cases described above show how journalists contributed to the construction of a narrative that offered clear "lessons" concerning the consequences of deviant behavior. In these cases, the press illustrated how the behavior of "bad" and "unnatural" mothers could result not only in the potential death of their children but also in the punishment of their wrongdoing at the hands of enraged neighbors or witnesses.

That the press focused plainly on condemning the actions of the "negligent" mothers rather than on the illegal conduct of the lynchers reinforced the notion that lynching was not a crime but an act of justice. The crime in these news stories was clearly the behavior of women who, because of alcoholism and carelessness, were violating the gendered ideal of "responsible motherhood" promoted by postrevolutionary politicians and health practitioners.[55] Furthermore, the use of adjectives such as *unnatural* to describe the behavior of these women added to the gravity of their offense. The word *desnaturalizada* suggested that "by nature" mothers were good and caring and that these women were, therefore, not only contravening the norms of society, but the laws of nature.[56]

The mistreatment of parents by their sons was also presented as "unnatural" even when the press referred to the social and economic circumstances that underpinned these stories of domestic abuse. Such circumstances included consumption of alcohol, lack of education, and conditions of poverty and economic depravity. For instance, Rafael Saavedra, a man who was lynched in a working-class neighborhood of Mexico City for having assaulted his mother, was described as a drunkard who had recently added marijuana to his list of vices.[57] (See figure 4.) *La Prensa*

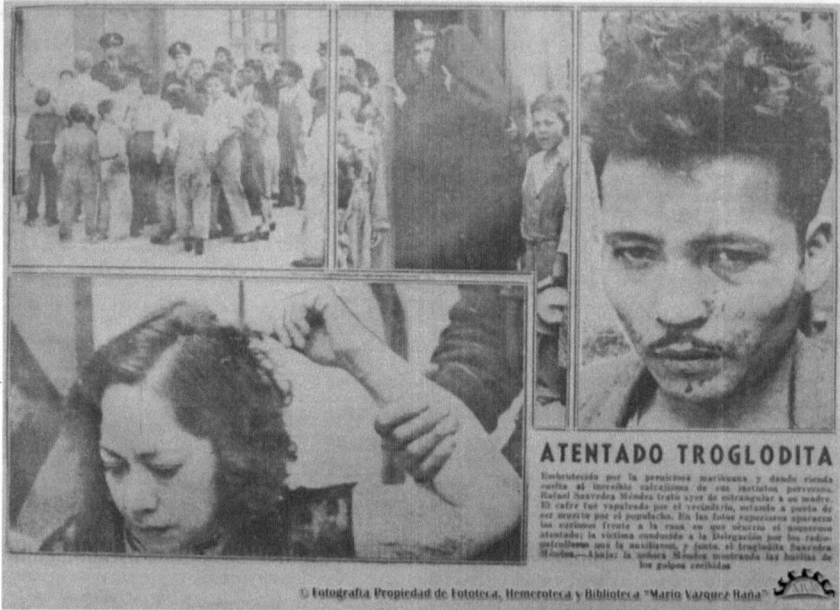

FIGURE 4. "Hombre fiera que intentó matar a su madre, iba a morir linchado" (Beast-Man Who Tried to Kill His Mother Was Going to Die Lynched), *La Prensa*, June 30, 1941. Credit: Fototeca, Hemeroteca y Biblioteca Mario Vázquez Raña, Organización Editorial Mexicana S.A. de C.V. © Fotografía Propiedad de Fototeca, Hemeroteca y Biblioteca "Mario Vázquez Rana."

reported that, despite his mother's best intentions, Rafael had dropped out of school and was often seen in the local cantina in the company of gangsters and vagabonds. Under the influence of alcohol, Rafael started to verbally and physically mistreat his mother and, according to witnesses, even tried to strangle her. A group of women that heard Rafael's mother screaming in pain broke into their home and started to beat the "fierce animal and imbecile son" with clubs and stones.

The press explained that the outrage generated by the incident was such that a group of passersby wanted to join the mob when they heard that "a bad son had tried to strangle his mother." An almost identical sequence of events characterized the lynching of Ruperto Cruz Rangel in Mexico City.[58] Ruperto had also tried to strangle his mother and, like Rafael Saavedra, was described as an alcoholic and a marijuana user. When nearby residents heard the screams of Ruperto's mother, Manuela, they broke into their home and, armed with clubs, brooms, and other home utensils, seized Manuela and started to beat Ruperto. According to the press, when the police arrived, "the lynchers had disbanded, leaving the criminal lying in a puddle of his own blood."

The press's emphasis on the presence of alcohol and drugs in these types of incidents was not accidental.[59] As with press reports of "bad mothers," a certain pedagogical overtone was part of the news coverage of abusive sons. Such pedagogy centered on the violence generated by alcohol and drugs but also on the unproductive and irresponsible behavior associated with substance abuse.[60] The press stressed that alcohol and drug consumption led to aggressiveness and to the triggering of what were described as "animalistic instincts."[61] Furthermore, the individuals who were the subjects of this news were portrayed as unemployed and lazy adult men who lived off their mother's or father's income and spent their days drinking and fighting.[62] As such, their behavior was clearly set in opposition to the ideal of the "sober," "productive," and "rational" citizen promoted by elites and public opinion during this period.[63]

It was against the deviancy of these "unnatural mothers" and "abusive sons" that the morality of lynching was constructed. Although lynching also involved the adoption of aggressive and brutal acts, the press referred to it as a righteous response that, even if far from ideal or commendable, was to be tolerated in the face of atrocious crimes.

This seeming tolerance of lynching was also present in cases involving violent men who mistreated their wives or intimate partners. Like lynchings perpetrated against unnatural mothers and bad sons, those directed against violent men pertained to the control of people's behavior in the private sphere. They entailed the actions of residents and neighbors who, acting outside the purview of the state, drew the boundaries between acceptable and unacceptable conduct. Furthermore, these cases were also underpinned by press narratives that emphasized the presence of alcohol in contexts characterized by economic depravity. What makes these cases distinct, however, is that they offer a counterpoint to the overall indifference that surrounded violence against women in post-revolutionary Mexico.[64]

Violence against women was widespread, and its occurrence seemed normalized under the notion of women's "natural" fragility and men's "inherent" violent instincts. And yet the lynching of abusive partners and the positive press coverage it received suggests that violence against women did not go unchallenged. On February 19, 1941, for instance, the press reported the attempted lynching of Benito García Narvaez in a working-class neighborhood of Mexico City.[65] Inebriated with pulque, Benito had tried to murder his wife, Joaquina, with a machete. After hearing Joaquina's shouts, a group of neighbors tried to lynch the "brutal drunkard," who had already delivered a machete blow to Joaquina's arm. Two policemen prevented the lynching and took Benito to prison. Joaquina was sent to the Juárez Hospital to recover from her injuries.

In a similar incident of domestic violence, the victim was less fortunate. Tomasa Rodríguez was also attacked by her partner with a machete but did not survive. According to *La Prensa* she was murdered in the locality of Estación Terrazas,

Chihuahua, on December 19, 1942.⁶⁶ The "blood-curdling jackal" had killed Tomasa with a machete and had scattered parts of her mutilated body, including her head, in different places. Once the perpetrator was in police custody, a group of villagers broke into the prison and tried to lynch him. The police rescued him, even though one of the rioters managed to put a noose around his neck and was ready to turn the man over to the mob.

Although these stories highlighted the vulnerability of women in the face of violent and abusive men, the participation of women in these and other lynchings suggests that women were not passive victims. For instance, in October 1943, the press reported that a group of women had lynched Carlos Padilla Maza in retaliation for having attacked his partner, Angela Rodríguez, in a Mexico City neighborhood. This was not the first time Carlos used violence against Angela, so when the group of women heard Angela crying for help, they broke into her house and started to beat the man.⁶⁷

Women were also responsible for the lynching of Rafael Saavedra mentioned above. It was a group of women who, hearing Rafael's mother's cries, armed themselves with stones and clubs in order to lynch the abusive son. Similarly, the press reported that a group of women tried to lynch five men who were accused of murdering a fourteen-year-old girl in Mexico City.⁶⁸ After the criminals reconstructed the crime scene in front of bystanders, journalists, detectives, and policemen, a group of women demanded that the police let them take justice into their own hands and started to throw stones at the five men, prompting the police to form a perimeter around them.⁶⁹

Crime news of lynchings of so-called rapists further exemplified the gendered dimensions of violence in post-revolutionary Mexico. Newspaper coverage of these men as "satyrs" who like this figure of Greek mythology possessed uncontrollable and instinctual sexual desires reflected anxieties regarding the vulnerability of girls to sexual violence.⁷⁰ These stories also shed light on communities' propensity to punish this type of crime by swift and collective means. The case of Olga Camacho, which as discussed earlier prompted the attempted lynching of a soldier, Juan Castillo Morales, is illustrative of the outrage these crimes generated among neighbors and villagers alike.

Similar cases were reported elsewhere during the 1930s. The rape of thirteen-year-old Luisa Aguilar in May 1930 in the town of San Baltasar Campeche, Puebla, for instance, caused residents' indignation and led to the attempted lynching of the perpetrator.⁷¹ According to a local newspaper, Maximino Cerezo, with the help of his accomplice, Amado López, assaulted Luisa after threatening to kill her with a knife. Brought to the scene by the girl's screams, a group of neighbors gathered around the men and attempted to "take justice into their own hands."⁷² In San Pedro, Coahuila, Guadalupe Torres was also on the verge of being lynched by a group of neighbors who found out he was trying to abuse Catalina Fabela, a seven-year-old girl.[73] Catalina escaped Guadalupe's attack thanks to family members and neighbors who heard her screaming for help.[74]

Press accounts of the lynching of rapists and other criminals pointed to neighbors' capacity to react swiftly to prevent or punish those acts they deemed intolerable. Surely, these accounts contrasted with the neglectful and ineffective responses the press ascribed to state authorities and contributed to rendering lynching an understandable, even appropriate, response. On April 26, 1949, for instance, *El Nacional* reported the lynching of the sátiro Pedro Bobadilla in a small town close to Mexico City. Bobadilla was caught by a group of neighbors when he was abusing a three-year-old girl.[75] Convinced that he was guilty of many other incidents that ocurred in the town, a mob of more than fifty people—mostly women—surrounded Bobadilla and, after putting a noose around his neck, dragged him with a horse down the highway between Mexico City and Cuernavaca. Personnel from the Red Cross who were going to the town to take the girl to the nearest hospital saved Bobadilla. The rape of a four-year-old girl by Felipe Jimenez Romero also provoked a swift reaction among residents of the Xochimilco neighborhood of Mexico City.[76] When a group of residents heard rumors about the sexual assault, they chased Jimenez Romero and, armed with stones and clubs, broke into a pulquería where the man was hiding. In this instance, too, the man, bleeding and badly injured, was saved by police officers and taken to the police station.

Even when the police managed to prevent the lynching of these so-called satyrs, the press built a narrative around these "failed" cases of lynching that centered on the public indignation generated by rapes. The rapist Miguel Pimentel was said to have caused such outrage among Coatzacoalco villagers that they tried to kill the "satyr old geezer" to set an example of how to deal with such criminals.[77] The newspaper added that policemen struggled to prevent the lynching, although they themselves "would have wanted to hand him over to the mob's wrath." Likewise, in Tlalnepantla, Estado de México, under the headline, "Outraged Women Were Going to Lynch the Jackal Santín," *La Prensa* reported that a large group of women chased José Natividad Santín with the intention of lynching him.[78] (See figure 5.) The man tried to abuse Teresa Arias and was reportedly part of a criminal organization that committed various crimes, including rapes and homicides, against other girls in the area. An image of the criminal next to two policemen who "rescued him from the enraged mob" was printed by the newspaper, together with an image of Teresa Arias held by her distressed mother.

The reaction of readers exposed to these types of stories is not difficult to imagine. The explicit and eloquent language used by crime news to communicate the gravity of these offenses, together with the publication of images that re-created the suffering of the victim as well as the brutality of the alleged criminal, surely contributed to an understanding of lynching as a proportional form of justice. And yet at the center of these stories were dozens of men and women whose

FIGURE 5. "Mujeres indignadas iban a linchar al chacal Santín" (Outraged Women Were Going to Lynch the Jackal Santín), *La Prensa*, January 25, 1944. Credit: Fototeca, Hemeroteca y Biblioteca Mario Vázquez Raña, Organización Editorial Mexicana S.A. de C.V. © Fotografía Propiedad de Fototeca, Hemeroteca y Biblioteca "Mario Vázquez Rana."

culpability was presumed but never proved or investigated, as well as people who, despite not having committed any crime, were punished merely for their alleged intent to do so. Although mentioned only at the margins of crime news, suspected wrongdoers often voiced their innocence. Journalists, however, were quick to disregard their claims and focus on the atrocity of the crime as well as the presumed culpability of the suspect, which was, more often than not, built around the testimony of a few witnesses.

The actual or potential violence of these crimes was central to journalists' representations of lynching as a fair form of punishment. However, crimes precipitating lynching did not necessarily involve violence. Salient among these "bloodless crimes" were robberies and cattle rustling.[79] Compared to the murders or violent assaults described above, these acts seem trivial or inconsequential, especially since some involved the stealing of small items or inexpensive possessions. And yet crime news continued to create a narrative that rendered these lynchings morally acceptable or understandable. Such morality, which also served to legitimate these lynchings in the eyes of perpetrators, was predicated on the economic needs of those who were deprived of their goods and possessions, however small. The excess of lynching was thus subsumed under a certain "moral economy"[80] that appealed to the proper norms of behavior among neighbors and villagers regarding those goods that were seen as essential to their subsistence.[81]

That lynching driven by robberies concerned possessions of little economic value surfaces in various instances perpetrated against so-called rateros, the degrading term used to refer to thieves or people accused of petit theft in post-revolutionary Mexico.[82] In July 1931, for instance, Serafín Flores was accused of stealing a sewing machine from Serapio Mejía in the city of Puebla.[83] Having confessed to his crime, the police took Serafín to the nearby town where he had sold the stolen item. Once in the town, a group of villagers recognized Serafín as the person responsible for a series of robberies that had taken place during the previous days. The press reported that the police were able to save the "professional ratero" from being lynched. The robbery of a watch and some clothes precipitated another lynching in Puebla years later, this time in Atlixco.[84] When Adolfo Aguilar and his wife discovered that someone had taken these items from their home, they alerted a group of neighbors who, armed with pistols, quickly joined Adolfo in pursuit of the criminal. On a road a few miles outside Atlixco the group saw a man walking alone and took him for the burglar. They then mobilized against him, "lassoing him" (*a cabeza de silla*) and dragging him with a horse. Acknowledging that there was no evidence that the man was actually responsible for the robbery, the press stated that the "raterillo" (little rat) was hanged from a tree and shot by the mob.

Crime news showed little if any sympathy for thieves. Instead, journalists called attention to robbers' sneaky and deceitful character and implicitly celebrated people's prompt and direct actions against them, even if these entailed excessive use of violence.[85] News stories about vendors accused of stealing or deceiving people further exemplify these dynamics of representation. They also offer a window into the norms and expectations that regulated people's everyday interactions. On July 8, 1937, for instance, the press reported that a group of women lynched a merchant who had sold them charcoal mixed with stones in the city of Puebla.[86] The article lamented the merchant's "lack of scruples" and described how the "rightly outraged" group of women threw stones at the vendor to punish his fraudulent behavior. In the Mixcoac neighborhood in Mexico City, another "dishonest" and "shameless" charcoal vendor was lynched by a group of women in December 1941.[87] The press described the incident in the context of a series of debates taking place in the city—among politicians and business organizations—regarding the scarcity of basic goods, such as beans, rice, wheat, and charcoal. The article described next how a group of women had attacked an "immoral charcoal vendor" in the belief that the man was tampering with the merchandise to increase his profits.[88]

The moral economy of lynching is particularly salient in collective violence against cattle rustlers (*abigeos*). Cattle were of fundamental value to families and communities. They were considered a basic means of subsistence, particularly in the countryside. The fierce resistance encountered by the government's campaign to eradicate foot-and-mouth disease by killing cattle in various communities in post-revolutionary Mexico is a clear expression of this.[89] So are the various cases of lynching of cattle rustlers reported by the press, particularly during the 1940s.[90] One such case took place in the town of Santa Clara, Puebla, in September 1940.[91] The victim, Fortunato López, had stolen cattle many times before in the same town but was always released from prison due to lack of evidence and, according to the press, due to the complicity of a local judge. When villagers found out that Fortunato had once again stolen livestock, they rang the church bells and dragged him to the center of the town's plaza where they stoned him "like a dog." Fortunato's mutilated corpse was afterward "exhibited" outside the municipal palace.[92]

A year later, in the town of San Mateo, Estado de México, two hundred people lynched six men and one woman suspected of cattle rustling. The lynch mob seized the seven individuals from the hands of a group of police officers who were transporting them to the Toluca prison. Armed with clubs, knives, and stones, the mob attacked the criminals. Three of them, including the woman, were killed and their bodies mutilated; the others survived but died a few hours later in the Toluca hospital. Interviewed by *La Prensa,* family members of the victims listed the names of the villagers who had instigated the attack and also accused a group of policemen who, they claimed, had tormented the criminals when in their custody.[93] The correspondent for *El Nacional* wrote that the lynching served as a warning to both criminals and the authorities. Although the act itself was reproachable, the journalist reasoned it also set an important precedent that made it clear that justice needed to be swift to be effective.[94]

Press coverage of the lynching of another cattle rustler in the town of Santa Catarina, Estado de México, suggested a similar "lesson."[95] The article stated that, tired of the inertia and leniency of authorities, villagers had decided to lynch a cattle thief who they had caught in flagrante. It added that after stoning and hanging the man, the mob had taken his body to Texcoco and placed it in front of the municipal palace to send the following message to authorities:

> Since there is no one to protect us from the bandits and thieves, and since we are tired of working and sacrificing ourselves so that others take advantage of us, we bring you "this." . . . [I]f you do not know or you do not want to punish the bandits, [we tell you] we do know how and we are willing to continue doing it every time the occasion arises.[96]

Crime news, in essence, presented lynching as a necessary corrective to the authorities' inability to deliver justice. This inability, however, did not stem only from the state's failure to punish criminals. It was also grounded in the notion that swift and lethal forms of punishment were a better and more effective way to attain justice. Although in the case of the lynchings of murderers the press justified the practice as a proportional form of punishment that matched the violence of the crime, crimes against property (including cattle rustling and robberies of smaller items) were also vindicated. In this case, lynching was justified by the notion that robbers somehow violated the norms of behavior regarding those goods that were essential for people's economic subsistence. Similar to lynchings perpetrated against unnatural mothers, bad sons, or violent men, the press offered clear lessons through its storytelling. Such lessons were meant to warn criminals about the consequences of their actions and the government about the costs that their failed responses to crime could have.

CONCLUSION

Crimes eliciting lynching reflected people's understandings of deviancy, morality, and danger. They revealed the type of behavior that neighbors and townsfolk considered unacceptable or intolerable, so much so as to be punished outside the legal mechanisms sanctioned by the state. The stories that occupied the crime pages reflected an understanding of the law as something that could be bent and bypassed in order to attain justice. They exposed a citizenry that demanded harsher and swifter punishments from the very same authorities it criticized and distrusted because of their abusive and corrupt practices.

The narratives presented by the press suggest lynching did not happen in a vacuum of state authority. Police officers, in particular, were present during many instances of lynching and even intervened and prevented the killing of so-called criminals at the hands of the mob. Although the press presented these cases as an example of the brave and law-abiding performance of the police, evidence suggests that policemen were not foreign to the use of extralegal and brutal forms of punishment. The use of the ley fuga against suspected criminals was a clear example of authorities' disregard for the rule of law as well as of the existence of a precarious consensus between the state and citizens regarding the use of extralegal violence.

The public support of lynching and the ley fuga, alongside public demands for the reinstatement of the death penalty to punish criminals, indicates that lynching was not merely a corrective to the state's inability to provide justice. Instead, it reflected citizens' inclination to apply swift and lethal forms of punishment. The morality of lynching was grounded in the notion that this practice constituted a legitimate, even moral response to crimes that were regarded as unnatural and immoral. In this sense, lynching was not merely a result of impunity. Rather, it was an expression of the culture of punishment that had taken root in post-revolutionary Mexico.

4

The Lynching of the Wicked

*Fat Stealers, Bloodsuckers, and Witches
in Post-Revolutionary Mexico*

In March 1955, U.S. and Mexican newspapers reported the occurrence of two lynchings in the state of Querétaro in north central Mexico. The first was directed against two federal road engineers who were beaten to death in a town called La Lira, close to the city of Querétaro. The press reported, "Villagers were told the engineers were stealing children and extracting their blood to be sent abroad to make serum."[1] More than fifty people were arrested in connection with the lynching. The second case occurred scarcely one week later in the locality of Juárez, just a few hours from La Lira. The incident involved the hanging of two brothers, Alejo and Martiniano Sánchez, who were known as witches.[2] After accusing them of having harmed some people through their witchcraft, dozens of neighbors seized the brothers and lynched them in what newspapers described as a "macabre spectacle."[3] An article in the Mexican magazine *Criminalia* celebrated the fact that federal authorities acted promptly in response to both cases by prosecuting those responsible for such "primitive and savage" acts.[4]

Driven by transgressions that pertain to the realm of the supernatural, these two instances of lynching offer a window into the role that mythical beliefs and mythlike figures played in the incidence of mob violence in post-revolutionary Mexico.[5] In particular, they are illustrative of the types of allegations that were made against people who were perceived as bearers of magical deeds and powers and were lynched in retaliation for their misdemeanors. Although victims of these lynchings were linked to otherworldly doings and events, accusations made against them reflected rather earthly preoccupations. Mythical figures such as bloodsuckers and fat stealers, for instance, revealed anxieties regarding modernization processes that often entailed the presence of people who were external to the community. Imagined as foreign, harmful, and greedy creatures that fed off the blood or fat of humans, including children, these figures have surfaced in Latin America since colonial times. Rumors surrounding their existence usually took the form of mythlike narratives that involved the exploitation of local "resources"—human bodies or bodily fluids—either by foreign individuals or by foreign countries. Lynchings of these mythical figures were extremely rare. And yet rumors that informed their occurrence emerged at different points in post-revolutionary Mexico, in the context of modernization projects promoted by the central state, the introduction of modern machinery, or the building of modern infrastructure, including roads and bridges.

Lynchings of people accused of witchcraft were more common, although they were far from being ordinary occurrences. While accusations of witchcraft could be directed against men, the vast majority of cases of lynching involved women, particularly older women.[6] Respected and feared by people due to their mystical powers, witches occupied an ambiguous position in communities. Through their use of herbs, potions, or invocation of spirits, witches were capable of both alleviating problems and providing magical remedies and inflicting the most terrible maladies, including death.[7] Referred to interchangeably as *hierberas* (herbalists), *curanderas* (healers), and *espiritistas* (spiritists), witches were not lynched because of their use of supernatural powers. Rather, when witches became the target of lynch mobs, it was because of their alleged misuse of such powers or for having inflicted insidious harm on a member of the community. Victims of witchcraft included both women and men but also children and infants who were made ill or kept ill by a witch's curse.

Similar to lynchings of bloodsuckers and fat stealers, the collective killing of witches was driven by fantastical beliefs that were intertwined with earthly concerns, including the unexpected and persistent sickness of children, family members, and partners or a person's sudden and inexplicable economic misfortune. Precipitated by these adverse situations, the punishing of witches was also driven by envy, personal vendettas, and intracommunal conflicts, including political differences.[8]

The overrepresentation of women in witchcraft accusations leading to lynching suggests gender played an important role in the occurrence of these acts of mob violence. Female witches, healers, and spiritists defied notions of submissiveness, domesticity, and motherly care associated with women in post-revolutionary Mexico. Feared and pursued by members of the community, witches were influential individuals who could behave in deceitful, greedy, and wicked ways. They had the power to deceive men, to make them lose their minds, or to manipulate them in order to make them return the affection of women who paid for their services. They could also inflict pain and death on their enemies and put a curse on a family's children, provoking their premature death. In a context in which, despite the revolution's promises of greater gender equality, men continued to exercise control over the private and public spheres the powers attributed to female witches were certainly subversive of this social order.[9]

Taken together, lynchings of bloodsuckers, fat stealers, and witches illuminate the impact that mythical beliefs had in the organization and legitimation of mob violence in post-revolutionary Mexico. First, there is the issue of scapegoating. Rumors and accusations regarding the existence and deeds of mythical figures provided an effective means to explain certain events that seemed random, threatening, or inexplicable. By identifying a scapegoat, people were able to provide order and meaning to situations that would otherwise seem too stressful or overwhelming. They were also able to place the blame on others for whatever misfortune affected them, concealing their own responsibility or denying the importance of more mundane reasons for their physical or material troubles. Mythical beliefs offered a powerful and effective narrative to fabricate scapegoats in post-revolutionary Mexico. Mythical figures were imagined either as external to the community or as possessing magical powers that situated them at the margins of society or outside the norms of sociability that regulated the rest of the people. They were, in this sense, already regarded as transgressors of the established social order.

The identification of some people as malicious or wicked was never random.[10] Fat-stealing and bloodsucking figures were associated with foreign individuals or with people who came from, or were in contact with, the "outside world" (e.g., the federal government or the United States). Witches included older women living alone, individuals who performed "strange" rituals, and men and women who claimed to be able to produce good and harm through the use of otherworldly powers. In other words, these were individuals who were already considered deviant or as somehow living outside communities' norms of behavior. Seeing them as guilty of performing a misdeed was thus just the expected and natural result of the characteristics people already ascribed to these fantastic figures.

In addition to providing an effective narrative for scapegoating, mythical beliefs contributed to justifying the use of particularly cruel forms of torment against victims. The mutilation and burning of witches, for instance, were seen as preferred methods of punishment. These forms of torment offered a more painful death, but, most important, they guaranteed the witch was unable to continue performing evil after being killed. It was important, then, not just to kill the witch, but "overkill" him or her through the disfigurement and defacement of the body. The use of brutal forms of violence in lynchings of mythical figures was thus sanctioned by otherworldly mandates or beliefs.

Furthermore, mythical beliefs were usually held to be true by several members of a given community. As such, accusations made against mythical figures as well as their corresponding punishment were more susceptible to being tolerated by neighbors and villagers alike. Because the harm done by wicked figures to one member of the community had the very real potential to affect others, mythical beliefs made the collectivization of violence more feasible. In other words, the lynching of the wicked was justified under the premise that stopping his or her misbehavior guaranteed the safety of the whole community.

Lynchings driven by mythical beliefs were reported during the 1930s and 1940s and continued well into the 1950s, as suggested by the two cases mentioned in the opening paragraph of this chapter. Similar to lynchings motivated by religious beliefs and practices, the press was quick to present these cases as a sign of the backwardness and ignorance of communities that were somehow thought of as living outside modernity. And yet evidence suggests that it was precisely these communities' exposure to modernization processes what triggered the circulation of mythlike narratives. This is most evident in bloodsucking and fat-stealing accusations but can also be observed in the case of witchcraft allegations, particularly those driven by political conflicts—including conflicts surrounding the agrarian reform introduced by the federal government. Moreover, witchcraft beliefs were not confined to isolated towns but were reported in urban areas experiencing rapid economic changes as well as in rural communities exposed to the introduction of modern medicine and technological innovations. Regardless of where they took place, for the myth believer, witchcraft allegations offered more compelling explanations for the sudden presence of sickness and economic misfortune than those provided by modern medicine or market-based rationales.

Below, I develop these arguments based on the analysis of various cases of lynching of mythical figures. I divide my discussion into two sections. The first focuses on the lynching of bloodsuckers and fat stealers. Because such events were rare, I center my discussion on the rumors that made these cases possible and draw on anthropological and historical studies that allow me to elucidate further the origin and weight of these beliefs in post-revolutionary Mexico. The second section analyzes lynchings perpetrated against witches. Here the number of cases is more substantial, thus allowing me to delve deeper into the potential fears and anxieties that informed accusations of witchcraft. The examination of these cases, together with the insights offered by literature on witchcraft in Mexico, suggests a pattern of scapegoating in which women, particularly older women, took center stage. It further reveals that illness and the death of a family member were the most prevalent reasons for accusations of witchcraft and their corresponding punishment. Each section presents the cases, whenever possible, in chronological order. However, because lynchings perpetrated against wicked individuals followed a consistent pattern across the post-revolutionary period (as did lynchings against criminals) the chapter privileges a synchronic over a diachronic analysis.

FAT STEALERS, BLOODSUCKERS, AND THE LYNCH MOB

On April 24, 1930, close to three hundred people brutally lynched Edgar Kullmann, a Norwegian geologist who was visiting the town of Amozoc as part of his larger exploration of the state of Puebla.[11] Kullmann had arrived in Puebla City a few days before, with a permit signed by Puebla's governor authorizing him to explore and research the whole state.[12] Described by the press as a "man of science," Kullmann traveled from Puebla City to Amozoc to study the traditions of the town's indigenous people. Once there, he introduced himself to the mayor, who welcomed him and recommended a place to stay. After grabbing something to eat and greasing his boots, Kullmann walked toward the town's main *zócalo* (plaza). A few blocks from there, he stopped to talk to a few local children to ask them for directions and give them some candies. Quickly thereafter, Kullmann found himself surrounded by dozens of villagers, who accused him of being one of those "decapitators" (*cortacabezas*) who abducted children in order to extract their body fat and power airplanes. The main instigator, Balbina de la Rosa, known as "la Borrega," pointed at the grease on Kullmann's boots as proof of the beheadings of children he had already perpetrated "in the name of progress." Kullmann reached out for the official permit that the governor had granted him, but the piece of paper was useless. An accusation had been made, and Kullmann, a foreigner never before seen in town, was the perfect scapegoat.

Kullmann was lynched with conspicuous cruelty. A crowd of men and women, which now numbered thousands, threw stones at him, beat him, and cut him with machetes. They next put a rope around his neck and dragged him toward a well, located one hundred meters from the place where Kullmann was first seen with the children. The press, making reference to the fact that Kullmann was lynched on a "Holy Thursday," described that walk as a Via Crucis and compared his suffering to that undergone by Jesus Christ. After throwing Kullmann's body into the well, some of the men and women who minutes before were tormenting the Norwegian geologist went to the local church to continue the religious celebrations of Holy Week.

The next day, villagers extracted Kullmann's body from the well to hide it and cover their crime. A group of agraristas that participated in the lynching extracted the body. The town's judge oversaw the body's exhumation, fearing that news about the lynching would reach Puebla City. Despite villagers' efforts to conceal Kullmann's assassination, news of the incident reached the governor of Puebla, who sent police officers to investigate. Although several villagers had participated in the collective killing, only three people were arrested. Balbina de la Rosa, the main suspect, was nowhere to be found.[13]

The press attributed the lynching of Kullmann to the ignorance of indigenous people whose superstition and backwardness constituted an affront to the state of Puebla and the nation as a whole.[14] And yet evidence suggests that the rumors leading to Kullmann's lynching circulated among both rural and urban dwellers and were amplified by Puebla's newspapers themselves. A week before the incident, the press reported that several children and adults had gone missing from various towns and cities in Puebla, including the state's capital. The inexplicable disappearances had given shape to a rumor, propagated by people in the city and the countryside, that the missing had been abducted in order to extract their body fat and use it as oil to propel the engine of an airplane.[15] At night and at dawn, a wicked creature would fly over villages and towns in order to abduct the victims who would power its fantastic airplane. The alarm provoked by the legend was such that parents refused to send their children to school. Despite authorities' efforts to ease people's fears by denying the existence of such a creature and explaining that only one disappearance had been officially reported in the previous months, the mythlike narrative of the fat sucker persisted.

How can one make sense of the rumors behind Kullmann's lynching? What were the elements that made this fantastic story credible in the eyes of Amozoc townsfolk and villagers from other towns in Puebla? Rumors allow people to communicate their anxieties and to exercise a certain level of control over stressful situations.[16] When reiterated over time, rumors acquire a plot and structure that emulates that of legends or myths.[17] Far from being random or arbitrary, the narrative invokes a plausible and collectively crafted version of reality.[18] It contains elements of reality that, as argued by James C. Scott, are embellished in a way "that brings it more closely into line with the hopes, fears, and worldview of those who hear it and retell it."[19]

In addition to the apparent disappearance of at least one person in Puebla, there is another element that helps explain the rumor's credibility as well as the potential reasons for villagers' anxieties. Newspapers explained that there was indeed an airplane flying every night over certain towns in Puebla. The airplane belonged to the distinguished Mexican pilot Pablo Sidar, who was performing flight tests in preparation for what was expected to be the first direct flight from Mexico to Argentina.

Sidar's flight generated a great deal of expectation and was celebrated among political and economic elites as an expression of the country's progress.[20] In an interview with the press, Sidar expressed his confidence in becoming the first man to perform the audacious trip, beating the American pilots who had announced a similar enterprise.[21] In the midst of Sidar's flying tests, Edgar Kullmann, who was neither a pilot nor the feared mythical figure, was brutally assassinated. In a further twist of events, Pablo Sidar, the renowned pilot, would die only a couple of weeks after Kullmann's untimely death, in a tragic accident during his failed attempt to perform the first direct flight to Argentina.[22]

The credibility of the mythlike rumors precipitating Kullmann's lynching can be further brought to light by looking deeper into the meanings and manifestations of this and similar myths. For instance, the fat-sucker creature that villagers associated with Kullmann resembles the mythical figure known as the "cortacabezas." With a particularly strong presence in the state of Chiapas, the figure of the cortacabezas is thought to be a man, either a foreigner or someone external to the community, who decapitates and mutilates people at night or in lonely places.[23] Driven by greed and selfishness, the cortacabezas uses his victims' body parts as the foundation for the construction of bridges and roads or to fabricate mechanical objects.[24] In one version of the myth, the body parts are sold to the United States to make watches; in another one, the cortacabezas are government engineers who require body parts to prevent their structures from collapsing.[25]

In addition, fat-stealer figures are rooted in Hispanic traditions and practices. One of these figures is the *pishtaco,* whose origins can be traced to colonial Peru and whose characteristics strikingly resemble those attributed to Kullmann. The pishtaco is conceived as a tall white man who beheads and dismembers his victims, most of them children, in order to extract their body fat and sell it "for the lubrication of machines of the modern world or to pharmacies to cure certain types of diseases."[26]

The myth of the pishtaco has been linked to the use, by some Spanish colonizers in Peru, of Indians' body fat to cure wounds or broken bones.[27] Although the practice ceased to exist among Spaniards, the fears associated with it lived on in the myth of the pishtaco.[28] The use of body fat, or *unto,* was also present during Mexico's colonial period. The Spanish chronicler Bernal Díaz del Castillo described how Spanish soldiers cut up Indians' corpses and used their fat to treat their wounds and those of their horses.[29] In Spain, knowledge about this practice gave rise to a belief among peasants about a child-stealer creature known as the *sacamantecas,* which is literally translated as "the one who extracts fat."[30]

In post-revolutionary Mexico rumors and mythical beliefs regarding the abduction of people and the use of their bodily fluids emerged in the context of the state's modernization efforts and the dynamics of exploitation and extraction brought about by the advent of modern capitalism. During the 1930s, the cultural and economic policies promoted in Mexico's countryside led to the circulation of rumors that claimed the federal government was kidnapping children in order to be "sent to the United States and turned into oil for planes."[31] Likewise, the construction of roads and bridges during the 1930s and 1940s raised concerns among villagers of Tepoztlán, Morelos, regarding the presence of engineers who they believed had offered 245 souls to a devil hiding in a cave in order to construct the road to their town in an expedited way.[32] And in San Juan Chamula, Chiapas, Tzotzil Maya villagers held that giants "roamed the region, capturing and selling Indians to ladino road crew chiefs who turned them into grease to lubricate their road-building machinery."[33]

Sanitation campaigns and health care policies promoted by the central state generated parallel rumors among indigenous villagers and town doctors during the 1930s and 1940s. According to such rumors, "state medics sought to kidnap local children, extract their fat, and use it to grease cars, airplanes and other machines."[34] To these accounts we can add the rumor leading to the lynching of the two federal road engineers described in this chapter's introduction. The latter rumor followed the same plot: state representatives were abducting children and removing their bodily fluids (in this case, blood instead of fat) to be sent overseas or to provide fuel for modern machinery.

These accounts reveal three characteristics that bring these rumors together. First, the extraction and consumption of bodily fluids (fat or blood) suggests, in all these narratives, a logic of exploitation or domination by external actors. Thus the protagonists in these rumors were either agents of the federal government or foreigners who were male, white, and of European descent. Alternatively, local "resources" were sent away to a powerful country, usually the United States, to lubricate or fuel modern machines. Second, children figured prominently in these narratives, even though adults were also considered potential victims of the mythical figures. And third, these rumors articulated a clear narrative of refusal or rejection of modernization projects. This narrative is manifested in the portrayal of those in charge of carrying out these projects as wicked individuals who possess otherworldly powers. In other words, this rejection crystallized in the form of mythical or nonhuman figures that snatched, decapitated, and consumed human bodies and fluids.

Rumors are made of narratives that borrow elements from reality, which are then elaborated in accordance with people's fears and anxieties. The 1930s through 1950s were characterized by rapid economic and technological changes, which were introduced by federal elites in an effort to incorporate and modernize rural communities. As discussed in chapter 1, several communities regarded the state's intervention in local affairs as intrusive and threatening and thus resisted these changes by violent means, including lynching. The changes introduced by the state included the construction of roads, bridges, and other public infrastructure works. Although these modernization efforts involved Mexican elites, foreign investment and foreign engineers—particularly from the United States—were a necessary step in building Mexico's own technical skills and tools.[35] The reference to foreign or strange elements in these narratives against modernization was thus not at all random.

Furthermore, the presence of children as victims of these mythical figures mirrored a constant feature of post-revolutionary Mexico: the actual or imagined presence of *robachicos* (child snatchers).[36] Reflected in the various newspaper reports about child theft that were published at the time, the centrality of fears surrounding child theft was also evident in the fierce reaction that these crimes provoked, which included the lynching or attempted lynching of robachicos.[37] The accusation made against the two engineers in La Lira, Querétaro, which claimed they were sending children's blood abroad to make serum, had thus enough elements to make it seem credible, even logical, in the eyes of perpetrators.[38] As in the case of Kullmann's lynching, there were elements of reality that gave consistency to the fears and anxieties that made the collectivization of violence possible.

That some people found in these mythical beliefs a plausible explanation for given situations does not rule out the fact that others might have used such beliefs for political purposes. It is impossible to know the extent to which all those who participated in the lynching of Kullmann, for instance, believed that he was actually a fat sucker. Was Balbina de la Rosa, the main instigator, convinced of this belief? Were there political tensions or conflicts in Amozoc and the particular neighborhood where the lynching took place that were aired or resolved by Kullmann's killing? We do not have enough information to be certain.

As the next section shows, however, political tensions and personal vendettas indeed informed accusations of witchcraft and the lynching of individuals who were thought to be vested with magical powers. The existence of such political and personal reasons does not negate the weight of these mythical beliefs. Rather, it demonstrates that mythlike fears and accusations were informed by earthly concerns and that, as such, they reflected existing personal and political conflicts.

THE COLLECTIVE KILLING OF WITCHES, HEALERS, AND SPIRITISTS

In August 1930, just a few months after Kullmann's death, Isabel León, a woman known as a witch, was nearly lynched by a group of neighbors in what the press described as a sordid area in Puebla City.[39] Isabel had been seen offering candies and toys to a little boy named Gaspar. The boy's mother, Leonor Rojas, felt uneasy about the woman's intentions. Isabel's "mysterious behavior" had led her and others in the neighborhood to believe she was a witch. When the boy went missing one afternoon, Leonor instinctively went looking for him at Isabel's house. What she found there was a horrid spectacle: "She saw her son, firmly tied to a bed, and the strange woman extracting a large amount of blood with an old and dirty syringe." Terrified and outraged by this sight, Leonor called a group of neighbors and, with them, tried to lynch the woman, whose killing was prevented by the police.

Although the press provided no further details about Isabel León and her so-called mysterious behavior, there are certain aspects of this story that deserve attention. The first has to do with neighbors' shared feelings of animosity to and distrust of Isabel prior to the incident. From the newspaper account, it is clear that the alleged act of witchery that precipitated Isabel's near-lynching only confirmed what neighbors already believed: she was an evil witch. More interesting perhaps is the specific accusation made against her. Isabel was allegedly extracting the little boy's blood in order to, so the press presumed, prepare one of her potions. As discussed above, accusations of child theft and rumors about mythical beings that used children's bodily fluids were not uncommon in post-revolutionary Mexico.[40] Similar figures were thought to exist in the neighboring state of Tlaxcala. So-called bloodsucking witches, or *tlahuelpuchis,* were believed to extract children's (usually infants') blood in order to survive and invigorate themselves.[41] It is thus plausible that when Leonor saw Isabel extracting blood from her son, she and her already prejudiced neighbors referred back to existing rumors regarding child snatchers as well as bloodsucking and fat-sucking creatures.

Even more common than bloodsucking accusations, however, were allegations made against witches who had put a curse on neighbors or members of a family–either children or adults—making them ill or causing their death. For instance, a few months before the incident described above, a group of neighbors accused María Jimenez Medina of being a witch and carrying out various misdeeds in Mexico City.[42] According to one woman, María had given her husband a beverage that caused his death shortly after he drank it. Another woman claimed that María would go out at night and venture into the mountains to prepare potions made of wild tobacco that caused harm to people she disliked. Yet another accuser asserted that she was capable of making people lose their minds and then take control of them. Although in this case neighbors decided to denounce the witch's misdeeds to local authorities,[43] most witchcraft accusations were dealt with "privately" or through the use of communal and extralegal forms of punishment, including lynching.

In January 1931, for instance, in a small town in Estado de México, a group of men armed with clubs lynched the town's witch, "an aged Indian woman," who was known for preparing potions and love charms for women who wanted to get back their husbands' affections.[44] Disgruntled by the witches' potions, which they claimed made them foolish, the men decided to beat her to death. The police prevented her murder, but the witch was expelled from the town in retaliation for her actions.[45] In an interview published years later, José Farah, former attorney general of Nayarit, recounted a similar lynching.[46] Perpetrated around 1935 by a group of Coras in San Juan Peyotán, the incident involved a male witch who had failed to deliver one of his spells and was punished accordingly. Farah stated that he suspended the investigation of the lynching after realizing that he would need to imprison all the inhabitants of San Juan Peyotán to punish the killing.

Witches occupied an ambiguous position in communities. Their capacity to use magical powers to cure diseases or secure the affection of a loved one made them particularly influential among villagers, who often sought their favors and protection. Witches' ability to use those same powers to provoke physical and economic maladies, however, made them the object of villagers' constant fears and suspicions. Thus when neighbors or former "patrons" of their magic turned those fears into actual accusations, witches became susceptible to particularly cruel forms of torment.

The lynching of the witch Lucero Curiel in August 1941 in San Juan del Mezquital, Zacatecas, brings to light witches' dual status in communities. An older woman who was sought after by various villagers, Lucero was known for her ability to cure diseases and secure people's good fortune through the use of potions and herbs.[47] Days before her killing, however, a number of neighbors accused her of causing several deaths in the town. Considering the situation unbearable, a group of men, women, and children dragged Lucero out of her home and beat her with stones and clubs. They then took her to a place where they had placed several pieces of wood. Once there, they tied her hands and, despite Lucero's cries for mercy, set her on fire. According to the press, the authorities of San Juan de Mezquital did not prevent Lucero's murder because, they conceded, this was the only way in which the witch could pay for her wrongs. Lucero Curiel was burned alive.

The use of fire to kill a witch surfaces as a preferred method of punishment in other cases reported during these years. In December 1943, for example, residents of the Villa de Guadalupe neighborhood in Mexico City threatened to burn two witches to make them pay for their wrongdoings.[48] The witches, Catalina Hidalgo Ramírez and Vicente Moctezuma Ramírez, who lived together and were sixty and fifty-seven years old, respectively, were accused of bewitching one of their neighbor's children. A group of men and women, including the accuser, managed to break into their home, dragging one of them by the hair and beating the other. The two witches escaped their assailants and returned to their home in the middle of the night. People outside continued to threaten them, shouting that they would come back and burn them using green wood, which ensured a slower and more painful death. The next morning, feeling that they were finally safe, Catalina and Vicente went to the nearest police station to denounce the incident.[49]

Although the lynching of these witches was not consummated, the threat against them, together with the actual death by burning of Lucero Curiel, illuminates the ways in which accusations against so-called wicked individuals served to justify the use of cruel forms of torment. The burning and mutilation of a witch's body was believed to prevent this supernatural being from continuing to inflict harm after the human form was neutralized.[50] Villagers from rural towns in Tlaxcala, for instance, believed that bloodsucking witches needed to be mutilated and their bodies left unburied. The description provided by Hugo Nutini and John M. Roberts regarding the "appropriate" method to kill a tlahuelpuchi is worth quoting at some length:

> First of all, when a person has been singled out as a tlahuelpuchi . . . she is swiftly put to death. The mob quickly runs to the house of the tlahuelpuchi, immobilizes her . . . so she cannot transform herself into an animal, and on the spot she is clubbed and/or stoned to death. Once she is dead, two men with knives symbolically kill her again by depriving her of her physical sense organs. The two chosen men drag the naked body of the tlahuelpuchi to a deserted spot where she is left to rot, for she cannot be buried.[51]

This incident bears all the hallmarks of a lynching and brings to the fore the ways in which mythical beliefs contributed to the sanctioning of excessive violence against individuals bestowed with magical powers. Through their use of magical potions and herbs or their communication with the world beyond, healers and spiritists were often referred to, interchangeably, as witches and were subjected to similar torments.[52] Healers' failure to provide an effective cure, in particular, called into question their powers and provoked the suspicion and rage of the disgruntled party. Accusations that healers were charlatans could thus carry fatal consequences. A case in point was the lynching of the healer and spiritist Mario Rodríguez Castillo in the town of Nopala, Estado de México, in July 1942. Mario had been asked to cure an old woman who was suffering severe stomach pain.[53] While he was invoking the spirits in order to remedy her pain, a group of around sixty men, led by the Nopala police chief, broke into the place and seized him. Accusing him of being a charlatan, the men shot him multiple times and then lassoed him and dragged him with a horse. His dead body was left abandoned on the road. None of those responsible for the lynching was apprehended. In addition to the chief of police, the lynching was perpetrated by a group of influential agraristas, thus suggesting probable political reasons for the healer's murder.[54]

The lynching of Clara Fonseca in the town of La Purísima, Puebla, in July 1944 further exemplifies the vulnerability of healers who were accused of being imposters.[55] The day before her lynching, Clara had been asked by an influential family to cure their three-year-old son, Pedro Ventura, who was dying of meningitis. The boy's father told Clara that if she was a real healer, she would cure the boy. If she did not cure him, he would know she was a charlatan. While Clara was giving him one of her powerful potions, the boy died in her arms. Alas, Clara was declared guilty of his death. As the news spread among the townsfolk, a group of people instigated by the boy's father went looking for the now-shunned healer, dragged her outside her house, and, after tying her to a tree, beat her to death with stones, sticks, and daggers. Clara presented at least seventy wounds on different parts of her body, and her skull was virtually destroyed. Puebla's attorney general traveled to La Purísima to investigate the crime, but the boy's parents had already fled the town, and local authorities, so the local press hinted, were complicit in Clara's assassination.[56]

In spite of the constant accusations against healers, spiritists, and witches, villagers regularly sought their favors. Their popularity was such that during the 1940s, medical students received a manual that warned them about the presence of "witches, sorcerers, and charlatans" in Mexico's countryside.[57] Their duty, the manual explained, was to eradicate the "false beliefs" on which these individuals had built their reputation. Although they were cautioned against the dangers these individuals posed for the advancement of modern medicine, medical students were also advised to familiarize themselves with the traditions of the people. In order to introduce the "new magic" of modern medicine, it seemed, doctors had to learn the ways of the old one. In addition to getting to know traditional forms of healing, doctors and nurses were supposed to bring curanderos closer to modern medicine. Thus cultural missions were sent to the countryside to teach local healers to cure and treat simple maladies according to scientific practices.[58]

Although a more sensitive approach to local traditions developed during the 1940s, assimilation and incorporation still dominated the state's approach to the customs and practices of Mexico's rural communities.[59] Moreover, witchcraft beliefs, in particular, were deprecated and regarded as a sign of the backwardness and ignorance of townsfolk and indigenous people. The film *The Forgotten Village* (1941), directed by Herbert Kline and based on John Steinbeck's story, was particularly revealing of the contempt for witchcraft and mythlike beliefs that existed during the period. Produced in the United States, the film was supported by the Mexican government.[60] Set in the town of Santiago, between the states of Tlaxcala and Puebla, *The Forgotten Village* reproduced some of the basic themes of the indigenista films that were so popular at the time.[61] In Steinbeck's own words, in the film "civilization and modern medicine served as the protagonist, with witch doctoring as the antagonist."[62] Although the film does not concern a lynching, its plot, as well as the fact that an actual "witch doctor" or "wise woman" was part of the cast, provides a revealing background to the narratives of witchcraft analyzed thus far.[63]

At the center of the film is the village's curandera, Trini. When an epidemic strikes the town, causing a number of children to get sick, villagers seek out the healer and ask for her help. Juan Diego, protagonist of the film, does the same. The healer tells Juan Diego that her son has "the airs" and treats the child with her "herbs and magic." The scene shows the healer chewing some herbs and pressing an egg against the boy's stomach to "extract" his malady (the curandera was asked to emulate the way in which she normally treated sickness in order to add realism to the scene).[64] After finishing her ritual, Trini gives the boy's mother the egg where the bad airs got trapped and assures her that the little boy will now get better. In spite of her promise, and Juan Diego's faith in her, the wise woman's remedy fails, and the boy dies.

Unlike the cases described in this chapter, Trini is not punished for her failed magic. Instead, Juan Diego, seeing other of his children get sick, resorts to modern medicine for the answers that magic could not give him.[65] With the help of the local teacher, he brings a doctor from Mexico City who, with a microscope, shows Juan Diego and others the real cause of the children's sickness: bacteria in the water. Although villagers scorned Juan Diego for having betrayed their traditions, the story is one in which modern medicine and scientific knowledge triumph over superstition and magic. As if to show that modernity triumphed over magic even beyond the "big screen," *El Nacional* reported that the witch doctor had, in real life, fallen sick with septicemia and, instead of treating herself with magic, decided to see an actual doctor. The woman, the newspaper celebrated, was saved by modern medicine.[66]

Despite the triumphal narrative of modernization surrounding the film, evidence suggests that at the time of the film's release and in the ensuing years, witchcraft beliefs continued to have a central place among Mexican villagers.[67] The film rightly suggests villagers sought healers to cure and make sense of the maladies that affected them. Similar to Juan Diego and the film's characters, people found in the otherworldly a feasible explanation for their illnesses and difficulties. But contrary to the film's narrative, when healers' and witches' remedies failed, it was not modern medicine that provided the next plausible explanation for people's troubles but rather the evil doings of the very same individuals they regarded as bestowed with magical powers. In other words, whenever their magic did not deliver the expected results, individuals who were otherwise respected and feared became loathed and vulnerable to the collective rage of those who felt betrayed by their powers.

The paradox underpinning these cases seems obvious. Despite their otherworldly abilities, these men and women could not escape their own death. The lynching of Patricio de la Cruz Jimenez, in Chalchicomula, Puebla, in August 1945 shows once more how witches' failure to provide an effective cure for people's maladies exposed them to swift forms of punishment. De la Cruz was known as a witch and herbalist. His fame was such that villagers from Chalchicomula and neighboring towns sought his help whenever they were ill.[68] When he proved unable to cure a respectable neighbor, though, the whole town became infuriated and decided to lynch him. Villagers attacked De la Cruz armed with stones, clubs, and machetes. They then dragged him to a place where they intended to crucify him. But the man had already died. The press blamed lack of education and the "cerebral darkness" under which the residents of Chalchicomula lived for such "unconceivable tragedy."

Similar to the healer Clara Fonseca who was lynched after being unable to cure the boy of an influential family, De la Cruz became the target of a lynch mob after a respectable neighbor accused him of failing to deliver his magic.[69] In other words, the status of the accuser was relevant in the organization of these lynchings. It is not difficult to envision why this was the case. An accusation made by an influential neighbor against a witch gave it veracity and contributed to collectivized violence, as people were more prone to show their solidarity when a witch's curse affected someone who was well regarded. As argued by the anthropologist Mary Douglas, in order for a witchcraft accusation to be effective, the right circumstances must be in place. In addition to the status of the accuser, the accused must be recognized as someone capable of inflicting harm on others. Douglas writes, "To be successful an accusation should be directed against victims already hated by the populace."[70]

An example of a "successful accusation" took place in September 1945, only a month after the lynching of Patricio de la Cruz, in the town of Rancho Blanco in the central state of San Luis Potosí. The case involved María Palencia, a young woman who started to experience convulsions and acute pains in different parts of her body for no apparent reason.[71] Before the amazed eyes of neighbors, María screamed in pain and asserted she could feel how some invisible force was strangling her and dragging her by her feet. Scratches and marks on her body attested to her torment.

On witnessing María's critical condition and based on the victim's own allegations, villagers became convinced that Gregoria García, a woman who was known to all residents of Rancho Blanco as a powerful witch, was to blame for the young woman's maladies. After identifying Gregoria as the guilty party, villagers headed to her house with the intention of lynching her. Once there, the civil defense chief (*jefe de la defensa civil*) joined the crowd and ordered Gregoria to liberate María from her pains, or otherwise he would let people hang her from a tree. Although María did not get better, the civil defense chief helped Gregoria escape the crowd, not before receiving a generous bribe from the witch in exchange for the favor. According to the press, when the police of San Luis Potosí city arrived to investigate the case, they witnessed in awe how María Palencia "was possessed by the evil spirits."

A few days later, with María continuing to feel sick, another witch was blamed for the evil curse, this time with fatal consequences. In the middle of one of her spasms, María pronounced the name Teresa Camacho, leading neighbors to believe that the latter was responsible for the young woman's condition.[72] That the mere uttering of the name by the bewitched young woman sufficed as proof of the so-called witch's wrongdoing suggests María's status in the community was not insignificant. The press also reported that, similar to previous cases, the accused party, Teresa Camacho, was regarded with suspicion by neighbors, making her an easy scapegoat. Villagers decided, once again, to avenge María and dragged Teresa out of her house. This time nobody was able to prevent the lynching. After beating her to death, neighbors threw Teresa into a well. After the lynching of Teresa Camacho, a group of doctors from the city of San Luis Potosí, together with a group of medical students, determined that the origins of María's maladies were not supernatural but syphilis.

Witchcraft beliefs offered plausible explanations for people's maladies. Such ideas provided order and meaning to situations that were otherwise perceived as too overwhelming. Despite the central government's efforts to advance modern medicine among rural and indigenous communities,[73] witchcraft beliefs continued to be part of people's worldview throughout the 1940s and 1950s.[74] Examples abound. In Puebla City, Rosendo Gómez accused an indigenous woman of bewitching him, under orders from his wife.[75] Feeling acute pains in his stomach and having lost more than 50 kilos, he sought the help of another witch doctor, who gave him a strange potion prepared with oil, sea salt, and a black hen. The man vomited a great amount of strange animals that, he asserted, originated with the witch's curse.[76]

Likewise, in Mexico City, Enriqueta Nieves Alejandro accused the witch Tomasa N. of provoking the death of her sister, who had cancer.[77] Enriqueta had visited the witch in search of a cure. Tomasa gave Enriqueta a potion made of different herbs and charged her 72 pesos for it. Enriqueta's sister died a week later, leading her to believe the witch (not the cancer) caused her death. In yet another case, a man named José Trinidad Zapotitla accused a seventy-year-old woman of having bewitched his children and keeping them ill.[78] The woman, Micaela Juárez Serrano, was known as a witch in the neighborhood of Nueva Malintzi in Puebla City. Convinced that his children would continue to be sick unless she was killed, the man took matters into his own hands and shot Micaela in her own house and in front of her grandchild.[79]

That people attributed their maladies and misfortunes to the deeds of witches does not mean that witchcraft accusations were necessarily free of personal or political interests. Witchcraft accusations could indeed be deployed to resolve political disputes or air personal vendettas. For instance, ethnographic research carried out by the anthropologists Carmen Viqueira and Ángel Palerm from 1948 to 1951 in two Totonaca communities in the states of Veracruz and Puebla illustrates the impact of intracommunity conflicts on witchcraft beliefs and accusations. According to the authors, witchcraft beliefs were informed by enviousness, distrust, and cycles of vengeance. In the town of Eloxochitlán, Puebla, in particular, where witchcraft was part of villagers' everyday lives, people constantly feared neighbors and enemies would harm them through the use of magical powers. The following finding is worth quoting at length, as it reveals the pervasive nature of these beliefs as well as their use to resolve personal disputes and conflicts:

> In Eloxochitlán ... people live in constant fear of the workings of witches and the wickedness of supernatural beings. But they pursue, all the same, witches in order to make people sick, ruin them, or even make their enemies die. The procedures are limitless, knowledge about them is generalized, and witches are abundant and fertile in resources. [Witches] bury dead chickens and dolls made of wood in the enemy's land; the dead are sent to visit him (which is always harmful); they send naguales[80] and sickness; animals, the water, their tools are bewitched; they make women sterile, and provoke children's death, etc. . . . Those who feel affected by witchcraft—which is in fact everybody, one way or another—use counter-magic and more powerful witches, to collect evils against the presumed guilty party.[81]

Neighbors used witches and magical curses to cause the suffering of others or to protect themselves from the potential harm inflicted on them by their enemies. That witches could be "used" by neighbors for different purposes surely contributed to the ambiguous position that witches had in communities. It furthermore added to their vulnerability and victimization.

In a context wherein neighbors became suspicious of one another, witches and people associated with magical powers provided the perfect scapegoats to air intracommunity conflicts.[82] The lynching of a male witch in the town of Aljojuca,

Puebla, in August 1945 can be explained according to this logic. Once respected and sought after for his healing powers, Patricio Cruz Martínez became suddenly despised and distrusted by villagers.[83] While some villagers claimed he had caused the death of their relatives by giving them pernicious herbs, others said that he had poisoned them or made them lose their minds. The witch, they claimed, performed these evil deeds either when villagers failed to pay for his services or when one neighbor paid him to bewitch another one. In the latter case we see how neighbors used Patricio's powers to retaliate against each other, yet it was he who was punished. Following the pattern of killing other witches, Patricio received several machete blows that left him dead and mutilated.

A similar case was reported the previous year, in a town close to Acatlán, also in Puebla.[84] The case involved forty-four-year-old Hermelinda Fuentes, a healer known for her "mysterious rites" and her use of herbs. Hermelinda had arrived from Saltillo, Coahuila, in 1940 and had become popular even among young girls from the middle and upper classes, who looked to the healer to help them cover up their "indiscretions." Her good fame, however, came to an end when different people started accusing her of using the *mal de ojo* (evil eye) on them. Although according to most beliefs a witch is not the only person who can give the curse of the evil eye,[85] villagers directed their anger against Hermelinda. Like Patricio Cruz Martínez, Hermelinda was killed with machetes and her body brutally mutilated.

In addition to personal vendettas, the lynching of witches and of people who claimed to have magical powers could be informed by political conflicts. The lynching of Micaela Ortega in November 1934, discussed in chapter 2, is a clear example of this. As described in that chapter, Micaela was known as a socialist, a spiritist healer, and an anticlerical. She was also known for her close friendship with an agrarista who had allegedly stolen the harvest that belonged to indigenous communal lands. When neighbors broke into Micaela's home with the intention of lynching her, she was curing Pascual Salazar, a villager who was mute and suffered partial paralysis in his legs that made him walk with a limp.[86]

As they broke into her property, villagers shouted, "Viva Cristo Rey," "Death to socialism," and "Death to the spiritist Doña Micaela," expressing their discontent with all those things that Micaela represented. That Micaela was identified as a spiritist becomes clear in the investigation that followed the events. Inspector Fernando A. Rodríguez asked villagers if it was true that Micaela could cure, to which they replied, yes, she could cure, with water and by invoking spirits from beyond. Pascual Salazar's son-in-law, who spoke on Pascual's behalf because Micaela's assailants had also injured him, asserted that the healer claimed to be able to cure paralytics. The conspicuous cruelty used against Micaela further suggests that villagers believed she had otherworldly powers. Like other healers and witches who were lynched at the time, Micaela was killed with machetes, and her body presented several wounds, some of which were made with pieces of hot iron.

According to the autopsy, Micaela's body showed several cuts close to her ears and mouth, her skull had various wounds, and her torso was lacerated "in numbers that makes it impossible to count."[87] Furthermore, villagers set her ablaze. Micaela's daughter, Enedina, reported that after dragging her outside her house, the lynch mob (including the town's mayor) had poured gasoline on Micaela's body and set her on fire.

Another case illustrating the political dimensions of witchcraft accusations took place just a year before Micaela Ortega's lynching, in the neighboring state of Veracruz. The case was denounced by Agustín de la Cruz, who addressed the president to condemn a group of men who, in complicity with the municipal authorities, threatened to kill him after accusing him of being a witch and provoking the death of one of the men's children through the use of magic.[88] De la Cruz asserted the men were after him because he defended the agrarista cause and stated the same individuals were responsible for assassinating his father and brother, also for political reasons. He asked the president if there was justice for agrarista and indigenous peasants like him in the country, or just for those who had enriched themselves "in the shadow of the revolution." De la Cruz concluded his letter by calling the witchcraft accusations against him "stupid" and explained his enemies were only trying to justify their murderous actions.[89]

The fact that personal vendettas and political conflicts could inform villagers' allegations against witches and healers does not necessarily negate people's genuine beliefs in these individuals' otherworldly powers. The popularity of these beliefs is evidenced by the fact that people accused of witchcraft—even in the face of danger—did not themselves refute being witches. What they denied was having caused harm through the use of their magic. In other words, unlike the case of Agustín de la Cruz, the accused party did not usually repudiate his or her status as a witch or healer.

Given their vulnerability and exposure to violence, one might wonder why people identified themselves as witches or claimed to be capable of curing or affecting others through magical powers.[90] The anthropologist Julian Pitt-Rivers offers a plausible interpretation. He argues that although witches could become social outcasts, they were also feared and respected by people around them and thus enjoyed a great deal of power. In this sense, although accusations against witches could and indeed often did produce a "premature death," being regarded as a witch also provided people with a considerable level of influence that they did not possess otherwise. In Pitt-Rivers's words, "The stakes might be high, but the prize is dear."[91]

For women, in particular, being vested with the capacity to heal or hurt others through the use of magical potions or herbs or the invocation of spirits provided an opportunity to occupy a position of power that was often denied to them based on their gender. For a woman to be considered the town's healer, witch, or spiritist meant being able to inspire the respect but also the fear of others. As illustrated by the examples presented in this chapter, however, when these fears translated into accusations, retaliation could follow. If the witch herself threatened others, the risks of retaliation were even higher. This much is clear in the case of María Juana Dolores, an old woman and self-proclaimed witch of Temoaya, Estado de México. According to the press, María Juana had threatened Aurelio Álvarez with "causing him a harm"(*causarle un daño*) if he did not cease pursuing a land dispute he had initiated against her.[92] After Aurelio started to feel ill, he became convinced that María Juana had fulfilled her promise and decided to put an end to her curse by killing her. Although other villagers supported María Juana and even tried to avenge her killing by lynching Aurelio, the damage was done. María Juana's alleged curse had cost her her life.

If on the side of the accused there could be "advantages" in being perceived as a person vested with magical powers, on the side of the accusers the gains offered by such mythical beliefs were equally important. Witchcraft beliefs enabled people to attribute their misfortunes to an individual who was already identified as a transgressor of communities' accepted norms of behavior. In this sense, witchcraft accusations allowed those who suffered the illness or death of a loved one to cope with the pain and attract the solidarity (and complicity when an accusation was followed by collective murder) of other members of the community who shared the same beliefs.[93]

As suggested by the lynching of the witch brothers Alejo and Martiniano Sánchez in La Lira, Querétaro, in 1955, witchcraft beliefs and incidences of mob violence precipitated by them continued well into the 1950s. Men and women who were regarded as possessing otherworldly powers to cure and hurt others were particularly susceptible to accusations that led to collective forms of violence. Not only were they seen as individuals who could use their powers for wicked purposes, but they were also regarded as people who needed to be killed through particularly cruel forms of violence in order to prevent them from exercising their powers after death. To those who held witchcraft accusations to be true, then, the lynching of witches, healers, and spiritists who had abused their powers was justified.

CONCLUSION

This chapter has analyzed the ways in which mythical beliefs and mythlike figures contributed to the occurrence of lynching in post-revolutionary Mexico. Although the press represented mythical beliefs as premodern or irrational, these beliefs were actually precipitated by people's exposure to modernization processes. Rumors regarding the existence of fat-stealing and bloodsucking figures, in particular, reflected people's collective responses to modernization projects, which were regarded as intrusive and exploitative. Rather than being irrational, mythlike narratives provided a logical explanation for otherwise incomprehensible situations. The sudden kidnapping and disappearance of children, for instance, which appears as a constant source of anxiety in post-revolutionary Mexico, translated into collectively crafted narratives that enabled people to identify a clear culprit and react against him.

Witchcraft beliefs were also driven by people's efforts to make sense of difficult situations. The sudden sickness of a family member, the death of a child, or a person's unexpected emotional distress could all prompt one or more members of a community to blame those who, vested with magical powers, were already perceived with suspicion. Mythical beliefs contributed to sanctioning the use of particularly cruel forms of torment. In the case of witches especially, burning and mutilation were considered necessary methods to prevent the wicked from continuing to exercise their magic from the afterworld. Furthermore, they contributed to collectivized violence and facilitated scapegoating. People were more prone to support the punishment of someone who in the eyes of the believer had the potential to harm them in the same way that they had already harmed others.

The fact that these individuals were thought to have otherworldly powers meant that they were already considered at the margins of society or outside the community's norms of behavior. In the case of fat-stealer and bloodsucking figures, their status as foreigners or as people in contact with foreign countries further confirmed their otherness. In the case of witches, this otherness was rooted either in their self-proclaimed powers or in their condition as women who, against their expected gender roles, were able to cause harm, manipulate men, and inflict illness and death on women, men, and even children.

Scapegoating was certainly not exclusive to cases of lynching of mythical figures. As I discussed in previous chapters, victims of lynching were usually singled out as being responsible for a wrongdoing without more proof than the circulation of rumors or the statement of one or more people who claimed to have witnessed the wrongdoing. What is distinct in the case of the lynching of wicked individuals is the narrative or system of belief that gave the scapegoating credibility and effectiveness.

Conclusion

Lynching Past and Present: Notes on Mexico and Latin America's Trajectory of Violence

On August 6, 1943, in the town of Paso de Macho, Veracruz, a group of villagers lynched a police commander and four other policemen.[1] The commander had been accused hours earlier of the assassination of two young men who belonged to an esteemed local family. After learning about the double murder, a large group of neighbors armed with pistols, machetes, and stones dragged the commander and the four policemen out of the police station. The lynch mob killed the commander and proceeded next to mutilate his corpse to the point that it became unrecognizable. The other police officers were also lynched, as were two people who were being held in custody at the police station and had no involvement in the assassination.

More than seventy years later, four police officers—again including a police commander—were lynched under similar circumstances. The case took place on April 12, 2019, in the town of Tlilapan, also in Veracruz. The lynching followed acusations regarding the commander's alleged involvement in protecting a group of state police officers that had assaulted an elderly couple and broken into their home hours earlier. Dozens of villagers, including family members of the victims, forced the commander and the other three policemen out of the police station while another group rang the town's church bells to summon more people. After tying the commander to a pole, the lynch mob poured gasoline on him and the other three policemen while they tortured them and demanded to know the location of the guilty police officers. The lynching turned into a riot, with people vandalizing and setting a police patrol car on fire. The policemen were saved only after representatives of the government of the state of Veracruz negotiated their release with villagers.[2]

Situated in two distant and apparently dissimilar historical moments, these two cases bring to the fore the historical tenacity of lynching in Mexico and its persistence as a collective, public, and particularly cruel form of violence used by neighbors and communities to punish individuals considered offensive or threatening. Like the cases mentioned in the introduction of this book (i.e., Puebla in 2015 and Mexico City in 1957), the lynchings of these police officers follow a similar script and are driven by analogous motives. Such motives include citizens' distrust of state authorities as well as communities' belief in the legitimacy of extralegal forms of violence to punish illegal or immoral conduct. These two cases further illustrate people's explosive interactions with public officials who, today as much as in the past, are perceived as abusive or as being directly involved in criminal behavior.

It would be tempting to interpret these continuities in the light of a linear or even fatalistic narrative of violence in Mexico, a narrative wherein mob violence would be thought of as something that has and will remain an integral part of how justice is done in this country. Nonetheless, as this book has shown, lynching cannot be interpreted as a static, predetermined, or transhistorical phenomenon. Rather, lynching represents a form of violence that is sociologically and historically significant and that, despite its persistence across different periods, is propelled by contentious, erratic, and ultimately political processes. These processes include the dynamics of coercion, negotiation, and resistance that characterized state-society relations, as well as the logics of power and sources of legitimation that contributed to construing lynching as a form of justice. In other words, the occurrence of lynching in post-revolutionary Mexico was neither natural nor overdetermined but dependent on political and historical processes that were and continue to be subject to change.

Acknowledging that the history of lynching is neither static nor linear does not mean that we cannot draw connections between the past and the present. The history of lynching in the post-revolutionary period offers important insights into Mexico's contemporary challenges of violence and insecurity. In particular, this history shows that the violence the country is experiencing today has deeper roots in the country's trajectory of state building and in citizens' understanding of extralegal violence as a legitimate form of justice.

Driven by an upsurge in drug-related violence, the first two decades of the twenty-first century have witnessed the onslaught of pervasive violence, including graphic and brutal expressions such as hangings, decapitations, mutilations, and mass killings.[3] Mexico's present context of violence has spurred a national debate over the reasons for this apparent escalation in levels of violence and overt forms of cruelty. While some scholars have interpreted this context as a clear departure from a national trajectory of political stability and pacification, others have seen in it elements that call into question the characterization of this very trajectory. In particular, an emergent body of literature has highlighted the multiple expressions of violence underlying the country's post-revolutionary process of state building and democratization.

By focusing on the violent and terrorizing practices used by regular armed forces, pistoleros, crooked politicians, narcotraffickers, and self-defense forces, this new historiography has been able to recalibrate the place that violence holds in Mexico's twentieth and twenty-first centuries.[4] Rather than interpret violence as an anomaly that struck the country only in the past two decades, these works have shown that violence in fact has been a constant and central force in shaping the political, social, and institutional fabric of the country's recent history. By going beyond a state-centered and center-centered understanding of violence and politics, this literature has also demonstrated that the monopolization of the legitimate use of violence has remained a partial, fragmented, and imperfect process that has run parallel to forms of governance and social control enacted by different state and nonstate actors at the local and regional levels.[5] Hence, these works have revealed that Mexico's apparent political stability or so-called pax-priísta was not the result of a steady and successful process of centralization of violence but was actually built on a plural and decentralized exercise of violence, coercion, and precarious rule of law.[6]

The present work can be read as a contribution to this scholarship. Through the examination of numerous cases of lynching and attempted lynching during the post-revolutionary period, *In the Vortex of Violence* has underscored the ways in which violence was at the epicenter of the politics of state making throughout these decades. The continuation of lynching well after the 1940s, a decade that had until recently been regarded as a watershed moment in the institutionalization, centralization, and overall decline in levels of violence, speaks to the ongoing challenges the post-revolutionary state faced in the wake of its core claim of the monopoly over the legitimate use of violence and punishment.

The fact that public officials—mayors and police officers—participated in the organization of lynching in both overt and covert ways points to the fact that the use of extralegal violence continued to be a central feature of the coercive tactics utilized by the state. Furthermore, the occurrence of state-sponsored lynchings reveals that public officials and state representatives were far from being mere purveyors of a "civilizing process." Similar to the historical trajectory of the United States, wherein sheriffs, judges, and police officers participated in and condoned mob killings, the history of lynching in Mexico suggests that public officials contributed to amplifying the use of "uncivilized" forms of violence as a means to exercise social control in given communities.

References to mayors who rang the town's church bells to summon perpetrators or stories about police officers who turned a blind eye while villagers seized a suspect from prison and took justice into their own hands illustrate how lynchings cannot simply be attributed to the absence of state authority. Even when public officials did not directly participate in a lynch mob, letters of complaint written by families of victims of lynching suggest perpetrators acted, in more than a few cases, with the acquiescence of local authorities. The latter is particularly true of lynchings that involved individuals who were perceived as a threat to the political and economic status quo of local communities. These included agrarista peasants and socialist teachers but also suspected criminals, including cattle rustlers and common thieves. In the case of the lynching of Protestants, the apparent complicity of municipal authorities was heightened by the actions or omissions of parish priests who portrayed Protestantism as a foreign force that would do nothing less than undermine the moral and spiritual integrity of the community and the nation.

The history of lynching in post-revolutionary Mexico shows that extralegal violence was certainly not wielded exclusively by the state or by influential figures. In fact, lynchings were for the most part perpetrated by citizens who experienced economic deprivation and lacked access to the institutional channels of justice. Moreover, victims and perpetrators of lynching shared, overall, similar socioeconomic backgrounds. Still, communities also utilized lynching to resist the presence of powerful state actors or local power brokers whose actions were perceived as disruptive, abusive, or threatening. This necessarily complicates our understanding of violence as a top-down or state-centered phenomenon. Lynchings of police officers, powerful caciques, and military personnel, in particular, show that citizens were not simply passive victims of political abuse, even if the former actors had the upper hand in this relationship. Moreover, these cases reveal that citizens contested and resisted the legitimacy of state authorities, not only in regard to the so-called modernization projects promoted by the federal government, but also in terms of the authorities' abuse of power and perceived unwillingness to provide the type of justice people deemed appropriate to redress criminal conduct.

By the same token, instances of mob violence that were in effect prevented by the police reveal that even in those cases that were not "successful," citizens showed agency to express their discontent with the state's provision of security and justice. By threatening suspected criminals with lynching, people sent a powerful message to both potential criminals and state actors as far as it concerned citizens' willingness to take direct action in the face of "weak," "soft," or "neglectful" authorities. Equally, through their coverage of both successful and unsuccessful cases of lynching, the press played a key role in magnifying a critique of state authorities' capacity to provide security and justice to citizens. That this critique could be articulated and put into circulation through press coverage of lynching furthermore confirms that this period—particularly the 1940s and 1950s—cannot be easily characterized as one of uncontested or stable priísta hegemony.

If lynchings of state authorities or local power brokers complicate a narrative of top-down or state-centered violence, other cases of mob violence suggest that lynching does not fit into a clear-cut narrative of bottom-up resistance either. Although there were indeed cases directed against state actors and power brokers, lynchings were by and large directed against people who were considered at the margins of society or whose conduct defied the dominant values, beliefs, or practices of given communities. At the center of the stories of mob violence examined by this book we find socialists, communists, Protestants, so-called witches, and suspected criminals—from "monstrous" murderers to "unnatural" mothers—whose behavior went against communities' accepted ideologies and norms of behavior.

To make sense of the different and at times contradictory dynamics of exclusion and domination that gave rise to lynching, I have suggested moving beyond bottom-up or top-down characterizations of violence and focusing instead on the logics of power informing this practice. Accordingly, the chapters in this book have shown that lynchings were by and large driven by perpetrators' attempts to preserve the political, economic, and religious status quo of their communities. Thus, instead of characterizing lynching as a "weapon of the weak," I have advanced an understanding of lynching as a form of social control that was, for the most part, informed by conservative and defensive politics rather than by emancipatory or revolutionary claims.

The history of lynching presented here has further brought to light the ways in which citizens themselves contributed to the reproduction of extralegal forms of violence in post-revolutionary Mexico. Citizens' support for extralegal violence was vividly expressed in press coverage of lynching and attempted lynching of so-called criminals. It was also evident in people's approval of the use of the ley fuga by state authorities. The parallel occurrence of lynchings and cases of the ley fuga, together with citizens' support of both practices, reveals the existence of a consensus among citizens and authorities regarding the acceptability of violence to respond to crimes that went largely unpunished.[7] Nonetheless, as exemplified by cases of lynching of public officials who abused their power or by cases wherein perpetrators broke into a police station to lynch an alleged criminal, this consensus was far from stable. Citizens did not always agree with authorities on the desirability of the punishment or on the culpability of the suspect. Hence this consensus remained precarious and subject to a process of negotiation between the state and authorities.

The state's inability to provide security and justice was then, as it is now, at the center of people's support of lynching. However, impunity alone does not fully explain citizens' inclination to support extralegal violence. Instances of lynchings that unfolded after perpetrators seized a suspected criminal from the police suggest people were not only interested in just any punishment, but one that would entail a swift, corporeal, and most likely lethal form of retribution. Most important, the excessive use of violence utilized in lynching, especially in cases in which the victim was not only killed but also overkilled by maiming, dragging, or burning the corpse substantiates the notion that lynching was not merely a corrective to the state's incapacity to administer punishment. Instead, perpetrators regarded lynching as a preferred means to attain justice. Its communal, spectacular, and particularly cruel dimensions made lynching a seemingly more apt instrument to deal with criminals and transgressors who violated the moral, economic, or political integrity of communities.

The acceptability of lynching and other forms of extralegal violence in postrevolutionary Mexico resonates with Latin America's contemporary context. Numerous studies have documented citizens' overall acceptance of extralegal forms of violence to punish criminal conduct in different countries across the region.[8] Such expressions of violence include lynching but also social cleansing, torture, vigilante killings, and extrajudicial assassinations carried out by the police or the military. That some of these violent responses to crime entail the direct involvement of the same state actors that Latin Americans deeply distrust points to one of the greatest paradoxes characterizing the region's current context of insecurity: namely, citizens' willingness to tolerate and promote the abuse of force by the very same actors they distrust, all in exchange for an ephemeral sense of security and justice predicated on immediate retribution and violence.

Scholars have explained citizens' support of extralegal violence mainly by looking at current crime and insecurity levels, as well as at citizens' perceptions of these countries' security and justice systems as ineffective or illegitimate. The evidence discussed by this book, however, suggests that crime, insecurity, and citizens' perceptions of state actors as illegitimate or ineffective have a longer history as drivers of mob violence and vigilante justice. It also points to the importance that alternative motivations, beyond crime and state responses to crime, have had in rendering this practice an acceptable form of justice. By bringing to the fore the role that religion, politics, and mythical beliefs had in the legitimation and organization of lynching, *In the Vortex of Violence* has exposed an array of cultural and political aspects that shaped the history of lynching and that are ignored in the extant literature on the subject. Future studies centered on the history of this practice both before and after Latin America's "democratic turn" (1980s–1990s) could further document the role of religious, mythical, and political transgressions in sanctioning mob violence in other countries across the region. The impact that Latin American processes of state making have had in the emergence and surge of lynching and other forms of vigilantism also deserves to be further explored.

The apparent absence of historical studies on lynching in Latin America prior to the 1980s contrasts with the rich and vast historiography of lynching in the United States. Because of the power dynamics that characterized lynching in the United States, scholars examining this practice north of the Río Bravo have paid more attention to the victims of mob violence and to the pernicious effects of this practice than have scholars working on its contemporary expressions in Latin America.[9] My understanding of lynching as a form of social control rather than as an emancipatory form of violence has sought precisely to place greater weight on the dynamics of power and exclusion enabled by this practice. Even when lynching in post-revolutionary Mexico was not informed by racial and ethnic forms of domination as in the United States, it was nevertheless directed at those who were, for the most part, considered unworthy, dangerous, and potentially polluting.

Scholars working on lynching and violence more broadly in Latin America and the United States would benefit greatly from making more explicit connections between the motivations and political dynamics shaping the history of this and related practices across the Americas and beyond. This would not only demonstrate that lynching is a global phenomenon rather than an "American exception," but it would also situate contemporary cases of lynching in a broader historical perspective. The history of lynching in Mexico offers a comparative basis for historians working on U.S. lynchings, particularly as it pertains to the overt and covert participation of state actors in the organization of mob killings, communities' distrust and rejection of the formal system of justice, and the impact of modernization and centralization efforts on escalating processes of scapegoating and social control. It also sheds light on other social orders that, beyond those predicated on racial domination or control, have served to legitimate the use of lynching as a means to defend the status quo of given communities.

Scholars working on Latin America would benefit from some of the insights that the U.S. historiography on lynching has to offer in terms of explaining continuities and changes in this practice across different periods. For instance, various studies on U.S. lynching have linked the rise of lynchings motivated mainly by racial dominance in the 1890s to the perceived threats to white rule that economic and political changes, such as the end of slavery and the Civil War, presented to communities of the American South.[10] At the same time, they have discussed how changes in sensibilities and cultural norms among the elites created the political conditions to criminalize and effectively prosecute lynchings.[11] How have motivations of lynching changed across time in Latin American countries? How has the profile of victims and perpetrators shifted and why?

This book has identified patterns of both continuity and change in the history of lynching in post-revolutionary Mexico. In terms of patterns of change, it has identified a decline, especially during the late 1940s, in lynchings perpetrated against state actors who represented the modernization efforts promoted by the central state. This change revealed a process of resistance and accommodation that made the state's interference in local affairs more acceptable and desirable. By the same token, by the 1950s, the overt participation of state officials in the organization of lynching had significantly receded as central elites privileged more covert forms of repression and were also more able and willing to "tame" regional and local power brokers' use of violence and political repression.

In contrast, lynchings motivated by religious beliefs and witchcraft accusations, together with cases directed against so-called criminals and individuals that were either de jure or de facto responsible for enforcing social control, continued well into the 1950s. The persistence of these cases not only reveals how, when observed from below, the so-called centralization and institutionalization of violence at the national level followed a different path and pace. It also illuminates the ways in which public attitudes that contributed to sanctioning the use of lynching did not change significantly from the 1930s to the 1950s. The fact that lynchings were not unequivocally condemned but presented as acceptable and even desirable by the press and public opinion offers a window into the reasons that made lynching such a pervasive practice throughout this period.

Future studies could examine the modalities and drivers of lynching during the years leading up to the 1980s and 1990s, the moment most scholars have associated with a surge in the number of lynchings in Latin America. The 1960s and 1970s saw an intensification of armed forms of insurgency and political repression informed by Cold War politics as well as by Mexico's own dirty war (ca. 1969–78).[12] The state's responses to political dissidence among peasants, students, and urban workers included the use of torture, targeted assassinations, illegal detentions, and forced disappearances. The lynching of five university workers who were accused of being communists on September 14, 1968, in San Miguel Canoa, Puebla, suggests lynching continued to be driven by defensive politics and religious motivations, as well as by a context wherein local power brokers were complicit in the production of extralegal violence.[13] A more systematic examination of other cases during the 1960s and 1970s would allow for a more complete picture of the history of lynching throughout Mexico's twentieth century.

The history of lynching presented in this book is in many ways not circumscribed to the history of post-revolutionary Mexico. The processes of scapegoating, exclusion, and violence I have discussed are shared by different countries and have been present in different periods. In addition to the United States and Latin America, lynchings have been documented and examined in countries as different as South Africa, India, Indonesia, and the Philippines. On the other hand, the history of lynching offered here is indeed one that reflects the particularities of Mexico's post-revolutionary period. Lynchings reflected not only the dynamics of coercion, negotiation, and resistance that shaped the country's process of state building during these decades but also the ways in which contemporaries' conceptions of religion, crime, politics, and mythlike fears shaped the acceptability of violence.

Today, as in the past, lynchings have been rationalized as a necessary means to punish those "others" that threaten to undermine citizens' sense of security. In Mexico, Guatemala, Argentina, Brazil, and Ecuador, among other countries, the criminal, the gang member, and the narcotrafficker have been construed as those outsiders against which, paraphrasing Michel Foucault, "society must be defended." In this defense of society, not only the state but also citizens and communities have helped deepen the seeming vortex of violence affecting Latin America.

Appendix
Definitions, Methods, and Sources for the Study of Lynching in Post-Revolutionary Mexico

The definition of lynching advanced by this book (see introduction) reflects some of the minimum criteria I used to determine which cases I would analyze as lynching, independently of the name given by contemporaries to describe this practice. In security reports, press articles, and letters of complaint, contemporaries referred to most incidents of lynching by the Spanish word *linchamiento*. Throughout the 1930s, several cases were described, using the English spelling, as *lynchamientos*, signaling the importance of the U.S. trajectory of lynching for Mexico's understanding of this practice.[1] Nevertheless, other events that matched the criteria used in my research to identify cases of lynching were described under different names, such as *justicia por mano propia* (self-help justice), *zafarrancho* (disarray), *tumulto* (tumult), or even *crimen salvaje* (savage crime). These expressions point to the diverse opinions or sentiments provoked by mob violence among a given public or readership. The incidents described by the word *linchamiento* involved cases justified by the press as a means to attain justice as well as cases portrayed as expressions of the alleged savagery, backwardness, or ignorance of those who perpetrated them. In other words, the use of the word *linchamiento* in itself implied neither support nor rejection of this practice.

In order to consider an event a lynching, I decided that the number of perpetrators had to outnumber the number of victims by a ratio of 3 to 1 and violence had to be unilateral, meaning that victims did not reciprocate or respond to a given attack.[2] Also, attacks had to be perpetrated publicly, in plain sight and in front of witnesses. Furthermore, the incident had to involve an attempt to punish a behavior that offended a *community* and not just one individual.[3] Although most cases of lynching involved the participation of ordinary citizens rather than state actors or public officials, periodicals and other primary sources also referred to collective killings perpetrated by and with the support of state actors as "linchamientos," particularly when such cases involved the use of public, cruel, and overt forms of torment. This book recognizes and incorporates this seeming elasticity of the term "lynching" as it allows me to highlight the state's complicity in the perpetration of lynching as well as to trace the complex connections between state and non-state forms of violence in Mexico.[4]

The latter aspect of this definition demands clarification of yet another term, "community." I use the term "community" to refer to individuals or groups of individuals that, beyond sharing a locality, neighborhood, or town, were united by a hegemonic cultural, political, or religious identity. A community, then, includes villagers who interacted with considerable regularity in their everyday lives, as well as urban dwellers who, despite their limited interaction, shared a common understanding of what constituted criminal or immoral conduct.[5] Far from being conflict-free or static, a community is thus understood as a dynamic and internally divided entity whose political, religious, and social boundaries are constantly being negotiated or redefined. As a communal or collectively sanctioned form of violence, lynching can thus be seen as an instrument by which the actual or imagined boundaries of a given community are enforced.

Despite the minimum criteria used to characterize an event as a lynching, there are important variations among the cases discussed in this book. These variations include differences in the number of perpetrators as well as in the level of premeditation, ritualization, and violence.[6] Whereas some cases involved only three or four perpetrators, others involved dozens and even hundreds. By the same token, some cases entailed brutal forms of violence and torment such as maiming, stoning, and burning, whereas others involved collective beatings that did not cause fatal injury. Premeditation and level of organization also differed from case to case, with some being more impulsive and unstructured and others merging with more organized forms of vigilante justice.[7]

In terms of ritualization, there are also important variations to consider. On one side of the spectrum, there are lynchings that unfolded swiftly, from the moment in which an accusation was voiced against an individual to the moment in which the mob was able to seize and lynch the suspect or accused party. These lynchings usually involved neighbors as well as passersby who overheard or witnessed the wrongdoing and rapidly proceeded to punish the offender. On the other side, there are lynchings that took place over a longer period, with perpetrators gathering not only by word of mouth but also by tolling of the church bells.[8] In this type of lynching there are usually a greater number of perpetrators and the victims are often tortured at length, maimed, and their bodies or corpses set on fire. In other words, the cruelty used against the victims tended to increase with the level of ritualization.[9] These are, of course, ideal types. The cases examined in this book fall somewhere in the middle of this spectrum.

Primary sources used in this work include local, national, and international newspapers; government records; security reports; judicial cases; official correspondence; and letters of complaint addressed to the president or other high-level officials.[10] Newspapers were crucial for tracing the historical trajectory of lynching as well as for capturing how this practice was represented, condemned, or legitimated by public opinion.[11] Because lynching was not formally classified as a crime in post-revolutionary Mexico,[12] and because cases of lynching were rarely brought before the courts, the utility of judicial archives to trace both the occurrence and the shifting modalities of lynching was rather limited.

Nota rota, or crime news, stories were of particular importance to this study.[13] Because they were not directly occupied with "high politics" or with traditional politics such as elections or party disputes, nota roja journalists—even those reporting for more mainstream newspapers—were able to print stories that would normally be subject to censorship.[14] Such stories involved public officials and state representatives who, as part of their "law and order" activities, made use of repression, corruption, and extralegal violence, including lynching.[15] Paradoxically, then, stories of nota roja could engage in political critique because they were not dealing with politics as usual but rather with the "undergrowth" of crime and local politics.[16]

That crime news and coverage of lynching reported more overtly on cases of state violence and abuse does not mean they were free from power dynamics or from politics in a broader sense. Newspapers contributed to reifying the notion that perpetrators of violence were to be found among the lower and uneducated classes, as well as among indigenous, Catholic, or rural communities that were prone to irrational and uncivilized behaviors. Such representations of violence obscured the manifold forms of extralegal violence perpetrated either directly or indirectly by state actors against peasants, workers, and political dissidents. They furthermore contributed to a discourse that construed state violence as legal, modern, and civilizing while portraying communal forms of violence as illegal and backward. That these same newspapers printed stories about politicians and state authorities who participated in mob killings points to the dissonance of press discourses and representations, as well as the open-ended field of interpretation they offer.

Newspapers, however, present a number of limitations. In addition to the biases described above, newspapers tend to exaggerate or minimize certain events in order to make a story more appealing or attractive for a given audience. Overt forms of violence such as murder and lynching, which lend themselves to gruesome and morbid descriptions, are particularly susceptible to these dynamics of narration and representation.[17] Nonetheless, other sources are also susceptible to similar biases. Official statistics on crime may reflect the inclination of police and judicial authorities to prioritize certain crimes over others. Similarly, judicial records may ignore or underrepresent conduct that is not classified as criminal but that individuals and communities might consider central to their security and well-being.[18] Conversely, newspapers and crime news can in fact offer certain advantages for a study centered on violence. The sensationalist description of lynching, for instance, offered a window into the sequencing and enactment of the event that other sources did not always include, such as how the victim was tortured and what was done to the corpse. Newspapers also allowed me to document how journalists and readers reacted to different cases of lynching and how victims, perpetrators, and local authorities were represented.

The second most important primary sources used by this study consisted of documents that were either produced or received by government agencies. These included security reports, official correspondence, and letters of complaint and petitions addressed to high-level officials, as well as cases that were being reviewed by Mexico's Supreme Court of Justice.

Like newspapers, these sources were characterized by dynamics of representation that were specific to both the authors of these documents and the audience to which these documents were addressed. Security reports that dealt with lynchings, for instance, were prepared by federal inspectors who were supposed to inform central authorities about the existence of conflicts that surfaced in the countryside as a result of the implementation of state policies. These reports usually included a description of the context, quotations from the different actors involved in a given conflict, and the interpretation provided by the inspector himself. Reference to the religious fanaticism or the ignorance of perpetrators of lynching in these documents were not uncommon, and they reflected these actors' inclination to subscribe to a view of rural communities as places that needed to be "modernized" and "tamed" by the post-revolutionary state.[19] In contrast to these security reports, the authors of letters of complaint sent to high-level officials were either relatives or friends of lynching victims. These accounts were usually less concerned with providing a detailed description of the context and more concerned with decrying these acts and demanding justice. When the victim was someone who defended the policies promoted by the post-revolutionary state, these letters included phrases of support and praise for the federal government and for the "authentic" values of the revolution.[20]

In sum, despite their limitations, these sources provide a substantive basis to reconstruct and examine the sources of legitimation, politics, and logics of power that shaped the history of lynching in post-revolutionary Mexico.

NOTES

ABBREVIATIONS FOR ARCHIVAL SOURCES

AGN, ALR	Archivo General de la Nación, Fondo Presidentes, Abelardo L. Rodríguez
AGN, ARC	Archivo General de la Nación, Fondo Presidentes, Adolfo Ruiz Cortines
AGN, DAP	Archivo General de la Nación, Documentación de la Administración Pública
AGN, DFS	Archivo General de la Nación, Fondo Secretaría de Gobernación, Dirección Federal de Seguridad
AGN, DGG	Archivo General de la Nación, Fondo Secretaría de Gobernación, Dirección General de Gobierno
AGN, DGIPS	Archivo General de la Nación, Fondo Secretaría de Gobernación, Dirección General de Investigaciones Políticas y Sociales
AGN, LC	Archivo General de la Nación, Fondo Presidentes, Lázaro Cárdenas
AGN, MAC	Archivo General de la Nación, Fondo Presidentes, Manuel Ávila Camacho
AGN, MAV	Archivo General de la Nación, Fondo Presidentes, Miguel Alemán Valdés
SCJ, AH	Archivo Histórico de la Suprema Corte de Justicia de la Nación
SRE, AH	Secretaría de Relaciones Exteriores, Archivo Histórico "Genaro Estrada"

INTRODUCTION

1. Redacción Animal Político, "Habitantes linchan a dos encuestadores en Ajalpan, Puebla"; Olmos, "El linchamiento en Ajalpan"; Arce, "In Frightened Mexico Town, a Mob Kills 2 Young Pollsters"; Martínez García, "Los linchados de Ajalpan, Puebla"; Ramsés, "Linchamiento en Ajalpan"; De Llano, "José y Rey, la inocencia linchada."

2. Azam and Villegas, "As Frustrations with Mexico's Government Rise, So Do Lynchings."

3. In terms of the media attention it received, the lynching of José Abraham and Rey David Copado is comparable to the lynching of three police officers in the borough of Tláhuac in Mexico City on November 23, 2004. In that case the policemen were also accused of child theft and trafficking of human organs. Binford and Churchill, "Lynching and States of Fear in Urban Mexico"; Davis, "Undermining the Rule of Law."

4. On the notion of lynching as a performance or ritual that is recognizable to both perpetrators and witnesses, see Garland, "Penal Excess and Surplus Meaning"; Wood, *Lynching and Spectacle,* 315–16.

5. "Tomándolo por robachicos, una turba trató de linchar a un agente secreto," *Excélsior,* April 10, 1957.

6. See Fuentes Díaz, *Linchamientos,* 83; Rodríguez Guillén, "Crisis de autoridad y violencia social"; Rodríguez Guillén and Veloz Ávila, "Linchamientos en México." Recent studies have also identified the existence of substantial public support for this practice in Mexico. See Schedler, "Ciudadanía y violencia organizada en México," 65; Zizumbo-Colunga, "Explaining Support for Vigilante Justice in Mexico," 2.

7. Three different studies suggest lynchings are concentrated in the central and southern regions of Mexico and single out Mexico City, Estado de México, Chiapas, Oaxaca, and Puebla as having higher numbers of lynchings. Mexico City and Estado de México are ranked first and second. If we arrange these states according to lynch rate (based on 2010 population data from INEGI), Morelos, Estado de México, and Hidalgo are the most prominent cases. See Fuentes Díaz, "Violencia y Estado, mediación y respuesta no estatal," 117; Rodríguez and Veloz, "Linchamientos," 57; Gamallo, "Crimen, castigo y violencia colectiva," 92.

8. According to the World Bank, Mexico's economy is the second largest in Latin America after Brazil. Politically, alternation of power, electoral competition, and an active civil society point to a healthy democracy. Yet Mexico's current levels of economic inequality, the size of its informal market, and its high levels of crime, insecurity, and corruption suggest a different story. See Bailey, *The Politics of Crime in Mexico.*

9. When a country reaches an average of more than one thousand battle deaths per year, it is considered to be at war. In Mexico the number of deaths attributed to organized crime in the year 2013 alone, was 10,095 (a midlevel estimate). Shirk et al., "Drug Violence in Mexico," 23.

10. Based on levels of homicide, Latin America is considered one of the most violent regions in the world today. Scholars have explained this in terms of these countries' weak justice systems, their high levels of inequality, and their growing victimization rates. See Arias and Goldstein, *Violent Democracies in Latin America;* Santamaría and Carey, *Violence and Crime in Latin America;* Auyero, Bourgois, and Scheper-Hughes, *Violence at the Urban Margins;* Holston and Caldeira, "Democracy and Violence in Brazil"; Koonings and Kruijt, *Armed Actors.*

11. Snodgrass Godoy, "When 'Justice' Is Criminal"; Goldstein, "In Our Hands"; Binford and Churchill, "Lynching and States of Fear in Urban Mexico"; Krupa, "Histories in Red."

12. This is in contrast to the U.S. context, where lynching is often understood as lethal or "community-sponsored murder." See Waldrep, "War of Words"; Pfeifer, *Rough Justice,* 6–7. On the ritualization of lynchings and their spectacular character in contemporary Latin America, see Fuentes, *Linchamientos,* 104–12; Goldstein, *The Spectacular City;* Krupa, "Histories in Red."

13. Compared to self-defense forces and vigilante groups, lynchings entail a lower level of organization and institutionalization. Whereas a lynch mob usually dissipates after

attacking a so-called offender, self-defense forces continue to operate beyond a single event, offering some sort of protection against crime to communities or towns. Despite this difference, these are all examples of vigilantism, which refers to "the collective use or threat of extra-legal violence in response to an alleged criminal act." See Moncada, "Varieties of Vigilantism," 403; see also Senechal de la Roche, "Why Is Collective Violence Collective?"

14. Statistical evidence from the 2012 AmericasBarometer suggests that, besides Mexico, support for lynching and other forms of extralegal violence to punish suspected criminals is significant in various Latin American countries, including Honduras, Haiti, Bolivia, Guatemala, El Salvador, and Peru. See Cruz and Santamaría, "Determinants of Support for Extralegal Violence in Latin America and the Caribbean."

15. This scholarship includes the work of sociologists, anthropologists, and political scientists. Historians have been absent from this conversation, with a few exceptions, including Hinnerk Onken's work on nineteenth-century Peru and a few works dealing, either directly or indirectly, with specific cases of lynching in twentieth-century Mexico. See Onken, "Lynching in Peru in the Nineteenth and Early Twentieth Centuries"; Meaney, *Canoa*; Melgarejo, *La violencia como fenómeno social*. Some of the most relevant works from the social sciences are Huggins, *Vigilantism and the State in Modern Latin America*; Snodgrass Godoy, *Popular Injustice*; Goldstein, *The Spectacular City*; Davis, "Undermining the Rule of Law"; Handy, "Chicken Thieves, Witches, and Judges"; Binford and Churchill, "Lynching and States of Fear in Urban Mexico"; Rodríguez, "Los linchamientos en México"; Rodríguez and Veloz, "Linchamientos en México."

16. Binford and Churchill, "Lynching and States of Fear in Urban Mexico," 301–12. Fuentes Díaz, "El Estado y la furia"; Binford and Churchill, "A Failure of Normalization"; Rodríguez, "Crisis de autoridad y violencia social," 43–74; Davis, "Undermining the Rule of Law."

17. Cf. Fuentes, "El Estado y la furia," 7; Binford and Churchill, "Lynching and States of Fear in Urban Mexico," 302; Binford and Churchill, "A Failure of Normalization," 132; Rodríguez, "Crisis de autoridad y violencia social," 47.

18. Binford and Churchill, "A Failure of Normalization," 125.

19. For an examination of the cultural and political hegemony that characterized the post-revolutionary period, see Joseph and Nugent, *Everyday Forms of State Formation*; Vaughan and Lewis, *The Eagle and the Virgin*; Rubin, "Decentering the Regime"; Vaughan, *Cultural Politics in Revolution*.

20. This book is based on the systematization of a total of 366 cases of lynching and attempted lynching. The cases include both fatal and nonfatal incidents. The distribution of cases is as follows: 100 were fatal, 130 were nonfatal, and 136 were attempts. I use the term "attempted lynching" to refer to cases that were prevented by the police, villagers or neighbors or the suspect's ability to escape the lynch mob. Although these are "unsuccessful" cases, they were highly communicative acts, as they sent a clear message to alleged wrongdoers and authorities regarding people's willingness to take justice into their own hands. For a similar argument about the importance of incorporating "lynching threats" in the study of lynching, see Tolnay and Beck, "'Racialized Terrorism' in the American South."

21. For a similar argument that goes against the notion that lynchings signal state absence, see Smith, *Contradictions of Democracy*.

22. For a similar argument, see Snodgrass Godoy, "When Justice Is Criminal."

23. The Mexican Revolution is considered the first major social revolution of the twentieth century. The revolution was driven by several grievances that included opposition to the authoritarian rule of Porfirio Díaz, resistance to an increasingly centralized state, and peasants' and workers' attempts to fight economic exploitation and mounting social inequalities. See Knight, *The Mexican Revolution*.

24. The Cristero War was triggered by the anticlerical measures promoted by President Plutarco Elías Calles. The conflict involved violent confrontations between peasants who held opposing views about the place of religion in the social, political, and economic organization of local communities. Cristeros, or supporters of the Cristero War, regarded the government's actions against the church as impious, heretical, and a violation of communal life. See Meyer, *The Cristero Rebellion*, 92–110; Butler, *Popular Piety*, 7–9.

25. Gillingham, "Who Killed Crispín Aguilar?"

26. The death penalty was formally abolished during the 1930s. Meade, "From Sex Strangler to Model Citizen."

27. According to the Equal Justice Initiative there were a total of 3,959 African Americans victimized by lynching in the United States between 1877 and 1950. Robertson, "History of Lynchings in the South Documents Nearly 4,000 Names." To this number, one should add the thousands of cases perpetrated against different racial minorities, including Chinese, Italians, Native Americans, and especially Mexicans. According to the historians William D. Carrigan and Clive Webb there were at least 547 lynchings perpetrated against people of Mexican origin or descent in the United States between 1848 and 1928. Carrigan and Webb, *Forgotten Dead*, 5–6; see also Pfeifer, *Roots of Rough Justice*, 33–53; Tolnay and Beck, *A Festival of Violence*, 271–72.

28. By the 1930s lynching had become less frequent and more covert and involved fewer perpetrators. In 1952 there were no cases of lynching reported by the press. See Garland, "Penal Excess and Surplus Meaning," 802.

29. Pfeifer, *Rough Justice*; Wood, *Lynching and Spectacle*, 4–27.

30. For examples of recent literature that has tried to "globalize" or expand the study of lynching beyond the United States, see Pfeifer, *Global Lynching and Collective Violence*, vols. 1 and 2; see also Wendt and Berg, *Globalizing Lynching History*; Carrigan and Waldrep, *Swift to Wrath*.

31. My reference to the "sources of legitimation" of lynching echoes E. P. Thompson's examination of eighteenth-century crowds in England as groups of men and women who believed they were "defending traditional rights or customs; and, in general that they were supported by the wider consensus of the community." In my analysis, however, the morality of lynching did not stem only from the belief in the unfairness of certain economic practices, but on transgressions that pertained to the realms of the political, religious, and even mythical. Thompson, "The Moral Economy of the English Crowd in the Eighteenth Century," 78.

32. The Second Cristiada was motivated by both religious and political interests, and it included attacks against socialist teachers as well as against agrarista peasants on behalf of armed groups of vigilantes known as Segunderos, many of whom were former Cristeros. Although it did not reach a national dimension, scholars have increasingly recognized the importance of La Segunda as a conflict that expressed communities' resistance to socialism, anticlericalism, and the central state's interference in local affairs. See Fallaw, *Religion and*

State Formation in Post-Revolutionary Mexico; Salinas, "Untangling Mexico's Noodle," 474; Guerra Manzo, "The Resistance of the Marginalized"; Bantjes, *As If Jesus Walked on Earth;* Becker, *Setting the Virgin on Fire.*

33. Knight, "The End of the Mexican Revolution?," 47–69; Joseph and Zolov, eds., *Fragments of a Golden Age,* 8–9; Niblo, *Mexico in the 1940s: Modernity, Politics, and Corruption,* 89.

34. Carey, *Plaza of Sacrifices.*

35. Pointing at the contradictions of Mexico's so-called economic miracle, Oscar Lewis described how "the disparity between the incomes of the rich and the poor (were) more striking than ever before." Lewis, *The Children of Sánchez,* xxix.

36. See Knight, "The Weight of the State in Modern Mexico"; Vaughan, *Cultural Politics;* Vaughan and Lewis, *The Eagle and the Virgin;* Padilla, *Rural Resistance in the Land of Zapata;* Carey, *Plaza of Sacrifices,* 23–25; Gillingham and Smith, "Introduction: The Paradoxes of Revolution"; Joseph, Rubenstein, and Zolov, "Assembling the Fragments," 8.

37. On homicide levels during this period, see "Estadísticas del crimen en México: Series históricas, 1901–2001," Columbia University, www.columbia.edu/~pp143/estadisticascrimen/EstadisticasSigloXX.htm; accessed October 31, 2017.

38. Smith, *The Mexican Press and Civil Society,* 1–17; Meade, "The Plaza Is for the *Populacho,* the Desert Is for Deep-Sea Fish," 314–16; Piccato, *A History of Infamy,* 3–4; Santillán Esqueda, "Mujeres delincuentes e imaginarios."

39. Wood, *Lynching and Spectacle,* 5.

40. Speckman, "Instituciones de justicia y práctica judicial"; Pulido Esteva, "Los negocios de la policía."

41. Pulido Esteva, "Los negocios de la policía."

42. In contrast to the communal character of lynching, cases of the ley fuga, even when supported by public opinion and ordinary citizens, were perpetrated only by military or police officials.

43. Reflecting on the similarities between lynching and the ley fuga, an article about the killing of a cattle rustler in León, Guanajuato, in *Time* magazine stated, "The lynch law of Latin American justice is the 'ley de fuga' (law of flight)." "Mexico: Ley de Fuga," *Time,* February 15, 1937.

44. On citizens' support of lynching in contemporary Mexico, see Schedler, "Ciudadanía y violencia organizada en México"; Zizumbo-Colunga, "Explaining Support for Vigilante Justice in Mexico." On the importance of public attitudes to lynching on its occurrence and eventual decline in the United States, see Dray, *At the Hands of Persons Unknown,* 19–20; Wood, *Lynching and Spectacle,* 27. On how discourses and representations of violence contribute to reproducing violent practices, see Carey and Santamaría, "The Politics and Publics of Violence and Crime in Latin America."

45. That is, lynchings have been interpreted as acts that reassert a sense of agency and entitlement to traditionally deprived and oppressed communities, in ways that resemble James Scott's rendering of the subordinated classes and their means of resistance. Scott, *Domination and the Art of Resistance;* cf. Snodgrass, "When 'Justice' Is Criminal," 623; Goldstein, "Flexible Justice"; Binford and Churchill, "Lynching and States of Fear in Urban Mexico." For a critique of these interpretations, see Krupa, "Histories in Red."

46. Socialists, communists, witches, rural teachers, Protestants, and criminals were all subjected to this form of torment due to the challenge they posed to the so-called material,

political, and spiritual integrity of communities. The profile of these victims coincides with those that René Girard identifies as sharing a "sacrificeable" character: "exterior or marginal individuals, incapable of establishing or sharing the social bonds that link the rest of the inhabitants." Girard, *Violence and the Sacred*, 12.

47. Although the press often referred to lynching as a practice that belonged to the "pueblo," it could and did involve the participation of figures of authority.

48. In 322 of the 366 cases examined, the victims were male. In 14 cases, the victims included both women and men, and only 29 were directed exclusively against women (in one case the gender of the victim is unspecified). Perpetrators, whenever indicated by the source, include both women and men.

49. Women appear as the main perpetrators of lynching in cases that involved religious offenses but also in those that involved state authorities as well as suspected criminals. For some representative examples, see the lynching in Senguio, Michoacán, in 1947 described in chapter 1 and the 1930 lynching of Edgar Kullmann analyzed in chapter 4.

50. This understanding of lynching echoes William B. Taylor's notion of rebellions as collective acts of violence whose intention is to restore a "customary equilibrium" rather than to subvert a given social or political order. See Taylor, *Drinking, Homicide, and Rebellion in Colonial Mexican Villages*, 114.

51. On lynching as social control in the United States, see Ward, *Hanging Bridge*, 13–14; Gorn, *Let the People See*, 45–55; Wood, *Lynching and Spectacle*, 24–26. On lynching as social control from a sociological perspective, see Senechal de la Roche, "Collective Violence as Social Control"; Black, "Crime as Social Control."

52. Rubin, "Decentering the Regime," 112. Although a number of cases of lynching analyzed in this book took place in the country's capital, the examination provided is not centered on mainstream politics and events but rather on how power relations and politics are articulated "from below" and based on everyday interactions between people and representatives of the state.

53. A large number of cases reported by the press, for instance, took place in neighborhoods of Mexico City and Puebla City where citizens enjoyed access to public services, including the provision of security by the police. At the same time, lynchings were also reported in rural communities that were certainly more isolated both politically and economically.

54. Cases driven by religious beliefs were also referred to as an expression of people's customs and traditions in a way that implicitly—or sometimes explicitly—identified them as belonging to indigenous communities that had for too long lived under the influence of the Catholic Church. Gendered notions of women as fanatical, irrational, and pious also informed representations of communities' attempts to resist the state's secularizing efforts, with women being referred to as "viejas beatas" (pious old women) who were easily manipulated by priests. On gendered representations of female fanaticism, see Wright-Rios, *Searching for Madre Matiana*. Discourses that equate lynching with indigenous traditions continue to reverberate today. When he was mayor of Mexico City (2000–2005), Mexican president Andrés Manuel López Obrador referred to the lynching of a man accused of stealing religious images from a church in Tlalpan, Mexico City, "as part of the beliefs of the native pueblos that represent a Mexico that has not entirely disappeared, the deep Mexico." Quoted in Sarmiento, "México profundo."

55. After Mexico City (152), Puebla (68), and Estado de México (32), the states with a large number of cases are Veracruz (15), Guanajuato (10), Michoacán (7), Oaxaca (6), Jalisco (6), and Hidalgo (6). The geography of lynching during the post-revolutionary period coincides with that indicated by studies of lynching in contemporary Mexico. See note 7 above.

56. According to the INEGI's 1940 census, for instance, the most populated states (with more than one million inhabitants) were Distrito Federal (Mexico City), Puebla, and Estado de México. Other states with more than one million inhabitants were Veracruz, Oaxaca, Michoacán, Jalisco, and Guanajuato. See INEGI, "Sexto censo general de población."

57. This book is based on the examination of several primary sources including government records; security reports; judicial cases; official correspondence; and letters of complaint; as well as local, national, and international newspapers. For a more detailed discussion of these sources, see the appendix.

58. In general, lynchings that took place in the periphery made it into national newspapers only when they were a result of a political conflict or dispute that involved federal authorities and programs (e.g., socialist education, military conscription, agrarian reform) or some "infamous" cacique or local powerbroker who was somehow related to central political elites. For an analysis of the press in post-revolutionary Mexico in terms of coverage, readership, and distribution, see Gillingham, Lettieri, and Smith, *Journalism, Satire, and Censorship in Mexico;* see also Smith, *The Mexican Press and Civil Society.*

59. Statistics compiled on contemporary lynching in Mexico are actually based exclusively on the analysis of newspaper materials published at the national level. See Vilas, "(In)Justicia por mano propia"; Fuentes, "Violencia y Estado, mediación y respuesta no estatal"; Rodríguez, "Crisis de autoridad y violencia social"; Gamallo, "Crimen, castigo y violencia colectiva." Statistics on violence and crime in contemporary Latin America have several limitations, including underreporting, biases in the ways in which statistics are collected, and lack of systematization. In Mexico's post-revolutionary period, official statistics on crime were shaped by similar challenges, including underreporting and lack of data for certain years. See Gillingham, "Who Killed Crispín Aguilar?"

CHAPTER ONE. BETWEEN CIVILIZATION AND BARBARITY

1. For a discussion of the cinematographic representations of the post-revolutionary state, see Chávez, "The Eagle and the Serpent." On the assimilationist project of mestizaje envisioned by the post-revolutionary state, see Alonso, "Territorializing the Nation and 'Integrating the Indian'"; Lund, *The Mestizo State,* 15.

2. The term *indigenista* makes reference to Fernández's both celebratory and assimilationist representation of indigenous people. Fernández's indigenista films include *María Candelaria* (1943), *La Perla* (1945), *Río Escondido* (1947), *Maclovia* (1948), and *Paloma herida* (1962). See Mraz, *Looking for Mexico,* 148.

3. The "Golden Age of Mexican cinema" refers to the impetus experienced by the film industry during the 1940s and 1950s. The films produced during this period were characterized by their folkloric themes, their use of melodrama, and their celebration of "lo mexicano." See Schmidt, "Making It Real Compared to What?"; Mraz, *Looking for Mexico,* 107–8; Chávez, "The Eagle and the Serpent," 120.

4. Chávez, "The Eagle and the Serpent," 119–23.

5. As argued by Mraz, *Maclovia* was certainly not the only film that depicted "Indian hordes attacking defenseless individuals who had somehow violated their customs." Mraz, *Looking for Mexico,* 148. Carlos Navarro's film *Janitzio* (1935) had introduced this theme, and its basic plot served as the basis of Fernández's earlier film *María Candelaria* (1943) and later of *Maclovia. Río Escondido* (1947) also included a scene of mob violence at the end. These four films presented a highly ritualized version of lynching that followed a recognizable script, starting with an accusation, followed by the ringing of church bells, and ending in a group of Indians carrying torches and encircling the victims. This representation is also present in Felipe Cazals's *Canoa* (1976), based on the actual lynching of five university workers from Puebla City on September 14, 1968. The same script can be found in the more recent film *La ley de Herodes* (1999) by Luis Estrada, which begins with the lynching of a mayor during the 1940s by a group of indigenous people.

6. According to INEGI, in 1930, 7 of 10 Mexicans lived in rural communities. The percentage of the population living in cities was 33.5 in 1930, 33.1 in 1940, and 42.7 in 1950. During the first half of the twentieth century, then, the country was predominantly rural. INEGI, *Indicadores sociodemográficos de México (1930–2000),* 21.

7. Weber, *Politics as Vocation;* Loveman, "The Modern State and the Primitive Accumulation of Symbolic Power." The literature dealing with the history of state formation in postrevolutionary Mexico is rich and growing. Some of the most influential works dealing with both the cultural and the coercive aspects of this process are Joseph and Nugent, *Everyday Forms of State Formation;* Rubin, "Decentering the Regime"; Vaughan, *Cultural Politics in Revolution;* Knight, "The Weight of the State in Modern Mexico"; Knight and Pansters, *Caciquismo in Twentieth-Century Mexico;* Joseph, Rubenstein, and Zolov, "Assembling the Fragments"; Vaughan and Lewis, *The Eagle and the Virgin;* Piccato, *A History of Infamy;* Padilla, *Rural Resistance in the Land of Zapata;* McCormick, *The Logic of Compromise in Mexico;* Smith, *Pistoleros and Popular Movements;* Rath, *Myths of Demilitarization;* Pansters, "Zones of State Making," 24; Gillingham, "Who Killed Crispín Aguilar?"; Pensado, *Rebel Mexico;* Aviña, *Specters of Revolution.*

8. Joseph and Nugent, *Everyday Forms of State Formation.*

9. Loveman, "Blinded Like a State"; Sieder, "Contested Sovereignties"; Rubin, "Decentering the Regime."

10. Due to their influence and political knowledge caciques could facilitate the state's penetration of local and regional arenas, thus embodying the "parainstitutional forms of social and political control" that have been central to Mexico's state-making processes. See Pansters, "Zones of State Making," 25–26; see also Pansters, "Goodbye to the Caciques?," 361. On the resilience of the phenomenon of *caciquismo* in Mexican politics, see Knight and Pansters, *Caciquismo in Twentieth-Century Mexico,* 14–20.

11. Whereas those actors associated with the federal government were usually in charge of promoting the policies designed by the central elites (e.g., literacy campaigns, conscription, vaccination campaigns), their implementation was made possible by the mediation and facilitation of local authorities such as mayors, caciques, and even local police officers.

12. I am using the terms "coercion" and "hegemony" in reference to Pansters's characterization of Mexico's process of state formation as one that entailed both "zones of coercion" and "zones of hegemony." Whereas the former refers to the use of violence and repression by state or parainstitutional actors, the latter entails the dynamics of incorporation and

negotiation promoted by the state, either through cultural politics or the institutionalization of dissent. Pansters, "Zones of State Making," 26–27.

13. As argued by Taylor, such riots were communal in scope and defensive in character, and their goal was to restore "a customary equilibrium" rather than to transform the norms of a society. Taylor, *Drinking, Homicide, and Rebellion*, 115–18.

14. "Social control" refers to people's understanding of and responses to a given conduct that is considered deviant or wrongful. Senechal de la Roche, "Collective Violence as Social Control," 97. As explained by Migdal, "state social control"—the one asserted by, say, police officers—implies the "successful subordination of people's own inclinations of social behavior . . . in favor of the behavior prescribed by state rules." Migdal, *Strong Societies and Weak States*, 22.

15. In plain words, whereas lynchings of, say, federal teachers, were driven by people's outright rejection of their presence because of the socialist ideas that they disseminated, lynchings of police officers did not imply people's opposition to the police per se but their disapproval of the behavior of a particular police officer.

16. I borrow the term from Norbert Elias, for whom the process of state building in Western Europe involved a shift in the sensibilities of elites and, eventually, in the social dispositions and attitudes toward public acts of suffering and punishment. Elias, "On Transformations of Aggressiveness."

17. The effect of this representation was to render rural violence as rooted in regional cultures as well as to remove regional and federal elites' agency in making this violence possible. Gillingham, "Who Killed Crispín Aguilar?," 100.

18. Hernández Rodríguez, "Strongmen and State Weakness"; Knight, "Habitus and Homicide."

19. See the introduction for a characterization of these two periods.

20. "Mexicans Hang Teacher," *New York Times*, March 27, 1935. A year earlier, in a town near Jonacatepec, Puebla, an inspector from the Secretaría de Educación Pública together with two teachers were nearly lynched by a group of men and women armed with machetes and pistols. See Salinas, "Untangling Mexico's Noodle," 492–93.

21. Raby, *Educación y revolución social en México*, 188.

22. "Fue asaltado un maestro rural cerca de Chilchotla," *La Opinión*, July 11, 1936.

23. The exact number of teachers who were either killed or injured during this period is difficult to establish. Meyer estimates that about 100 teachers were assassinated and close to 200 suffered severe injuries. Raby, for his part, documented 139 cases of teachers who were assaulted or killed. In December 1935, after less than two years of the implementation of socialist education, *El Universal* referred to 50 assassinated teachers. And in July 1938, the SEP estimated that one teacher was killed every ten days in Mexico. See Meyer, "An Idea of Mexico," 291; Raby, "Los maestros rurales y los conflictos sociales"; "Unificación del magisterio nacional: Se instaló la convención de maestros," *El Universal*, December 1935; "Un maestro es asesinado cada diez días en el país," *El Diario de Puebla*, July 19, 1938.

24. Lewis, *The Ambivalent Revolution*, 115; Vaughan and Lewis, "Introduction," 10–11; Vaughan, *Cultural Politics in Revolution*, 5–8.

25. Lerner, *La educación socialista*, 13.

26. Vaughan, "Nationalizing the Countryside"; Bantjes, "Idolatry and Iconoclasm in Revolutionary Mexico." As argued by Knight, some of these modernization efforts (revolving

around anticlericalism, education, nationalism, and promoting sobriety and hygiene) can be traced to the nineteenth century and to the Porfiriato. See Knight, "Popular Culture and the Revolutionary State in Mexico, 1910–1940."

27. As asserted by Salinas, during the 1920s rural teachers' instruction focused on basic knowledge like mathematics and grammar; in the 1930s, however, teachers "expressed a new missionary zeal and stepped deeper into village politics and agrarian matters." Salinas, "Untangling Mexico's Noodle," 487. On responses to post-revolutionary health care in Mexico, including those measures implemented with the support of teachers, see Smith, "Towards a Typology of Rural Responses to Healthcare in Mexico, 1920–1960,"; Soto Laveaga, "Bringing the Revolution to Medical Schools"; Aguilar Rodríguez, "Alimentando a la nación."

28. Although my focus is on violent forms of resistance, a rich body of literature has documented various forms of nonviolent resistance articulated by those opposing socialist education, including petitions to the government, absenteeism or nonattendance, public protests, and the circulation of rumors regarding teachers' behavior. See Lewis, *The Ambivalent Revolution*, 95; Vaughan, *Cultural Politics in Revolution*, 122.

29. Bantjes, "Saint, Sinners, and State Formation," 488; Butler, "Keeping the Faith in Revolutionary Mexico," 25–26; Becker, *Setting the Virgin on Fire*, 327.

30. The entwinement of political and religious issues is clear in the case of Trinidad Ramírez, a teacher who was lynched in May 1935 in Contepec, Michoacán. Ramírez was lynched because of his opposition to the celebration of religious rituals and his animosity to the parish priest but also because of his active defense of agrarian reform. See Becker, *Setting the Virgin on Fire*, 125; Raby, *Educación y revolución social en México*, 187–88. The case is also mentioned by Guerra, "The Resistance of the Marginalized," 128. A letter sent to President Cárdenas in June 1936 by teachers in Tlalpujahua de Rayón, Michoacán, complained about the fanaticism of villagers and stated that they had heard some locals saying that they should be afraid of suffering the same fate as the teacher in Contepec. See AGN, DGG, 2/340(13)/18159, Caja 56, Exp. 9.

31. Leopoldo Méndez (1902–69) was one of the most influential printmakers and political activists of this period. He created images that celebrated the Mexican Revolution and the life and work of peasants and the urban poor. See Caplow, *Leopoldo Méndez*.

32. Méndez, *En nombre de Cristo*.

33. Caplow, *Leopoldo Méndez*, 148.

34. The case is similar to the one reported in April 1936 in Tlapacoyan, Veracruz, where seventy armed men burned the teacher Carlos Toledano alive, cut the ears off another teacher, Pablo Jimenez, and set the school on fire. "Fue quemado vivo un maestro rural y otro más fue vilmente mutilado,"*Excélsior*, April 22, 1936; "Fue duramente batida la gavilla que quemó a un maestro y amputó las orejas a otro en Tlapacoya," *Excélsior*, April 23, 1936.

35. The quote is from *El Universal*, April 7, 1937. For more on this case, see Telegram to the Ministry of Interior by Fausto Molina, AGN, DAP, Serie Asesinatos, Caja 54, 2/012.2(18)24674, Exp. 54.

36. Méndez also represented the death and hanging of the teacher José Martínez Ramírez on February 28, 1938, in Tochimilco, Puebla. Next to his depiction of Martínez Ramírez's inert hanging body, Méndez included the written message assailants had left behind as a warning to other socialist teachers. For the original message, signed by Enrique Rodríguez, known as "El Tallarín," see "Se protesta enérgicamente por el asesinato del compañero Prof.

José Ramírez Martínez, Maestro del Estado de Puebla," Letter to the president signed by Jesus Ceja, AGN, DAP, Serie Asesinatos, Caja 55, 2/012.2 (18), Exp. 30. For a detailed discussion of this case, see chapter 2. On Méndez's representation of socialist teachers, see Caplow, *Leopoldo Méndez*, 148–49.

37. The image of teachers as martyrs can be understood as a manifestation of what Bantjes calls the "transfer of sacrality" (from the religious to the civil realm) promoted by the government. Bantjes, "Idolatry and Iconoclasm in Revolutionary Mexico," 90; see also Caplow, *Leopoldo Méndez*, 151.

38. Vaughan and Lewis use this term to refer to the "reciprocal interaction between elites and popular culture in creating, disseminating, and appropriating symbols of national identity." See Vaughan and Lewis, "Introduction," 2–3.

39. Similar to the film *Maclovia*, these expressions of visual art both reflected and contributed to producing an "aesthetics of nation building" that was in tune with the postrevolutionary state. The Liga de Escritores y Artistas Revolucionarios (LEAR), for instance, to which both Méndez and Reyes belonged, supported Cárdenas's government and his policies, even if the organization was critical at first.

40. The mural depicts a female teacher being attacked by two men. One of them is shown carrying money in his hands and stepping over some books while he drags the teacher by the hair; the other one, shown wearing a scapular around his neck, brutally strokes her face with the butt of a rifle.

41. For instance, Hermelinda Rendón was shot and killed with machetes by a group of men in November 1935 in Jalancingo, Veracruz. "Otra maestra que ha sido asesinada," *Excélsior*, November 23, 1935. The same month, Micaela and Enriqueta Palacios were attacked and had their ears cut off in San Martín Hidalgo, also in Veracruz. "Maestros socialistas sin orejas," *Excélsior*, November 19, 1935; "Llegaron las maestras a quienes les cortaron los alzados las orejas," *Excélsior*, November 25, 1935. Simón Villanueva, a former teacher, recalls that a female teacher was raped and had her breasts mutilated in the state of Durango for propagating antireligious ideas. Villanueva, "El maestro rural en la educación," 185. Other female teachers were kidnapped and raped. See Raby, *Educación y revolución social*, 182–83; López, "Women Teachers of Post-Revolutionary Mexico," 68–69.

42. Guardias blancas operated like paramilitary groups and were usually hired by local landowners. Their violence was mainly directed at agrarista peasants, although, due to their defense of agrarian reform, teachers were also susceptible to their attacks. See Fallaw, *Religion and State Formation in Postrevolutionary Mexico*, 6. For more on violence against agraristas, see Santoyo, "La Mano Negra en defensa de la propiedad y el orden," 81; Knight, "Habitus and Homicide."

43. For a discussion of the relation between more organized forms of vigilantism against teachers and lynch mobs, see chapter 2.

44. "El sacrificio de los maestros," *Excélsior*, December 27, 1935. Tellingly enough, the article compared the mission of teachers to that of Bartolomé de Las Casas, who attempted to both civilize and protect the Indians.

45. "No es posible declarar si se ha logrado algo con la desfanatización de indios," *Excelsior*, September 11, 1935.

46. Diario Oficial, México, December 13, 1934. Quoted in Raby, "Ideología y construcción del Estado," 318.

47. See Salinas, "Untangling Mexico's Noodle"; Bantjes, *As If Jesus Walked on Earth*, 43–52; Lewis, *The Ambivalent Revolution*, 119–35; see also Morris, "The World Created Anew," 145–46.

48. The government's mouthpiece, *El Nacional*, for instance, referred to lynching as a strategy used by fanatics against the "modernizing labor of the government." See "Sistemática violencia," *El Nacional*, January 3, 1935; "El linchamiento, táctica de lucha de los fanáticos," *El Nacional*, January 7, 1935.

49. Vaughan and Lewis, "Introduction," 10. Newcomer offers a similar reflection on the state's self-portrayal as a modernizing force that had to fight the religious fanatics who opposed its policies during the 1940s. Newcomer, *Reconciling Modernity*, 183–84.

50. In her work on nineteenth-century Brazil, Loveman provides a similar reflection based on central elites' portrayal of popular resistance to civil registration as an expression of people's ignorance. See Loveman, "Blinded Like a State."

51. "Todo un pueblo amotinado: Alcalde en peligro de ser linchado," *La Prensa*, March 25, 1931.

52. "En Cholula iban a ser linchados dos ingenieros por el populacho enfurecido," *La Opinión*, September 26, 1931.

53. Some of the armed men who participated in the lynching of maestros during the Second Cristiada, for instance, targeted not only anticlerical teachers but also state officials. A representative case took place in December 1940, in the town of Hueyapan, Puebla, when El Tallarín and his men killed a tax collector in the main plaza after ringing the church bells and mobilizing the villagers. Friedlander, *Being Indian In Hueyapan*, 47–49.

54. "Inspector agredido por veinte pillos," *El Nacional*, October 9, 1931.

55. For instance, two policemen were nearly lynched in July 1934, also in Mexico City, because they were trying to shut down a *toreo*, an illicit pulque distillery, and fine the vendors. The press mentioned that the policemen had been beaten badly after two women had alerted the pulque vendors about their arrival. "Dos gendarmes iban a morir linchados," *El Nacional*, June 31, 1934.

56. Pierce, "Parades, Epistles and Prohibitive Legislation."

57. In Chiapas, for example, the manufacture and sale of alcohol was protected not only by municipal authorities but also by the state governor, Victórico Grajales (r. 1932–36). Furthermore, alcohol played a central role in religious and communal life. As such, federal teachers' efforts to counter the presence of alcohol were unwelcome, as shown by the case of two teachers who were attacked by a group of inebriated Chamulans carrying machetes. Lewis, *The Ambivalent Revolution*, 132; Vaughan, "Nationalizing the Countryside," 163–67.

58. "En Nopalucan se iban a registrar los mismos sucesos que en Quimixtlan," *La Opinión*, August 24, 1939.

59. In the context of Sonora, Bantjes discusses how anti-agrarista sentiments combined with opposition to anticlericalism and socialist education provoked various acts of violence in 1935, including the attempt to lynch the mayor of Huatabampo and a riot in Quiriego. See Bantjes, *As if Jesus Walked on Earth*; see also Bantjes, "Saints, Sinners, and State Formation," 150–51; Vaughan, "Nationalizing the Countryside," 162–63; Salinas, "Untangling Mexico's Noodle."

60. For instance, in the town of Tepatlaxco, Puebla, a man from the neighboring town of Acajete was hanged from a tree and shot by a group of villagers because of a land dispute dating to 1929. See "Fue lynchado un vecino de Acajete por los del Poblado de Tepatlaxco,"

La Opinión, June 1, 1937. In the municipality of Zacatlán, Puebla, Cristeros killed the president of the agrarian committee in September 1937. "Los crímenes habidos en Amoltepec fueron por los cristeros," *La Opinión,* September 28, 1937. In Espinazo, Nuevo León, peasants who supported land reform attempted to lynch two men who were accused of murdering the president of the agrarian committee. "Los agraristas de Espinazo pretendieron linchar a Cirilo Ruiz y a Santos Jalomo," *El Porvenir,* June 13, 1939. Several years later, the press reported the lynching of a rural teacher, Carlos Fonseca, because he refused to give back some lands that belonged to local peasants. "Aprehendieron al que instigó un linchamiento," *El Nacional,* August 17, 1955.

61. "Espantosa carnicería en Alpuyecac," *La Opinión,* November 20, 1936.

62. The year before, villagers from Tomatlán, in the municipality of Zacatlán, Puebla, hanged the president of the agricultural commission as well as the mayor. The rural teacher was also tortured and tied to a rock. "Mayor Hanged in Mexico," *New York Times,* June 2, 1935.

63. In Puebla, political elites opposing agrarian reform included the governor himself, Maximino Ávila Camacho. Maximino privileged the interests of landowners and promoted the organization of militias (*defensas rurales*) and paramilitary forces (*guardias blancas*) in order to control agrarista peasants in the state. For examples of extralegal killings perpetrated against agraristas in Puebla that were linked to Maximino, see AGN, DAP, Serie Asesinatos, Caja 54, 2/012.2(18)120006, Exp. 15; AGN, DAP, Serie Asesinatos, Caja 52, 2/012.2(18)1101, Exp. 56. For a broader discussion of violence against agraristas in Puebla, see Pineda, "La formación de la liga de comunidades agrarias y sindicatos campesinos en Puebla (1935–1938)," 62–66; Quintana, *Maximino Ávila Camacho and the One-Party State,* 74–102. For violence against agraristas in Veracruz, see Santoyo, "La Mano Negra," 94. And for Sonora, see Bantjes, *As If Jesus Walked on Earth,* 131–34.

64. The state's sanitary brigades in charge of promoting vaccination programs were also met with resistance. In March 1940, for instance, in Huazulco, Morelos, a group of villagers shot a colonel and two other men who had been called on by the sanitary brigade to help them "persuade" locals to get the meningitis vaccine. The press reported that villagers received the three men with gunshots. "Informe acerca de grave zafarrancho," *Excélsior,* March 23, 1940. For more examples, see Smith, "Towards a Typology of Rural Responses to Healthcare in Mexico, 1920–1960."

65. Put into effect in December 1942, the new system of military conscription was based on the Law of National Military Service approved in August 1940. The law established that military service was mandatory for all able-bodied eighteen-year-old men, who were to receive military training every Sunday morning or twice a week, whenever possible. A recruitment committee headed by the municipal authorities organized a public lottery to select a pool of these young men to go into the Federal Army for a year. Rath, "'Que el cielo un soldado en cada hijo te dio . . . ,'" 514; Cruz García, "Gobierno y movimientos sociales mexicanos," 475–76; Torres Ramírez, *México en la segunda guerra mundial,* 109–12.

66. Cruz García, "Gobierno y movimientos sociales mexicanos," 477.

67. Although my focus is on lynching, as explained by Rath most forms of resistance to military conscription involved nonviolent strategies, including young men's refusal to have their picture taken or simply vanishing from their town. Rath, "'Que el cielo un soldado en cada hijo te dio . . . ,'" 520.

68. Message from Ezequiel Navarro, Comité Regional Campesino, Tuxtepec, Oaxaca, to Antonio Gómez Velazco, 29 Zona Militar, December 22, 1942, AGN, MAC 545.2/14–19. See reference also in Rath, "'Que el cielo un soldado en cada hijo te dio . . . ,'" 517.

69. Extract from complaint sent to the president by Rosenda A. de Méndez and Saturnina R. de Miller, December 30, 1943, Ixtlán de Juárez, Oaxaca, AGN, MAC 545.2/14–19.

70. Letter addressed to Secretaría de la Defensa Nacional by Agustina Gutiérrez, October 23, 1949, Santa María Petapa, Oaxaca, AGN, MAC 545.2/14–19.

71. Letter addressed to the president by Luisa García, copied to the Recruitment Office of the 28th Military Zone, July 29, 1943, Oaxaca, AGN, MAC 545.2/14–19.

72. Other grievances expressed by recruits themselves included having to travel long distances to get to the towns where military training took place, missing work and pay, and being unfairly drafted or incarcerated by members of the recruitment committee for political or personal reasons. AGN, MAC 545.2/14–19.

73. Memorandum written by inspectors Clodomiro Morales Camacho and Ríos Thivol addressed to Lamberto Ortega Peregrina, Jefe del Departamento de Investigaciones Políticas y Sociales, September 4, 1947, AGN, DGIPS, Caja 84, Exp. 1.

74. Ledbetter, "Fighting Foot-and-Mouth Disease in Mexico," 405–6.

75. Memorandum written by inspectors Clodomiro Morales Camacho and Ríos Thivol addressed to Lamberto Ortega Peregrina, Jefe del Departamento de Investigaciones políticas y Sociales, September 4, 1947, AGN, DGIPS, Caja 84, Exp. 1.

76. Because they were rarely punished, it is extremely rare to find judicial evidence on cases of lynching. In this case, however, the fact that the victims were soldiers might help explain the punishment of the perpetrators and the corresponding paper trail left behind. See SCJ-AH, Exp. 531/51, Amparo Directo presentado por parte de José Guadalupe López; Exp. 5331/51, Amparo Directo presentado por Simón López Venegas; Expediente 529/51 presentado por Clemente Santos de la Rosa.

77. SCJ-AH, Exp. 531/51 Amparo Directo presentado por José Guadalupe López, Acuerdo, May 29, 1950.

78. SCJ-AH, Exp. 5331/51, Amparo Directo presentado por Simón López Venegas, Amparo, January 20, 1950.

79. SCJ-AH, Exp. 529/51 presentado por Clemente Santos de la Rosa, Demanda, January 20, 1950.

80. SCJ-AH, Exp. 531/51 Amparo Directo presentado por José Guadalupe López, Sentencia, December 18, 1954.

81. Memorandum written by inspectors Clodomiro Morales Camacho and Ríos Thivol addressed to Lamberto Ortega Peregrina, Jefe del Departamento de Investigaciones Políticas y Sociales, September 4, 1947, AGN, DGIPS, Caja 84, Exp. 1. In the memorandum, the inspectors denied the mayor's involvement in the incident; however, in the judicial files quoted above, the mayor is referred to as a known Sinarquista.

82. Ledbetter, "Fighting Foot-and-Mouth Disease in Mexico," 406. As mentioned above, Sinarquistas were also critical of military conscription on the basis of their reluctance to send troops to fight on behalf of a foreign government. For instance, in Nieves, Zacatecas, a group of Sinarquistas lynched a military instructor, cutting his ears off, the same form of

torment used by Cristeros against socialist teachers during the 1930s. "Martirizaron y asesinaron a un instructor en Zac. los Sinarquistas," *La Prensa,* January 5, 1943. See also Cruz García, "Gobierno y movimientos sociales mexicanos," 479.

83. It was based on this nationalistic and defensive politics that Sinarquistas mobilized opposition to military conscription. They were actively involved in acts of resistance to the conscription lotteries in states like Puebla, Morelos, Durango, Estado de México, and Guerrero. See Cruz García, "Gobierno y movimientos sociales mexicanos," 493-94; Rath, "'Que el cielo un soldado en cada hijo te dio . . . ,'" 517.

84. See chapter 2 for a discussion of how villagers' political inclinations echoed those promoted by vigilantes who participated in the Second Cristiada.

85. Ledbetter, "Fighting Foot-and-Mouth Disease in Mexico," 401.

86. In a letter written to the president, for instance, a group of peasants from the Costa Chica of Guerrero denounced the fact that the state government had denied their petition to name the members of the anti-foot-and-mouth disease committee (Comité Estatal Anti-Aftoso). Instead of allowing peasants and farmers to participate in the committee, the governor, who they distrusted, had chosen its members arbitrarily. Letter addressed to President Miguel Alemán Valdez, signed by the president of the agrarian commission, October 31, 1947, AGN, MAV 542.1/366.

87. A similar process of resistance and accommodation between rural villagers and central elites took place in regard to other health care and sanitation efforts promoted by the federal government. See Smith, "Towards a Typology of Rural Responses to Healthcare in Mexico, 1920-1960."

88. Although Mexican officials started to promote vaccination rather than the killing of cattle by the end of 1947, the shift in policy took years to take full effect. See Ledbetter, "Fighting Foot-and-Mouth Disease in Mexico," 407-8.

89. The commission comprised agricultural specialists and veterinarians. Their job was to visit rural areas to raise awareness about the disease as well as kill infected stock. See Ledbetter, "Fighting Foot-and-Mouth Disease in Mexico," 398.

90. "Robert L. Proctor, Inspector de la Comisión México-Americana Contra la Aftosa, Asesinado de Forma Salvaje," *El Porvenir,* February 3, 1949; "Mexicans Kill American," *New York Times,* February 3, 1949; "Cattle Vaccinators Attacked," *New York Times,* February 2, 1949.

91. "Detuvieron a los que lincharon al Dr. Proctor," *El Informador,* April 14, 1949.

92. "Mexicans Kill American," *New York Times,* February 3, 1949.

93. "Brigada anti-aftosa iba a ser linchada," *La Opinión,* August 12, 1949.

94. Despite the newspaper's characterization of Jolalpan villagers, in this case, and in contrast to the cases in Senguio and Temascalcingo, a group of soldiers that was sent to protect the inspectors was able to convince villagers of the need to accept the vaccine. The year before, *El Porvenir* reported that nine soldiers, who were escorting a sanitary brigade bringing smallpox vaccines to a town in Estado de México, had been lynched. The press first blamed the incident on the "pueblo ignorante," or ignorant people; it then retracted its report and quoted the military commander stationed in Toluca who denied that there was any sanitary brigade in Estado de México. "Linchamiento," *El Porvenir,* June 11, 1948; "Se desmiente lo del linchamiento," *El Nacional,* June 11, 1948.

95. The term served as a symbolic portrayal of a hierarchical and patriarchal family at both the national and the intimate level, with the president as the father and the family as a hierarchical and gendered unit. Zolov, *Refried Elvis,* 12.

96. The press reported a few isolated cases during the 1950s, but their occurrence was exceptional. For instance, in November 1951 indigenous villagers ambushed a group of alcohol inspectors on a road close to San Cristobal de las Casas, Chiapas. The assailants were producing alcohol clandestinely and opposed paying taxes to the government. "Emboscaron a un grupo de inspectores de alcoholes," *La Prensa,* November 11, 1951.

97. Ledbetter, "Fighting Foot-and-Mouth Disease in Mexico," 408.

98. Marcos Cueto refers, for instance, to how anthropological studies carried out during the 1940s and 1950s contributed to a better understanding of local practices as well as to greater integration of rural and indigenous traditions into mainstream medicine. See Cueto, *Cold War, Deadly Fevers,* 120–22; see also Opperman, "Modernization and Rural Health in Mexico"; Smith, "Towards a Typology of Rural Responses to Healthcare in Mexico, 1920–1960."

99. Rath, "'Que el cielo un soldado en cada hijo te dio . . . ,'" 529.

100. "Un voceador ha sido herido villanamente," *El Combate,* July 24, 1932.

101. Rath, "Camouflaging the State," 100–103.

102. See Vanderwood, *Juan Soldado.*

103. "Thirty-Two Held at Tijuana in Lynching Mob Roundup," *Los Angeles Times,* February 17, 1938.

104. Vanderwood, *Juan Soldado,* 15–27.

105. "Troops Battle Mexican Mob; Save Sex Killer," *Chicago Daily Tribune,* February 16, 1938.

106. "Alleged Girl Slayer Executed in Mexico," *New York Times,* February 18, 1938.

107. "Dos miembros del ejército fueron asesinados," *La Opinión,* December 1, 1936.

108. "Soldados a punto de ser linchados ayer, " *La Opinión,* July 20, 1939.

109. In August 1944, for instance, three drunken soldiers who had beaten a woman in a cantina and then assaulted two police officers were nearly lynched by infuriated bystanders in Mexico City. "Escandalazo en Tlanepantla: Iban a linchar a 3 soldados," *La Prensa,* August 7, 1944. Similarly, the press reported the attempted lynching of a soldier who was caught trying to kidnap an eight-year-old girl, also in Mexico City. "Por criminal acción iba a ser linchado un soldado," *La Prensa,* August 9, 1950. And in February 1951, villagers from Cautepec, Hidalgo, lynched two soldiers who had killed a worker during a cantina brawl. "Dos soldados linchados," *La Prensa,* February 26, 1951.

110. There were, nonetheless, a good number of letters of complaint written by citizens that reflected the army's collusion with the interests of political elites, both at the municipal and state levels. Moreover, the army was a key agent of rural repression "in a confused world of half formal policing missions and informal political maneuvering." Gillingham, "Who Killed Crispín Aguilar?," 101. And yet, as Rath asserts, by the 1940s and 1950s, people did not ask for the removal of the military but rather reflected the belief that "the army could perform a legitimate policing role, provided it was controlled by democratic, civilian authorities." See Rath, *Myths of Demilitarization in Postrevolutionary Mexico,* 130.

111. For an analysis of the dynamics of abuse and corruption characterizing the police, see Piccato, *City of Suspects;* Davis, "Policing and Regime Transition"; Pulido Esteva, "Los negocios de la policía en la ciudad de México durante la posrevolución."

112. "Gendarme víctima de brutal atentado por una horda de desalmados en el barrio de S. Matías," *La Opinión*, September 27, 1937.

113. As discussed by Piccato, neighbors often resisted police intervention in what seemed ordinary matters such as breaking up fights or arresting drunkards for creating a public disturbance. See Piccato, *City of Suspects*, 44.

114. "Comandante policíaco sufre una paliza," *La Opinión*, August 4, 1942. Similarly, in June 1942, the press reported the lynching of a policeman by sixteen individuals, including ten "mujeres bravísimas" (very brave women). The lynching, which took place in Guanajuato, was prompted by the officer's attempt to stop a street brawl. See "Linchamiento de un gendarme que fue a aplacar un mitote," *La Prensa*, June 12, 1942. Only two months later, inspector Javier González from the Office of Rules of the Federal District (Oficina de Reglamentos del Distrito Federal) was nearly lynched by a group of infuriated neighbors after his partner, inspector José Rodríguez, killed a butcher who refused to pay a bribe. "Tragedia a causa de los precios de la carne entre inspectores y dueños de expendios," *La Prensa*, August 20, 1942.

115. "Querían linchar al inspector de policía de Tecuala," *El Informador*, September 1, 1944.

116. "Comisario de policía linchado por matón," *La Prensa*, March 2, 1943.

117. The same newspaper reported just two days after the incident that local authorities were harassing unionized salt workers in retaliation for the lynching of a police commander, Adolfo Jimenez. The workers responded by asking the governor to remove local authorities who were responsible for "the robberies, murderers, and scandals committed" in the town. "Puede haber un linchamiento en Estación 'Carrillo,'" *La Prensa*, March 3, 1943.

118. "El policía asesino, a punto de ser linchado por indignada multitud," *La Prensa*, August 17, 1943. The attempted lynching of Trinidad Robles, a policeman who shot a man when he was trying to break up a fight in Mexico City, unfolded along similar lines. "Policía a punto de ser linchado por lesionar a agresivo rijoso," *La Prensa*, April 30, 1951. Other reports include "Espantosa matanza de un comandante y 4 policías," *La Prensa*, August 6, 1943; "Enfurecida turba trato de linchar a dos funcionarios," *La Prensa*, March 3, 1944; "Dos patrulleros iban a ser linchados por unos cafres," *La Prensa*, June 5, 1950.

119. "Cobarde asesinato cometido por un agente de la policía, ebrio," *La Prensa*, February 25, 1945.

120. Davis, "Policing and Regime Transition"; Piccato, *A History of Infamy*, 107–25.

121. There were of course other strategies adopted by citizens in the face of police abuse that did not involve the use of violence. These included letters of complaint to federal authorities, citizens' reports of police misconduct, or refusing to cooperate with the police in their investigations. See Piccato, *City of Suspects*, 43–45.

122. For instance, in September 1931, inhabitants of the town of San Martín Texmelucan, Puebla, lynched former mayor Felipe Valencia and four of his *pistoleros* (gunmen). "Cuatro individuos fueron linchados ayer en el pueblo de Texmelucan," *La Opinión*, September 28, 1931. In June 1934, a group of agrarista peasants lynched Mayor Antonio Lopez in a town in the state of Michoacán. "Troop Units Stationed in All Mexican Villages," *New York Times*, June 23, 1934. A year later, a man who proclaimed himself the mayor of Coxquihuic, Veracruz, was lynched and hanged from a tree. "Fue muerto un individuo que se autoeligió alcalde," *El Universal*, November 5, 1935; "Head of Committee Lynched," *New York Times*,

November 6, 1935. The same year, the press reported the attempted lynching of Everardo Topete, the brother of the anticlerical governor of Jalisco. "Milagrosamente se salvó de morir el Sr. Manuel Topete," *Excélsior,* November 25, 1935; "Lynch Mob in Mexico Flees from Air Bombs," *Washington Post,* November 27, 1935. In July 1941, villagers of Chilón, Chiapas, lynched the mayor in retaliation for various murders he had committed. "Alcalde linchado por multitud enfurecida," *La Prensa,* July 11, 1941. Years later, a group of villagers stoned and then hanged the *síndico* (city attorney) of El Apomal, in Sinaloa. "Un síndico de ayuntamiento fue linchado por enfurecido pueblo," *La Prensa,* January 21, 1945.

123. According to Rath, Governor Betancourt proclaimed Colonel Martínez Cairo head of the municipal council in order to gain control of the town's electoral process, discipline the *ejidatario* (common land) peasants and mill workers, and ensure that they voted for the official candidate in the next election for governor in 1951. See Rath, *Myths of Demilitarization,* 134–35.

124. For instance, *La Opinión* reported that a man who had sent letters of complaint to Puebla's governor and to Mexico City regarding the behavior of Martínez Cairo was badly beaten by a group of police officers in the presence of Martínez Cairo and the town's police commander. "Atentado en Matamoros," *La Opinión,* May 11, 1949. The next year, in August, a group of villagers accused Martínez Cairo of having planned the assassination of a wealthy farmer, J. Guadalupe Ariza. According to a letter published by *La Prensa,* villagers claimed that the police commander, under the orders of Martínez Cairo, had killed Ariza with clubs. They furthermore stated that the people of Izúcar de Matamoros, Puebla, were defenseless against the embarrassing spectacle of "the coronel cacique" Martínez Cairo. "Intolerables desmanes comete un coronel en Izúcar de Matamoros," *La Prensa,* August 1, 1950. See also "Cayó, por fin, el coronel protegido de Betancourt," *Excélsior,* October 20, 1950.

125. Civilians were protesting the imposition of the official candidate in the municipal elections in León, Guanajuato. Newcomer, *Reconciling Modernity,* 182; Rath, *Myths of Demilitarization in Postrevolutionary Mexico, 1920–1960,* 138; "Ayuntamiento depuesto por el pueblo amotinado," *La Prensa,* October 21, 1950.

126. "Ayuntamiento depuesto por el pueblo amotinado," *La Prensa,* October 21, 1950.

127. Press reports also indicated that Rafael Ávila Camacho, PRI candidate and future governor of Puebla, had intervened in order to force the resignation of Martínez Cairo. "Cayó, por fin, el coronel protegido de Betancourt," *Excélsior,* October 20, 1950.

128. For instance, in November 1951, the former mayor of San Andrés Papalutla, Oaxaca, was lynched by villagers in retaliation for having sold some communal lands to the neighboring town. "Fue linchado un ex Alcalde que vendió terrenos ajenos," *Excélsior,* November 14, 1951. In January 1955 villagers from Tlapehuala, Guerrero, lynched the mayor, who was installed in office by the PRI, as a way to protest authorities' disregard for the popular vote. See "Fue linchado un alcalde impuesto por el P.R.I.," *El Porvenir,* January 19, 1955. Just a couple of years later, the press reported the lynching of the mayor of San Andrés Dinicuiti, Oaxaca. The incident was prompted by the mayor's assassination of a man named Arturo Martínez Dolores, in a context characterized by people's exasperation with a political system that imposed PRI candidates against their will. "Un alcalde linchado," *El Porvenir,* February 24, 1957; "Motivos del linchamiento," *El Informador,* February 24, 1957.

129. Telegram signed by Rodolfo Chávez Carrillo, governor of the state of Colima, sent to President Adolfo Ruiz Cortinez, January 1, 1956, AGN, ARC, Exp. 541.1/33.

130. Letter by Luis Aguilar Gutiérrez, on behalf of the Comité Nacional Campesino Emiliano Zapata, sent to President Adolfo Ruiz Cortinez, January 6, 1956, AGN, ARC, Exp. 541.1/33.

131. Quintana, *Maximino Ávila Camacho and the One-Party State*, 3–5; Pansters, "Zones of State Making," 25–26.

132. A former local and federal congressman and mayor of Ciudad Hidalgo, Aquiles de la Peña had controlled this town for more than two decades (since the mid-1930s). He chose and deposed mayors at will and, in tune with the behavior of other strongmen, surrounded himself by pistoleros. In the earlier years of his political career he had been a known agrarista who had aggressively fought the presence of Cristeros in Michoacán. He was a personal friend, a compadre, of Lázaro Cárdenas.

133. Several press articles covered the incident: "Sinarcas y comunistas en contubernio, matan y queman en Michoacán," *La Prensa*, April 7, 1959; "Brutalidad derivada de la ignorancia, causa de los sangrientos hechos de C. Hidalgo, habla don Lázaro," *La Prensa*, April 8, 1959; "Falsa versión sobre envenenamiento de agua, causó las cuatro muertes," *Excélsior*, April 8, 1959; "Cuidadosamente premeditaron los hechos sangrientos de Hidalgo," *Excélsior*, April 9, 1959.

134. Benitez's representation of the priest as a "voice of reason" is in contrast to the actual role of parish priests in the organization of lynchings (see chapter 2).

135. In his place they designated José G. Rueda, a teacher, who was supported by most villagers.

136. There were other cases of people getting sick during the days before the lynching. According to press reports, those cases were caused by a gastrointestinal disease outbreak that had hit the town.

137. "Zafarrancho en Cd. Hidalgo: Hubo 4 Muertos y 4 Heridos," *Excélsior*, April 7, 1959; "Falsa versión sobre envenenamiento del agua, causó las cuatro muertes," *Excélsior*, April 8, 1959; "Sinarcas y comunistas en contubernio, matan y queman en Michoacán," *La Prensa*, April 7, 1959; Benítez, *El agua envenenada*, 145–48.

138. At first *La Prensa* suggested that it was a group of Sinarquistas, in alliance with communist elements, that had planned and executed the lynching. The newspaper itself then questioned this version when it printed an interview with David Lomelí, national leader of the UNS, in which he denied that Sinarquistas would engage in acts of violence and blamed the cacique himself for the events in Ciudad Hidalgo. Members of the Coalición Nacional Revolucionaria who had instigated the overthrow of the mayor were also mentioned as potential instigators of the lynching. *Excélsior* cited an investigation by the state police that pointed to members of the Alianza Juvenil as those responsible for the incident. It stated that bottles of alcohol and gasolina (allegedly used to set fire to De la Peña's house and sawmill) had been found in the offices of the organization. In his novel, which was based on his investigation of the case, Benitez also writes that it was young members of a political asociación who spread the rumor about the poisoned water. See "Sinarcas y comunistas en contubernio, matan y queman en Michoacán," *La Prensa*, April 7, 1959; "Brutalidad e ignorancia como causas del hecho en Michoacán," *La Prensa*, April 8, 1959; "Cuidadosamente premeditaron los hechos sangrientos de Hidalgo," *Excélsior*, April 9, 1959; Benitez, *El agua envenenada*, 114–15.

139. Martín, "Ya no había a quien matar," 35.

140. "Un triple linchamiento fue perpetrado en el pueblo de Tepetzala ayer," *La Opinión*, May 11, 1930. Three months later, in the same town and also under the orders of the mayor, two men were hanged by a group of drunken men in the main plaza. The mayor had mobilized the villagers by ringing the church bells and then had the men beaten up and hanged. "Prodigiosos crímenes en Santa Isabel Tepetzala," *La Opinión*, August 12, 1930.

141. The organization of this lynching mirrors the collective killing of the alcohol inspectors in Nopalucan, Puebla, in August 1939. The town's mayor also summoned villagers by ringing the church bells.

142. Remarkably enough, the three men survived the attack. An engineer from the local agrarian commission dissuaded the crowd from killing the men and convinced them to take them to the authorities of Puebla city. The fact that the engineer was in charge of dividing and distributing some lands among villagers helps explain why villagers listened to him.

143. In the case of the lynching of Micaela Ortega in the town of Acajete, Puebla, on November 11, 1934, the mayor himself was among the perpetrators of the killing. See chapter 2.

144. These practices persisted throughout the period analyzed by this book and were used during later decades, particularly the 1960s and 1970s. For examples, see Piccato, *A History of Infamy*; Pansters, *Violence, Coercion, and State-Making in Twentieth-Century Mexico*; McCormick, "The Last Door"; Hernández Rodríguez, "Strongmen and State Weakness"; Smith, *Pistoleros and Popular Movements*; Padilla, *Rural Resistance in the Land of Zapata*.

145. Cases of police killings that were covered up as lynchings go back at least to the 1890s. Perhaps the most famous case is the assassination of Arnulfo Arroyo, a man accused of attacking President Porfirio Díaz in 1897. The police asserted at first that they had been unable to control a crowd that had broken into the prison and lynched Arroyo. The investigation later revealed they themselves had stabbed Arroyo to death. See "Mexican Police Arrested," *New York Times*, September 20, 1897; "The Lynching of Arroyo," *New York Times*, September 22, 1897; see also Barrera Bassols, *El Caso Villavicencio*; Lomnitz, "Mexico's First Lynching."

146. "El alcalde de San Aparicio cometió un grave delito," *La Opinión*, September 9, 1931.

147. "Exigirán responsabilidades a quienes lyncharon a 4 hombres en Huitzilan," *La Opinión*, May 21, 1937.

148. Letter signed by Martina Vázquez addressed to the local judge (March 20, 1933); letter signed by Manuel Martínez Romero and Francisco Morales addressed to the public prosecutor (March 20, 1933); and letter signed by Timoteo Lujón on behalf of the Comité Ejecutivo Agrario addressed to the state governor (March 22, 1933). AGN, ALR, Exp. 524/280 Veracruz.

149. "Tremendo zafarrancho en Axocopan," *Diario de Puebla*, May 24, 1938.

150. The congressman was Antonio Castillo, a former textile worker turned union leader and then local congressman. Castillo was known for abusing his power and using police officers to advance his own political agenda. Evidence suggests this was not the first time Castillo was involved in an incident of this kind. The year before, in Atlixco, Puebla, the press reported that he was involved in the killing of two indigenous peasants that was perpetrated by a police commander. The commander hanged the two men because they opposed local authorities and had denounced the abuses perpetrated by Castillo and his gunmen. "Atropellos en Atlixco," *La Opinión*, August 19, 1937; "Será desaforado el dip. Castillo para poder consignarlo," *La Opinión*, May 25, 1938.

151. "Los esbirros del Dip. Castillo cometen un bárbaron crimen en el pueblo de Axocopan," *La Opinión,* May 24, 1938.

152. See also the extrajudicial killings of Pedro Fomperosa perpetrated by police officers under the command of the mayor of San Andrés Tuxtla, Veracruz, mentioned in chapter 3. For other examples of abuses committed during the 1940s and 1950s, see Gillingham, "Who Killed Crispín Aguilar?"; Piccato, "Ley Fuga as Justice"; McCormick, *The Logic of Compromise in Mexico.*

153. Letter addressed to the president, signed by M. Rodriguez Espíndola on behalf of the Partido Revolucionario de Unificación Nacional, June 18, 1940. AGN, DAP, Serie Asesinatos, Caja 52, 2/012.2(18–81)/1, Exp. 43.

154. Maximino fiercely supported Manuel's candidacy for the presidency and kept tight control of his political opponents through coercion and intimidation. See Quintana, *Maximino Ávila Camacho and the One-Party State,* 95–97. The election generated other violent episodes. In February 1940, for instance, a riot broke out between "almazanistas" and "avilacamachistas" in Querétaro. The press reported that, provoked by avilacamachistas, a crowd that supported Almazán started to throw stones at political opponents and were close to lynching them. "Lapidaron a camachistas," *Excélsior,* February 17, 1940.

155. Letter addressed to President Lázaro Cárdenas signed by Albina Hernández and Francisca García, AGN, DAP, Serie Asesinatos, Caja 52, 2/012.2(18)113/2, Exp. 39.

156. Gayosso Ríos, *Mi Palabra,* 110–14; the case is also quoted in Rath, *Myths of Demilitarization,* 127.

157. Another case perpetrated with the acquiescence of a mayor took place in January 1944 in Teocalcingo, Estado de México. A mob of seventy people, who allegedly had "authorization" from the mayor, lynched a man and his wife. They first dragged the man with a rope and then shot him in the head. His wife was also shot but survived the attack. "Una turba inconsciente 'fusiló' a un matrimonio," *La Prensa,* January 29, 1944.

158. "Un ejecutor de hacienda a punto de ser linchado cerca de Chalco," *El Porvenir,* October 16, 1949.

159. Gillingham, "Who Killed Crispín Aguilar?," 100.

160. Rubin, "Decentering the Regime," 86–87, 103–4; Quintana, *Maximino Ávila Camacho and the One-Party State,* 5–6.

161. As mentioned before, Governor Betancourt appointed Martínez Cairo as mayor of Izúcar de Matamoros. And Aquiles de la Peña's close friendship with Lázaro Cárdenas shielded him from having to face justice. The list of post-revolutionary caciques who enjoyed the support of federal elites, at least until they broke some of the unwritten rules of acceptable behavior, included Maximino Ávila Camacho in Puebla, Gonzalo N. Santos in San Luis Potosí, Saturnino Osornio in Querétaro, and Tomás Garrido Canabal in Tabasco. See Knight and Pansters, *Caciquismo in Twentieth-Century Mexico;* Quintana, *Maximino Ávila Camacho and the One-Party State,* 6.

162. An exception to this trend was the 1968 lynching of five university workers in San Miguel Canoa, Puebla, which was organized and perpetrated with the support of the mayor. See AGN, DFS, "San Miguel Canoa," Versión Pública, Foja 11. In contemporary Mexico there are seldom references to lynchings being organized or perpetrated directly by public officials. For an analysis of lynchings in present-day Mexico, see Davis, "Undermining the Rule of Law"; Fuentes, *Linchamientos, fragmentación y respuesta en el México neoliberal;*

Binford and Churchill, "Lynching and States of Fear in Urban Mexico"; Rodríguez, "Crisis de autoridad y violencia social."

163. In a letter denouncing the events, Feliciano Pita (brother of the victims) explained that the killing was carried out in retaliation for the victims' opposition to the indiscriminate logging of the Sierra Madre del Sur of Guerrero, which was promoted by local authorities despite its damaging impact on the lives of villagers. Letter addressed to President Adolfo Ruíz Cortínez, signed by Feliciano Pita, San Nicolás del Oro, Guerrero, July 25, 1957, AGN, ARC, 541/346.

164. Copy of an article published in the newspaper *Adelante,* July 25, 1957, "Las autoridades de Otatitlán al margen de la ley," AGN, ARC 541/518.

165. Central elites became increasingly susceptible to public opinion and thus opted for more covert and selective forms of violence that would allow them to deny having committed political assassinations. Gillingham, "Who Killed Crispín Aguilar?," 104–11. On the use of pistoleros and agents provocateurs by political elites in order to cover their involvement, see Pensado, "The Rise of a 'National Student Problem' in 1956"; Piccato, *A History of Infamy,* 162–71.

CHAPTER TWO. IN THE NAME OF CHRIST

With the permission of *The Americas* parts of this chapter are reproduced and adapted from Gema Kloppe-Santamaría, "The Lynching of the Impious: Violence, Politics, and Religion in Post-Revolutionary Mexico (1930s–1950s)," *The Americas: A Quarterly Review of Latin American History* 77, no. 1 (2020): 101–28.

1. AGN, IPS, Informe dirigido al C. Jefe de la Sección III y firmado por el Inspector Fernando A. Rodríguez, Caja 70, Exp. 11.

2. Fallaw, *Religion and State Formation in Post-Revolutionary Mexico,* 31; Salinas, "Untangling Mexico's Noodle," 474; Guerra, "The Resistance of the Marginalized"; Bantjes, *As If Jesus Walked on Earth;* Becker, *Setting the Virgin on Fire;* Vaughan, *Cultural Politics in Revolution.*

3. While focused primarily on lynchings, the present chapter also highlights the intersections between lynching and more organized forms of vigilantism, such as when armed groups of Cristeros or Segunderos participated in the organization of communal lynchings.

4. For the purposes of this chapter, I use the term "Protestant" to refer to all non-Catholic Christian denominations, including Evangelicals, Pentecostals, and Mormons.

5. De la Luz García, "Ciudadanía, representación y participación cívico-política de los evangélicos mexicanos," 18.

6. Violence was certainly neither the main nor the only means used by Catholics to express their discontent with anticlericalism. Particularly after the Cristero War, Catholics privileged the use of civil forms of resistance, such as street protests, underground masses, and religious instruction, as well as public petitions and letters of complaint addressed to federal authorities demanding their right to exercise religion. See Fallaw, *Religion and State Formation in Postrevolutionary Mexico,* 4–5; Becker, *Setting the Virgin on Fire,* 129–32; Aspe Armella, *La formación social y política de los católicos mexicanos.*

7. As argued by Blancarte, the 1929 accords only brought a formal end to the Cristero conflict. An actual modus vivendi between state and church was reached at the end of the 1930s, when the government adopted a more tolerant approach to Catholicism and when

the church decided to develop a strategic relationship with the state centered on national values. Blancarte, *Historia de la Iglesia católica en México*, 31–58. See also Knight, "Habitus and Homicide," 118; Camp, *Cruce de espadas*, 48–49; Dávila Peralta, *Las Santas Batallas*, 91–92.

8. I use the terms "folk religiosity" and "popular religiosity" to refer to practices and beliefs observed by lay members of the Catholic Church that were not necessarily sanctioned by the church's hierarchy. Some examples are the devotion of images of saints not accepted by the Catholic Church, syncretic practices such as healing with herbs, and, of particular relevance for this study, the use of violence in the name of religion. I am aware that the divide between popular and official might lead to an understanding of religion as a "two-tier system" that defines the first as superstitious and emotional and the latter as true and rational. My use of the term "popular" versus "official" or "institutional," however, is meant to be descriptive rather than normative. For a critique of the two-tier system approach, see Vanderwood, "Religion: Official, Popular, and Otherwise"; Bantjes, "Religion and the Mexican Revolution."

9. I focus on Catholicism for two main reasons. First, Catholic groups and individuals were the main religiously informed perpetrators of lynchings, riots, and vigilante killings in post-revolutionary Mexico. Second, Catholicism had and continues to have a predominant presence in Mexico. During the period 1930s–1950s, the proportion of Mexicans who identified as Catholics varied between 97 and 98 percent. At the regional level, these percentages were similar, with the exception of the states of Quintana Roo and Tabasco, where, on average, the proportion of people who identified as Catholic was 81 and 88 percent, respectively, according to the 1940 census. See INEGI, *La diversidad religiosa en México*, 3–5.

10. This understanding of religion acknowledges that for the believer religion is experienced as part of everyday life and thus cannot be confined to Sunday Mass or to the private sphere. It further recognizes that religion is not only present in communal ceremonies and traditions, but also in communities' political and economic dynamics. See Vanderwood, "Religion: Official, Popular, and Otherwise," 412; Van Young, *The Other Rebellion*, 453; Nutini and Barry, *Social Stratification in Central Mexico 1500–2000*, 189–91.

11. Natalie Zemon Davis's influential work on religious riots in sixteenth-century France also explores the relation between the material and symbolic aspects of religion. In her view, both Catholic and Protestant rioters intended to purify communities of polluted elements and false religious doctrines. At the same time, their aim was political: to send a message to the authorities who had failed to punish idolaters and wrongdoers. See Davis, "The Rites of Violence," 61.

12. For a detailed examination of the relation between parish priests and villagers in the context of eighteenth-century Mexico, see Taylor's classic study, *Magistrates of the Sacred*.

13. The agrarian reform and the promotion of socialist ideas were considered particularly disruptive, as was the presence of people who professed Protestantism, a religion perceived as foreign, spurious, and closer to liberal and socialist ideologies, each rejected by Catholicism. Blancarte, *Historia de la Iglesia católica en México*, 75; Bastian, *Los disidentes*; Bastian, "Protestants, Freemasons, and Spiritists."

14. Fallaw, *Religion and State Formation in Postrevolutionary Mexico*, 13.

15. On the potential divisions and disagreements between the faithful and the clergy regarding Catholic practices, see Wright-Rios, *Revolutions in Mexican Catholicism*.

16. Members of the LNDLR, which had taken up arms during the Cristero War, were particularly critical of the agreement, or *arreglos*, between the state and the church. They considered the actions of the archbishops in charge of the negotiation treacherous and did not give up the idea of taking up arms again; many did during the 1930s. Meyer, *La Iglesia católica en México*, 6–7. During the 1940s similar tensions would emerge between the higher ranks of the church and members of the UNS.

17. The church hierarchy openly supported those who took up arms during the Cristero revolt but became critical of armed resistance during the Second Cristiada. This shift was probably based on lessons learned from the Cristero War, including the difficulty of controlling the actions of vigilantes and other violent entrepreneurs. As Blancarte and Fallaw argue, from the 1930s on the church privileged pacific and civic expressions of dissent through different lay organizations that operated under the umbrella of ACM. Fallaw, *Religion and State Formation in Postrevolutionary Mexico*, 25–27; Blancarte, *Historia de la Iglesia católica en México*, 33; Aspe, *La formación social y política de los católicos mexicanos*, 90. See also Butler, *Popular Piety*; Salinas, "Untangling Mexico's Noodle," 474.

18. For instance, in his pastoral letter published on April 12, 1936, Archbishop José Garibi Rivera condemned socialist education as a source of immorality and danger that needed to be resisted by faithful Catholics. AGN, DGG, Serie Asesinatos, Caja 69, Exp. 4, 2. 340/11 10506. Even more belligerent was the pastoral letter written by the archbishop of Mexico, Luis María Martínez, in 1944, which openly called Catholics to fight the foreign and pervasive influence of Protestantism. See De la Luz, "Ciudadanía, representación y participación cívico-política de los evangélicos mexicanos," 13; Pérez Rosales, "Censura y control," 93–94. The denunciation of "foreign" or "immoral" ideologies would continue during the following decades. In 1961, for instance, the archbishop of Puebla devoted an entire pastoral letter to the issue of communism and the vital threat this ideology posed for Christian civilization as well as for the motherland. Dávila Peralta, *Las Santas Batallas*, 135.

19. Women played a particularly active role in the organization of lynchings perpetrated in the name of religion. Their participation can be understood in the context of the central role they played in the defense and revitalization of Catholic religion in post-revolutionary Mexico. See Wright-Rios, "Visions of Women"; see also Miller, "The Role of Women in the Mexican Cristero Rebellion."

20. For folk Catholicism in particular the veneration of religious images, including those of patron saints, is a central aspect of religious rites as well as community celebrations and festivals. Nutini and Issac, *Social Stratification in Central Mexico, 1500–2000*, 186–87. See also Bantjes, "Idolatry and Iconoclasm in Revolutionary Mexico"; Fallaw, "Varieties of Mexican Revolutionary Anticlericalism."

21. As has been argued by Finchelstein, religious fervor may become intertwined with ideologies that sanctify the use of violence. Envisioned as an "instrument of the sacred," Argentinean fascists came to regard violence as a legitimate and even "sacred" means to rid the motherland of "internal enemies," represented by communists, Jews, and Protestants. Finchelstein, *Transatlantic Fascism*, 125–28. See also Girard, *Violence and the Sacred*. This is not to say that religion is unequivocally related to violence. For a critique of one-sided and simplistic interpretations of religion as inherently drawn to violent and irrational conducts, see Cavanaugh, *The Myth of Religious Violence*.

22. For examples of how anticommunist and anti-Protestant sentiments intersected with intracommunity conflicts in certain communities identified as Catholic, see Romanucci-Ross, *Conflict, Violence and Morality in a Mexican Village*, 159–60; Lewis, *Five Families*, 41–42.

23. Literature on lynching in the United States has also explored how religion, in that case, southern Protestantism, promoted a theological framework centered on retribution, sacrifice, and redemptive violence that aimed at safeguarding the "purity" of white communities. See Evans, *Cultures of Violence*, 124–53; Mathews, "The Southern Rite of Human Sacrifice"; Patterson, *Rituals of Blood*.

24. For an analysis of the sanctioning and sanctification of the use of violence during the Cristero War, see González, *Morir y matar por Cristo Rey*; on martyrdom during the Cristiada, see López-Menéndez, *Miguel Pro*.

25. The philosopher René Girard offers an important theoretical insight into the relationship between religion, sacrifice, and communal violence. In his view, the religious rite of sacrifice allows a community to prevent cycles of vengeance and reprisal. By directing violence against a scapegoat, a victim that is "sacrificeable," the community reaffirms its unity and cohesion and redirects the use of violence against outsiders. Girard, *Violence and the Sacred*.

26. Some level of overlap between these categories is inevitable as some socialist teachers engaged in acts of iconoclasm and as violence against Protestants was, to some extent, driven by the alleged links between these religious groups and socialist or communist ideas. Bantjes, "Idolatry and Iconoclasm in Revolutionary Mexico," 111–12; Raby, *Educación y revolución social en México: 1921–1940*, 163.

27. A number of newspapers, including the government's mouthpiece, *El Nacional*, and the *New York Times* reported the incident. "Cura de Santa Ana Maya, Michoacán, y cuatro señoritas están en la penitenciaria de Morelia," *El Porvenir*, June 18, 1931; "Crímenes de la intolerancia religiosa," *El Nacional*, July 5, 1931; "Alemán linchado," *La Prensa*, June 17, 1931; "Era holandés el comunista que fue linchado," *La Prensa*, June 18, 1931; "German Red Reported Lynched in Mexico," *New York Times*, June 17, 1931.

28. On liberalism and its concern with the creation of a modern and secular society, see Hale, "Jose Maria Luis Mora and the Structure of Mexican Liberalism," 196; Van Young, *The Other Rebellion*, 484. For examples of collective forms of resistance, including rioting, precipitated by the anticlericalism of liberal reforms, see Vanderwood, *The Power of God against the Guns of Government*; Bazant, "La Iglesia, el Estado y la sublevación conservadora de Puebla en 1856," 101–3.

29. Although defanaticization campaigns vary considerably from region to region (being particularly strong in states such as Tabasco, Veracruz, Yucatán, Michoacán, and Sonora), they were part of a fairly coherent revolutionary project that aimed at eliminating both the political and economic and the symbolic and cultural power of the church. See Bantjes, "Saints, Sinners, and State Formation"; Bantjes, *As If Jesus Walked on Earth*.

30. As indicated by Butler, revolutionaries were not necessarily irreligious, and some of them promoted anticlericalism as a means to purify the Catholic faith. Butler, "Sotanas Rojinegras."

31. Fallaw, *Religion and State Formation in Postrevolutionary Mexico*, 4.

32. Some examples of desecration of churches included turning them into government offices and public schools or, in more extreme cases, using them as stables or latrines. Bantjes also mentions the temporary use of convents as brothels in order to mock the nun's mandate of celibacy. Bantjes, "Saints, Sinners, and State Formation," 488. To see further examples of iconoclasm during the revolution, see Bastian, "Protestants, Freemasons, and Spiritists," 80–81.

33. Bantjes, *As If Jesus Walked on Earth*, 12. See also Moreno Chávez, "Quemando santos para iluminar conciencias," 41; Becker, *Setting the Virgin on Fire*, 129; Fallaw, "Varieties of Mexican Revolutionary Anticlericalism," 485–86; Knight, "Popular Culture and the Revolutionary State in Mexico, 1910–1940."

34. For prior incidents of revolutionary anticlericalism and offenses to Catholic symbols, see "First Lynching in Mexico: Man Accused of Robbing Image of Virgin Tortured by Mob," *Washington Post*, August 17, 1919. See also the attempted lynching of a man who caused an explosion in Mexico City's basilica on November 14, 1921, mentioned in Bantjes, "Saints, Sinners, and State Formation," 137. On contemporary examples of mob violence driven by the stealing of religious images, see "Le robó a Dios," *El Sol de Puebla*, December 16, 2013; "'Encueran' a imagen religiosa en parroquia de La Resurrección," *El Sol de Puebla*, January 14, 2015.

35. Cárdenas's conciliatory approach to the church can be explained as the result of four interrelated factors: a strategy to escape Calles's anticlerical grip; a deliberate attempt to reorient the government's efforts toward socioeconomic issues, including agrarian reform and the modernization of the countryside; a response to the opposition that anticlerical measures generated and that therefore pushed him to reconsider his religious policy; and Cárdenas's childhood friendship with Luis María Martínez, who became archbishop of Mexico in 1937. Blancarte, *Historia de la Iglesia católica en México*, 48; Bantjes, *As If Jesus Walked on Earth*, 11–12; Bantjes, "Idolatry and Iconoclasm in Revolutionary Mexico," 115–19; Pérez, "Censura y control," 92–93.

36. This much we can infer from the sources, especially newspapers. Although it is possible to imagine that some of these individuals indeed had a contentious relationship with religion, without more access to their voices it is difficult to be certain about this. In any event, I am aware that a seemingly economic motivation does not exclude a religious one. As Davis argues, the fact that religious rioters engaged in acts of pillaging does not negate the religious dimension of their actions. See Davis, "The Rites of Violence," 65.

37. "El linchamiento ocurrido en Tetla," *El Nacional*, May 17, 1933; *Periódico oficial del estado de Tlaxcala*, September 10, 1933.

38. A week after the incident, a newspaper reported that two hundred villagers had written the president, acknowledged their participation in the lynching, and justified the lynching as an act of justice. "El linchamiento de Fructuoso Concha, va a ser investigado," *El Nacional*, May 25, 1933.

39. Similarly apolitical or lacking an apparent ideological intent was the behavior of a woman who danced on the altar of the Virgin of Guadalupe Basilica in Mexico City. Offended by her irreverence, churchgoers, together with a group of men in charge of looking after the temple, rushed the woman outside the basilica. As the woman continued dancing erratically and shouting offensive phrases, churchgoers attempted to lynch her. The irreverent woman, who was saved by the police, was described as a "loca," a crazy woman,

by the press. "Dama loca que bailaba en un altar de la basílica," *La Prensa,* July 7, 1931. As stated before in reference to thieves, a political rendering of this type of behavior could be possible. Marjorie Becker's work demonstrates, for instance, that dancing in a space considered holy could be politically motivated. In her retelling of the torching of the image of La Purísima in northwestern Michoacán in July 1935, she explains how a group of young women danced on the altar in front of the ashes of La Purísima, signaling their willingness to cooperate—albeit in their own terms—with the anticlericalism of the post-revolutionary project. Becker, "Torching La Purísima, Dancing at the Altar."

40. "Iban a linchar a un supuesto rata sacrílego," *La Prensa,* October 18, 1930.

41. Samper, "Cannibalizing Kids," 4. Samper's work analyzes a series of lynchings directed against foreign women in Guatemala during the 1990s. The women were accused of stealing children in order to traffic with their body parts.

42. "Dos detenidos en la iglesia de Santa María," *Excelsiór,* November 13, 1935.

43. "Una falsa versión originó un tumulto al ser sacadas las imágenes de un templo," *Excelsior,* May 7, 1936.

44. Both of these riots resemble the attempted lynching of two engineers in Cholula in September 1931. As explained in chapter 1, the engineers were falsely accused of wanting to destroy the church. Rus refers to a similar case in Chiapas in 1934, when a group of Chamulas organized guards after rumors circulated that anti-Catholic "quemasantos" (people who burn saints) would go to their town and burn the saints' images. See Rus, "The 'Comunidad Revolucionaria Institucional,'" 271–72.

45. Bantjes, "Idolatry and Iconoclasm in Revolutionary Mexico," 109–11.

46. As explained by Fallaw, there were important differences even among those revolutionaries who embraced iconoclasm. Some regarded it as a means to weaken the church's presence but did not necessarily oppose organized religion or even religious beliefs. Others, however, saw it as an instrument to eradicate religion altogether. Fallaw, "Varieties of Mexican Revolutionary Anticlericalism," 483–85.

47. Although Garrido Canabal's iconoclasm was particularly fierce, we should not forget that revolutionaries such as Obregón, Calles, and Cárdenas celebrated his actions and referred to Tabasco as an exemplar of the revolution. See Moreno, "Quemando santos para iluminar conciencias"; Kirshner, "Tomás Garrido Canabal and the Mexican Red Shirt Movement."

48. Kishner, "Tomás Garrido Canabal and the Mexican Red Shirt Movement," 102.

49. "Zafarrancho en la Villa de Coyoacán," *El Nacional,* December 31, 1934; "Responsables de crímenes en Coyoacán," *El Porvenir,* January 4, 1935; "Mexico Holds 40 for Killing of Five at Church," *Chicago Daily Tribune,* January 4, 1935; "War on Red Shirts In Mexico Follows Catholic Slayings," *Washington Post,* January 2, 1935; "Churchgoers Shot in Clash with Reds at Mexico Suburb," *Christian Science Monitor,* December 31, 1934; "62 Reds Are Held in Mexican Killing," *New York Times,* January 1, 1935.

50. The red and black flag symbolized the anticlerical and antireligious tendencies of socialist and communist ideas and came to epitomize, particularly after the 1940s, the infiltration of foreign ideas that were considered destabilizing for the nation. See Kirshner, "Tomás Garrido Canabal and the Mexican Red Shirt Movement," 103; Bantjes, *As If Jesus Walked on Earth,* 10. Revealing the tenacity of the red and black flag as an offensive symbol for Catholics, on September 15, 1968, more than three decades after the lynching of Ernesto

Malda, a mob incited by the local priest lynched five university workers in the small town of Canoa in the state of Puebla after being accused of attempting to hoist a red and black flag in the town's main plaza. They were also accused of wanting to remove the image of the town's patron saint, San Miguel, as well as of intending to kill the local priest, Enrique Meza Pérez.

51. "Zafarrancho en la Villa de Coyoacán," *El Nacional*.

52. Although the Red Shirts denied having used any weapons, subsequent reports indicated that the delegate from Coyoacán, who happened to be a close associate of Garrido Canabal, hid the weapons. See Kirshner, "Tomás Garrido Canabal and the Mexican Red Shirt Movement," 106. The *Christian Science Monitor* does report, based on interviews with unnamed officials, that it was the Red Shirts who opened fire against Catholics. "Churchgoers Shot in Clash with Reds at Mexico Suburb," *Christian Science Monitor*, December 31, 1934.

53. Kirshner, "Tomás Garrido Canabal and the Mexican Red Shirt Movement," 105.

54. Taracena, *La verdadera revolución mexicana*, 1.

55. "62 Reds Are Held in Mexican Killing," *New York Times*, January 1, 1935.

56. Malda's coffin was wrapped in the red and black flag. President Cárdenas sent a wreath of flowers for Malda's funeral and Garrido Canabal sent a telegram with his condolences to Malda's parents in which he praised the virility of the young Red Shirt. See Kirshner, "Tomás Garrido Canabal and the Mexican Red Shirt Movement," 110; "Responsables de crímenes en Coyoacán," *El Porvenir*, January 4, 1935.

57. "War on Red Shirts in Mexico Follows Catholic Slayings," *Washington Post*, January 2, 1935.

58. Catholics were particularly keen on the story of María de la Luz Camacho, a young female member of Acción Católica Mexicana, whose last words as she was being shot were "¡Viva Cristo Rey!" Camacho became the first martyr of the ACM, and Catholics saw in the story of her killing a testament to the state's ongoing war against Catholicism. See Parsons, *Mexican Martyrdom*, 239; López Melendez, "Mártires abandonados."

59. As discussed in chapter 1, violence against socialist teachers was particularly relevant for the narratives of martyrdom articulated by public officials.

60. It is important to note, however, that President Cárdenas made it clear that he would not continue to tolerate the provocations and recalcitrant actions of the Red Shirts. In June 1935, he pushed Garrido Canabal to step down from his position as minister of agriculture.

61. "Sistemática violencia," *El Nacional*, January 3, 1935.

62. "El linchamiento, táctica de lucha de los fanáticos," *El Nacional*, January 7, 1935.

63. This representation of lynchings as acts that reflected the ignorance and fanaticism of people contrasts with that articulated by the press in reference to lynchings driven by crime. In those cases, the press tended to emphasize the moral economy of lynching as well as justify their occurrence in light of crimes that were presented as abnormal and monstrous. See chapter 3.

64. The Mexican criminologist Carlos Franco Sodi offered an alternative representation of religious riots and lynchings. Rather than define them as pure frenzy, Sodi asserted that when mobs assaulted authorities in charge of applying the ley de cultos, they were committing a political crime, regardless of their reactionary and spontaneous character. See Sodi, "Muchedumbres delincuentes y delitos políticos."

65. A similar argument is offered by Salinas in reference to violence against teachers in Morelos. In his words, "Local devotees, and not the clergy per se, presented a grassroots bulwark against anticlerical impositions from the outside." Salinas, "Untangling Mexico's Noodle," 494.

66. In fact, the legitimacy of the use of violence became, at different points in time, a contentious issue between laypeople and clergy. At least officially, the church adopted a more critical stance toward violence at the end of the Cristero War and later on during the Second Cristiada, as well as during the 1940s in light of the actions carried out by recalcitrant Sinarquistas. See Butler, "Keeping the Faith in Revolutionary Mexico," 12–22; Blancarte, *Historia de la Iglesia católica en México*, 85.

67. AGN, IPS, Informe dirigido al C. Jefe de la Sección III y firmado por el Inspector Fernando A. Rodríguez, Caja 70, Exp. 11.

68. Although the federal inspector does not make much of it, the fact that Micaela was a spiritist probably also contributed to Catholics' hostility to her. As analyzed by Bastian, spiritists were, together with Protestants and Freemasons, among the religious practices that threatened Catholicism religion as they promoted pluralism, individualism, and the adoption of secularized moral values. See Bastian, "Protestants, Freemasons, and Spiritists."

69. "Numerosos muertos y heridos en Ciudad González," *Excélsior*, March 31, 1936; "Investigación de los sucesos en C. González," *Excélsior*, April 2, 1936. The town was also known as San Felipe Torres Mochas. The incident was represented in the collection of lithographs commissioned by the SEP and created by the graphic artist Leopoldo Méndez, under the title *Matanza de campesinos y maestros en San Felipe Torres Mochas, Gto*. See Méndez, *En nombre de Cristo*.

70. As explained by Bantjes, the organization of "cultural Sundays" and other cultural activities taking place at the time when religious rites were usually celebrated was not accidental. Rather, it was part of the government's attempt to replace religious festivals with civic and so-called patriotic rituals. Bantjes, "Idolatry and Iconoclasm in Revolutionary Mexico," 103.

71. For instance, the parish priest was directly responsible for the organization of the lynching of three sacrilegious robbers in the town of Los Reyes de Juárez, Puebla, in April 1959. Two men (former seminarians) and a woman were caught stealing icons from the church. The priest rang the town's church bells, prompting at least two hundred villagers to try to lynch the robbers. "Tres ladrones sacrílegos fueron linchados en Los Reyes," *La Prensa*, April 9, 1959; "Detienen al alcalde de Los Reyes, por el linchamiento," *La Prensa*, April 9, 1959.

72. Because priests were highly regarded by believers, it was not uncommon for physical assaults of priests to result in lynchings perpetrated by churchgoers against the alleged assailants. For examples, see "Escándalo al interior de una iglesia," *Excélsior*, January 28, 1936 (in San Miguel Allende, Guanajuato); "Un sacristán que amenaza de muerte a un cura," *La Prensa*, July 19, 1942 (in Gómez Palacio, Durango); "Bárbaro asesinato del señor cura de San Pablo," *La Prensa*, February 20, 1943 (in Mexico City); "Ocho mil feligreses rescataron a un cura," *La Prensa*, December 16, 1943 (in Dolores, Hidalgo); "Sacerdote católico a punto de morir en su templo acuchillado por un marihuano," *La Prensa*, May 23, 1944 (in Torreón, Coahuila); "Crece la indignación contra Valentino y quieren lincharlo," *La Opinión*, January 30, 1957 (in Mexico City).

73. Knight, "Popular Culture and the Revolutionary State in Mexico, 1910–1940," 416.

74. Blancarte, *Historia de la Iglesia católica en México*, 32.

75. *Diario Oficial*, México, December 13, 1934. Quoted in Raby "Ideología y construcción del Estado," 318.

76. Fallaw, *Religion and State Formation in Postrevolutionary Mexico*, 19. According to the Catholic Church, the right to private property had been given to men by God and could not be taken away by the state. Moreover, there were economic factors behind the church's opposition to agrarian reform as priests depended on tithes and had clientelistic relationships with landowners. See Blancarte, *Historia de la Iglesia católica en México*, 50; Fallaw, *Religion and State Formation in Postrevolutionary Mexico*, 6; Becker, "Torching La Purísima," 251.

77. Because it was a highly contentious issue that antagonized peasants, landlords, and priests, agrarian reform precipitated violent attacks against socialist teachers as well as agrarista peasants. Violence against agraristas was particularly pervasive in Veracruz. There, guardias blancas and the paramilitary organization known as Mano Negra (Black Hand) hanged, tortured, and assassinated hundreds of agrarista peasants. See Santoyo, "La Mano Negra en defensa de la propiedad y el orden"; Gillingham, "Who Killed Crispín Aguilar?"; Rashkin, "Representations of Violence in Testimonies of the Campesino Movement in Veracruz"; AGN, Ramo Presidentes, Lázaro Cárdenas, Serie Asesinatos, Caja 752, Exp. 541/262.

78. Bantjes, "Idolatry and Iconoclasm in Revolutionary Mexico," 112; Salinas, "Untangling Mexico's Noodle," 487; Becker, *Setting the Virgin on Fire*.

79. As argued by Vaughan, teachers' anticlericalism depended on a number of factors, which included their level of organization, their relationship with local and regional actors, and the strength of the clergy in given contexts. For instance, Puebla's teachers were generally less anticlerical than those of Sonora for these reasons. See Vaughan, "El papel político del magisterio socialista de México"; Fallaw, "Varieties of Mexican Revolutionary Anticlericalism," 502.

80. Becker, *Setting the Virgin on Fire*; Fallaw, "Varieties of Mexican Revolutionary Anticlericalism"; Vaughan, "El papel político del magisterio socialista de México."

81. "Trámite queja del C. Ildefonso Vega," April 9, 1938, AGN. DGG, Caja 56, Exp. 13, Foja 1.

82. The case is narrated in an essay written by the former teacher Simón Villanueva. The essay is part of a book series published by the SEP, which collected the testimonies of rural teachers during the years 1920–52. Villanueva, "El maestro rural en la educación," 185. The case is also quoted in Bantjes, "Idolatry and Iconoclasm in Revolutionary Mexico," 116.

83. Less dramatic in its consequences was the iconoclastic behavior of Francisco de Jesús, a teacher in the town of Yoloxóchitl, Guerrero. In his retelling of the event, Fallaw explains that when de Jesús set fire to a small cross, hoping to undermine villagers' religious reverence, he reached the opposite result: villagers tried to lynch him. Fallaw, *Religion and State Formation in Postrevolutionary Mexico*, 123.

84. Davis observes that, in contrast to Protestant rioters, Catholics tended to direct their violence more at the bodies of Protestants than at their material objects. In her words, "Injury and murder were a preferred mode of purifying the body social." Her explanation

for this is that for Catholics, "the persons of heretics" were the main source of danger and defilement, whereas for Protestants, it was Catholics' use of images and symbols that was considered heretical. Davis, "The Rites of Violence," 77.

85. Clemente Mendoza was a well-known vigilante leader who participated in the Second Cristiada and was also a veteran of the Cristero rebellion. He was particularly active in Puebla and Veracruz. "Tres maestros fueron asesinados en Puebla," *El Universal*, November 17, 1935; "Los asesinos de maestros muertos por las tropas," *El Universal*, November 27, 1935.

86. "Maestros socialistas sin orejas: Se las cortó un núcleo de gente alzada," *Excélsior*, November 19, 1935; "Fue horriblemente mutilada una Srita. Profesora," *El Universal*, November 19, 1935.

87. "Otra maestra que ha sido asesinada," *Excélsior*, November 23, 1935.

88. "Fue quemado vivo un maestro rural y otro más fue vilmente mutilado," *Excélsior*, April 21, 1936.

89. In a rally organized by teachers to denounce the violence perpetrated against them, they made special mention of teachers who had had their ears mutilated, particularly in the state of Veracruz. "Unificación del magisterio nacional: Se instaló la convención de maestros," *El Universal*, December 9, 1935.

90. Odilón Vega was responsible for the killing of a number of rural teachers in Puebla, including Alfonso Durán and Arnulfo Sosa. After being apprehended in 1940, he managed to escape from prison. Telegram to the Ministry of Interior from Fausto Molina, AGN, DAP, Serie Asesinatos, Caja 54, 2/012.2(18)24674, Exp. 54 ; "Se fugó ayer de la 'peni' Odilón Vega," *La Opinión*, July 20, 1940; "Está probada la fuga de Odilón Vega," *La Opinión*, July 24, 1940.

91. The insurgents Francisco Villa and Emiliano Zapata and their followers resorted to particularly gruesome forms of violence that included maiming prisoners' bodies, including removing the ears. Knight, *The Mexican Revolution*, 40. An even earlier reference to this practice appears in Beals's biography of Porfirio Díaz, in connection with the war against the Yaquis around 1896. Beals recounts that during this bloody war, "the soldier who could kill a Yaqui warrior and produce his victim's ears obtained a bounty of a hundred pesos." Beals, *Porfirio Díaz* 311. This is not to suggest that ear cropping was a distinctively "Mexican" practice but rather to point to the fact that perpetrators tended to use past enactments of violence in order to make their acts recognizable to a given audience. For instance, the prominent *segundero* El Tallarín was a former Zapatista militant and was thus probably exposed to this form of violence. See Salinas, "Untangling Mexico's Noodle."

92. The picture was taken when the two teachers visited Mexico City to demand from President Cárdenas justice and protection for teachers. Interestingly enough, one could argue that the picture also helped assert the image of teachers as martyrs of the revolution or even as pious elements, as the sisters look more like nuns than "subversive" teachers. "Llegan las maestras a quienes les cortaron los alzados las orejas," *Excélsior*, November 24, 1935.

93. "Mexicans Hang Teacher," *New York Times*, March 27, 1935.

94. "Mayor Hanged in Mexico," *New York Times*, June 2, 1935.

95. "Maestro víctima de unos vecinos," *Excélsior*, September 18, 1935.

96. The reference to these lynchings was published by the magazine *El maestro rural*, quoted in Raby, *Educación y revolución social en México*, 159–60.

97. Fallaw, *Religion and State Formation in Postrevolutionary Mexico*, 120.

98. Ibid., 121.
99. Raby, *Educación y revolución social en México*, 187–88.
100. Ibid., 197.
101. Salinas's characterization of El Tallarín is useful. As he suggests, the motivations of this segundero were as much about religion as they were about politics and agrarian grievances. Clemente Mendoza is also an interesting case. After executing him, federal troops found a note in which Mendoza stated his allegiance to the Virgin of Guadalupe and to Christ: "I do not want to fight, nor live, nor die, if it is not for the church and for you. Holy mother of Guadalupe, join this poor sinner in his agony; let his last breath on earth and his first song in heaven be: Viva Cristo Rey." See "Rinde informes de la investigación practicada en la Zona de Teziutlán, Puebla," AGN, IPS, Caja 71, Exp. 2.
102. "Otros asesinatos de la banda que manda el criminal Tallarín cometidos anteayer," *La Opinión*, March 2, 1938.
103. "Informando sobre el atentado en que perdieron la vida el profesor rural federal y los regidores del Ayto. de Tochimilco," Letter to the Minister of the Interior signed by Gov. Maximino Ávila Camacho, AGN, DAP, Serie Asesinatos, Caja 55, 2/012.2 (18), Exp. 28.
104. "Se protesta enérgicamente por el asesinato del compañero Prof. José Ramírez Martínez, Maestro del Estado de Puebla," Letter to the president signed by Jesus Ceja, AGN, DAP, Serie Asesinatos, Caja 55, 2/012.2 (18), Exp. 30.
105. In Michoacán, the assassination of the teacher María Salud Morales in June 1937 seems equally opaque as far as the identity of the victimizers. Whereas one source indicated that she was beaten with stones and sticks by a group of religious fanatics, another suggested she was attacked by a group of armed Cristeros supported by the local priest, Cipriano Zarpién. The case is discussed in Raby, "Los maestros rurales y los conflictos sociales," 193.
106. "Fue serio lo acaecido en Tochimilco según dice la Comandancia de la zona," *La Opinión*, March 3, 1938.
107. AGN, DAP, Serie Asesinatos, "Rinde informes de la investigación practicada en la Zona de Teziutlán, Puebla," Caja 53, Exp. 62; see also "Tres maestros más fueron asesinados en el ed. de Puebla," *Excélsior*, November 17, 1935.
108. Catholic villagers also supported the actions of El Tallarín against anticlerical teachers in the state of Morelos. See Salinas, "Untangling Mexico's Noodle," 492. Likewise, Catholic activists provided logistical support and arms to the Cristero leader Lauro Rocha, who operated in the region of Los Altos de Jaliscos during the 1930s and was probably responsible for attacking Micaela and Enriqueta Palacios. In November and December 1935, for instance, newspapers reported the detention of various members of the LNDLR in connection with Rocha's seditious activities against socialist teachers. Although some of them denied their involvement, María Luisa Ruiz Velazco Mier, a Catholic woman in her fifties, proudly accepted her responsibility for buying and providing arms to Rocha in order to fight against socialist education. See "Declararon ayer los católicos detenidos," *El Universal*, November 24, 1935; "Declararon los católicos ante el juez," *El Universal*, December 1, 1935.
109. Fallaw, *Religion and State Formation in Postrevolutionary Mexico*, 120.
110. Letter addressed to President Cárdenas and signed by Juan Efraín González on behalf of the Unión de Maestros Federales of the 11th Zone, November 17, 1935, AGN, DAP, Serie Asesinatos, "Rinde informes de la investigación practicada en la Zona de Teziutlán, Puebla," Caja 53, Exp. 62.

111. Letter addressed to President Cárdenas and signed by José Parra, October 14, 1935, AGN, DGG, Serie Asesinatos, 2. 340/11 10515, Exp. 13.

112. "Fue detenido un Sr. Presbítero," *La Opinión*, July 2, 1936.

113. Claiming that Tonalá had always been "a den of Cristeros," Rodríguez claimed that priests had mobilized everyone in the town, including señoritas, parents, and children. He also stated that the priest had told parents that "it is better for children to enter glory like donkeys than enter wise to hell." Letter addressed to the Minister of the Interior and signed by teacher Luis N. Rodríguez, May 20, 1938, AGN, DGG, Serie Asesinatos, 2. 340/11 10515, Exp. 13.

114. From the 139 attacks against socialist teachers that Raby documents during 1932 and 1940, there were only 20 cases that took place after 1938, between 1939 and 1940. The vast majority of cases are concentrated in the years 1935-38. See Raby, "Los maestros rurales y los conflictos sociales," 216-25. The latest example that I found of an attack on a teacher was reported in 1941 in Temoaya, Estado de México. The victim had opened a school for indigenous children. Two hundred villagers participated in the lynching. "Como represalia por la actitud que se adopte contra los que ultrajaron la bandera, han quemado más escuelas," *El Porvenir*, May 29, 1941.

115. Beginning in 1936, Cárdenas started to stress that the main goal of socialist education was not to fight religion but to promote modernization of the countryside. Bantjes, "Idolatry and Iconoclasm in Revolutionary Mexico," 119.

116. As explained by Blancarte, one of the events that marked the beginning of a new modus vivendi between state and church was the exhortation to Catholics, by the archbishop of Guadalajara, José Garibi Rivera, to contribute to the payment of Mexico's foreign debt in the context of the nationalization of oil reserves. Blancarte, *Historia de la Iglesia católica en México*, 58-59.

117. See, e.g., "Bárbaro linchamiento de ladrones sacrílegos," *La Prensa*, October 17, 1941; "Los ladrones sacrílegos fueron linchados en Los Reyes," *Excélsior*, April 9, 1959 (Los Reyes, Tepeaca, Puebla); "A manos de la plebe enfurecida pereció el ladrón de un templo," *La Prensa*, August 24, 1941; "La multitud linchó a uno de los 3 bravucones que profanaron la iglesia," *La Prensa*, September 7, 1941 (Veracruz); "Iban a linchar a uno que robó candelabros en pequeño templo," *La Prensa*, April 20, 1943 (Mexico City); "Horripilante linchamiento de un muchacho sacrílego," *La Prensa*, June 5, 1943 (Estado de México); "Ladrón sacrílego sorprendido cuando robaba una capilla," *La Prensa*, December 9, 1944 (Mexico City).

118. "Templo protestante atacado por exaltados," *La Prensa*, April 21, 1944. The use of the national flag by Sinarquistas signaled their appropriation of national symbols and their deployment of a nationalist ideology.

119. The UNS was characterized by the use of aggressive and even militaristic strategies. Driven by concerns about the advancement of socialism, modern capitalism, and the encroachment of a centralized state, Sinarquistas were strongest in the Bajío region, but their presence expanded during the 1940s to central and southeastern Mexico. Although the Catholic Church considered it part of its strategy to regain "social authority in the wake of leftist revolutions," it lacked control over its actions and did not officially approve of its use of violence. Fallaw, *Religion and State Formation in Postrevolutionary Mexico*, 145; see also Blancarte, *Historia de la Iglesia católica en México*, 85; Serrano Álvarez, "El sinarquismo en el Bajío mexicano," 199; De la Luz, "Ciudadanía, representación, y participación cívico-política de los evangélicos mexicanos," 16; Dormandy, *Primitive Revolution*, 108-11.

120. During the same month (May 1944), the press reported that a young woman, Jacinta García, had been burned alive by a group of Catholics in the town of Guadalupe Victoria, Puebla. "Joven quemada viva como en los tiempos de la inquisición," *La Prensa*, May 25, 1944. The news, however, turned out to be false. De la Luz, "Ciudadanía, representación, y participación cívico-política de los evangélicos mexicanos," 2.

121. De la Luz, "Ciudadanía, representación, y participación cívico-política de los evangélicos mexicanos," 21–22. We are reminded here that, in contrast to Catholics, Protestants do not use crosses when they bury their dead.

122. Sandoval Forero, "Familias indígenas conversas," 23–24.

123. Anti-Protestant sentiments were certainly not new. Closely linked to the anti-American attitudes that had developed over the years following the Mexican-American War of 1846, anti-Protestantism grew as a result of the success of Protestant missionaries in converting Mexicans. See Bloch and Ortoll, "¡Viva México! ¡Mueran los Yanquis!" For previous examples of lynching and rioting against Protestants, including cases involving American nationals, see SRE-AH, Fondo Embajada de Estados Unidos, Tomo 445 (Aguascalientes, September 15, 1896); "Report 2 Preachers Lynched in Mexico," *New York Times*, February 7, 1923; "Report American Lynched," *New York Times*, August 3, 1926.

124. It also enabled the reopening of Catholic schools that had been closed down under the previous post-revolutionary governments. Camp, *Cruce de espadas*, 48–49; Dávila, *Las Santas Batallas*, 91–92.

125. Niblo, *Mexico in the 1940s*, 89.

126. The letter was published on November 8, 1943, and it was meant to promote Catholics' support of the Mexican government's decision to participate in World War II. Quoted in Meyer, *La Iglesia católica en México*, 22.

127. De la Luz García, "El pentecostalismo en México," 204.

128. Quoted in Pérez, "Censura y control," 93–94.

129. For instance, in March 1950, a group of Catholics from the town of San Gabriel Ometoxtla in Cholula, Puebla, addressed the president to denounce the presence of two temples of the Mormon church which, they claimed, operated without the proper permit of the minister of the interior. They furthermore stated that unless the government took the necessary measures to expropriate these temples, "serious incidents" would continue to take place in the town, as "members of this church have disregarded national symbols, including the image of the Virgen Guadalupana." AGN, MAV, Serie Conflictos Religiosos, Exp. 547.4/167

130. De la Luz, "Ciudadanía, representación, y participación cívico-política de los evangélicos mexicanos," 14.

131. Anti-Protestant violence was not limited to Mexico. In Colombia, during the period of "La Violencia" (1940s–1950s), anticommunist Catholics sympathetic to the Conservative Party harassed, intimidated, and killed Protestants who were accused of supporting the Liberal Party. In Brazil, anti-Protestant violence was also present during the 1930s and 1940s following Catholics' attempt to restore Catholicism as the national religion. In all three countries, violence against Protestants appears to be underpinned by nationalist sentiments as well as by Catholics' anxieties regarding the increasing presence of Protestant religions. See Dailey, "Religious Aspects of Colombia's 'La Violencia'"; Helgen, *Religious Conflict* .

132. "Iba a ser linchado un propagandista protestante en Guanajuato," *La Prensa*, December 8, 1944.

133. "Iban a linchar a dos propagandistas protestantes en templo de Coyoacán," *La Prensa*, March 31, 1945. Just a month after this incident, a riot broke out between groups of Catholics and Protestants after the latter entered a Catholic church in the town of Soyaniquilpan, Estado de México, and started to distribute leaflets while the parish priest was giving his sermon. Members of both religious groups were killed during the riot. "Encuentro a balazos entre católicos y protestantes," *La Prensa*, June 3, 1945.

134. *El Universal* referred to this case a few years later, when it reported that a man accused of instigating the attack had been found guilty and that the Supreme Court had confirmed the charges against him. "El que emepezó a linchar a un policía fue aprehendido," *El Universal*, November 9, 1951.

135. In 1940, 96.6 percent of the country's total population identified as Catholic. In contrast, 1.2 percent identified as non-Catholic. Although this percentage is very low, it had more than doubled in relation to the last decade of the nineteenth century (by 1895, this percentage was only 0.3). INEGI, *La diversidad religiosa en México*, 5–8. More specifically, the proportion of Protestants in Mexico went from 0.4 percent in 1900 to 0.91 percent in 1940. See Gross, "Protestantism and Modernity," 481; De la Luz, "El pentecostalismo en México," 205.

136. As explained by Blancarte, Mexico's entry into World War II and its cooperation with the United States triggered the Catholic Church's fears regarding the potential arrival of Protestant missioners and the corresponding expansion of this religion's adherents. Blancarte, *Historia de la Iglesia católica en México*, 105. On the expansion of Protestantism (particularly Pentecostalism) as a result of U.S.-Mexico migration and the Catholic Church's efforts to prevent it, see Ramírez, *Migrating Faith*.

137. Protestants, together with Freemasons and spiritists, were part of those "non-Catholic religious sociabilities" that, according to Bastian, allowed revolutionaries to break with the traditional structures promoted by the Catholic Church. Bastian, "Protestants, Freemasons, and Spiritists," 83–85; Blancarte, *Historia de la Iglesia católica en México*, 75. Protestants strongly identified with and actively participated in the Mexican Revolution, particularly under Francisco Madero and Venustiano Carranza. On the ideological affinities between Protestants and revolutionaries during the 1910s and 1920s, see Baldwin, "Broken Traditions."

138. Fallaw, "Varieties of Mexican Revolutionary Anticlericalism," 504; Vaughan, "Cultural Politics in Revolution," 91. On Protestants' support of agraristas and socialism in postrevolutionary Oaxaca, see McIntyre, "'All of Their Customs Are Daughters of Their Religion.'"

139. De la Luz, "El pentecostalismo en México y su propuesta de experiencia religiosa e identidad nacional," 201. On Mexico's antialcohol campaigns, see Pierce, "Parades, Epistles and Prohibitive Legislation"; Fallaw, "Dry Law, Wet Politics."

140. These types of festivities usually involve the consumption of alcohol and the veneration of religious images. Sandoval, "Familias indígenas conversas," 18.

141. The cargo system was particularly relevant to the organization of religious festivities. Although it initially functioned as a means to enable communal integration and economic redistribution, it evolved into a system that contributed to the reproduction of the dynamics of power and inequality that benefited local caciques. According to scholars such as Bastian and Dow, the religious conversion of indigenous Catholics to Protestantism—especially during the 1970s—can be explained as a means to break with the burden imposed

by the cargo system. See Bastian, "Violencia, etnicidad y religión entre los mayas del estado de Chiapas en México," 304–5; Dow, "The Expansion of Protestantism in Mexico."

142. "Otro sangriento zafarrancho entre católicos y protestantes, ocurrió," *La Prensa*, March 24, 1945.

143. "Sangriento ataque contra un grupo de protestantes," *La Prensa*, May 29, 1945.

144. AGN, MAC, Serie Asesinatos/Atropellos, Exp. 542.1/1221.

145. Two telegrams were sent in the following days to the president and to the governor of Puebla stating that Sinarquistas had threatened to burn down their houses within the next seventy-two hours if they did not leave the town. See AGN, MAC, Serie Asesinatos/Atropellos, Exp. 542.1/1221. A similar case had taken place in Puebla the year before. On December 30, 1944, in the municipality of Huatlatlahuca, a group of Evangelicals claimed that local authorities, including the local judge, had imprisoned them only for practicing their religion. AGN, MAC, Serie Asesinatos/Atropellos, Exp. 547.5/22.

146. David G. Ruesga was a Pentecostal priest who had converted to Protestantism while in Dallas, Texas, and had returned to Mexico in the 1920s. He would become one of the leading voices in denouncing violence against Protestants and was an active member of the Evangelicals' National Defense Committee. De la Luz, "El pentecostalismo en México," 200. To see further examples of Ruesga's petitions and telegrams sent to the federal authorities, see AGN, MAV, Serie conflictos religiosos, Exp. 547.5/3.

147. AGN, MAC, Serie Asesinatos/Atropellos, Exp. 547.5/22. During July and August 1945, Evangelicals denounced the occurrence of more incidents of violence in Puebla. In July 1945, in a telegram sent to the president, Evangelicals urged federal authorities to intervene as a large group of Sinarquistas had surrounded their church and killed many of their members.

148. Letter signed by José María González and Marcelino Vargas, addressed to the Minister of the Interior, AGN, DGIPS, Caja 98, Exp. 20.

149. Informe de Ing. Carlos Reyes Retana, AGN, DGIPS, Caja 98, Exp. 20.

150. A similar case is discussed in Oscar Lewis's *Five Families*. In that case Pedro Martínez, the father of one of the families interviewed by Lewis, had converted to Protestantism, igniting the anger of his neighbors. Once, a rumor spread about Pedro's intention to "burn the saints," resulting in a series of attacks on him and his family. Pedro was stoned, and his children were vilified at school. His daughter was once "dragged by her hair toward the church to force her to kiss the priest's hand." See Lewis, *Five Families*, 42.

151. In August 1947, in the towns of Xonacatlán and Cuyuaco, Puebla, Catholics incited by the local priest engaged in acts of religious persecution against Evangelicals. See Telegram to President Miguel Alemán by David G. Ruesga, AGN, MAV, Serie conflictos religiosos, Exp. 547.5/. In August 1948, José Octavio Dávila demanded protection for Santiago Mena, who had been seriously injured for being a member of the Church of Jesus Christ of Latter-Day Saints in the town of San Nicolás de los Ranchos, Puebla. See AGN, MAV, Serie conflictos religiosos, Exp. 547.5/6. In December 1948, a group of Catholics who had been incited by the local priest assassinated the Evangelical Antonio de la Cruz Carmona in Almoloya de Juárez, Estado de México. Evangelicals also denounced the arbitrary detention of Espiridión Carmona by local authorities. See AGN, MAV, Serie Homicidios, Exp. 541/502. On July 3, 1949, in the town of Coronago in Cholula, Puebla, a group of more than twenty people attacked a family of Evangelicals, with the support of the mayor, the police commander, and

the president of the agrarian commission. "Tremendo zafarrancho en un pueblo," *La Opinión,* July 7, 1949; "Se averigua un nefando crimen," *La Opinión,* July 13, 1949. On June 10, 1955, Protestants protested that a group of Catholics had threatened to expel them from their town, Santa Úrsula, despite the fact that they did not worship in public but only in the privacy of their homes, as established by the law. See AGN, ARC, Serie Conflictos Religiosos, Exp. 547.1/73. On August 11, 1958, a "Catholic crowd" armed with pistols and stones attacked several Evangelicals in the middle of the night in Hueytamalco, Puebla. The crowd was led by Sixto Rojas and Silvestre Bandala. See AGN, ARC, Serie Conflictos Religiosos, Exp. 571.1/167.

152. De la Luz, "Ciudadanía, representación, y participación cívico-política de los evangélicos mexicanos," 15.

153. Attacks against Protestants continued to occur throughout the 1940s, 1950s, and subsequent decades. For examples, see the following articles on cases in Hidalgo, Puebla, and Estado de México: "Agitador al que se inculpa de un bestial linchamiento," *El Nacional,* April 16, 1960; "Alcalde inquisidor," *El Liberal Poblano,* September 4, 1963; "1,500 fanáticos intentaron linchar a 1,700 protestantes," *El Porvenir,* August 6, 1963; "Persecusión de evangelistas," *Novedades de Puebla,* September 20, 1968. See also AGN, DGIPS, Caja 1505C, Exp. 10–11, for lynchings and attempted lynchings in Toluca and Oaxaca in 1979 and 1980, respectively.

CHAPTER THREE. THE LYNCHING OF ATROCIOUS CRIMINALS

1. "¡Muerte al chacal! La multitud pidió al monstruo para lincharlo," *La Prensa,* April 22, 1943; "El entierro de las víctimas convertido en un mitin de protesta," *La Prensa,* April 22, 1943.

2. "Violento careo del chacal y las niñas," *La Prensa,* May 14, 1943.

3. Granted, Anguiano Armenta and Cárdenas Hernández came from very different social backgrounds. Whereas the latter was a chemistry student from a middle-class family, Anguiano Armenta was a working-class man with no apparent education. For a comprehensive discussion of the Cárdenas Hernández case and its implications for public debates surrounding the death penalty, see Meade, "From Sex Strangler to Model Citizen."

4. In 1940 nationally, approximately 42 percent of adults could read and write. This percentage increased in the following decades, making newspapers the main means to transmit information, even more than the radio. See Piccato, "Notes for a History of the Press in Mexico," 45–48; Meade, "The Plaza Is for the *Populacho,*" 315; Smith, *The Mexican Press and Civil Society,* 13–14.

5. In the U.S. South, newspapers also contributed to rendering lynching as an inevitable and suitable response to hideous crimes that could not be punished accordingly by legal means. See Dray, *At the Hands of Persons Unknown,* 4–5.

6. Tabloids were particularly popular during the period, with *La Prensa* being the most successful daily in terms of sales. Smith, *The Mexican Press and Civil Society,* 14–15; Piccato, "Murders of Nota Roja," 203–4.

7. On the role of crime news in public debates about justice in post-revolutionary Mexico, see Piccato, "Murders of Nota Roja"; Meade, "From Sex Strangler to Model Citizen," 323–77; Santamaría, "Legitimating Lynching," 44–60.

8. As argued by Buffington and Piccato, press coverage of social transgressions, even when characterized by its sensational and "entertaining" character, also provided "lessons"

about the moral and social implications of crime." They further contributed to delineating the boundaries between tolerable and intolerable behavior. Buffington and Piccato, "Introduction," 8.

9. See Piccato, "Ley Fuga as Justice"; see also Gillingham, "Who Killed Crispín Aguilar?"

10. According to crime statistics compiled by Piccato, the homicide rate at the national level went from 38 per 100,000 inhabitants in 1936–40 to 31 per 100,000 between 1941 and 1946. Homicide levels continued to decrease nationally until well into the twenty-first century. This trend was reversed only in 2008. See Piccato, "Estadísticas del crimen en México"; see also INEGI, Comunicado de Prensa Núm. 374/19.

11. "El primer criminal linchado en México," *La Prensa*, April 21, 1930.

12. "Primer caso de linchamiento," *El Porvenir*, April 24, 1930.

13. Historical evidence of lynchings in the country goes back at least to the eighteenth century in the form of communal, extralegal, and cruel forms of punishment perpetrated against authorities—from tax collectors to parish priests and mayors. See Taylor, *Drinking, Homicide and Rebellion in Colonial Mexican Villages*, 115–18.

14. "Fue linchado un asesino," *La Opinión*, April 15, 1930.

15. Meade, "From Sex Strangler to Model Citizen," 353. President Manuel Ávila Camacho temporarily reinstated the death penalty through an emergency decree in the context of World War II but only for cases of robbery on highways or deserted areas.

16. As stated by Piccato, murder was seldom punished in post-revolutionary Mexico: only 38 percent of indicted murderers were found guilty between 1926 and 1952. Piccato, "Murders of Nota Roja," 227.

17. "Crimen sin nombre se cometió en la persona de una niña," *La Opinión*, July 9, 1933.

18. For instance, on July 16, 1934, a man accused of having raped an eight-year-old girl in Puebla was shot twice by two police officers while he was being taken to prison. The press and public officials claimed the so-called rapist was trying to escape. "Pagó con su vida el ultraje a una niña," *La Opinión*, July 16, 1934. To see an analysis of other cases, see Piccato, "Ley Fuga as Justice."

19. "¿Se aplicó la ley fuga a los asesinos de una niña?," *La Opinión*, July 16, 1933.

20. "Alleged Girl Slayer Executed in Mexico," *New York Times*, February 18, 1938. In his account of the events, Vanderwood explains Castillo Morales was made to run for his life as two execution squads shot at him in front of hundreds of people. In this sense, his execution was a sort of "staged" ley fuga with some but not all elements required by martial law for the execution of a convicted soldier. See Vanderwood, *Juan Soldado*, 49, 54–55.

21. See Vanderwood, *Juan Soldado*, 51–72.

22. "El sanguinario alcalde de San Andrés Tuxtla y su pistolero de confianza, presos y apunto de ser linchados por el pueblo," *La Prensa*, December 5, 1941.

23. "El asesino de Ixtlahuaca, a punto de ser linchado por la multitud poseída de coraje," *La Prensa*, August 27, 1942.

24. "El populacho indigando iba a linchar a dos chacalazos," *La Prensa*, September 4, 1944.

25. It is highly unlikely that the Herrera brothers would have been punished with the death penalty as it had been only temporarily reinstated for cases of highway robbery or assault. Besides, as argued by Meade, the president pardoned most of those who were sentenced to death. See Meade, "From Sex Strangler to Model Citizen," 375.

26. For some examples of so-called murderers who were threatened with lynching but were saved by the police, see "Desalmado sujeto que estuvo a punto de ser linchado por un grupo numeroso de gentes," *El Nacional*, April 9, 1933; "Guarnición federal en el sur del estado," *El Porvenir*, March 29, 1935; "Horrible tragedia ocurrió ayer en la calle del General Regules," *La Prensa*, March 23, 1942; "A pedradas le dieron muerte a un nevero," *La Prensa*, April 29, 1942; "Estuvo a punto de ser linchado por el asesinato de un individuo," *La Prensa*, September 1, 1942; "Cabareteras y clientes iban a lincharlo por asesino," *La Prensa*, January 13, 1943; " "Un asesino estuvo a punto de ser linchado por la multitud," *El Universal*, May 13, 1952; "El estrangulador a punto de ser linchado por una turbamulta," *El Porvenir*, December 1, 1956.

27. In addition to participating in the settlement of political vendettas in post-revolutionary Mexico, police officers worked as pistoleros for local power brokers and profited directly from criminal activities. See Rath, *Myths of Demilitarization*, 115–43; Davis, "Policing and Regime Transition"; Águila and Bortz, "The Rise of Gangsterism and Charrismo"; Smith, *Pistoleros and Popular Movements*; Piccato, *A History of Infamy*, 161–90.

28. Extract of letter written by Juana Gonzalez, March 8, 1933, AGN, ALR, Exp. 542/253.

29. Letter addressed to the president, signed by Delfina Castro de García, July 1940, AGN, DAP, Serie Asesinatos, Caja 52, 2/012.2(18–132)/1, Exp. 46; "Se inserta informe del C. Presidente Mpal. en el que comunica la muerte del extinto bandolero José García Pinto," August 17, 1940, AGN, DAP, Serie Asesinatos, Caja 52, 2/012.2(18–132)/1, Exp. 46. For other examples, see AGN, ARC, Exp. 541/484 (telegram to the president signed by Servando Espinosa regarding the criminal activities of policemen in Matamoros, Tamaulipas, March 17, 1955); AGN, ARC, Exp. 541/518 (transcription of an article that describes the torture and assassination of Miguel Prieto Mora by a group of policemen in Otatilán, Veracruz, July 25, 1957).

30. "Furiosa multitud quiso aplicar tremenda sanción a individuo que hirió a otro," *Excélsior*, October 23, 1940.

31. "Monstruoso ebrio balaceó a un niño por ridículos celos," *La Prensa*, January 23, 1943.

32. "Un pistolero de políticos linchado por la multitud de la Ciudad de Torreón," *Excélsior*, Februrary 21, 1940.

33. As this example suggests, many victims of lynching were not simply killed but "overkilled." The lynching of José Galván, a man who was responsible for killing at least six people in Jilotepec, Estado de México, also involved excessive use of violence. After being lynched by a crowd of dozens of people who stabbed and shot him until he showed no sign of life, Galván's "bloody corpse" was dragged by horse through the main streets of the town. "Fue linchado un asesino de negra historia y se arrastró su cadaver," *La Prensa*, September 20, 1943. A related newspaper article told of people from Jilotepec and surrounding towns celebrating a mass thanking God for the lynching of this man, who was known also as "Pancho Villa." "Acción de gracias por el linchamiento de Pancho Villa," *La Prensa*, September 21, 1943.

34. "Una multitud de quinientas personas trató de linchar en Jilotepec a infame asesino," *La Prensa*, June 1, 1943. The press reported that a few days earlier Dolores Alcántara had shot a man in front of hundreds of people at the town's street market (*tianguis*). On that occasion, the press reported villagers were infuriated and had already tried to seize the criminal in order to lynch him but could not do so because the mayor had him taken into police custody. "Brutal asesino iba a ser linchado en Jilotepec," *La Prensa*, May 18, 1943.

35. Santiago Burgos Brito, "Un linchamiento en Yucatán," *El Informador,* June 5, 1942.

36. "Linchamiento," *El Nacional,* May 22, 1945.

37. According to *La Prensa* the two men had murdered close to forty people. The men were stoned and clubbed to death by men, women, and even children. "Linchamiento de 2 torvos chacales," *La Prensa,* May 22, 1945.

38. "La multitud quiso linchar a los descuartizadores," *La Prensa,* July 30, 1950.

39. The collective killing of Leonardo Blancas, a murderer who was shot by a group of peasants was also described as a case of ley fuga, even though it did not involve state authorities and was presented as an act of "popular vengeance." See "Venganza colectiva contra un asesino," *La Prensa,* August 10, 1943.

40. The public indignation caused by the killing of Mr. Urbano was such that weeks later the press reported the murderers were threatened with lynching inside the Lecumberri prison. "Los chacales amenazados," *La Prensa,* August 3, 1950. This was not the first time crime news mentioned the danger that criminals would be lynched inside prison by other inmates. On April 15, 1941, for instance, *La Prensa* reported that inmates at the women's prison at Lecumberri awaited Felicita Sánchez Aguillón, aka "la hyena," in order to lynch her. Felicita was accused of helping kill and disappear the bodies of infants that had been born to unmarried mothers. "Van a linchar si pueden a la mujer hiena," *La Prensa,* April 15, 1941. On the crimes of Felicita Sánchez Aguillón and other female transgressors, see Santillán Esqueda, "Mujeres delincuentes e imaginarios."

41. Mónico Neck, "Apuntes de actualidad," *El Nacional,* August 2, 1950.

42. Piccato, "Estadísticas del crimen en México."

43. Tellingly, Meade narrates that the first convicted criminal who was spared the death penalty due to its recent elimination was shot "while trying to escape" from the Islas Marías penal colony. Meade, "From Sex Strangler to Model Citizen," 355–56; see also Piccato, *A History of Infamy,* 122.

44. "Protección contra el crimen," *Excélsior,* November 12, 1953.

45. "Bestial orgía de ocho chacales," *La Prensa,* February 5, 1944.

46. "La pena de muerte," *El Informador,* September 21, 1956. The same newspaper published an analogous editorial a few months earlier: "Consideraciones sobre la pena de muerte," *El Informador,* July 29, 1956.

47. Accusations of child theft played a prominent role in the organization of lynchings. Albeit less frequent, car accidents, especially those that resulted in the injury or death of a child, also precipitated mob violence.

48. Buffington and Piccato, *True Stories of Crime in Modern Mexico,* 11–15; Castillo, Lucero, and Swedberg, *Voices of Crime,* 3–4; Santamaría and Carey, *Violence and Crime in Latin America,* 4–18.

49. Snodgrass Godoy, for instance, has argued, "Lynchings are more a reaction to fear and insecurity than they are to crime *per se.*" The former observation is based on the fact that in the context of Guatemala lynching does not necessarily happen in those places where levels of crime are greater but where perceptions of insecurity are higher. Snodgrass, "When 'Justice' Is Criminal," 628.

50. See Garland, "Penal Excess and Surplus Meaning," 813–16.

51. "Iba a ser linchada una madre que dejó a su hija," *La Prensa,* June 16, 1930.

52. "Iban a matar a una madre cruel," *La Prensa,* March 12, 1930.

53. "Una madre convertida en hiena quería matar a palos a su propia hija," *La Prensa*, March 31, 1943.

54. "Desnaturalizada madre abandonó a sus hijos, muriendo uno de ellos," *El Nacional*, June 1, 1953.

55. The notion of "responsible motherhood" implied that mothers were to be the main caregivers in the family and that they had to undertake child-rearing practices that ensured the good health of their children as well as the "quality" of future generations. See Stern, "Responsible Mothers and Normal Children," 375; Bliss, "Mothers of Invention," 249–50.

56. The gendered dimension of these narratives of motherhood becomes evident in the fact that there was no mention in the news about "careless" or "abandoning" fathers, despite the fact that many of the women in these stories were described as single mothers. For a discussion of how gender informed representations of violent or "deviant" women in the press, see Santillán Esqueda, "Mujeres delincuentes e imaginarios."

57. "Hombre fiera que intentó matar a su madre, iba a morir linchado," *La Prensa*, June 30, 1941. A similar case of a man who tried to strangle his mother and was nearly lynched by a group of neighbors in Mexico City was reported only a month later. See "Hijo infame estuvo a punto de ahorcar a su madre y la multitud iba a lincharlo," *La Prensa*, July 28, 1941.

58. "Lo medio mató la multitud furibunda cuando iba a ultrajar a su madre," *La Prensa*, March 31, 1942.

59. For other examples of "bad children" who were lynched or threatened with lynching due to their abusive behavior, see "Iba a ser linchado un salvaje hijo que golpeó a su padre," *La Prensa*, July 30, 1930; "Iba a matar a su madre un degenerado," *La Prensa*, December 5, 1930; "Agredió a su padre y la multitud irritada trató de lincharlo," *La Prensa*, January 17, 1941; "Un hijo desnaturalizado que golpeó a su padre fue muerto por el pueblo indignado," *La Prensa*, April 11, 1941; "Holgazán y brutal tipo acuchilló a su madre," *La Prensa*, January 10, 1944.

60. The notion of alcohol as a substance that had a pernicious effect on the social order and on people's "proclivity" to commit crimes was not new but had been advanced by various criminologists at the turn of the twentieth century. See Buffington, *Criminal and Citizen in Modern Mexico*, 99–102.

61. As in the case of murderers, references to the animal-like behavior of abusive sons were not uncommon. In the case of Rafael Saavedra mentioned above, for instance, the press described how Rafael's hands were transformed into the "claws of a beast" when he was strangling his mother. "Hombre fiera que intentó matar a su madre, iba a morir linchado," *La Prensa*, June 30, 1941.

62. See "Un hijo desnaturalizado trataba de degollar a su padre con una navaja," *La Prensa*, June 21, 1942; "A machetazos asesinó a su madre," *La Prensa*, September 3, 1942; "Mató a su madre a pedradas," *La Prensa*, September 21, 1943.

63. See Pierce, "Parades, Epistles and Prohibitive Legislation"; Fallaw, "Dry Law, Wet Politics," 40–42; Campos, *Home Grown*, 197–200.

64. Piccato, *City of Suspects*, 105.

65. "Iban a linchar a un cafre que macheteó a su infeliz mujer," *La Prensa*, February 19, 1941. A similar case took place in the neighborhood of La Estrella in Mexico City against a drunkard who had beaten his wife and stepson. Neighbors armed with stones tried to lynch the man, but the police prevented the incident. See "Energúmeno a punto de ser linchado por la multitud," *La Prensa*, July 27, 1950.

66. "Espeluznante 'chacal' despedazó a hachazos a su mujer y los trozos macabros los arrojó a los coyotes," *La Prensa*, December 20, 1942.

67. "Un golpeador de mujeres a punto de ser linchado," *La Prensa*, October 17, 1943.

68. "Indignación popular contra los autores de salvaje atentado," *La Prensa*, September 22, 1940.

69. Another case involved a group of female vendors who tried to lynch J. Inés Rizo Orozco in the market of La Merced in Mexico City after he threatened them with a knife. According to the press, the police had to intervene to save the man from the group of women, who left their assailant's face beaten and badly scratched. "Mercaderes que iban a linchar a un valiente," *La Prensa*, January 23, 1931.

70. That someone suspected of raping girls would be called a "satyr" reinforced a notion of masculinity predicated on men's "uncontrollable" and "instinctual" sexual desires. Crime news also used the word *instinct* to refer to a rapist's sexual conduct, which reiterated his behavior as somehow natural or inescapable. For instance, the press referred to a man accused of having raped eight girls as "the Satyr of Duesseldorff" and stated that he had "fed his beastly instincts in eight innocent girls from six to eight years." The man was attacked by a group of women that included some of the victims' mothers. See "8 pequeñas víctimas de un chacalote," *La Prensa*, September 14, 1943. On the notion of men as "naturally" inclined to sexual promiscuity, see also Bliss, "Mothers of Invention," 252.

71. "Incalificable crimen se cometió con una niña de 13 años," *La Opinión*, May 14, 1930.

72. The same newspaper reported two similar incidents in the following years. On August 5, 1937, it reported that the "disgusting rapist" of seven-year-old Refugio Simo was almost killed in an attempted lynching incited by his vile actions and the "justified popular rage" it generated. And on June 24, 1938, in the town of San Martín Tlapala, Atlixco, it reported that Lorenzo Gómez had been lynched by a group of people who "were forced" to carry out such an action because the man had raped two young women. See "Asqueroso sátiro que estuvo a punto de morir linchado," *La Opinión*, August 5, 1937; "Lyncharon a un sátiro en Tlapala, ayer," *La Opinión*, June 24, 1938.

73. "El sátiro iba a ser linchado por la multitud," *La Prensa*, June 5, 1942.

74. A similar case was reported in Mexico City the same month. In this case, a man was accused of trying to rape a three-year-old girl named Tomasita. After seeing how the man cornered the girl, a neighbor, Estela Espino, had alerted the other residents. The press reported that had the police not intervened the neighbors would surely have killed the "barbarous criminal." "Un sátiro de oficio bolero estuvo a punto de ser linchado por la multitud," *La Prensa*, June 29, 1942.

75. "Un sátiro a punto de ser linchado," *El Nacional*, April 26, 1949.

76. "La multitud enfurecida iba a linchar a repugnante sátiro," *La Prensa*, June 7, 1949.

77. "Asqueroso sátiro a punto de ser linchado en Coatzacoalcos," *La Prensa*, June 23, 1943. Similar examples were reported the same year. See "Bestial sátiro, lapidado," *La Prensa*, July 8, 1943; "Fue linchado un asesino y prófugo en San Francisco Ocotlán, Cholula," *La Opinión*, August 3, 1943; "Mediante el toque a rebato fue aprehendido un sátiro," *La Prensa*, August 15, 1943.

78. "Mujeres indignadas iban a linchar al chacal Santín," *La Prensa*, January 25, 1944.

79. It should be noted that according to various studies, robberies constitute the main offense eliciting lynching in Mexico and the rest of Latin America today. In countries as

different as Guatemala, Bolivia, Ecuador, and Brazil, lynchings are not driven mainly by murders, rapes, or other serious offenses but by minor property crimes. See Snodgrass, "When 'Justice' Is Criminal"; Krupa, "Histories in Red"; Goldstein, "'In Our Own Hands'"; Vilas, "(In)Justicia por mano propia"; Rodríguez, "Crisis de autoridad y violencia social."

80. The concept "moral economy" suggested by E. P. Thompson to analyze eighteenth-century food riots in England is useful here. It refers to the social norms and obligations that defined and regulated the "proper economic functions of several parties within the community." In this view, a riot resulted from a violation of those shared moral assumptions and was thus perceived as a legitimate course of action: "Men and women in the crowd were informed by the belief that they were defending traditional rights or customs." See Thompson, "The Moral Economy of the English Crowd," 78–79. For a sociological discussion of collective violence (including riots and lynching) as a "moralistic response to deviant behavior," see Senechal de la Rocha, "Collective Violence as Social Control," 98; Black, "Crime as Social Control."

81. In reference to contemporary Bolivia, Goldstein makes a similar observation, noting that the robberies that precipitate lynching involve items of little economic value, such as gas tanks, clothing, and food. This, he argues, "attests to the direct impact of these thefts on people's attempts to preserve basic domestic economy." Goldstein, "'In Our Own Hands,'" 39.

82. The term continues to be used today to refer to so-called robbers, and it is used on banners announcing that if caught in flagrante, "rateros" will not be taken to the authorities but will be lynched. See, e.g., "Vecinos en Álvaro Obregón lanzan advertencia a ladrones," *Milenio*, September 8, 2014; "Ratero que sea sorprendido será linchado: vecinos GAM," *El Universal*, December 27, 2015.

83. "Un ratero profesional estuvo a punto de ser lynchado en un pueblo," *La Opinión*, July 2, 1931.

84. "Horripilante crimen cerca de Atlixco," *La Opinión*, September 25, 1941.

85. Even the fatal story of the Hernandez family in the Azcapotzalco neighborhood of Mexico City was reported with certain disdain. In August 1951, Guadalupe Rodríguez and José Hernández tried to commit suicide, fearing that their neighbors would lynch them. The parents hanged their five-year-old daughter and then tried to kill themselves with a knife. Both parents, who lived in a one-room shack, were accused of stealing clothes. "Sangriento drama de una familia en Azcapotzalco," *La Prensa*, August 20, 1951.

86. "Un carbonero fue lapidado en el barrio de el Montón," *La Opinión*, July 8, 1937.

87. "Auto de fe con un carbonero. Mujeres indignadas a punto de lincharlo," *La Prensa*, December 25, 1941.

88. Similar incidents were reported against milk and meat vendors who sold their produce at unfair prices. See, e.g., "Motín popular contra un lechero avorazado," *La Prensa*, October 28, 1944; "Dos conocidos hambreadores en peligro de ser linchados," *La Prensa*, Feburary 5, 1944.

89. See Rath, *Myths of Demilitarization,* 124–25; Ledbetter, "Fighting Foot-and-Mouth Disease in Mexico." For some examples of lynching of health inspectors in the context of this campaign, see chapter 1.

90. An earlier case was reported by Puebla's newspaper, *La Opinión,* in 1933. The case took place in the town of Santa María Xonacatepec, Puebla, where a group of villagers armed

with pistols and machetes lynched a cattle rustler. "Crimen en el pueblo de Xonacatepec," *La Opinión,* July 21, 1933. The following excerpt of testimony collected by Friedlander in his study of Hueyapan, Puebla, reveals how common the practice of lynching criminals and cattle rustlers in particular was during the 1930s and 1940s: "Around here, that's how it's done. When there's a robbery in a *pueblo,* people get help from the surrounding *pueblos.* They ring the bells, people come down to the center of the town to receive instructions, and then go out in search of the thieves." Friedlander, *Being Indian in Hueyapan,* 47.

91. "Lincharon a un ladrón de ganado en Santa Clara," *Excélsior,* September 26, 1940.

92. A similar incident was reported in the town of Apanguito, Guerrero, in June 1944. The case involved a group of neighbors that lynched a cattle rustler and left his body hanging on the outskirts of town next to the cattle he had stolen as a warning to passersby and visitors. "Aplicaron la ley del Talión a un desalmado bandolero," *La Prensa,* June 4, 1944.

93. "Linchamiento colectivo en el Estado de México," *La Prensa,* July 11, 1941. As discussed in the previous section, the use of extralegal violence by the police against so-called criminals was not unusual. For instance, the press reported that a man accused of cattle rustling was hanged and tortured by the police in Galeana, a municipality in the state of Nuevo León, in order to force him to confess his crime. The widow said the man was found dead by his son in the prison cell, with his teeth broken and his back and abdomen severely injured. See "Martirizado y colgado para que confesara crimen que no cometió," *La Prensa,* March 19, 1943.

94. "Criminal acto de linchamiento en el poblado de San Mateo, Mex.," *El Nacional,* July 11, 1941.

95. "Lincharon a un robavacas," *La Prensa,* April 2, 1951.

96. The message does not seem to be a literal quote from the perpetrators but rather the journalists' interpretation of what the perpetrators intended to communicate with the lynching.

CHAPTER FOUR. THE LYNCHING OF THE WICKED

1. "Arrest 52 in Lynching of Mexican Engineers," *Chicago Daily Tribune,* March 29, 1955; "Otros dos salvajes linchamientos en el estado de Querétaro," *El Porvenir,* March 29, 1955.

2. "2 Brothers Lynched in Mexico," *New York Times,* March 30, 1955.

3. "Otros dos salvajes linchamientos en el estado de Querétaro," *El Porvenir,* March 29, 1955.

4. *Criminalia,* April 1, 1955, 14.

5. By "mythical beliefs," I am referring to those narratives that entail otherworldly events and occurrences. With the term "mythical figures," I am alluding to those beings whose deeds transcend the rules of the natural world.

6. This overrepresentation of women in accusations of witchcraft and in the punishment of witch-related misdeeds is consistent with the vast literature on witchcraft in Mexico and other Latin American countries, as well as with that written in reference to premodern Europe, seventeenth-century New England, and contemporary South Africa. In the context of colonial Guatemala and Mexico, the actual or perceived involvement of women in witchcraft has been associated with shifting gender relations, to women's defiance of "traditional" gender roles and "proper" sexual conducts, and to the anxieties generated by such behaviors among men, the church, and secular authorities. See Behar, "Sex and Sin, Withcraft and the

Devil in Late-Colonial Mexico"; Few, *Women Who Live Evil Lives*. For similar arguments in connection with different contexts, see Demos, *Entertaining Satan;* Bever, "Witchcraft, Female Aggression, and Power in the Early Modern Community"; Reed, "Why Salem Made Sense"; Austen, "The Moral Economy of Witchcraft." For an exception to this, see the work of Pitt-Rivers who, in reference to witchcraft accusations in Chiapas, asserts that women were rarely thought of as witches because they "do not possess sufficient spiritual power." Pitt-Rivers, "Spiritual Power in Central America," 230.

7. This contrasts with the ways in which seventeenth-century New Englanders conceived witches. As analyzed by John Putnam Demos, in that case, witches' association with the devil meant that they were irremediably linked to evil deeds and thus being a witch was already seen as an unaccepted transgression. In Mexico, in contrast, the syncretism of Spanish folk culture and indigenous traditions resulted in the idea of witches as being capable of performing both good and evil deeds, of using their magical powers to heal or to inflict harm. Furthermore, even when a witch or a healer was associated with evil, such evil was understood as the "natural counterpart" of her association with that which is good. Their ability to perform evil was in this sense inescapable. See Demos, *Entertaining Satan;* Signorini and Lupo, "The Ambiguity of Evil among the Nahua of the Sierra," 87; Nutini and Roberts, *Bloodsucking Witchcraft*, 55–56; Pitt-Rivers, "Spiritual Power in Central America."

8. A rich literature on witchcraft accusations and their motivations confirms these assertions. Here I provide only a few examples. For witches and their punishments in colonial Mexico and Guatemala, see Behar, "Sex and Sin, Witchcraft and the Devil in Late-Colonial Mexico." On witchcraft in twentieth-century Mexico, see Viqueira and Palerm, "Alcoholismo, brujería y homicidio en dos comunidades rurales de México," 194; Signorini and Lupo, "The Ambiguity of Evil among the Nahua of the Sierra"; Nutini and Roberts, *Bloodsucking Witchcraft;* García Valencia, "Religión, política y brujería"; Pinto Durán and López Moya, "Comunidad diferenciada," 94; González Chévez, "Brujería," 24; Pitt-Rivers, "Spiritual Power in Central America"; Knab, *A War of Witches*. On witches and their persecution in medieval Europe and seventeenth-century New England, see Douglas, "Witchcraft and Leprosy," 723; Demos, *Entertaining Satan;* Reed, "Why Salem Made Sense." On witchcraft in contemporary South Africa, see Comaroff and Comaroff, "Policing Culture, Cultural Policing"; Harnischfeger, "Witchcraft and the State in South Africa."

9. On gender relations and constructions of femininity in the post-revolutionary period, see López, "Women Teachers of Post-Revolutionary Mexico"; Stern, "Responsible Mothers and Normal Children"; Bliss, "Mothers of Invention."

10. Scholars agree that in order for an accusation of witchcraft to be effective, the "right circumstances" need to be in place. As explained by Douglas, "To be successful an accusation should be directed against victims already hated by the populace." In reference to postapartheid South Africa, Comaroff and Comaroff explain that older women who are thought to possess conspicuous amounts of wealth are the most vulnerable to accusations of witchcraft, as perpetrators (often younger men) blame them for their economic misfortunes. See Douglas, "Witchcraft and Leprosy," 726; Comaroff and Comaroff, "Policing Culture, Cultural Policing," 525.

11. "La leyenda de los degolladores motiva un horripilante asesinato," *La Opinión*, April 25, 1930; "Todo el peso de la ley caerá sobre los asesinos de Van Edgard Kullman," *La Opinión*, April 26, 1930; "A través de la semana," *La Opinión*, April 27, 1930.

12. As asserted by Vaughan and Lewis, during the 1930s the government supported the investigation of indigenous cultures and traditions in order to develop programs that would promote the incorporation and assimilation of indigenous people into modernity. It is thus not surprising that the governor had granted Kullmann permission to study the customs of the Indians of Puebla. Vaughan and Lewis, "Introduction."

13. "Todo el peso de la ley caerá sobre los asesinos de Van Edgard Kullmann," *La Opinión*, April 26, 1930; "Una condena mínima se aplicó a los asesinos del profesor Kullman," *La Opinión*, August 31, 1931.

14. "A través de la semana," *La Opinión*, April 27, 1930; "Una condena mínima se aplicó a los asesinos del profesor Kullmann," *La Opinión*, August 31, 1931.

15. "Misteriosa desaparición de varios niños y adultos," *La Opinión*, April 18, 1930; "Ha despertado temor entre los timoratos una fábula," *La Opinión*, April 23, 1930.

16. Samper, "Cannibalizing Kids," 2.

17. Ibid., 4.

18. On narratives and rumors and their credibility, see Stoler, "'In Cold Blood.'"

19. Scott, *Domination and the Arts of Resistance*, 145.

20. "Pablo Sidar será el primero que vuelo a Buenos Aires," *La Opinión*, April 11, 1930; "Pablo Sidar aterrizó en el aeródromo de Balbuena," *La Opinión*, April 28, 1930; "Pablo L. Sidar sigue haciendo preparativos," *La Opinión*, April 29, 1930.

21. "Pablo Sidar será el primero que vuelo a Buenos Aires," *La Opinión*, April 11, 1930.

22. "Ha muerto Pablo Sidar," *La Opinión*, May 12, 1930.

23. Speed and Collier, "Limiting Indigenous Autonomy in Chiapas." A similar legend exists in Oaxaca in the form of a man-eagle that eats children, as well as in contemporary narratives that refer to the kidnapping of children by the government in order to sustain a dam or build large projects. See Eckart, *Los mazatecos ante la nación*.

24. Speed and Collier, "Limiting Indigenous Autonomy in Chiapas"; Pinto Durán and López Moya, "Comunidad diferenciada," 96; Bortoluzzi, "Crisis social y orden narrativo."

25. According to historical and anthropological studies, the sacrifice of individuals in order to use their body parts as cement in large constructions was common among the Maya in the Pre-Columbian period. See Bortoluzzi, "Crisis social y orden narrativo," 19–21.

26. Oliver-Smith, "The Pishtaco," 363. In the context of Bolivia, the figure of the ñak'aq incarnates similar powers and is associated with similar processes of modernization. Bortoluzzi, "Crisis social y orden narrativo." A more recent iteration of this myth can be found in the figure of the *chupacabras*, a bloodsucking creature who feeds off of animals, particularly goats, and sometimes humans. According to Lauren Derby, the chupacabras served to articulate anxieties regarding processes of economic exploitation, extraction, and U.S. imperialistic power. In the Mexican case, the rumor coincided with Mexico's signing on to NAFTA. See Derby, "Vampiros del imperio o porqué el chupacabras acecha a las Américas."

27. Smith, "The Pishtaco."

28. The myth has persisted in contemporary Peru in connection with cases involving the stealing of children's body fat or organs. It has also led to instances of mob violence. On December 9, 1988, for instance, in a Lima shantytown, three French tourists (all men) were almost lynched after being accused of kidnapping twenty children. The men were thought to be either pishtacos or a recent iteration of this mythical figure called "sacaojos" (the one that pokes the eyes out). See Williams, "Death in the Andes," 273–74.

29. Conklin, *Consuming Grief*, 10–11.
30. Pitt-Rivers, "Spiritual Power in Central America," 200.
31. Vaughan, *Cultural Politics in Revolution*, 122.
32. Waters, "Remapping Identities," 225.
33. Ibid., 226.
34. Smith, "Towards a Typology of Rural Responses to Healthcare in Mexico, 1920–1960," 44. According to a former nurse who participated in the sanitary brigades sent to rural Guanajuato during the 1950s, villagers would resist her presence because they thought nurses could give an "evil eye" to their children. Although less dramatic than the fat-sucking rumors, the example is equally telling of the function of rumors as a means to resist the introduction of modern medicine in villages. See Aguilar, "Alimentando a la Nación," 35.
35. Waters, "Remapping Identities," 223.
36. According to the anthropologists Robert Shadow and María Rodríguez-Shadow, the fear of robachicos and violent reactions to them are driven by communities' attempts to defend their "reproductive resources," which are symbolically and materially embodied by children. See Shadow and Rodríguez-Shadow, "Los 'robachicos.'"
37. For examples, see "Robachicos a punto de ser linchado ayer," *La Prensa*, February 3, 1931; "Iba a ser quemado vivo un robachicos en las calles de Dr. Balmis," *La Prensa*, February 12, 1931; "Amargo rato de un robachicos," *Excélsior*, June 11, 1940; "Robachicos a punto de ser linchado," *La Prensa*, June 27, 1945; "Por poco era linchado un robachicos," *La Prensa*, July 2, 1945. See also Vanderwood's discussion of anxieties regarding children's kidnappings and murders in the 1930s along the Tijuana–San Diego border. Vanderwood, *Juan Soldado*.
38. The fear of robachicos has continued to produce its share of mythlike rumors in contemporary Mexico. These rumors claim children's bodily organs are being sold abroad or given to sick wealthy American children. See Quiñones, *True Tales from Another Mexico*, 33; see also Fuentes Díaz, "El Estado y la furia," 7–8; Vilas, "(In)Justicia por mano propia," 22. For similar fears and anxieties in other Latin American countries, see Samper, "Cannibalizing Kids."
39. "Una hechicera iba a ser linchada el día de ayer," *La Opinión*, August 2, 1930.
40. These beliefs continued to surface in the 1940s and 1950s, in the form of legends about bloodsucking creatures in León, Guanajuato, and the belief in Michoacán about the existence of people who kidnapped children in order to use their blood and cure their diseases. See "Demoníaco vampiro asuela las calles de la ciudad de León," *La Prensa*, June 25, 1945; AGN, Fondo Presidentes, Letter addressed to President Adolfo Ruiz Cortinez, signed by Amparo Baez de Brijil, March 27, 1957, ARC 541/853.
41. Bloodsucking witches are imagined as shape-shifting beings that need the blood of infants to survive. When in their human form, these witches live as regular women among their neighbors. They have been held responsible for the death of dozens of infants in different periods. Nutini's fieldwork was carried out during the first years of the 1960s, whereas Romero and Pech examined this phenomenon during the 1970s and 1980s. Nutini recorded the lynching of one witch in 1961 and two more plausible cases in 1965 and 1972. See Nutini and Roberts, *Bloodsucking Witchcraft*; Romero and Pech, "La muerte violenta de los niños por las brujas en Tlaxcala." Though some of the communities studied by Nutini and Roberts observed more traditional Indian traditions, the belief in bloodsucking witches and in

witchcraft more generally is not limited to Indian or rural communities. In his study on the urban poor in Mexico City and its surrounding areas, Oscar Lewis also alludes to this belief. One of Jesús Sánchez's children actually recalls the lynching of a bloodsucking witch in Chalma, Estado de México. See Lewis, *The Children of Sánchez*, 20–21, 207–8, 214.

42. "Mexico Throws Spell Casting 'Witch' into Cell," *Chicago Daily Tribune*, May 11, 1930.

43. The press offers no details regarding the charges against María Jimenez Medina. Witchcraft was certainly not classified as a crime in post-revolutionary Mexico, so it is doubtful that she was held prisoner based merely on these deeds. On the other hand, evidence suggests authorities did not necessarily disagree with these beliefs, so it is possible that they took the accusations to be true but arrested her on different charges.

44. "Indians Rebel at Love Potions; Beat 'Witch' Supplying Wives," *New York Times*, January 12, 1931.

45. A parallel incident was reported in July 1936, though the case was perpetrated by two individuals and not by a lynch mob. In a border town close to Helena, Texas, two American brothers of Mexican descent assaulted an elderly Mexican woman who they claimed had bewitched their sister. The sister woke up several times with "finger marks on her throat," and they demanded that the witch end her curse. When she refused, the brothers decided to kill her. The Rangers took them to Mexico where authorities wanted them. A Texas Ranger quoted the two brothers saying, "They don't hang men in Mexico for killing a witch." "Mexicans Lash 'Witch,' Surrender," *Washington Post*, July 24, 1936.

46. "Penitencias en el dominio de los coras," *Excélsior*, March 13, 1952.

47. "Como en los tiempos de la inquisición, hicieron auto de fe con hechicera," *La Prensa*, August 10, 1941.

48. "Dos brujos lapidados en la Villa de Guadalupe," *La Prensa*, December 11, 1943.

49. Interestingly enough, according to the press, once in the police station, Catalina and Vicente did not deny being witches. They simply explained to authorities that because they were known as brujos, they had been unjustly accused of causing the illness of one of the neighbor's children.

50. For instance, María Isabel Cervantes, a witch who was accused of causing the death of a neighbor in the town of La Calera, Jalisco, was stabbed to death and her body set on fire to prevent her from continuing to perform her witchcraft from the "afterlife." "Quemaron una mujer en Jalisco," *La Prensa*, July 4, 1945. Although the press did not refer to them as witches, the killing of various older women at the time with machetes or with burning objects suggests there were probably witchcraft accusations involved. For instance, in Lagos de Moreno, Jalisco, a fifty-five-year-old woman was mutilated with machetes and had her face skinned on January 1944. "Anciana descuartizada," *La Prensa*, January 6, 1944. Likewise, in 1951, in Zaragoza, Nuevo León, a group of neighbors armed with clubs lynched a woman and after killing her, sliced her belly open and introduced pieces of burning coal. "Mujer quemada viva tras de aplicarle tormentos," *La Prensa*, September 25, 1951.

51. During his fieldwork in the municipality of San Diego Tlalocan, in Tlaxcala, Nutini saw the corpse of a tlahuelpuchi who had been lynched. According to his account, the woman had all her bones broken, and her ears, tongue, and nose had been severed. Nutini and Roberts, *Bloodsucking Witchcraft*, 74–75.

52. According to the traditions of the town of Hueyapan, Puebla, for instance, a person could only be a healer if they had returned from the dead. Only this guaranteed that they

had "the gift of healing." Friedlander *Being Indian In Hueyapan*, 45. Further references to the fluidity between healers and witches can be found in Knab, *A War of Witches*, 167.

53. "Salvaje linchamiento de un espiritista," *La Prensa*, July 25, 1942.

54. As discussed later, political reasons could contribute to acts of collective violence against witches and mystical healers in post-revolutionary Mexico.

55. "Linchamiento espantoso en un poblado," *La Opinión*, July 24, 1944; "Bruja cruelmente martirizada y muerta," *La Prensa*, August 2, 1944. A similar case was reported a year earlier. It involved a man who had lost five children and his parents due to the wrongdoings of a witch in Toluca, Estado de México. When the man started to experience the same stomachaches that his family members had before dying, he decided to take matters into his own hands and stoned the witch, a seventy-year-old woman, to death. The article explains that villagers of this and surrounding towns came to see her for remedies to cure evils but that she was also known for doing wrongs. "A pedradas fue muerta una bruja," *La Prensa*, September 23, 1943.

56. "El procurador comprobó el linchamiento," *La Opinión*, July 25, 1944.

57. Soto, "Bringing the Revolution to Medical Schools," 414.

58. In his work on Hueyapan, Puebla, Friedlander recounts the story of Doña Zeferina, the town's curandera, who was trained in the 1940s by government-sponsored nurses to give injections and bandage wounds according to the "modern ways." The nurses, impressed by Doña Zeferina's qualities, invited her to go with them to Mexico City to get more training, but the healer declined. According to local beliefs, Doña Zeferina's powers were attested by the fact that she was able to "return from the dead." Friedlander *Being Indian In Hueyapan*, 45–46.

59. Opperman, "Modernization and Rural Health in Mexico," 49.

60. Soto, "Bringing the Revolution to Medical Schools," 423. That Mexican officials liked the film is not entirely surprising. After all, as discussed in chapter 1 on state formation, the Mexican government supported the production of films that contributed to an image of the state as a civilizing force that had to battle against the forces of ignorance and fanaticism in local communities.

61. See chapter 1 for a discussion of the assimilationist undertone of indigenista films such as *Janitzio, María Candelaria,* and *Río Escondido,* all directed by Emilio "El Indio" Fernández.

62. "Hollywood Reports," *New York Times*, January 26, 1941.

63. The healers' real name was Trini. Telling of the influence she had in the town, the film's director recounted in his diary that Trini's agreeing to work in the film was instrumental to getting other villagers to work with him. "Diary of a Document," *New York Times*, March 23, 1941.

64. Ibid.

65. "'The Forgotten Village,'" *Christian Science Monitor*, October 17, 1942.

66. "El drama de la medicina rural en la república," *El Nacional*, December 22, 1944, quoted in Soto, "Bringing the Revolution to Medical Schools," 424.

67. There were certainly exceptions. For instance, Protestants usually rejected the work of healers and witches and, like post-revolutionary modernizers, regarded them as a sign of backwardness and ignorance. See McIntyre, "'All of Their Customs Are Daughters of Their Religion,'" 484–85.

68. "Un brujo condenado a morir crucificado," *La Prensa*, August 7, 1945.

69. The press uses the terms "vecinos connotados" in the case of Clara Fonseca's accusers and "destacado" in Patricio de la Cruz's. Such words denote people who are respectable or have a certain status within a community.

70. Douglas, "Witchcraft and Leprosy," 726.

71. "Un caso de brujería de los más espeluznantes que se han visto," *La Prensa*, September 4, 1945.

72. "Echaron al pozo a la bruja para vengar sus maleficios," *La Prensa*, September 9, 1945.

73. Smith, "Towards a Typology of Rural Responses to Healthcare in Mexico, 1920–1960"; Aguilar Rodríguez, "Alimentando a la nación," 35.

74. Anthropological studies carried out during the 1950s and 1960s and in subsequent decades provide evidence of the weight that witchcraft beliefs had in post-revolutionary Mexico. In these studies, the states of Chiapas, Tlaxcala, Puebla, and Oaxaca receive greater attention. See Viqueria and Palerm, "Alcoholismo, brujería y homicidio," 10–11; Pitt-Rivers, "Spiritual Power in Central America"; Nutini and Roberts, *Bloodsucking Witchcraft*; Kaplan, "Tonal and Nagual in Coastal Oaxaca, Mexico," 363.

75. "Entre la maritornes y la esposa tenían al pobre, embrujado," *La Prensa*, August 21, 1944.

76. Lola Romanucci-Ross alludes to similar beliefs in Morelos at the time of her study (around 1958–1960). A villager referred to how "some women" had the power to make a man dull or unperceptive due to jealousy and reported a man had vomited worms and other unidentified specimens as a result of the spell. Romannuci-Ross, *Conflict, Violence and Morality in a Mexican Village*, 108.

77. "Bruja causante de la muerte de una mujer," *La Prensa*, April 29, 1945. The next day, the press reported a similar incident in the town of Obispo in Culiacán, Sinaloa. The case involved Roberto Mendoza, who was convinced of being under the "bad" influence of a male witch, Isabel Espinosa. The man beat the witch to death and after killing him, stabbed him with a sharp stake through the heart, as the belief was that otherwise witches would live again to continue their witchcraft. "Un hechicero fue asesinado, ayer," *La Prensa*, April 30, 1945.

78. "Una 'bruja' asesinada a tiros," *La Opinión*, June 28, 1959.

79. Kaplan offers another example based on her investigation of *nagualismo* among black mestizos of coastal Oaxaca during the 1950s. According to her account, after excessive rains ruined their crops, Negro villagers started to talk about murdering a Mixtec woman whose *nagual* (animal counterpart) was a *culebra de agua* (water snake). It was the woman's animal counterpart who was producing the destructive rains, and villagers believed the only way to stop this was to kill the woman. Kaplan, "Tonal and Nagual in Coastal Oaxaca, Mexico," 366.

80. According to Pitt-Rivers, a nagual is usually described as an "animal-soul," a "spirit-counterpart," or a "transforming witch." It is "a means of representing individuals in the spiritual realm and of relating their fortunes to the power structure of the community." Pitt-Rivers, "Spiritual Power in Central America," 194; see also Kaplan, "Tonal and Nagual in Coastal Oaxaca."

81. Viqueria and Palerm, "Alcoholismo, brujería y homicidio," 10–11. My translation.

82. For instance, in November 1945, a local newspaper reported that in various towns in Puebla it was becoming common practice to accuse women of bewitching neighbors either because they were known for preparing "mysterious beverages" or simply because they behaved in a hostile and suspicious way. The article also reported the assassination of Delfina Hernández in San Andrés Calpan, Puebla, by a group of men who broke into her house and shot her in the chest and stomach while she was sleeping. "Otro salvaje crimen en Calpan," *La Opinión,* November 25, 1945. The anthropologist Timothy J. Knab provides a useful examination of how witchcraft beliefs intersect with intracommunity conflicts and cycles of vengeance in Puebla. Situated in the Sierra of Puebla during the 1970s, Knab's study refers to the lynching of a powerful witch in the 1920s. The man, the uncle of one of the villagers (identified as "Doña María," a healer and also a witch), was lynched after being accused of murdering a boy from an influential family. The man was burned on his feet and arms, beaten, stoned, tied to a cross, and left bleeding for hours. Knab, *A War of Witches,* 198–200.

83. "Por creerlo brujo, fue asesinado un hombre en Jalapaxco, Aljojuca," *La Opinión,* August 6, 1945.

84. "Curandera sacrificada por terrible venganza," *La Prensa,* June 15, 1944.

85. Studies of mal de ojo in Mexico suggest that witches are not necessarily seen as responsible for this type of curse, as it can also be done by an envious person, strangers, neighbors, or menstruating women. See Molina and Gancedo, "El mal de ojo como enfermedad," 85; Weller et al., "Variation and Persistence in Latin American Beliefs about Evil Eye."

86. AGN, IPS, Informe dirigido al C. Jefe de la Sección III y firmado por el Inspector Fernando A. Rodríguez, Caja 70, Exp. 11.

87. AGN, IPS, Informe dirigido al C. Jefe de la Sección III y firmado por el Inspector Fernando A. Rodríguez, Caja 70, Exp. 11. The brutality used by her victimizers resembles other cases reported by the press in the following years. For instance, in February 1944, the witch Natividad Wences was stabbed 42 times in front of her six children. In Comitán, Chiapas, a male witch named Aurelio Rodríguez was lynched by a mob armed with machetes and knives. His left hand, nose, and ears were mutilated. He also had his eyes gouged out and his skull skinned. See "42 puñaladas le dieron por bruja," *La Prensa,* February 18, 1944; "Por venganza fue asesinado brutalmente infeliz brujo," *La Prensa,* August 4, 1951.

88. AGN, ALR, Letter addressed to President Abelardo L. Rodríguez, signed by Agustín de la Cruz, April 6, 1933, Exp. 254/256.

89. A similar case was denounced years later, in the state of Guerrero. A group of peasants from the town of Acapetlahuaya accused the mayor, the president of the PRI's municipal committee, and the police commander of having murdered several people, including a few innocent women. One of the victims was a woman who had been killed in her own house under the false accusation that she was a witch. Four more peasants were thrown into a well. AGN, ARC, Letter addressed to President Adolfo Ruiz Cortinez, signed by Arcadio Martinez and others, May 18, 1955, Exp. 542.1/701.

90. In the vast majority of cases discussed in this chapter people did not deny being witches; rather, they limited themselves to denying that they used their magic for evil purposes.

91. Pitt-Rivers, "Spiritual Power in Central America," 183–84.

92. "La mató seguro de que era una terrible bruja," *La Prensa,* July 5, 1945.

93. Nutini and Roberts's analysis of bloodsucking witchcraft in Tlaxcala and Puebla shows also that witchcraft accusations allowed parents to attribute the premature death of their newborn (probably caused by accidental asphyxiation while sleeping with their mothers) to these mythical beings. Nutini and Roberts, *Bloodsucking Witchcraft*, 238.

CONCLUSION

1. "Espantosa matanza de un comandante y 4 policías," *La Prensa*, August 6, 1943.
2. Ávila, "Queman patrulla y amenazan con linchar a policías en Veracruz"; Redacción Diario de Xalapa, "Intentan linchar a comandante; policías agredieron a pareja de ancianos."
3. One of the most recent manifestations of this surge in levels of brutality was the disappearance and massacre of forty-three male students in the Mexican city of Iguala, Guerrero, on September 26, 2014. By the end of 2019, parents and family members of the students were still awaiting justice.
4. There are several works that can be considered in this historiography. For some of the most recently published articles, books, or edited volumes, see Piccato, *A History of Infamy*; Knight, "Habitus and Homicide"; Pansters, "Zones of State-Making"; Gillingham, "Who Killed Crispín Aguilar?"; Rath, *Myths of Demilitarization in Postrevolutionary Mexico*; Padilla, *Rural Resistance in the Land of Zapata*; Smith, *Pistoleros and Popular Movements*; McCormick, *The Logic of Compromise*; Pensado, *Rebel Mexico*; Aviña, *Specters of Revolution*; Gillingham and Smith, *Dictablanda*; Pansters, *Violence, Coercion, and State-Making in Twentieth-Century Mexico*.
5. Rubin, "Decentering the Regime"; Knight, "Habitus and Homicide," 108–9; Gillingham, "Who Killed Crispín Aguilar?"; Piccato, *A History of Infamy*, 263; Gillingham and Smith, "Introduction," 12–15.
6. Pansters, "Zones of State-Making."
7. Piccato, "Ley Fuga as Justice."
8. Carreras, "The Impact of Criminal Violence on Regime Legitimacy in Latin America"; Ungar, "The Privatization of Citizen Security in Latin America"; Cruz and Santamaría, "Determinants of Support for Extralegal Violence"; Phillips, "Inequality and the Emergence of Vigilante Organizations"; Snodgrass, "When 'Justice' Is Criminal."
9. For a similar critique, see Kruppa, "Histories in Red," 24–25.
10. Ward, *Hanging Bridge*, 12–13; Pfeifer, *Rough Justice*, 13.
11. Wood, *Lynching and Spectacle*, 24–27.
12. On the repression and armed struggles characterizing this period, see Herrera Calderón and Cedillo, *Challenging Authoritarianism in Mexico*; McCormick, "The Last Door"; Aviña, *Specters of Revolution*.
13. Both the mayor and the town's priest supported the lynching. For an examination of this case, see Meaney, *El crimen impune*; Santamaría, "Lynching, Religion, and Politics in Twentieth-Century Puebla."

APPENDIX

1. The use of the term "linchamiento" or "lynchamiento" in Mexico surged during the second half of the nineteenth century, a period that coincides with the intensification of this

practice in the United States. In fact, a basic electronic search of the word *linchamiento* in the database Readex-Latin American Newspapers Series One, which covers several newspapers from Latin America from the nineteenth century up to the first two decades of the twentieth century, shows a total of 198 entries, with the earliest dating to the 1870s. The entries correspond for the most part to newspapers printed in Mexico, Argentina, and Panama. Although some of the lynchings reported by these newspapers referred to cases in the United States, many others reported on local occurrences. In the case of Mexico, newspaper coverage also included lynchings of Mexican nationals or people of Mexican descent in the United States.

2. I borrow this criterion from the sociologist Roberta Senechal de la Roche, who distinguishes unilateral acts of collective violence from bilateral and reciprocal expressions of violence such as brawls, feuds, and warfare. See Senechal de la Roche, "Why Is Collective Violence Collective?"

3. The question of defining lynching according to its communal or community-sanctioned dimension can of course be highly contentious. In the United States, for instance, defenders of lynching defined it as a justifiable response to crimes that offended the values of a given community. In turn, antilynching activists emphasized the racist and unjustifiable character of these acts and by the 1930s defined any racial killing of an African American as lynching, regardless of the communal support behind it. Christopher Waldrep, "War of Words," 75. See also Carrigan and Webb, *Forgotten Death*, 11–14; Gorn, *Let the People See*, 37–42. In this study, the communal support underpinning an incident is central to qualifying it as lynching and to distinguish this practice from plain murder or from forms of violence that had nothing to do with punishing conduct that offended a community. For instance, the collective killing of an individual in order to rob him or her would not fit the definition of lynching provided here, even if it satisfied all other criteria (being collective, public, and cruel). Nor would state-sanctioned extralegal killings that were neither supported nor perpetrated by members of the community.

4. Certainly not all overt and extralegal killings perpetrated by state actors should be considered lynching. To be considered as such, cases had to have communal support. A case that illustrates this point is the torture and hanging of the suspect Juan Rodríguez in December 1941 in Angangueo, Michoacán. The hanging was carried out outside the prison and perpetrated by the chief of the federal forces, the public prosecutor, and a few other policemen. Despite being collective, public, and cruel, the case was motivated by the authorities' intention to force Rodríguez's confession. Villagers decried the incident and demanded justice for what they considered a crime. Rodríguez's killing, then, was clearly not grounded in the community's interest in punishing the criminal and hence cannot be described as a lynching. "Para hacerlo confesar un delito que no cometió lo colgaron de la rama de un árbol," *La Prensa*, December 25, 1941. See, in contrast, the examples discussed in chapter 1 under the rubric "state-sanctioned lynchings." For a conceptual discussion on the blurred lines between state violence and non-state violence, see the notion of "gray zone" as described by Wil Pansters and as initially proposed by the sociologist Javier Auyero. Pansters, "Zones of State Making," 24; Auyero, *Routine Politics and Violence in Argentina*.

5. This expression of the community is most clearly illustrated by those cases of lynching that involved passersby or witnesses that, despite not knowing each other, came together as a result of the outrage they felt about certain criminal conduct.

6. As observed by W. Fitzhugh Brundage in reference to the United States, lynchings can assume a "variety of forms, ranging from secretive small groups to enormous crowds." Brundage, *Lynching in the New South*, 18.

7. Although some sociologists have drawn theoretical distinctions between lynching and vigilante groups, arguing that the latter involve a greater level of organization, in practice the relation between these expressions of violence is more fluid. In post-revolutionary Mexico lynch mobs could involve the participation of organized vigilantes, including Cristeros, Segunderos, and members of the Unión Nacional Sinarquista. This was particularly true for those cases of lynching motivated by religious and political conflicts that targeted Protestants, communists, and other "impious" individuals. For a discussion on the theoretical differences between various forms of collective violence, see Senechal, "Collective Violence as Social Control."

8. Similar to their function in the organization of colonial and nineteenth-century riots, the ringing of bells to summon lynchers in post-revolutionary Mexico reflected the centrality of the church in the organization of communal life and served to project these incidents as acts of violence that were sanctioned by the community. See Taylor, *Drinking, Homicide, and Rebellion*, 115–18; Van Young, *The Other Rebellion*, 484.

9. For a similar argument, see Fuentes Díaz, "Violencia y Estado," 114–15; Garland, "Penal Excess and Surplus Meaning," 45.

10. Instead of using electronic or searchable documents, I reviewed over a thousand newspaper issues manually, day by day, paying particular attention to news coverage of extralegal forms of violence. Other primary sources, from telegrams to security reports and letters of complaint, were examined following a similar methodology: an extensive selection of files or folders were reviewed in their totality rather than preselected based on an electronic search of the term "lynching." Because the titles or summaries of these files rarely included a direct reference to the word *lynching*, I revised those that contained related terms such as "zafarrancho" (disarray), "tumult" (tumult), "motín" (riot), or "asesinato en masa" (collective murder). Although this made the identification of cases of lynching more challenging, it allowed me to understand lynching and its representations in relation to other forms of extralegal violence, including cases of police torture, ley fuga, riots, vigilante killings, and murders that were not collective in nature. This methodology also proved crucial for identifying the porous divide between lynchings and killings perpetrated by vigilante groups, as well as the occurrence of police killings that emulated lynchings. An archive that did include the term "lynching" in its classification and index was the Genaro Estrada Archive from the Secretaría de Relaciones Exteriores' Historic Archive (SRE-AH). The cases in this archive refer for the most part to lynchings of Mexican Americans in the United States that go beyond the temporal scope of this book (e.g., 1850s–1920s). See, e.g., consular correspondence dealing with the lynching of Luis Moreno, Irineo González, and José Palomino in the United States, SRE-AH, Fondo Embajada de Estados Unidos, Tomos 445 (fojas 162–65), 421 (fojas 5–6), and 348 (fojas 249–50, 273–77).

11. "Public opinion" refers to the views and sentiments that prevail among the general public. It results from the interplay of personal predispositions, exposure to mass media, and group interactions. Newspapers are a partial expression of public opinion but one that is crucial for the historian who relies on printed rather than oral communications. On this, see Glynn and Huge, "Public Opinion"; on public opinion and the press in Mexico, see Piccato, *The Tyranny of Opinion*.

12. A few cases of lynching were investigated and prosecuted under the crimes of "motín" (riot) and "tumultuous homicide" (*homicidio tumultuario*), but neither of these legal categories was used exclusively to punish lynching. In this sense, lynching lacked legal specificity. See cases discussed in chapter 1: SCJ, AH, Expediente 531/51, Amparo Directo presentado por parte de José Guadalupe López; Expediente 5331/51, Amparo Directo presentado por Simón López Venegas; Expediente 529/51 presentado por Clemente Santos de la Rosa.

13. The newspapers examined for this book covered a variety of periodicals, from the highly popular tabloid *La Prensa* to mainstream dailies such as *Excélsior, El Universal,* and the government mouthpiece, *El Nacional*. Other periodicals examined include the newspapers *El Porvenir* and *El Informador* as well as the local newspaper *La Opinión* published in the state of Puebla. U.S. newspapers, mainly the *New York Times* and the *Los Angeles Times,* were also consulted. U.S. newspapers usually covered stories that had originally appeared in Mexican newspapers or that were based on Mexican government dispatches or reports.

14. Although the stories and narratives presented by Mexican newspapers had until recently been dismissed as an unequivocal expression of elites' opinions or the state's control over civil society, recent historiography on the subject has shown provincial newspapers and tabloids centered on crime news enjoyed a significant degree of autonomy. Even newspapers produced in the capital, which experienced greater levels of state control, were able to print stories that counter official policies. See Gillingham, Lettieri, and Smith, "Introduction: Journalism, Satire, and Censorship in Mexico," 10–13; Piccato, "Notes for a History of the Press in Mexico," 45.

15. Even the local newspaper *La Opinión,* which was effectively co-opted by Puebla's governor, Maximino Ávila Camacho, during his tenure (1937–41), continued to report on the abuses perpetrated by local officials—including mayors, judges, and police officers—with an openness that was rarely seen in stories on the governor. A case in point was *La Opinión*'s coverage of the killing of Aaron Tufiño by a group of police officers under the command of Pablo Castillo, brother of a local congressman, Antonio Castillo. The story was printed in 1938, after Maximino had established firm control of the newspaper. For more about this and similar cases, see chapter 1. On *La Opinión,* see Paxman, "Changing Opinions in *La Opinión*," 85–92.

16. See Piccato, "Murders of Nota Roja," 195; on this "undergrowth" of local politics, see Knight, "Habitus and Homicide."

17. Piccato, "Homicide as Politics in Modern Mexico," 116–23.

18. Examples of conduct that is usually not typified as a crime and yet may be deemed central by individuals and communities are witchcraft and rape within marriage (when not punishable by law).

19. For a useful analysis of both the history and characteristics of security archives in Mexico, see Padilla and Walker, "In the Archives."

20. The voices of perpetrators themselves only take center stage in a few of these official documents, either when they are interviewed and then quoted by federal inspectors as suspected members of a lynch mob or when they themselves provide their own versions of the events leading to a lynching

BIBLIOGRAPHY

FILMS (MEXICO)

Canoa: Memoria de un hecho vergonzoso. Directed by Felipe Cazals (1976)
Janitzio. Directed by Carlos Navarro (1935)
La ley de Herodes. Directed by Luis Estrada (1999)
Maclovia. Directed by Emilio Fernández (1948)
María Candelaria. Directed by Emilio Fernández (1943)
Río Escondido. Directed by Emilio Fernández (1947)

PERIODICALS (MEXICO)

Animal Político
El Diario
Diario de Puebla
Diario de Xalapa
Excélsior
El Informador
La Jornada
El Liberal Poblano
Milenio
El Nacional
Novedades de Puebla
La Opinión
El País
El Porvenir
Proceso

La Prensa
El Sol de Puebla
El Universal

PERIODICALS (UNITED STATES)

Chicago Daily Tribune
Christian Science Monitor
Los Angeles Times
New York Times
San Diego Tribune
Washington Post

PUBLISHED WORKS

Águila, Marcos, and Jeffrey Bortz. "The Rise of Gangsterism and Charrismo: Labor Violence and the Postrevolutionary Mexican State." In *Violence, Coercion, and State-Making in Twentieth-Century Mexico: The Other Half of the Centaur,* edited by Wil G. Pansters, 185–212. Stanford, CA: Stanford University Press, 2013.

Aguilar Rodríguez, Sandra. "Alimentando a la nación: Género y nutrición en México (1940–1960)." *Revista de Estudios Sociales,* no. 29 (2008): 28–41.

Alonso, Ana M. "Territorializing the Nation and 'Integrating the Indian': 'Mestizaje' in Mexican Official Discourses and Public Culture." In *Sovereign Bodies: Citizens, Migrants, and States in the Postcolonial World,* edited by Thomas Blom Hansen and Finn Stepputat, 39–60. Princeton, NJ: Princeton University Press, 2009.

Arce, Alberto. "In Frightened Mexico Town, a Mob Kills 2 Young Pollsters." *San Diego Tribune,* October 22, 2015.

Arias, Enrique Desmond, and Daniel M. Goldstein. *Violent Democracies in Latin America.* Durham, NC: Duke University Press, 2010.

Aspe Armella, María Luisa. *La formación social y política de los católicos mexicanos: La Acción Católica Mexicana y la Unión Nacional de Estudiantes Católicos, 1929–1958.* Mexico City: Universidad Iberoamericana, 2008.

Austen, Ralph A. "The Moral Economy of Witchcraft." In *Modernity and Its Malcontents,* edited by Jean and John L. Comaroff, 89–110. Chicago: University of Chicago Press, 1993.

Auyero, Javier. *Routine Politics and Violence in Argentina the Gray Zone of State Power.* New York: Cambridge University Press, 2007.

Auyero, Javier, Philippe Bourgois, and Nancy Scheper-Hughes, eds. *Violence at the Urban Margins.* New York: Oxford University Press, 2015.

Ávila, Édgar. "Queman patrulla y amenazan con linchar a policías en Veracruz." *El Universal,* April 13, 2019.

Aviña, Alexander. *Specters of Revolution: Peasant Guerrillas in the Cold War Mexican Countryside.* New York: Oxford University Press, 2014.

Azam, Ahmed, and Paulina Villegas. "As Frustrations with Mexico's Government Rise, So Do Lynchings." *New York Times,* January 26, 2016.

Bailey, John. *The Politics of Crime in Mexico: Democratic Governance in a Security Trap.* Boulder, CO: FirstForumPress, 2014.

Baldwin, Deborah. "Broken Traditions: Mexican Revolutionaries and Protestant Allegiances." *The Americas* 40, no. 2 (1983): 229–58.

Bantjes, Adrian A. *As If Jesus Walked on Earth: Cardenismo, Sonora, and the Mexican Revolution.* Wilmington, DE: Scholarly Resources, 2000.

———. "Idolatry and Iconoclasm in Revolutionary Mexico: The De-Christianization Campaigns, 1929–1940." *Mexican Studies / Estudios Mexicanos* 13, no. 1 (1997): 87–120. https://doi.org/10.1525/msem.1997.13.1.03a00040.

———. "Religion and the Mexican Revolution: Toward a New Historiography." In *Religious Culture in Modern Mexico*, edited by Martin Austin Nervig, 223–54. Lanham, MD: Rowman & Littlefield, 2007.

———. "Saints, Sinners, and State Formation: Local Religion and Cultural Revolution in Mexico." In *The Eagle and the Virgin: Nation and Cultural Revolution in Mexico, 1920–1940*, edited by Mary Kay Vaughn and Stephen Lewis, 137–56. Durham, NC: Duke University Press, 2006.

Barrera Bassols, Jacinto. *El caso Villavicencio: Violencia y poder en el Porfiriato.* Mexico City: Instituto Nacional de Antropología e Historia, 2016.

Bastian, Jean-Pierre. *Los disidentes: Sociedades protestantes y revolución en México, 1872–1911.* Mexico City: Fondo de Cultura Económica, 2015.

———. "Protestants, Freemasons, and Spiritists: Non-Catholic Religious Sociabilities and Mexico's Revolutionary Movement, 1910–20." In *Faith and Impiety in Revolutionary Mexico*, edited by Mathew Butler, 75–92. New York: Palgrave Macmillan, 2007.

———. "Violencia, etnicidad y religión entre los mayas del estado de Chiapas en México." *Mexican Studies / Estudios Mexicanos* 12, no. 2 (1996): 301–14.

Bazant, Jan. "La Iglesia, el Estado y la sublevación conservadora de Puebla en 1856." *Historia Mexicana* 35, no. 1 (1985): 93–109.

Beals, Carleton. *Porfirio Díaz: Dictator of Mexico.* Westport, CT: Greenwood Press, 1971.

Becker, Marjorie. *Setting the Virgin on Fire: Lázaro Cárdenas, Michoacán Peasants, and the Redemption of the Mexican Revolution.* Berkeley: University of California Press, 1996.

———. "Torching La Purísima, Dancing at the Altar: The Construction of Revolutionary Hegemony in Michoacán, 1934–1940." In *Everyday Forms of State Formation: Revolution and the Negotiation of Rule in Modern Mexico*, edited by Gibert Joseph and Daniel Nugent, 247–64. Durham, NC: Duke University Press, 1994.

Behar, Ruth. "Sex and Sin, Witchcraft and the Devil in Late-Colonial Mexico." *American Ethnologist* 14, no. 1 (1987): 34–54. https://doi.org/10.1525/ae.1987.14.1.02a00030.

Benítez, Fernando. *El agua envenenada.* Mexico City: Fondo de Cultura Economica, 2014.

Bever, Edward. "Witchcraft, Female Aggression, and Power in the Early Modern Community." *Journal of Social History* 35, no. 4 (January 2002): 955–88. https://doi.org/10.1353/jsh.2002.0042.

Binford, Leigh. "Lynching and States of Fear in Urban Mexico." *Anthropologica* 51, no. 2 (2009): 301–12.

Binford, Leigh, and Nancy Churchill. "A Failure of Normalization: Transnational Migration, Popular Justice and Police Repression in the Contemporary Neoliberal Mexican Social Formation." *Social Justice* 26, no. 3 (1999): 123–44.

Black, Donald. "Crime as Social Control." *American Sociological Review* 48, no. 1 (1983): 34–45.

Blancarte, Roberto. *Historia de la Iglesia católica en México: 1929–1982*. Zinacantepec: Colegio Mexiquense, 1993.

Bliss, Katherine E. "Mothers of Invention: Narratives of Maternity, Paternity, and Modernity in Early Twentieth-Century Mexico." In *True Stories of Crime in Modern Mexico*, edited by Robert Buffington and Pablo Piccato, 248–64. Albuquerque: University of New Mexico Press, 2009.

Bloch, Avital H., and Servando Ortoll. "¡Viva México! ¡Mueran los Yanquis! The Guadalajara Riots of 1910." In *Riots in the Cities: Popular Politics and the Urban Poor in Latin America 1765–1910*, edited by Silvia M. Arrom and Servando Ortoll, 195–223. Wilmington, DE: Scholarly Resources, 1996.

Boege, Eckart. *Los Mazatecos ante la nación*. Mexico City: Siglo XXI, 2015.

Bortoluzzi, Manfredi. "Crisis social y orden narrativo: La figura del 'degollador' en Perú, Bolivia y México." In *El hombre es el fluir de un cuento: Antropología de las narrativas*, edited by Manfredi Bortoluzzi and Witold Jacorzynski, 75–98. Mexico City: Publicaciones de la Casa Chata–CIESAS, 2010.

Brundage, W. Fitzhugh. *Lynching in the New South: Georgia and Virginia, 1880–1930*. Urbana: University of Illinois Press, 1994.

Buffington, Robert. *Criminal and Citizen in Modern Mexico*. Lincoln: University of Nebraska Press, 2000.

Buffington, Robert, and Pablo Piccato. "Introduction: Crime Stories." In *True Stories of Crime in Modern Mexico*, edited by Robert Buffington and Pablo Piccato, 1–23. Albuquerque: University of New Mexico Press, 2009.

Butler, Matthew. "Keeping the Faith in Revolutionary Mexico: Clerical and Lay Resistance to Religious Persecution, East Michoacán, 1926–1929." *The Americas* 59, no. 1 (2015): 9–32.

———. *Popular Piety and Political Identity in Mexico's Cristero Rebellion*. Oxford: Oxford University Press, 2004.

———. "Sotanas Rojinegras: Catholic Anticlericalism and Mexico's Revolutionary Schism." *The Americas* 65, no. 4 (2009): 535–58. https://doi.org/10.1353/tam.0.0108.

Camp, Roderic A. *Cruce de espadas: Política y religión en México*. Mexico City: Siglo XXI, 1998.

Campos, Isaac. *Home Grown: Marijuana and the Origins of Mexico's War on Drugs*. Chapel Hill: University of North Carolina Press, 2014.

Caplow, Deborah. *Leopoldo Méndez: Revolutionary Art and the Mexican Print*. Austin: University of Texas Press, 2008.

Carey, David, Jr., and Gema Santamaría. "The Politics and Publics of Violence and Crime in Latin America." In *Violence and Crime in Latin America: Representations and Politics*, edited by Gema Santamaría and David Carey Jr., 3–18. Norman: University of Oklahoma Press, 2017.

Carey, Elaine. *Plaza of Sacrifices: Gender, Power, and Terror in 1968 Mexico*. Albuquerque: University of New Mexico Press, 2005.

Carreras, Miguel. "The Impact of Criminal Violence on Regime Legitimacy in Latin America." *Latin American Research Review* 48, no. 3 (2013): 85–107. https://doi.org/10.1353/lar.2013.0040.

Carrigan, William D., and Christopher Waldrep, eds. *Swift to Wrath: Lynching in Global Historical Perspective*. Charlottesville: University of Virginia Press, 2013.

Carrigan, William D., and Clive Webb, eds. *Forgotten Dead: Mob Violence against Mexicans in the United States, 1848–1928*. Oxford: Oxford University Press, 2017.

Castillo, Luz Huertas, Bonnie A. Lucero, and Gregory J. Swedberg. *Voices of Crime: Constructing and Contesting Social Control in Modern Latin America*. Tucson: University of Arizona Press, 2016.

Cavanaugh, William T. *The Myth of Religious Violence: Secular Ideology and the Roots of Modern Conflict*. New York: Oxford University Press, 2009.

Chávez, Daniel. "The Eagle and the Serpent: The State as Spectacle in Mexican Cinema." *Latin American Research Review* 45, no. 3 (2010): 115–41.

Comaroff, John, and Jean Comaroff. "Policing Culture, Cultural Policing: Law and Social Order in Postcolonial South Africa." *Law & Social Inquiry* 29, no. 3 (Summer 2004): 513–45.

Conklin, Beth A. *Consuming Grief: Compassionate Cannibalism in an Amazonian Society*. Austin: University of Texas Press, 2011.

Cruz, José Miguel, and Gema Kloppe-Santamaría. "Determinants of Support for Extralegal Violence in Latin America and the Caribbean." *Latin American Research Review* 54, no. 1 (2019): 50–68. https://doi.org/10.25222/larr.212.

Cruz García, Mauricio. "Gobierno y movimientos sociales mexicanos ante la Segunda Guerra Mundial." *Foro Internacional* 51, no. 3 (2011): 458–504.

Cueto, Marcos. *Cold War, Deadly Fevers: Malaria Eradication in Mexico, 1955–1975*. Washington, DC: Woodrow Wilson Center Press, 2014.

Dailey, Susanne. "Religious Aspects of Colombia's 'La Violencia': Explanations and Implications." *Journal of Church and State* 15, no. 3 (1973): 381–405.

Dávila Peralta, Nicolás. *Las santas batallas: La derecha anticomunista en Puebla*. Mexico City: Gobierno del Estado, 2000.

Davis, Diane E. "Policing and Regime Transition." In *Violence, Coercion, and State-Making in Twentieth-Century Mexico: The Other Half of the Centaur*, edited by Wil G. Pansters, 68–90. Stanford, CA: Stanford University Press, 2012.

———. "Undermining the Rule of Law: Democratization and the Dark Side of Police Reform in Mexico." *Latin American Politics & Society* 48, no. 1 (2006): 55–86. https://doi.org/10.1353/lap.2006.0005.

Davis, Natalie Zemon. "The Rites of Violence: Religious Riot in Sixteenth-Century France." *Past & Present*, no. 59 (May 1973): 51–91.

De la Luz García, Deissy Jael. "Ciudadanía, representación y participación cívico-política de los evangélicos mexicanos." *Revista de el Colegio de San Luis* 24–25 (2006): 9–36.

———. "El pentecontalismo en México y su propuesta de experiencia religiosa e identidad nacional." *Cultura y Religión* 3, no. 2 (2009): 199–217.

De Llano, Pablo. "José y Rey, la inocencia linchada." *El País*, October 31, 2015.

Demos, John Putnam. *Entertaining Satan: Witchcraft and the Culture of Early New England*. Oxford: Oxford University Press, 2004.

Derby, Lauren. "Vampiros del imperio o porqué el chupacabras acecha a las Américas." In *Culturas imperiales: Experiencia y representación en América, Asia y África,* edited by Ricardo Salvatore, 317–45. Buenos Aires: Beatriz Vierbo Editora, 2005.

Dormady, Jason. *Primitive Revolution: Restorationist Religion and the Idea of the Mexican Revolution.* Alburquerque: University of New Mexico Press, 2011.

Douglas, Mary. "Witchcraft and Leprosy: Two Strategies of Exclusion." *Man* 26, no. 4 (1991): 723. https://doi.org/10.2307/2803778.

Dow, James. "The Expansion of Protestantism in Mexico: An Anthropological View." *Anthropological Quarterly* 78, no. 4 (2005): 827–50. https://doi.org/10.1353/anq.2005.0054.

Dray, Philip. *At the Hands of Persons Unknown: The Lynching of Black America.* New York: Modern Library, 2002.

Elias, Norbert. "On Transformations of Aggressiveness." *Theory and Society* 5, no. 2 (1978): 229–42. https://doi.org/10.1007/bf01702163.

Evans, Ivan. *Cultures of Violence: Racial Violence and the Origins of Segregation in South Africa and the American South.* Manchester: Manchester University Press, 2011.

Fallaw, Ben. "Dry Law, Wet Politics: Drinking and Prohibition in Post-Revolutionary Yucatán, 1915–1935." *Latin American Research Review* 37, no. 2 (2002): 37–64.

———. *Religion and State Formation in Postrevolutionary Mexico.* Durham, NC: Duke University Press, 2013.

———. "Varieties of Mexican Revolutionary Anticlericalism: Radicalism, Iconoclasm, and Otherwise, 1914–1935." *The Americas* 65, no. 4 (2009): 481–509. https://doi.org/10.1353/tam.0.0106.

Few, Martha. *Women Who Live Evil Lives: Gender, Religion, and the Politics of Power in Colonial Guatemala, 1650–1750.* Austin: University of Texas Press, 2002.

Finchelstein, Federico. *Transatlantic Fascism: Ideology, Violence, and the Sacred in Argentina and Italy, 1919–1945.* Durham, NC: Duke University Press, 2010.

Friedlander, Judith. *Being Indian in Hueyapan.* Basingstoke: Palgrave Macmillan, 2007.

Fuentes Díaz, Antonio. "El Estado y la furia." *El Cotidiano* 131 (2004): 7–19.

———. *Linchamientos: Fragmentación y respuesta en el México neoliberal.* Puebla, Mexico: Benemérita Universidad Autónoma de Puebla, 2006.

———. "Violencia y Estado, mediación y respuesta no estatal." PhD dissertation, Universidad Nacional Autónoma de México, 2008.

Gamallo, Leandro A. "Crimen, castigo y violencia colectiva: Los linchamientos en México en el Siglo XXI." Master's thesis, FLACSO, 2012.

García Valencia, Hugo. "Religión, política y brujería." *Dimensión Antropológica* 37 (2006): 151–80.

Garland, David. "Penal Excess and Surplus Meaning: Public Torture Lynchings in Twentieth-Century America." *Law Society Review* 39, no. 4 (2005): 793–834. https://doi.org/10.1111/j.1540-5893.2005.00245.

Gayosso Ríos, Filadelfo. *Mi palabra: A la vera de Tlacuilo.* Mexico City: Plaza y Valdés, 2004.

Gillingham, Paul. "Who Killed Crispín Aguilar? Violence and Order in the Postrevolutionary Countryside." In *Violence, Coercion, and State-Making in Twentieth-Century Mexico:*

The Other Half of the Centaur, edited by Wil G. Pansters, 91–111. Stanford, CA: Stanford University Press, 2012.

Gillingham, Paul, Michael Lettieri, and Benjamin T. Smith, eds. *Journalism, Satire, and Censorship in Mexico*. Albuquerque: University of New Mexico Press, 2018.

Gillingham, Paul, and Benjamin T. Smith, eds. *Dictablanda: Politics, Work, and Culture in Mexico, 1938–1968*. Durham, NC: Duke University Press, 2014.

———. "Introduction: The Paradoxes of Revolution." In *Dictablanda: Politics, Work, and Culture in Mexico, 1938–1968*, edited by Paul Gillingham and Benjamin T. Smith, 1–43. Durham, NC: Duke University Press, 2014.

Girard, René. *Violence and the Sacred*. Translated by Patrick Gregory. Baltimore, MD: Johns Hopkins University Press, 1977.

Glynn, Carroll J., and Michael E. Huge. "Public Opinion." In *The Concise Encyclopedia of Communication*, edited by Wolfgang Donsbach, 500–503. Chichester: John Wiley & Sons, 2015.

Goldstein, Daniel M. "Flexible Justice." *Critique of Anthropology* 25, no. 4 (2005): 389–411. https://doi.org/10.1177/0308275x05058656.

———. "'In Our Own Hands': Lynching, Justice, and the Law in Bolivia." *American Ethnologist* 30, no. 1 (2003): 22–43. https://doi.org/10.1525/ae.2003.30.1.22.

———. *The Spectacular City: Violence and Performance in Urban Bolivia*. Durham, NC: Duke University Press, 2005.

González, Fernando M. *Morir y matar por Cristo Rey: Aspectos de la Cristiada*. Mexico City: Plaza y Valdés, 2001.

González Chévez, Lilián. "Brujería: Códigos restringidos respecto a la causalidad de la enfermedad. Estudio de caso en la periferia urbana de Cuernavaca, Morelos." *Revista Pueblos y Fronteras Digital* 5, no. 10 (January 2010): 24–57. https://doi.org/10.22201/cimsur.18704115e.2010.10.146.

Gorn, Elliott J. *Let the People See: the Story of Emmett Till*. New York: Oxford University Press, 2018.

Gross, Toomas. "Protestantism and Modernity: The Implications of Religious Change in Contemporary Rural Oaxaca." *Sociology of Religion* 64, no. 4 (2003): 479–98.

Guerra Manzo, Enrique. "The Resistance of the Marginalised: Catholics in Eastern Michoacán and the Mexican State, 1920–40." *Journal of Latin American Studies* 40, no. 1 (2008): 109–33.

Hale, Charles A. "Jose Maria Luis Mora and the Structure of Mexican Liberalism." *Hispanic American Historical Review* 45, no. 2 (1965): 196. https://doi.org/10.2307/2510565.

Handy, Jim. "Chicken Thieves, Witches, and Judges: Vigilante Justice and Customary Law in Guatemala." *Journal of Latin American Studies* 36, no. 3 (2004): 533–61. https://doi.org/10.1017/s0022216x04007783.

Harnischfeger, Johannes. "Witchcraft and the State in South Africa." *Anthropos* 95, no. 1 (2000): 99–112.

Helgen, Erika. *Religious Conflict in Brazil: Protestants, Catholics, and the Rise of Religious Pluralism in the Early Twentieth Century*. New Haven, CT: Yale University Press, 2020.

Hernández Rodríguez, Rogelio. "Strongmen and State Weakness." In *Dictablanda: Politics, Work, and Culture in Mexico, 1938–1968*, edited by Paul Gillingham and Benjamin Smith, 108–25. Durham, NC: Duke University Press, 2014.

Herrera Calderón, Fernando, and Adela Cedillo, eds. *Challenging Authoritarianism in Mexico: Revolutionary Struggles and the Dirty War, 1964–1982*. New York: Routledge, 2012.
Hershfield, Joanne. "Screening the Nation." In *The Eagle and the Virgin: Nation and Cultural Revolution in Mexico, 1920–1940*, edited by Mary Kay Vaughan and Stephen E. Lewis, 259–79. Durham, NC: Duke University Press, 2006.
Holston, James, and Teresa Caldeira. "Democracy and Violence in Brazil." *Comparative Studies in Society and History* 41, no. 4 (1999): 691–729. https://doi.org/10.1017/s0010417599003102.
Huggins, Martha K. *Vigilantism and the State in Modern Latin America: Essays on Extralegal Violence*. New York: Praeger, 1991.
Instituto Nacional de Estadística y Geografía (INEGI). Comunicado de Prensa, Número 347/19. July 25, 2019. Available at www.inegi.org.mx/contenidos/saladeprensa/boletines/2019/EstSegPub/homicidios2018.pdf; last accessed September 1, 2019.
———. *La diversidad religiosa en México: XII Censo General de Población y Vivienda 2000*. Mexico City: INEGI, 2005.
———. *Indicadores sociodemográficos de México (1930–2000)*. Mexico City: INEGI, 2001.
———. "Sexto censo general de población." www.uv.mx/apps/censos-conteos/1940/menu1940.html; last accessed December 10, 2018.
Joseph, Gilbert M., and Jürgen Buchenau. *Mexico's Once and Future Revolution: Social Upheaval and the Challenge of Rule since the Late Nineteenth Century*. Durham, NC: Duke University Press, 2013.
Joseph, Gilbert M., and Daniel Nugent, eds. *Everyday Forms of State Formation: Revolution and the Negotiation of Rule in Modern Mexico*. Durham, NC: Duke University Press, 2006.
Joseph, Gilbert M., Anne Rubenstein, and Eric Zolov. "Assembling the Fragments." In *Fragments of a Golden Age: The Politics of Culture in Mexico since 1940*, edited by Gilbert M. Joseph, Anne Rubenstein, and Eric Zolov. Durham, NC: Duke University Press, 2001.
———, eds. *Fragments of a Golden Age: The Politics of Culture in Mexico since 1940*. Durham, NC: Duke University Press, 2004.
Kaplan, Lucille N. "Tonal and Nagual in Coastal Oaxaca, Mexico." *Journal of American Folklore* 69, no. 274 (1956): 363–68. https://doi.org/10.2307/536346.
Kirshner, Alan M. "Tomás Garrido Canabal and the Mexican Red Shirt Movement." PhD dissertation, New York University, 1970.
Knab, Timothy J. *A War of Witches: A Journey into the Underworld of the Contemporary Aztecs*. Boulder, CO: Westview Press, 1999.
Knight, Alan. "The End of the Mexican Revolution? From Cárdenas to Ávila Camacho, 1937–1941." In *Dictablanda: Politics, Work, and Culture in Mexico, 1938–1968*, edited by Paul Gillingham and Benjamin T. Smith, 47–64. Durham, NC: Duke University Press, 2014.
———. "Habitus and Homicide: Political Culture in Revolutionary Mexico." In *Citizens of the Pyramid: Essays on Mexican Political Culture*, edited by Wil G. Pansters, 107–30. West Lafayette, IN: Purdue University Press, 1997.
———. *The Mexican Revolution*, vol. 1: *Porfirians, Liberals and Peasants*. Lincoln: University of Nebraska Press, 1990.
———. *The Mexican Revolution*, vol. 2: *Counter-Revolution and Reconstruction*. Lincoln: University of Nebraska Press, 1990.

———. "Popular Culture and the Revolutionary State in Mexico, 1910–1940." *Hispanic American Historical Review* 74, no. 3 (1994): 393–444.

———. "The Weight of the State in Modern Mexico." In *Studies in the Formation of the Nation State in Latin America*, edited by James Dunkerley, 212–53. London: Institute of Latin American Studies, 2002.

Knight, Alan, and Wil G. Pansters, eds. *Caciquismo in Twentieth-Century Mexico*. London: Institute for the Study of the Americas, 2005.

Koonings, Kees, and Dirk Kruijt. *Armed Actors: Organized Violence and State Failure in Latin America*. London: Zed Books, 2013.

Krupa, Christopher. "Histories in Red: Ways of Seeing Lynching in Ecuador." *American Ethnologist* 36, no. 1 (2009): 20–39. https://doi.org/10.1111/j.1548-1425.2008.01107.x.

Ledbetter, John. "Fighting Foot-and-Mouth Disease in Mexico: Popular Protest against Diplomatic Decisions." *Southwestern Historical Quarterly* 104, no. 3 (January 2001): 386–415.

Lerner, Victoria. *La educación socialista*. Mexico City: Colegio de México, 1982.

Lewis, Oscar. *The Children of Sánchez: Autobiography of a Mexican Family*. New York: Knopf Doubleday Publishing Group, 1961.

———. *Five Families: Mexican Case Studies in the Culture of Poverty*. New York: John Wiley & Sons, 1962.

Lewis, Stephen E. *The Ambivalent Revolution: Forging State and Nation in Chiapas, 1910–1945*. Albuquerque: University of New Mexico, 2005.

———. "The Nation, Education, and the 'Indian Problem' in Mexico, 1920–1940." In *The Eagle and the Virgin: Nation and Cultural Revolution in Mexico, 1920–1940*, edited by Mary Kay Vaughn and Stephen E. Lewis, 176–95. Durham, NC: Duke University Press, 2006.

Lomnitz, Claudio. "Mexico's First Lynching: Sovereignty, Criminality, Moral Panic." *Critical Historical Studies* 1, no. 1 (2014): 85–123.

López, Oresta. "Women Teachers of Post-Revolutionary Mexico: Feminisation and Everyday Resistance." *Paedagogica Historica* 49, no. 1 (2013): 56–69. https://doi.org/10.1080/00309230.2012.746714.

López-Menéndez, Marisol. "Mártires abandonados: Militancia católica, memoria y olvido en México." *Sociedad y Religión: Sociología, Antropología e Historia de la Religión en el Cono Sur* 28, no. 48 (2017): 97–129.

———. *Miguel Pro: Martyrdom, Politics, and Society in Twentieth-Century Mexico*. London: Lexington Books, 2016

Loveman, Mara. "The Modern State and the Primitive Accumulation of Symbolic Power." *American Journal of Sociology* 110, no. 6 (2005): 1651–83.

———. "Blinded Like a State: The Revolt against Civil Registration in Nineteenth-Century Brazil." *Comparative Studies in Society and History* 49, no. 1 (2006): 5–39. https://doi.org/10.1017/s0010417507000394.

Lund, Joshua. *The Mestizo State: Reading Race in Modern Mexico*. Minneapolis: University of Minnesota Press, 2012.

Marín, Nidia. "Ya no había a quién matar." In *1968–2008, Los silencios de la democracia*, edited by Eduardo Cruz Vázquez, 31–45. Mexico City: Planeta, 2008.

Martínez García, Carlos. "Los linchados de Ajalpan, Puebla." *La Jornada*, October 28, 2015.

Matthews, Donald G. "The Southern Rite of Human Sacrifice: Lynching in the American South." *Mississippi Quarterly* 61, no. 1 (2008): 20–47.

McCormick, Gladys. "The Last Door: Political Prisoners and the Use of Torture in Mexico's Dirty War." *The Americas* 74, no. 1 (June 2017): 57–81. https://doi.org/10.1017/tam.2016.80.

———. *The Logic of Compromise in Mexico: How the Countryside Was Key to the Emergence of Authoritarianism*. Chapel Hill: University of North Carolina Press, 2016.

Mcintyre, Kathleen M. "'All of Their Customs Are Daughters of Their Religion': Baptists in Post-Revolutionary Mexico, 1920s–Present." *Sex, Gender and the Sacred* (April 2014): 83–103. https://doi.org/10.1002/9781118833926.ch4.

Meade, Everard. "From Sex Strangler to Model Citizen: Mexico's Most Famous Murderer and the Defeat of the Death Penalty." *Mexican Studies/Estudios Mexicanos* 26, no. 2 (2010): 323–77. https://doi.org/10.1525/msem.2010.26.2.323.

———. "The Plaza Is for the Populacho, the Desert Is for Deep-Sea Fish: Lessons from La Nota Roja." In *Journalism, Satire, and Censorship in Mexico*, edited by Paul Gillingham, Michael Lettieri, and Benjamin T. Smith, 299–331. Alburquerque: University of New Mexico Press, 2018.

Meaney, Guillermina. *Canoa: El crimen impune*. Mexico City: Editorial Posada, 1977.

Méndez, Leopoldo. *En nombre de Cristo—han asesinado más de 200 maestros*. Mexico City: Editorial Gráfica Popular, 1939.

Meyer, Jean A. *The Cristero Rebellion: The Mexican People between Church and State 1926–1929*. Cambridge: Cambridge University Press, 1976.

———. "An Idea of Mexico: Catholics in the Revolution." In *The Eagle and the Virgin: Nation and Cultural Revolution in Mexico, 1920–1940*, edited by Mary Kay Vaughn and Stephen E. Lewis, 281–96. Durham, NC Duke University Press, 2006.

———. *La Iglesia católica en México 1929–1965*. Cuadernos de Trabajo del CIDE. Mexico City: CIDE, 2005.

Migdal, Joel. *Strong Societies and Weak States: State-Society Relations and State Capabilities in the Third World*. Princeton, NJ: Princeton University Press, 1988.

Miller, Barbara. "The Role of Women in the Mexican Cristero Rebellion: Las Señoras y Las Religiosas." *The Americas* 40, no. 3 (1984): 303–23. https://doi.org/10.2307/981116.

Molina, Anatilde Idoyaga, and Mariano Gancedo. "El mal de ojo como enfermedad: Elite-lore y folklore en Iberoamérica." *Revista de Dialectología y Tradiciones Populares* 69, no. 1 (2014): 77–93. https://doi.org/10.3989/rdtp.2014.01.004.

Moncada, Eduardo. "Varieties of Vigilantism: Conceptual Discord, Meaning and Strategies." *Global Crime* 18, no. 4 (2017): 403–23. https://doi.org/10.1080/17440572.2017.1374183.

Moreno Chávez, José Alberto. "Quemando santos para iluminar conciencias: Desfanatización y resistencia al proyecto cultural garridista (1924–1935)." *Estudios de Historia Moderna y Contemporánea de México*, no. 42 (2012): 37–74. https://doi.org/10.22201/iih.24485004e.2011.42.30389.

Morris, Nathaniel. "The World Created Anew: Land, Religion and Revolution in the Gran Nayar Region of Mexico." PhD dissertation, University of Oxford, 2015.

Mraz, John. *Looking for Mexico: Modern Visual Culture and National Identity*. Durham, NC: Duke University Press, 2009.

Newcomer, Daniel. *Reconciling Modernity: Urban State Formation in 1940s León, Mexico*. Lincoln: University of Nebraska Press, 2004.

Niblo, Stephen R. *Mexico in the 1940s: Modernity, Politics, and Corruption*. Wilmington, DE: Scholarly Resources, 2001.

Nutini, Hugo G., and John M. Roberts. *Bloodsucking Witchcraft: An Epistemological Study of Anthropomorphic Supernaturalism in Rural Tlaxcala*. Tucson: University of Arizona Press, 1993.
Nutini, Hugo G., and Barry L. Isaac. *Social Stratification in Central Mexico 1500–2000*. Austin: University of Texas Press, 2009.
Oliver-Smith, Anthony. "The Pishtaco: Institutionalized Fear in Highland Peru." *Journal of American Folklore* 82, no. 326 (1969): 363. https://doi.org/10.2307/539781.
Olmos, José Gil. "El linchamiento en Ajalpan." *Proceso*, October 21, 2015.
Onken, Hinnerk. "Lynching in Peru in the Nineteenth and Early Twentieth Centuries." In *Globalizing Lynching History: Vigilantism and Extralegal Punishment from an International Perspective*, edited by Simon Wendt and Manfred Berg, 173–86. London: Palgrave Macmillan, 2011. https://doi.org/10.1057/9781137001245_11.
Opperman, Stephanie. "Modernization and Rural Health in Mexico: The Case of the Tepalcatepec Commission." *Endeavour* 37, no. 1 (2013): 47–55. https://doi.org/10.1016/j.endeavour.2012.10.005.
Padilla, Tanalís. *Rural Resistance in the Land of Zapata: The Jaramillista Movement and the Myth of the Pax-Priísta 1940–1962*. Durham, NC: Duke University Press, 2009.
Padilla, Tanalís, and Louise E. Walker. "In the Archives: History and Politics." *Journal of Iberian and Latin American Research* 19, no. 1 (2013): 1–10. https://doi.org/10.1080/13260219.2013.805715
Pansters, Wil G. "Goodbye to the Caciques? Definition, the State and the Dynamics of Caciquismo in Twentieth-Century Mexico." In *Caciquismo in Twentieth-Century Mexico*, edited by Alan Knight and Wil G. Pansters, 349–76. London: Institute for the Study of the Americas, University of London, 2005.
———, ed. *Violence, Coercion, and State-Making in Twentieth-Century Mexico: The Other Half of the Centaur*. Stanford, CA: Stanford University Press, 2012.
———. "Zones of State Making." In *Violence, Coercion, and Hegemony in Twentieth-Century Mexico: The Other Half of the Centaur*, edited by Wil G. Pansters. Stanford, CA: Stanford University Press, 2012.
Parsons, Wilfrid. *Mexican Martyrdom*. Charlotte, NC: Tan Books and Publishers, 2012.
Patterson, Orlando. *Rituals of Blood: Consequences of Slavery in Two American Centuries*. New York: Basic Civitas Books, 2006.
Paxman, Andrew. "Changing Opinions in *La Opinión*: Maximino Ávila Camacho and the Puebla Press, 1936–1941." In *Journalism, Satire, and Censorship in Mexico*, edited by Paul Gillingham, Michael Leitteri, and Benjamin T. Smith, 83–103. Albuquerque: University of New Mexico Press, 2018.
Pensado, Jaime M. *Rebel Mexico: Student Unrest and Authoritarian Political Culture during the Long Sixties*. Stanford, CA: Stanford University Press, 2013.
———. "The Rise of a 'National Student Problem' in 1956." In *Dictablanda: Politics, Work, and Culture in Mexico, 1938–1968*, edited by Paul Gillingham and Benjamin T. Smith, 360–78. Durham, NC: Duke University Press, 2014.
Pérez Rosales, Laura. "Censura y control: La campaña nacional de moralización en los años cincuenta." *Historia y Grafía*, no. 37 (2011): 79–113.
Pfeifer, Michael J. *Roots of Rough Justice: Origins of American Lynching*. Urbana: University of Illinois Press, 2011.

———. *Rough Justice: Lynching and American Society, 1874–1947.* Urbana: University of Illinois Press, 2004.
Pfeifer, Michael J., ed. *Global Lynching and Collective Violence,* vol. 1: *Asia, Africa, and the Middle East.* Urbana: University of Illinois Press, 2017.
———. *Global Lynching and Collective Violence,* vol. 2: *The Americas and Europe.* Urbana: University of Illinois Press, 2017.
Phillips, Brian J. "Inequality and the Emergence of Vigilante Organizations: The Case of Mexican Autodefensas." *Comparative Political Studies* 50, no. 10 (2016): 1358–89. https://doi.org/10.1177/0010414016666863.
Piccato, Pablo. *City of Suspects: Crime in Mexico City, 1900–1931.* Durham, NC: Duke University Press, 2001.
———. "Estadísticas del crimen en México: Series históricas, 1901–2001." December 8, 2013. Available at www.columbia.edu/~pp143/estadisticascrimen/EstadisticasSigloXX.htm; last accessed September 1, 2019.
———. *A History of Infamy: Crime, Truth, and Justice in Mexico.* Oakland: University of California Press, 2017.
———. "Homicide as Politics in Modern Mexico." *Bulletin of Latin American Research* 32, no. s1 (2013): 116–23. https://doi.org/10.1111/blar.12109.
———. "Ley Fuga as Justice: The Consensus around Extrajudicial Violence in Twentieth-Century Mexico." In *Violence and Crime in Latin America: Representations and Politics,* edited by Gema Santamaría and David Carey Jr., 23–43. Norman: University of Oklahoma Press, 2017.
———. "Murders of Nota Roja: Truth and Justice in Mexican Crime News." *Past and Present* 223, no. 1 (2014): 195–231. https://doi.org/10.1093/pastj/gtt044.
———. "Notes for a History of the Press in Mexico." In *Journalism, Satire, and Censorship in Mexico,* edited by Paul Gillingham, Michael Leitteri, and Benjamin T. Smith, 33–59. Albuquerque: University of New Mexico Press, 2018.
———. *The Tyranny of Public Opinion: Honor in the Construction of the Mexican Public Sphere.* Durham, NC: Duke University Press, 2010.
Pierce, Gretchen. "Parades, Epistles and Prohibitive Legislation: Mexico's National Anti-Alcohol Campaign and the Process of State-Building, 1934–1940." *Social History of Alcohol and Drugs* 23, no. 2 (2009): 151–80. https://doi.org/10.1086/shad23020151.
Pinto Durán, Astrid Maribel, and Martín De La Cruz López Moya. "Comunidad diferenciada: Linchamiento por brujería e imaginarios políticos en un pueblo Tojolabal." *LiminaR. Estudios Sociales y Humanísticos* 2, no. 1 (2013): 94. https://doi.org/10.29043/liminar.v2i1.146.
Pitt-Rivers, Julian. "Spiritual Power in Central America: The Naguals of Chiapas." In *From Hospitality to Grace: A Julian Pitt-Rivers Omnibus,* edited by Giovanni da Col and Andrew Shryock, 227–47. Chicago: Hau Books, 2017.
Pulido Esteva, Diego. "Los negocios de la policía en la Ciudad de México durante la posrevolución." *Trashumante: Revista Americana de Historia Social,* no. 6 (January 2015). https://doi.org/10.17533/udea.trahs.n6a02.
Quiñones, Sam. *True Tales from Another Mexico: The Lynch Mob, the Popsicle Kings, Chalino, and the Bronx.* Albuquerque: University of New Mexico Press, 2001.

Quintana, Alejandro. *Maximino Ávila Camacho and the One-Party State: The Taming of Caudillismo and Caciquismo in Post-Revolutionary Mexico*. Lanham, MD: Lexington Books, 2010.
Raby, David L. *Educación y revolución social en México: 1921–1940*. Mexico City: Secretaría de Educación Pública, 1974.
———. "Ideología y construcción del Estado: La función política de la educación rural en México: 1921–1935." *Revista Mexicana de Sociología* 51, no. 2 (1989): 305–20.
———. "Los maestros rurales y los conflictos sociales." *Historia Mexicana* 18, no. 2 (1968): 190–226.
Ramirez, Daniel. *Migrating Faith: Pentecostalism in the United States and Mexico in the Twentieth Century*. Chapel Hill: University of North Carolina Press, 2015.
Ramsés, Edmundo. "Linchamiento en Ajalpan: 'Ley de la selva.'" *Milenio*, October 29, 2015.
Rashkin, Elissa. "Representations of Violence in Testimonies of the Campesino Movement in Veracruz." *A Contracorriente* 9, no. 2 (2012): 134–69.
Rath, Thomas. "'Que el cielo un soldado en cada hijo te dio . . . ': Conscription, Recalcitrance and Resistance in Mexico in the 1940s." *Journal of Latin American Studies* 37, no. 3 (2005): 507–31. https://doi.org/10.1017/s0022216x05009442.
———. *Myths of Demilitarization in Postrevolutionary Mexico, 1920–1960*. Chapel Hill: University of North Carolina Press, 2013.
———. "Camouflaging the State: The Army and the Limits of Hegemony in PRIista Mexico, 1940–1960." In *Dictablanda Politics, Work, and Culture in Mexico, 1938–1968*, edited by Paul Gillingham and Benjamin T. Smith, 89–107. Durham, NC: Duke University Press, 2014.
Redacción Animal Político. "Habitantes linchan a dos encuestadores en Ajalpan, Puebla." *Animal Político*, October 20, 2015.
Redacción Diario de Xalapa. "Intentan linchar a comandante; policías agredieron a pareja de ancianos." *Diario de Xalapa*, April 13, 2019.
Reed, Isaac. "Why Salem Made Sense: Culture, Gender, and the Puritan Persecution of Witchcraft." *Cultural Sociology* 1, no. 2 (2007): 209–34. https://doi.org/10.1177/1749975507078188.
Robertson, Campbell. "History of Lynchings in the South Documents Nearly 4,000 Names." *New York Times*, February 10, 2015.
Rodríguez Guillén, Raúl. "Crisis de autoridad y violencia social: Los linchamientos en México." *Polis* 8, no. 22 (2012): 43–74.
Rodríguez Guillén, Raúl, and Norma Ilse Veloz Ávila. "Linchamientos en México: Recuento de un periodo largo (1988–2014)." *El Cotidiano*, no. 187 (2014): 51–58.
Romanucci-Ross, Lola. *Conflict, Violence, and Morality in a Mexican Village*. Chicago: University of Chicago Press, 1986.
Romero Melgarejo, Osvaldo. *La violencia como fenómeno social: El linchamiento en San Miguel Canoa*. Jorale: Colegio de Tlaxcala, 2006.
Romero Melgarejo, Osvaldo, and Alessa Pech. "La muerte violenta de los niños por las brujas en Tlaxcala." *Varia* 2, no. 3 (2013): 99–125.
Rubin, Jeffrey W. "Decentering the Regime: Culture and Regional Politics in Mexico." *Latin American Research Review* 31, no. 3 (1996): 85–126.

Rus, Jan. "The 'Comunidad Revolucionaria Institucional': The Subversion of Native Government in Highland Chiapas, 1936–1968." In *Everyday Forms of State Formation: Revolution and the Negotiation of Rule in Modern Mexico*, edited by Daniel Nugent and Gilbert M. Joseph, 265–300. Durham, NC: Duke University Press, 1994.

Salinas, Salvador. "Untangling Mexico's Noodle: El Tallarín and the Revival of Zapatismo in Morelos, 1934–1938." *Journal of Latin American Studies* 46, no. 3 (2014): 471–99. https://doi.org/10.1017/s0022216x1400073x.

Samper, David. "Cannibalizing Kids: Rumor and Resistance in Latin America." *Journal of Folklore Research* 39, no. 1 (2002): 1–32.

Sandoval Forero, Eduardo. "Familias indígenas conversas: Nuevas relaciones sociales y culturales. El caso de los Mazahuas en el Estado de México." *Papeles de Población* 12, no. 12 (1996): 15–22.

Santamaría, Gema. "Legitimating Lynching: Public Opinion and Extralegal Violence in Mexico." In *Violence and Crime in Latin America: Representations and Politics*, edited by Gema Santamaría and David Carey Jr., 44–60. Norman: University of Oklahoma Press, 2017.

———. "Lynching, Religion, and Politics in Twentieth-Century Puebla." In *Global Lynching and Collective Violence*, vol. 2: *The Americas and Europe*, edited by Michael J. Pfeifer, 85–114. Urbana: University of Illinois Press, 2017.

Santamaría, Gema, and David Carey Jr., eds. *Violence and Crime in Latin America: Representations and Politics*. Norman: University of Oklahoma Press, 2017.

Santillán Esqueda, Martha. "Mujeres delincuentes e imaginarios: Criminología, cine y nota roja en México, 1940–1950." *Varia Historia* 33, no. 62 (2017): 389–418. https://doi.org/10.1590/0104-87752017000200006.

Santoyo, Antonio. "La mano negra en defensa de la propiedad y el orden: Veracruz 1928–1943." *Secuencia*, no. 28 (January 1994): 81. https://doi.org/10.18234/secuencia.v0i28.452.

Sarmiento, Sergio. "México profundo." *El Diario*, October 21, 2015. Available at http://diario.mx/Opinion/2015-10-21_aed1570d/mexico-profundo/; accessed September 1, 2019.

Schedler, Andreas. "Ciudadanía y violencia organizada en México: Informe final del proyecto CONACYT-IFE: Balas y votos: Violencia, política y ciudadanía en México." Mexico City: CIDE, 2014.

Schmidt, Arthur. "Making It Real Compared to What? Reconceptualizing Mexican History since 1940." In *Fragments of a Golden Age*, edited by Gilbert M. Joseph, Anne Rubenstein, and Eric Zolov, 23–69. Durham, NC: Duke University Press, 2001.

Scott, James C. *Domination and the Arts of Resistance: Hidden Transcripts*. New Haven, CT: Yale University Press, 1992),

Senechal de la Roche, Roberta. "Collective Violence as Social Control." *Sociological Forum* 11, no. 1 (1996): 97–128. https://doi.org/10.1007/bf02408303.

———. "Why Is Collective Violence Collective?" *Sociological Theory* 19, no. 2 (2001): 126–44. https://doi.org/10.1111/0735-2751.00133.

Serrano Álvarez, Pablo. "El sinarquismo en el Bajío mexicano (1934–1951): Historia de un movimiento social regional." *Estudios de Historia Moderna y Contemporánea de México* 14 (1991): 195–236.

Shadow, Robert, and María Rodríguez-Shadow. "Los 'Robachicos.'" *México Indígena* 22 (1991): 41–46.

Shirk, David, et al. "Drug Violence in Mexico: Data and Analysis through 2013." Justice in Mexico Project, April 2014. https://justiceinmexico.org/drug-violence-in-mexico-data-and-analysis-through-2013/; last accessed January 31, 2020.

Sieder, Rachel. "Contested Sovereignties: Indigenous Law, Violence and State Effects in Postwar Guatemala." *Critique in Anthropology* 31, no. 3 (2011): 161–84.

Signorini, Italy, and Alessandro Lupo. "The Ambiguity of Evil among the Nahua of the Sierra." *Etnofoor* 5, no. 1–2 (1992): 81–94.

Smith, Benjamin T. *The Mexican Press and Civil Society, 1940–1976: Stories from the Newsroom, Stories from the Street*. Chapel Hill: University of North Carolina Press, 2018.

———. *Pistoleros and Popular Movements: The Politics of State Formation in Postrevolutionary Oaxaca*. Lincoln: University of Nebraska Press, 2009.

———. "Towards a Typology of Rural Responses to Healthcare in Mexico, 1920–1960." *Endeavour* 37, no. 1 (2013): 39–46. https://doi.org/10.1016/j.endeavour.2012.10.006.

Smith, Nicholas. *Contradictions of Democracy: Vigilantism and Rights in Post-Apartheid South Africa*. Oxford: Oxford University Press, 2019.

Snodgrass Godoy, Angelina. *Popular Injustice: Violence, Community, and Law in Latin America*. Stanford, CA: Stanford University Press, 2006.

———. "When 'Justice' Is Criminal: Lynchings in Contemporary Latin America." *Theory and Society* 33, no. 6 (2004): 621–51. https://doi.org/10.1023/b:ryso.0000049192.62380.29.

Sodi, Carlos Franco. "Muchedumbres delincuentes y delitos políticos." *Criminalia*, March 21, 1935.

Soto Laveaga, Gabriela. "Bringing the Revolution to Medical Schools." *Mexican Studies / Estudios Mexicanos* 29, no. 2 (2013): 397–427. https://doi.org/10.1525/msem.2013.29.2.397.

Speckman, Elisa. "Instituciones de justicia y práctica judicial (Ciudad de México: 1929–1971)." PhD dissertation, Universidad Nacional Autónoma de México, 2018.

Speed, Shannon, and Jane F. Collier. "Limiting Indigenous Autonomy in Chiapas, Mexico: The State Government's Use of Human Rights." *Human Rights Quarterly* 22, no. 4 (2000): 877–905. https://doi.org/10.1353/hrq.2000.0050.

Stern, Alexandra Minna. "Responsible Mothers and Normal Children: Eugenics, Nationalism, and Welfare in Post-Revolutionary Mexico, 1920–1940." *Journal of Historical Sociology* 12, no. 4 (1999): 369–97. https://doi.org/10.1111/1467-6443.00097.

Stoler, Ann Laura. "'In Cold Blood': Hierarchies of Credibility and the Politics of Colonial Narratives." *Representations* 37 (1992): 151–89. https://doi.org/10.1057/9780230360075_2.

Taracena, Alfonso. *La verdadera revolución mexicana*. Mexico City: Editorial Jus, 1975.

Taylor, William B. *Drinking, Homicide, and Rebellion in Colonial Mexican Villages*. Stanford, CA: Stanford University Press, 2004.

———. *Magistrates of the Sacred: Priests and Parishioners in Eighteenth-Century Mexico*. Stanford, CA: Stanford University Press, 1996.

Thompson, E. P. "The Moral Economy of the English Crowd in the Eighteenth Century." *Past and Present* 50, no. 1 (1971): 76–136. https://doi.org/10.1093/past/50.1.76.

Tolnay, Stewart Emory, and E. M. Beck. *A Festival of Violence: An Analysis of the Lynching of African-Americans in the American South, 1882–1930*. Urbana: University of Illinois Press, 1995.

———. "'Racialized Terrorism' in the American South: Do Completed Lynchings Tell an Accurate Story?" *Social Science History* 42, no. 4 (2018): 677–701. https://doi.org/10.1017/ssh.2018.22.

Torres Ramírez, Blanca. *México en la segunda guerra mundial*. Mexico City: Colegio de México, 1983.

Ungar, Mark. "The Privatization of Citizen Security in Latin America: From Elite Guards to Neighborhood Vigilantes." *Social Justice* 34, no. 3–4 (2007): 20–37.

Vanderwood, Paul J. *Juan Soldado, Rapist, Murderer, Martyr, Saint*. Durham, NC: Duke University Press, 2004.

———. *The Power of God against the Guns of Government: Religious Upheaval in Mexico at the Turn of the Nineteenth Century*. Stanford, CA: Stanford University Press, 1999.

———. "Religion: Official, Popular, and Otherwise." *Mexican Studies/Estudios Mexicanos* 16, no. 2 (2000): 411–41.

Van Young, Eric. *The Other Rebellion: Popular Violence, Ideology, and the Mexican Struggle for Independence, 1810–1821*. Stanford, CA: Stanford University Press, 2002.

Vaughan, Mary K. *Cultural Politics in Revolution: Teachers, Peasants, and Schools in Mexico, 1930–1940*. Tucson: University of Arizona Press, 1997.

———. "El papel político del magisterio socialista de México, 1934—1940: Un estudio comparativo de los casos de Puebla y Sonora." In *Memoria del XII Simposio de Historia y Antropología*, 175–97. Hermosillo: Instituto de Investigaciones Históricas, Universidad de Sonora, 1998.

———. "Nationalizing the Countryside: Schools and Rural Communities in the 1930s." In *The Eagle and the Virgin: Nation and Cultural Revolution in Mexico, 1920–1940*, edited by Mary Kay Vaughn and Stephen E. Lewis, 157–75. Durham, NC: Duke University Press, 2006.

Vaughan, Mary K., and Stephen E. Lewis, eds. *The Eagle and the Virgin: Nation and Cultural Revolution in Mexico, 1920–1940*. Durham, NC: Duke University Press, 2006.

———. Introduction to *The Eagle and the Virgin: Nation and Cultural Revolution in Mexico, 1920–1940*, edited by Mary K. Vaughan and Stephen E. Lewis, 1–21. Durham, NC: Duke University Press, 2006.

Vilas, Carlos M. "(In)Justicia por mano propia: Linchamientos en el México contemporáneo." *Revista Mexicana de Sociología* 63, no. 1 (2001): 131–60.

Villanueva, Simón. "El maestro rural en la educación." In Secretaría de Educación Pública, *Los maestros y la cultura nacional*. Mexico City: Secretaría de Educación Pública, 1987.

Viqueira, Carmen, and Ángel Palerm. "Alcoholismo, brujería y homicidio en dos comunidades rurales de México." *Revista Mexicana de Sociología* 18, no. 1 (1956): 194. https://doi.org/10.2307/3537588.

Waldrep, Christopher. "War of Words: The Controversy over the Definition of Lynching, 1899–1940." *Journal of Southern History* 66, no. 1 (2000): 75. https://doi.org/10.2307/2587438.

Ward, Jason Morgan. *Hanging Bridge: Racial Violence and America's Civil Rights Century*. New York: Oxford University Press, 2018.

Waters, Wendy. "Remapping Identities: Road Construction and Nation Building in Postrevolutionary Mexico." In *The Eagle and the Virgin: Nation and Cultural Revolution in Mexico, 1920–1940*, edited by Mary Kay Vaughan and Stephen E. Lewis, 221–42. Durham, NC: Duke University Press, 2006.

Weber, Max. "Politics as Vocation." In *From Max Weber: Essays in Sociology*, edited by H. H. Gerth and C. Wright Mills, 77–128. New York: Oxford University Press, 1946.

Weller, Susan C., Roberta D. Baer, Javier Garcia De Alba Garcia, Mark Glazer, Robert Trotter, Ana L. Salcedo Rocha, Robert E. Klein, and Lee M. Pachter. "Variation and Persistence in Latin American Beliefs about Evil Eye." *Cross-Cultural Research* 49, no. 2 (2014): 174–203. https://doi.org/10.1177/1069397114539268.

Wendt, Simon and Manfred Berg, eds. *Globalizing Lynching History: Vigilantism and Extralegal Punishment from an International Perspective*. London: Palgrave Macmillan, 2011.

Williams, Gareth. "Death in the Andes: Ungovernability and the Birth of Tragedy in Peru." In *The Latin American Subaltern Studies Reader*, edited by Ileana Rodríguez, 260–87. Durham, NC: Duke University Press, 2001. https://doi.org/10.1215/9780822380771-014.

Wood, Amy Louise. *Lynching and Spectacle: Witnessing Racial Violence in America, 1890–1940*. Chapel Hill: University of North Carolina Press, 2011.

Wright-Rios, Edward N. *Revolutions in Mexican Catholicism: Reform and Revelation in Oaxaca, 1887–1934*. Durham, NC: Duke University Press, 2009.

———. *Searching for Madre Matiana: Prophecy and Popular Culture in Modern Mexico*. Alburquerque: University of New Mexico Press, 2014.

———. "Visions of Women: Revelation, Gender and Catholic Resurgence." In *Religious Culture in Modern Mexico*, edited by Martin Austin Nesvig, 178–202. New York: Rowman & Littlefield, 2007.

Zizumbo-Colunga, Daniel. "Explaining Support for Vigilante Justice in Mexico." *AmericasBarometer Insights*, no. 39 (2010). Available at www.vanderbilt.edu/lapop/insights/I0839en.pdf; accessed September 1, 2019.

Zolov, Eric. *Refried Elvis: The Rise of the Mexican Counterculture*. Berkeley: University of California Press, 1999.

INDEX

Page numbers in *italics* denote illustrations. Incidents are listed by name of the victim under the headings "victims of lynching or attempted lynching," or "victims of other violence."

Acción Católica Mexicana, 32, 56, 60, 148n58
African Americans. *See* racism; United States—lynching in
agency, of the subordinated classes, lynching portrayed as, 10, 125n45
agrarian reform: abandonment of, Manuel Ávila Camacho and, 56; land distribution as welcomed, 22; and lynchings due to land disputes, 23, 132n60; and lynchings of local authorities, 22–23, 52, 132–33nn59–60,62; and lynchings of socialist teachers, 19, 41, 132–33nn60,62; and lynchings of witches, 92; opposition to, 21, 22–23, 132n59, 133n63; opposition to by the Catholic Church, 51, 150nn76–77; socialist education in implementation of, 19, 41, 51, 130n27, 150nn76–77. *See also agrarista* peasants
agrarista peasants: Catholic religion and attacks on, 40, 49; definition of, 35; *guardias blancas* and attacks on, 131n42, 133n63, 150n77; Mano Negra and attacks on, 150n77; militias (*defensas rurales*) and attacks on, 133n63; as perpetrators of lynchings, 93, 100; La Segunda and attacks on, 124–25n32; and witchcraft-related political killings, 105, 106
Aguascalientes (state), 18–19, 52

alcohol inspectors. *See* anti-alcohol campaigns
Alemán Valdés, Miguel, 7
Alianza Juvenil, 139n138
Almazán, Juan Andreu, 36, 141n154
anthropology, and resistance/accommodation processes, 136n98
anti-alcohol campaigns: lynchings motivated by, 22, 29, 132nn55,57, 136n96; socialist education and, 19, 132n57
archeological sites, 21
Argentina, 3, 116
Arroyo, Arnulfo, 140n145
art. *See* public art
"attempted lynching," definition of and importance of studying, 123n20
authorities, 16. *See also* local authorities; state actors
Auyero, Javier, 173n4
Ávila Camacho, Manuel: conservative politics of, 56; the death penalty brought back as "emergency decree" under, 72, 158nn15,25; letters to, protesting anti-Protestant attacks, 59; and Mexico's "economic miracle," 7; and military conscription, 23; and political murders, 36, 73, 141n154; and state détente with the Catholic Church, 55, 56, 154n124

195

Ávila Camacho, Maximino: and the local newspaper *La Opinión,* 175n15; opposition to agrarian reform, 133n63; and political violence, 36, 141nn154,161
Ávila Camacho, Rafael, 138n127

Bantjes, Adrian A., 131n37, 132n59, 146n32, 149n70
Bastian, Jean-Pierre, 149n68, 155–56n137,141
Beals, Carleton, 151n91
Becker, Marjorie, 146–47n39
bell ringing to summon lynchers, 118, 174n8
Benitez, Fernando, *El agua envenanada,* 33, 139nn134,138
Betancourt, Carlos, 31, 32, 138n123, 141n161
Blancarte, Roberto, 142–43n7, 144n17, 153n116, 155n136
bloodsucker figures. *See* mythical beliefs and mythical figures
Bolaina, Zenón, 35
Bolivia, 3, 123n14, 162–63n79, 166n26
Brazil, 3, 116, 154n131, 162–63n79
bribes, 72, 103, 137n114
brujos/brujas. See witches/healers/spiritists
Brundage, W. Fitzhugh, 174n6
Buffington, Robert, 157–58n8
Butler, Matthew, 145n30

caciques: the cargo system and power of, 155–56n141; as embodying the parainstitutional forms of social and political control, 128n10
—COMPLICITY WITH LYNCHINGS: and agrarian reform, 23; state-sanctioned lynchings, 17, 37–38, 141n161
—LYNCHINGS OF: overview, 10; for abuse of authority, 17, 32–34, 139nn132,134–136,138; definition of, 32; as persistent pattern, 11
Calles, Plutarco Elías, 124n24, 147n147
capitalist model of Mexico, 7
car accidents, lynchings for, 160n47
Cárdenas Hernández, Gregorio, 65, 157n3
Cárdenas, Lázaro: overview of social programs under, 7; and anticlericalism, abandonment of policy of, 45, 55, 146n35, 153n115; complaints to, by family members of lynching victims, 36; complaints to, on priests inciting violence, 55; and iconoclasm of Tomás Garrido Canabal, 47, 147n147, 148n60; and *ley fuga,* 28; and lynching of Aquiles de la Peña, 33, 141n161; and lynching of Ernesto Malda, 148n56; and socialist education, establishment of, 50; and socialist teachers, 50, 130n30, 151n92; support from artists and writers, 131n39
cargo system, 155–56n141
Carranza, Venustiano, 155n137
Carrigan, William D., 124n27
Catholic religion: anticommunism of, 56–57, 144n18, 154n131; anti-Protestantism of, 57, 58, 143n13, 149n68; defined as a field that involves both the spiritual realm and the material/political, 41–42, 61, 143nn9–11; distancing of higher ranks from armed resistance/violence, 41, 42, 56, 144n17, 149n66; divisions within the Catholic Church, 42–43, 144nn16–19; language of higher ranks as belligerent and legitimating violence, 42–43, 48, 57, 61–62, 144n18; opposition to agrarian reform, 51, 150nn76–77; percentage of population identifying as, 143n9, 155n135; reopening of Catholic schools, 154n124; state cooperation/collaboration with, 56–57, 61, 154n126; state détente (modus vivendi) with, 11, 41, 55, 56, 61, 62, 142–43n7, 153nn115–116, 154n124; thieves of religious images and, 146n36; vigilantes as motivated by, 53, 152n101; World War II supported by, 154n126. *See also* Catholic religion, parish priests
—AND ANTICLERICALISM: abandonment of policy of, 23, 45, 55, 56, 146n35, 153nn115–116, 154n124; article 3 of the constitution, 21, 56; civic religion sought, 44, 145n30; collective violence in opposition to, 45; Cristero War in opposition to, 42, 143n13; "cultural Sundays"/ demonstrations in front of churches, 47, 50, 149n70; defanaticization campaigns, 19, 21, 44, 47, 51, 145n29; as federal policy to reduce the power of the church, 44–45, 46–47, 145–46nn29–30,32, 147nn46–47; *ley de cultos* (1926; law of religious worship), 44; local authorities and, 21–22; nonviolent resistance to, 142n6; red and black flag symbolizing, 47, 147–48nn50,56; riots in protest of iconoclasm and, 41, 45, 46, 47, 49–50, 146n36, 147n44, 148n64; socialist education policy and, 19, 20–21, 23, 41, 51, 130n30, 150nn79,83. *See also* Catholic religion—and iconoclasm; Catholic religion—lynchings motivated by; Cristero War; Second Cristiada
—AND ICONOCLASM: abandonment of policy, 45; as federal policy to reduce the power of the church, 44–45, 46–47, 146n32, 147nn46–47; vs. importance of images, artifacts, and spac-

es to Catholics, 43, 144n20; by Protestants, 56; socialist education and, 19, 51, 150n83
—FOLK OR POPULAR: definition of, 143n8; festivals and rituals of, and Protestant refusal to participate in, 58, 155–56nn140–141; genuinely affective experiences due to threats against religion, 49, 50; importance in legitimating violence, 5, 41, 42–43, 48–49, 50, 60, 144n19, 149nn65–66; sacrificial ethos of, 43, 145n25; veneration of religious images, importance of, 144n20
—LAY COMMUNITY: Acción Católica Mexicana as pacific and civil mobilization of, 56, 60; and the conservative and reactionary ideology of the Church, 43; vigilantes, support for, 54, 152n108. *See also* Acción Católica Mexicana; Liga Nacional Defensora de la Libertad Religiosa
—LYNCHINGS MOTIVATED BY: overview, 13, 40–43, 61–62, 145n26; and conservative and reactionary ideology, 43, 144n21; cruelty in, 40, 51–53, 150–51n84; gender and, 144n19; and importance of religious images and spaces to Catholics, 43, 144n20; and legitimation of violence, 41, 42–43, 48–50, 144nn18–19, 145nn23,25, 149n66; as persistent pattern, 11; as resistance to anticlericalism, 44–45, 146n35; and the ringing of bells as projecting community sanction of violence, 174n8; sacrificial ethos of martyrdom and, 43, 145nn23,25; for theft of religious images, 41, 45–46, 55, 146n36,38, 149n71; vigilante group involvement in, 41, 142n3. *See also* Catholic religion—lynchings of impious individuals; Catholic religion, parish priests—complicity with lynching and vigilantism; Protestants—lynchings of; socialist teachers—lynchings of
—LYNCHINGS OF IMPIOUS INDIVIDUALS: overview, 41; and intracommunity conflicts over land and resources, 49; local priest involvement in, 44, 47, 48–50, 147–48n50, 149n65–66,71–72, 172n13; and martyrdom, conflicting stories of, 48, 148nn58–59; narratives of, 40, 43–44, 45, 47–49, 146–48nn38–39,44,50,52, 149n71; as political crime, 148n64; press representations of, 48–50, 148n63; rumor and, 45–46, 147n44; spiritists and other religious beliefs, 149n68; for theft of religious images, 41, 45–46, 55, 146nn35,38, 149n71
Catholic religion, parish priests: as lynching victims, 158n13

—COMPLICITY WITH LYNCHING AND VIGILANTISM: overview, 10, 43, 126n47; authority of local priests and, 50, 62, 149n72; legitimation of violence against Protestants, 58, 59–60, 112, 156–57n151; legitimation of violence against socialist teachers, 49–50, 54–55, 153n113; and lynchings of impious individuals, 44, 47, 48–50, 147–48n50, 149n65–66,71–72, 172n13; and religious vs. material interests, 53
cattle rustling, 86–87, 163–64nn90,92–93,96
cattle. *See* foot-and-mouth disease (cattle) eradication program
Cazals, Felipe, *Canoa, Memoria de un hecho vergonzoso*, 128n5
Ceja, Jesús A., 54
censorship: crime news stories as avoiding, 73, 119, 175nn14–15; of political murders, 73
Chiapas (state): anti-alcohol campaigners, attacks on, 132n57, 136n96; and the cargo system, 155–56n141; and geography of lynching, 3, 122n7; lynching of anticlericalists, 147n44; lynching of local authorities, 137–38n122; lynching of Protestants, 41; lynching of socialist teachers, 19; mythical figures in, 95; witchcraft and lynchings of witches in, 164–65n6, 170n74, 171n87
Chihuahua (state), 29, 77, 81–82
child snatchers (*robachicos*): fear of, as defense of reproductive resources, 167n36; lynchings of accused, 1–2, 67, 89, 96–97, 122n3, 136n109, 160n47; mythlike narratives as making sense of, 107–8; narrative of, the press and, 67; rumor and, 147n41, 167n38
Chinese people, lynchings of, 124n27
class: the press as reifying notions of violence based on, 119; shared status of perpetrators and victims of lynching, 112. *See also* economic inequality; elites; workers' and peasants' rights
Coahuila (state), 74, 82–83, 105
Coalición Nacional Revolucionaria, 139n138
Cold War, 116
Colima (state), 32
Colombia, anti-Protestant violence in, 154n131
Comaroff, Jean, 165n10
Comaroff, John, 165n10
Comité Nacional de Defensa Evangélica, 59
communism: anticommunist politics of Manuel Ávila Camacho, 56–57; Catholic Church's anticommunism, 56–57, 144n18

198   INDEX

communists: lynching of university workers (1968), 116, 141–42n162, 147–48n50, 172n13; lynchings of, organized vigilantes participating in, 174n7; as "sacrificeable" characters, 125–26n46
community-sanctioned dimension of lynching: overview, 113–14; and crime-related lynchings, 113; defined as term, 118; as defining incidents as lynching, 35, 118, 173nn3–4; and distrust of state actors, 2–3, 4, 114, 123n14; as enforcement of actual or imagined boundaries of a community, 118; and mythical beliefs, 5, 91–92, 108; and persistence of lynching, 116; as persistent, despite the abolition of the death penalty, 6, 11, 69–70; and police, lynching of, 110; press coverage of, 113; and shared notions of deviancy and danger, 4; and support for lynching in Latin American countries, 4, 114, 116, 123n14; the United States and, 173n3. *See also* extralegal violence; justice, lynching viewed as legitimate means to attain; public opinion
contemporary lynchings: for child theft allegations, 1–2; as global phenomenon, 6, 115, 116; of police officers, 109–10; for robberies, as main offense eliciting lynchings, 162–63n79; statistics on, and dynamics of representation, 127n59; surge in numbers of (1980s and 1990s), 116; and use of new technologies of communication (cell phone, social media), 4
corruption. *See* justice system, corruption in
crime: overview, 5; and consensus between citizens and state authorities on the use of extralegal violence, 67, 68, 69–71, 88, 113; and consensus between perpetrators and public opinion on the use of extralegal violence, 66; perceived increases in, 4, 69, 76; reconstructions of, 75, 82. *See also* crime news (*nota roja*); crime statistics; criminals (presumed), lynchings of; death penalty
crime news (*nota roja*): overview, 8; on "animalistic instincts," 65, 67, 72, 77, 81, 161n61; censorship as avoided by, 73, 119, 175nn14–15; censorship of political murders, 73; collective outrage as reflected and amplified in, 67, 69; as covered in both tabloids and mainstream newspapers, 66; didactic overtones of "lessons" on discerning acceptable and unacceptable conduct, 67, 78–79, 81, 87, 157–58n8; guilt as presumed in, 65; on *ley fuga* (law of flight) killings, 67, 70, 72, 75–76, 158nn18,20,

160nn39,43; on men's violent and/or sexual "instincts," 81, 82, 162n70; on mysterious disappearances and deaths of prisoners in police custody, 67, 70, 158n18, 164n93; on police prevention of lynchings, 71–72, 83; political messages urging "tough on crime" responses from politicians, 67, 73, 86–87; readership of, 65–66, 67, 157nn4,6; sensationalistic style of, 66, 67, 68, 69, 83; on substance abuse, 81, 161n60. *See also* crime news, representations of mob violence as legitimate form of justice; criminals (presumed), lynchings of; press
crime news, representations of mob violence as legitimate form of justice: overview, 66–67; and community-sanctioned dimension of lynching, 113; contrasted with news coverage on lynching cases involving religion, mythical beliefs, or opposition to modernization, 66; despite the brutal and uncivil character of lynching, 66; moral economy of lynching, narrative of, 85–87, 148n63, 163nn80–82,85,88; and morality of lynching, narrative of, 78, 81, 88; perceived inability of the state to deliver justice, 66, 74–75, 83, 86–87, 112; perception of "crime wave" and, 69, 76; proportional punishment claimed in, 66, 76–78, 83, 85, 87; swift and lethal forms of punishment as more effective, 83, 86, 87, 88; "unnatural" mothers as reinforcing, 79, 161nn55–56. *See also* press—representations of lynching
crime statistics: homicide rates, decreases in, 68, 158n10; as reflection of authorities' prioritization of crimes, 120; as underrepresenting non-criminal conduct that is critical to security of the community, 120, 175n18. *See also* statistics on lynching
Criminalia, 89
criminals (presumed), lynchings of: overview, 67–68, 87–88; abusive sons, 68, 79–81, 80, 82, 161nn57,60–61; child theft, 160n47; child thieves (*robachicos*), 1–2, 67, 89, 96–97, 122n3, 136n109, 160n47; and culture of punishment, 88; as disproportional and excessive form of punishment, 78, 85; for domestic violence against women, 68, 81–82, 161n65; gravity of crimes as differing greatly, 77–78, 85, 160n47; gravity of the crime as justification for, 65, 66, 75, 160n37; for inconsequential crimes, 66, 78, 85, 162–63n79; innocence voiced by suspects, as ignored, 85; for intent to commit

a crime, 66, 78, 85; justice system ineffectiveness as justification for, 65, 74–75; and *lex talionis* (eye for an eye), 65, 76–77; mayors complicit with, 36–37; as "natural" response to crime, 67, 157n5; norms of behaviors as violated by victims of, 68, 113; overkilling of victims, 159n33; and perceptions of insecurity and dangerousness, 78, 160n49; as persistent pattern, 11; police protection of lynching victims, 65, 71–72, 74, 75, 78, 79, 81, 82, 83, 85, 87–88, 161n65, 162n69; prisoners lynched by other inmates, 160n40; prisons, dragging victims out of, 74–75, 159n34; as "sacrificeable" characters, 125–26n46; for sexual violence against women, 28, 82–83, 162nn70,72,74; "unnatural" mothers, 67, 68, 78–79, 81, 161nn55–56; as warning, 78, 86, 87, 112, 164n92; women as participating in, 82, 83, 86, 162n69
—CRIMES AGAINST PROPERTY: overview, 67, 68; as "bloodless crimes," 85; cattle rustling, 86–87, 163–64nn90,92,96; as main offense eliciting lynching in contemporary Latin America, 162–63n79; and moral economy of lynching, 85–87, 148n63, 163nn80–82,85,88; *rateros* (robbers), as term, 85, 163n82
—MURDERS: overview, 67–68; animalistic instincts of killers, 65, 67, 72, 77, 161n61; impunity of murderers and, 69, 74–75, 77, 158n16; in lieu of death penalty, 63, 65, 69, 73, 76–77; narratives of, 63–65, 64, 68–69, 70, 71–72, 73–74, 75–76, 77, 82, 157n3; women as participating in, 82
Cristeros: definition of, 124n24; as vigilantes participating in lynch mobs, 142n3, 174n7
Cristero War (1926–29): overview, 6, 7, 124n24; end of, accords for, 41, 42, 142–43n7, 144n16, 149n66; and martyrdom, 43; and resistance to anticlericalism and socialism, 42, 143n13; support of church hierarchy for armed resistance during, 144n17
cruelty in lynchings: overview, 3, 4, 113–14; Catholic perpetrators and, 40, 51–53, 150–51n84; as increasing with level of ritualization, 118–19; and mythical figures, 91, 93, 108; overkilling of victims, 91, 113, 159n33; and witches, 91, 99–100, 105–6, 107, 108, 168nn50–51, 170n77, 171n87. *See also* torture
cruelty in state-sanctioned extralegal violence, 17, 35, 38

Cueto, Marcos, 136n98
culture of punishment, 88
curanderas. See witches/healers/spiritists

Davis, Natalie Zemon, 143n11, 150–51n84
death from lynching: as expected end result in the United States, 122n12; as not necessarily the end result in Latin America, 3, 123n20; statistics on, 123n20
death penalty: abolishment of, 6, 69; brought back as "emergency decree" under Manuel Ávila Camacho, 72, 158nn15,25; demands for reinstatement of, 65, 76, 88; *ley fuga* in lieu of, 77, 160n43; lynching criminals in lieu of, 63, 65, 69, 73, 76–77; pardons of those receiving, 158n25; persistence of lynching despite abolition of, 6, 11, 69–70
death squads, 3–4
Demos, John Putnam, 165n7
Derby, Lauren, 166n26
Díaz del Castillo, Bernal, 95
Díaz, Porfirio, 44, 124n23, 129–30n26, 140n145, 151n91
"dirty war" (ca. 1969–78), 116
Distrito Federal. *See* Mexico City (state)
domestic violence, lynchings of perpetrators of, 68, 81–82, 161n65
Douglas, Mary, 102, 165n10
Dow, James, 155–56n141
drug and alcohol abuse, representations of, 81, 161n60
drug-related violence, 110, 111, 116
Durango (state), 51, 131n41, 135n83

economic inequality: high contemporary rates of, 3, 122nn8,10; Mexico's "economic miracle" and increase in, 7, 125n35
Ecuador, 3, 116, 162–63n79
Elías Calles, Plutarco, 44, 50
Elias, Norbert, 129n116
elites: abandonment of anticlericalism by, 23; and authority of parish priests, 50; capitalist model of, 7; and criminalization of lynching, 115; impunity as guaranteed by, 38; impunity of, and political power, 8; military conscription as favored by, 23; newspapers assumed to be the unequivocal expression of, 175n14; opposition to agrarian reform, 23, 133n63; policies as designed by, 128n11; public opinion of and plausible denial by, 142n165; socialist education as upsetting the interests

elites (continued)
of, 19; state-sanctioned lynchings as tolerated by, 37–38, 141n161, 142n165
El Salvador, 123n14
engineers of modernization projects, 11, 21, 23, 89, 96–97, 147n44
England, food riots in, 163n80
Estado de México (state): among most populated states, 127n56; and geography of lynching, 3, 122n7, 127n55; lynching of anticlericalists/iconoclasts, 41; lynching of criminals, 71–72, 74, 83, 86–87, 159n33; lynching of foot-and-mouth eradication personnel, 26; lynching of local authorities, 57–58, 135n94; lynching of Protestants, 41, 57–58, 156n150, 157n153; lynching of socialist teachers, 153n114; lynching of witches, 98, 100, 107, 167–68n41, 169n55; Protestant riot in Catholic church, 155n133; resistance to military conscription, 135n83; state-sanctioned lynchings, 37, 141n157
Estrada, Luis, *La ley de Herodes*, 31, 128n5
Europe, witchcraft and women in premodern, 164–65n6
Evangelicals, 55–56, 59, 142n4, 156–57nn145–147,151
Excélsior: crime news and, 66, 77; representations of the state as civilizing force, 20–21; as source, 175n13. *See also* Catholic religion; press
extralegal violence: overview, 174n10; community approval of *ley fuga* (law of flight), 9, 69–70, 75–76, 88, 125nn42–43, 160n39; community support for, 114, 123n14; consensus between citizens and state authorities on the use of, 67, 68, 69–71, 88, 113; consensus between perpetrators and public opinion on the use of, 66; methodology and, 174n10; public support for, despite decrease in homicide and crime rates, 68, 158n10. *See also* homicide; riots; state-sanctioned extralegal violence; vigilantes

Fallaw, Ben, 42, 53, 144n17, 147n46, 150n83
fat-stealer figures. *See* mythical beliefs and mythical figures
Fernández, Emilio: *Maclovia*, 15, 127n2, 128n5, 131n39; *María Candelaria*, 127n2, 128n5; *Paloma herida*, 127n2; *La Perla*, 127n2; *Río Escondido*, 127n2, 128n5
film: anti-witchcraft, 101–2, 169nn60,63; Golden Age of Mexican cinema, 15, 31, 127n3; indigenista films, 15, 101, 127n2; and the narrative of the state as a "civilizing force," 15–16, 169n60
Finchelstein, Federico, 144n21
folk Catholicism. *See* Catholic religion, folk or popular
foot-and-mouth disease (cattle) eradication program: and importance of cattle for subsistence, 86; lynchings motivated by, 24–25, 26–27, 134n76; Mexican-American Commission for the Eradication of Foot-and-Mouth Disease, 26, 135n89; popular opposition to, as pragmatic vs. "fanatic," 25–26, 135nn86,88–89; resistance and accommodation and, 26, 27; and the Sinarquistas, 25, 134n81
Foucault, Michel, 116
France, religious riots in, 143n11
Freemasons, 149n68
Friedlander, Judith, 163–64n90, 169n58

Garibi Rivera, José, 144n18, 153n116
Garrido Canabal, Tomás, 47, 48, 141n161, 147n47
Gayosso Ríos, Filadelfo, *Mi palabra (A la vera de Tlacuilo)*, 37
gender: overview of lynchings and, 10, 126nn48–49; and crime news of rapists ("satyrs"), 82, 162n70; ideal of "responsible motherhood," 79, 161nn55–56; and lynchings perpetrated in the name of religion, 144n19; and normalization of domestic violence, 81; representations of female fanaticism, 126n54; and witchcraft, 90–91, 106–7, 108, 164–65n6. *See also* women
geography of lynching, 3, 11, 12, 122n7, 126n53, 127nn55–59
Gillingham, Paul, 136n110
Girard, René, 125–26n46, 145n25
Goldstein, Daniel, 163n81
Gómez Velasco, Antonio, 23–24
Grajales, Victórico, 132n57
Guanajuato (state): among most populated states, 126n56; and geography of lynching, 127n55; lynching of criminals, 125n43; lynching of local authorities, 31–32, 137n114, 138n125; lynching of Protestants, 41, 57, 58; lynching of socialist teachers, 19, 49–50; and mythical beliefs, 167nn34,40
guardias blancas, 20, 131n42, 133n63, 150n77
Guatemala: lynchings in, 3, 116, 147n41, 160n49, 162–63n79; support for extralegal violence in, 123n14; witchcraft, overrepresentation

of accusations against women in colonial, 164–65n6
Guerrero (state): disappearance and massacre of university students (2014), 172n3; lynching of anticlericalists/iconoclasts, 150n83; lynching of criminals, 164n92; lynching of local authorities, 138n128; lynching of Protestants, 41; resistance to foot-and-mouth disease eradication program, 135n86; resistance to military conscription, 135n83; state-sanctioned extralegal violence, 38, 142n163, 171n89

Haiti, 123n14
healers. *See* witches/healers/spiritists
health and sanitation programs: modern medicine's cultural mission to witches/healers, 100–101, 103, 169n58; mythical beliefs and resistance to, 167n34; resistance and accommodation and, 27, 135n87, 136n98; socialist education and, 19; vaccinations, lynching of sanitary brigades, 26–27, 133n64, 135n94g
heretics. *See* Catholic religion—lynchings of impious individuals
Hidalgo (state), 75, 99, 122n7, 127n55, 136n109
hierberas. See witches/healers/spiritists
homicide: decline in rates of, in the postrevolutionary period, 6, 7, 68, 158n10; high contemporary rate of, 3, 122n9; impunity of murderers, 1–2, 69, 74–75, 77, 158n16; rates in Latin America, 3, 122n10; statistics on unpunished murders, 1–2, 158n16. *See also* crime; extralegal violence; lynching
Honduras, 123n14
hygiene programs. *See* health and sanitation programs

impunity: of anti-Protestant perpetrators of violence, 60; and citizens' understanding of lynching as a legitimate form of justice, 8, 74, 77; of elites, and political power, 8; elites as guaranteeing, 38; as insufficient explanation of community support for extralegal violence, 88, 113; of lynching, 9–10, 34; of murderers, 1–2, 69, 74–75, 77, 158n16
India, 116
indigenous communities: anti-alcohol campaigns and lynchings by, 136n96; government study of traditions of, to promote incorporation and assimilation into modernity, 93, 100–101, 166n12, 169n58; incorporation of medical knowledge of, 136n98; lynching as a reaction to conduct held offensive by, 11; maiming of warriors from, in wars with, 151n91; the perception of lynching as expression of "traditions" of, 11, 15, 94, 126n54, 128n5; and representation of lynching as product of ignorance and barbarity, 11, 20–21, 94; Spanish colonialism and use of body fat of, 95, 166n28
Indonesia, 116
Informador, El: crime news in, 77; as source, 175n13
Italian people, lynchings of, 124n27

Jacobins, 45, 51
Jalisco (state): among most populated states, 127n56; and geography of lynching, 127n55; lynching, 19, 52, 55, 108n152, 137–38n122, 168n50; state-sanctioned extralegal violence, 73
justice: extralegal collective forms of, 3–4, 122–23n13; the press on received inability of the state to deliver, 66, 74–75, 83, 86–87, 112. *See also* death penalty; justice, lynching viewed as legitimate means to attain
justice, lynching viewed as legitimate means to attain: as corrective justice, 16, 17, 27–34, 39, 129nn14–15; corruption as structural and systemic and, 8–9; as defining factor in lynching, 3; as persistent pattern, 11, 110; press representations of, 112, 113, 116, 117. *See also* community-sanctioned dimension of lynching; crime news, representations of mob violence as legitimate form of justice; impunity; justice system, corruption in
justice system, corruption in: bribes, 72, 103, 137n114; and community approval of *ley fuga* (law of flight), 9, 69–70, 75–76, 88, 125nn42–43, 160n39; as endemic, and rise of lynching as legitimate form of justice, 8; impunity of murderers, 1–2, 69, 74, 77; and interpretations of lynching as a recent phenomenon, 4, 110–11, 123n15; as structural and systemic, 8–9. *See also* impunity

Kaplan, Lucille N., 170n79
Kline, Herbert, *The Forgotten Village*, 101, 169nn60,63
Knab, Timothy J., 171n82
Knight, Alan, 129–30n26

Latin America: anti-Protestant violence in, 154n131; community-sanctioned dimension of lynching and, 4, 114, 116, 123n14; death not necessarily the end result of lynchings in, 3, 123n20; democratic turn of, 114; homicide rates in, 3, 122n10; intensification of political repression in (1960s and 1970s), 116; Mexico claimed to be second largest economy in, 3, 122n8; mythical figures and, 89–90, 95, 166nn26,28; robberies as main offense eliciting contemporary lynchings, 162–63n79; and scapegoating, 116; support for extralegal violence in, 114, 123n14; surge in numbers of lynchings (1980s and 1990s), 116; vigilantism as generally increasing in, 3–4; witchcraft, overrepresentation of accusations against women in, 164–65n6
law of flight. *See* ley fuga (law of flight)
lay Catholics. *See* Catholic religion—lay community
legitimacy. *See* justice, lynching viewed as legitimate means to attain; sources of legitimation
León massacre (1946), 31–32
Lewis, Oscar, 125n35, 167–68n41; *Five Families*, 156n150
Lewis, Stephen, 131n38, 166n12
ley fuga (law of flight): overview, 69–70, 113; and authorities' disregard for the rule of law, 88; crime news coverage of, 67, 70, 72, 75–76, 158nn18,20, 160nn39,43; definition of, 9; in lieu of death penalty, 77, 160n43; perception of corruption and abuse in the justice system and community approval of, 9, 69–70, 75–76, 88, 125nn42–43, 160n39; soldiers executed under, 28; state actors as perpetrators of, as distinguished from lynching, 9, 34, 69, 125n42
Liga de Escritores y Artistas Revolucionarios (LEAR), 131n39
Liga Nacional Defensora de la Libertad Religiosa (LNDLR; National Defense League for Religious Liberty), 54, 144n16, 152n108
linchamientos/lynchamientos: and influence of U.S. trajectory of lynching, 117; as term, 117, 172–73n1. *See also* lynching
local authorities: autonomy of newspapers to cover, 175nn14–15; bribing of, 103; as mediating and facilitating the implementation of federal programs, 128n11; parish priests regarded as, 50, 149n72. *See also caciques*; mayors; police; state actors
—COMPLICITY IN LYNCHINGS: overview, 111–12, 116; and anti-Protestant violence, 59–61, 112, 156–57nn145,147,151; assassinations staged as lynchings, 34–35, 140n145; decline of, 38, 115, 141–42nn162,165; witchcraft-based lynchings, 98, 99, 100, 103, 106. *See also* state-sanctioned lynchings
—LYNCHINGS OF: for abuse of authority, 17, 31–32, 71, 138nn124,128; and agrarian reform, 22–23, 52, 132–33nn59–60,62; earliest historical evidence of, 158n13; for hostility to Catholicism, 21; as persistent pattern, 11; and top-down vs. bottom-up violence, complications of narrative of, 112–13
local priests. *See* Catholic religion: parish priests
logics of power: overview, 10; as decentered, 11, 126n52; definition of, 9; and lynching as "weapon of the weak"/resistance of subordinated classes, 10, 125n45; and perpetrators, authority figures as, 126n47; and police, lynchings of, 31; and political and historical processes that are subject to change, 110; and victims as authority figures, 10; and victims as marginalized individuals, 10, 91, 113, 125–26n46. *See also* Catholic religion; community-sanctioned dimension of lynching; gender; local authorities; state actors; status quo, lynching as community defense of
López Obrador, Andrés Manuel, 126n54
Los Angeles Times, as source, 175n13
Loveman, Mara, 132n50
Lutherans, 57
lynching: absence of the state assumed to create context for, 4–5; attempted, definition of and importance of studying, 123n20; collective, brutal, overt forms of violence as characterizing all, 3; criminalization of, 115; criteria used to define an incident as, 117–18, 173nnn2–5; definition of, 3; earliest historical evidence of, 158n13; geography of, 3, 11, 12, 122n7, 126n53, 127nn55–59; as global phenomenon, 6, 115, 116; increasing frequency of, 3; intracommunity conflicts and historical dynamics and, 4, 49, 59–60, 112; legal specificity as lacking for, 119, 175n12; *ley fuga* distinguished from, 9, 125nn42–43; number of perpetrators to victims in definition of, as ratio, 117; premeditation of, 3, 118; recognizable scripts of, 2; as reflection of local dynamics of coercion, resistance, and negotiation, 5; ringing of bells to summon lynchers, 118, 174n8; socioeconomic similarities of most perpetrators and victims of, 112; as status

quo defense by the community, 10, 61, 113, 115, 126n10; terms for, 117, 172–73n1, 174n10; and top-down vs. bottom-up violence, complications of narrative of, 53, 112–13; as unilateral vs. bilateral or reciprocal, 117, 173n2; variations among cases of, 3, 118–19, 174nn6–7; vigilantism distinguished from, 53–54, 122–23n13, 174n7; as "weapon of the weak," literature claiming, 10, 113, 125n45. *See also* Catholic religion—lynchings motivated by; community-sanctioned dimension of lynching; contemporary lynchings; criminals (presumed), lynchings of; cruelty in lynching; logics of power; marginalized status of lynching victims; mythical beliefs—lynchings motivated by; press—representations of lynching; ritualization of lynchings; sources of legitimation; state actors; state–sanctioned lynchings; statistics on lynching

Madero, Francisco, 155n137
Mano Negra (Black Hand), 150n77
marginalized status of lynching victims: overview, 112–13, 114–15; logics of power and, 10, 91, 113, 125–26n46; mythical figures, 91, 108; witches/healers/spiritists, 91, 97–98, 102, 108, 165n10
Marin, Nidia, 34
market vendors: fraudulent behavior of, 86, 163n88; women, attempted lynching of attacker, 162n69
Martínez, Luis María: anticommunism of, 57; anti-Protestantism of (Crusade for the Defense of the Catholic Faith), 41, 57, 144n18; and Cárdenas's abandonment of anticlericalism, 146n35; on cooperation/collaboration with the state, 57, 154n126
martyrs and martyrdom: conflicting stories of, and lynchings of impious individuals, 48, 148nn58–59; crime suspects killed by authorities as, 71; sacrificial ethos of Catholics, 43, 145nn23,25; socialist teachers as, 20, 131n37, 148n59, 151n92
Maya people, 95, 166n25
mayors: complicity with state-sanctioned extralegal violence, 38, 71; protecting Protestants, 60
—COMPLICITY WITH LYNCHINGS: overview, 10, 126n47; anti-alcohol campaigns and, 22; anti-Protestant violence, 156–57n151; assassinations staged as lynchings, 34–35, 140n145; and Catholicism as motivation, 40, 141–42n162, 172n13; state-sanctioned lynchings, 17, 34, 36–37, 72–73, 140nn140–141,143, 141nn157,161; witchcraft-related lynchings, 106, 140n143

—LYNCHINGS OF: overview, 10; for abuse of authority, 17, 31–32, 71, 138nn123–124,127–128; and agrarian reform, 133n62; earliest historical evidence of, 158n13; for hostility to Catholic religion, 21; as persistent pattern, 11; in protest of socialist education, 52
Meade, Everard, 158n25, 160n43
Méndez, Leopoldo, 20, 130–31nn31,36, 131n39; *In the Name of Christ . . . they have murdered 200 teachers*, 19–20
Mendoza, Clemente, 52, 54, 151n85, 152n101
methodology: "attempted lynching," definition of and importance of studying, 123n20; criteria used to define an incident as a lynching, 117–18, 173nnn2–5; judicial archives of limited utility in, 119, 120; literature review, 4–5, 110–11, 123n15; and *lynching* as term, 117, 172–73n1, 174n10; sources, 119–20, 127n57, 174nn10–11, 175nn12–15,18,20; and sources, dynamics of representation in, 12, 119–20, 127nn58–59, 175nn18,20. *See also* press—representations of lynching
Mexican-American War (1846), 154n123
Mexican Revolution (1910), 6, 7, 44, 124n23; maiming of opponents as common in, 52, 151n91
Mexicans in the United States, lynchings of, 124n27
Mexico: "dirty war" (ca. 1969–78), 116; economy of as claimed to be thriving, 3, 122n8; emergent historiography on continuity of violence in, 110–11; and geography of lynching, 3, 11, 12, 122n7, 126n53, 127nn55–59; literacy rates in, 65–66, 157n4; map of, *xvi*; most populated states in, 127n56; pax priísta, 7, 111, 112; post-revolutionary period, defined, 5; and scholarly perception of lynching as a recent phenomenon, 4–5; syncretism of Spanish folk culture and indigenous traditions, 165n7; university students, disappearance and massacre of (2014), 172n3. *See also* Catholic religion; censorship; contemporary lynchings; Cristero War (1926–29); economic inequality; local authorities; Second Cristiada (La Segunda, 1934–38); state actors; state formation; state-sanctioned extralegal violence

Mexico City (state): among most populated states, 127n56; and anti-alcohol campaigns, 29, 132n55; and geography of lynching, 3, 12, 122n7, 127n55; lynching of accused child stealers, 2; and lynching of anticlericalists/thieves of religious images, 41, 45, 47–48, 126n54, 146–47n39, 149n72; lynching of criminals, 63–65, 68–69, 72, 73–74, 75, 78–80, 81, 82, 83, 86, 161n57, 161n65, 162nn69,74, 163n85; lynching of local authorities, 22, 29–31, 122n3, 132n55, 137n118; lynching of Protestants, 41, 57; lynching of soldiers, 136n109; and national newspapers, 12; riots against anticlericalism, 46; and state-sponsored extralegal violence, 138n124; and urban lynchings, 126n53; witchcraft and lynching of witches, 98, 99, 103–4, 167–68n41

Meyer, Jean A., 129n23

Michoacán (state): among most populated states, 127n56; anticlericalist women in, 146–47n39; and defanaticization campaigns, 145n29; and geography of lynching, 127n55; lynching of anticlericalists/iconoclasts, 41, 43–44, 51; lynching of foot-and-mouth disease eradication brigade, 24–25, 27; lynching of local authorities, 33–34, 137–38n122, 139nn132,134–136,138; lynching of socialist teachers, 18, 19, 130n30, 152n105; mythical beliefs, 167n40; state-sanctioned extralegal violence, 173n4; state-sanctioned lynchings, 33; women as main perpetrators of lynching, 126n49

Migdal, Joel, 129n14

military: collusion with the interests of the political elite, 31–32, 136n110, 138nn123–124,127; complicity with lynchings, 17, 37, 73; death of suspects in custody of, 70; iconoclastic actions by, 44; lynchings of, 10, 17, 24, 28–29, 32, 70–71, 134n76, 136n109; protecting Protestants, 60; protecting socialist teachers, 18

military conscription: establishment of and opposition to, 23, 24, 133n65, 134n72; lynchings of authorities, 23–24; nonviolent resistance to, 133n67; resistance and accommodation processes and, 27; Sinarquista opposition to, 134–35nn82–83

militias, 133n63

modernization: lynching as the result of exposure to (vs. "premodern" practice), 8, 11; of medicine, and mythical beliefs, 92; narratives of mythical figures as revealing anxieties about, 11, 89–90, 92, 95–96, 107–8, 166n26, 167n34; nineteenth-century origins of goals of, 129–30n26; resistance to and accommodation of, and decline in number of lynchings on state actors, 10–11, 27, 115; security reports referring to need for, 120. *See also* agrarian reform; anti-alcohol campaigns; Catholic religion—anticlericalism; health and sanitation programs; military conscription; nationalism; secularization; socialist education

moral economy (E. P. Thompson), 124n31, 163n80

moral economy of lynching, 85–87, 148n63, 163nn80–82,85,88

morality of lynching: overview, 88, 124n31; the press and narrative of, 78, 81, 88

Morelos (state): and geography of lynching, 3, 122n7; lynching of sanitary brigade members, 133n64; lynching of socialist teachers, 19, 149n65, 152n108; mythical beliefs, 95; per capita rate of lynching, 122n7; resistance to military conscription, 135n83; witchcraft, 170n76

Mormon church, 142n4, 154n129, 156–57n151

murders. *See* homicide

mythical beliefs and mythical figures: bloodsucker figures, 89–90, 96, 97–98, 108, 166n26, 167n40; bloodsucking witches (*tlahuelpuchi*), 97–98, 99, 167–68n41, 172n93; children as figuring prominently in, 93, 95, 96–98, 166nn23,28, 167–68nn34,38,40,41; *chupacabras*, 166n26; colonial period and surfacing of, 90, 95; *cortacabezas* (decapitators), 93, 95; defined as terms, 164n5; evil eye (*mal de ojo*), 105, 167n34, 171n85; as explanation of threatening or inexplicable events, 91; fat-stealer figures, 89–90, 93–96, 108, 166n28; as foreign/external exploitation and domination, 89–90, 91, 95–96, 108, 166n26; man-eagle that eats children, 166n23; marginalized status of, 91, 108; medical use of stolen body fluids and organs, 89, 95, 96–97, 167nn38,40; and modernization, anxieties about, 11, 89–90, 92, 95–96, 107–8, 166n26, 167n34; *ñak'aq*, 166n26; *pishtaco*, 95, 166n28; rumors and, 94–95, 96, 167nn34,38; *sacamantecas*, 95; *sacaojos*, 166n28; and scapegoating, 91, 108; technology and infrastructure works, bodies used for, 93, 94, 95–96, 166nn23,25,26. *See also* witchcraft

—LYNCHINGS MOTIVATED BY: overview, 92, 107–8; as community-sanctioned, 5,

91–92, 108; cruelty of torments in, 91, 93, 108; earthly preoccupations reflected in, 89–90; marginalized status of victims, 91; and modernization projects, 11, 89–90, 92, 95–96, 107–8, 166n26, 167n34; narratives of, 89, 93–94; as persistent pattern, 11; political conflicts and, 97; press representations of, 93, 94, 107; prosecution of, 93; as rare, 90, 92

Nacional, El: crime news in, 66, 79, 83, 86; representation of religion-based lynchings as systematic campaign by high rank of the Catholic Church, 48; as source, 175n13; on witchcraft, 101. *See also* Catholic religion; press
NAFTA, 166n26
nationalism: Manuel Ávila Camacho and, 56; and cooperation/collaboration between church and state, 61; Sinarquistas and, 153n118
nationalization of oil reserves, 153n116
Native Americans, lynchings of, 124n27
Navarro, Carlos, *Janitzio*, 128n5
Nayarit (state), 20, 29, 98
newspapers. *See* crime news (*nota roja*); press
New York Times: and lynching as ignorance, 26; as source, 175n13
nonviolent resistance: to anticlericalism, 142n6; to military conscription, 133n67; options for, 32; to police abuse of authority, 71, 137n121; to socialist education, 130n28
nota roja. *See* crime news (*nota roja*)
Nuevo León (state), 132–33n60, 164n93, 168n50
Nutini, Hugo, 99, 167–68nn41,51, 172n93

Oaxaca (state): among most populated states, 127n56; and geography of lynching, 3, 122n7, 127n55; lynching in resistance to military conscription, 23–24; lynching of local authorities, 138n128; lynching of Protestants, 41, 157n153; mythical beliefs, 166n23; popularity of witchcraft beliefs, 170n74; witchcraft and lynching of witches, 170nn74,79
Obregón, Álvaro, 147n47
Onken, Hinerk, 123n15
Opinión, La: autonomy of, 175nn14–15; as co-opted by Maximino Ávila Camacho, 175n15; crime news in, 70; as source, 175n13
Osornio, Saturnino, 141n161

Palerm, Ángel, 104
Pansters, Wil G., 128–29n12, 173n4

paramilitary groups: *guardias blancas,* 20, 131n42, 133n63, 150n77; Mano Negra (Black Hand), 150n77; Red Shirts (Camisas Rojas, Bloques Juveniles Revolucionarios), 47–48, 147–48nn50,52,56,60. *See also* vigilantes
parish priests. *See* Catholic religion: parish priests
Partido Nacional Revolucionario (PNR; National Revolutionary Party), 7
Partido Revolucionario Institucional (PRI; Institutional Revolutionary Party): lynching of candidates and local authorities from, 32, 138n128; replacement of, and lynching, 5
patriarchy, 136n95
patterns of change: decline in lynching complicity by state actors, 115; decline in lynchings perpetrated against state actors, 10–11, 115
patterns of continuity: of opposition and resistance to the state's meddling in local affairs, 22; persistence of lynchings, 11, 110, 115–16
Pech, Alessa, 167–68n41
Pentecostals, 142n4
Peru, 95, 123n14, 166n28
Philippines, 116
Piccato, Pablo, 137n113, 157–58nn8,10,16
pistoleros, 33, 38, 73, 74, 77, 111, 137n122, 139n132, 159n27
Pitt-Rivers, Julian, 106, 164–65n6, 170n80
police: bribes and, 72, 137n114; and cattle rustlers, 86, 164n93; criminal activities of, 159n27; and impunity of murderers, 69; lynching as reflecting the dynamics of negotiation and accommodation between citizens and, 5; mysterious disappearances and deaths of crime suspects in custody of, 67, 70, 158n18, 164n93; and state-sponsored extralegal violence, 38, 87–88, 164n93
—ABUSE OF FORCE BY: and lynching perceived as legitimate form of justice, 8–9; lynchings of police as motivated by, 17, 29–31, 30, 36, 71, 109–10, 137n117–118; newspaper coverage of, 175n15; nonviolent resistance to, 71, 137n121; as structural and systemic, 8
—COMPLICITY WITH LYNCHINGS: overview, 10, 111–12, 126n47; anti-Protestant violence, 156–57n151; assassinations staged as lynchings, 72, 140n145; state-sanctioned lynchings, 17, 35–36, 72–73, 140n150, 159n27; Texas Rangers, 168n45

206   INDEX

—LYNCHINGS OF: overview, 10; and abuse of authority, 17, 29–31, 30, 36, 71, 74–75, 109–10, 137nn117–118; and anti-alcohol campaigns, 132n55; and child theft accusations, 2, 122n3; and citizens' distrust of state authorities, 74–75, 110; and community-sanctioned violence, 110; as disapproval of behavior of a particular officer, 129n15; for hostility to Catholic religion, 21; and logics of power, 31; mistaken as Protestant pastors, 57–58, 155n134; as persistent pattern, 11, 110; and unjust punishment of wrongdoers, 17, 29, 137nn113–114

—PROTECTING LYNCHING VICTIMS: anti-Protestant lynchings, 57; crime-based lynchings, 65, 71–72, 74, 75, 78, 79, 81, 82, 83, 85, 87–88, 161n65, 162n69; as fulfillment of formal mandate, 71–72; outnumbered by the mob, 1; witchcraft-based lynchings, 97, 98

popular Catholicism. *See* Catholic religion—folk or popular

Porvenir, El: crime news in, 66; representations of lynching in, 135n94; as source, 175n13. *See also* Catholic religion; press

post-revolutionary period: definition of, 5; greater political stability and lower levels of violence in, 6, 7. *See also* state formation

power. *See* logics of power

premeditation of lynchings, 3, 118

Prensa, La: crime news and, 66, 77, 79–80, 86; readership of, 157n6; as source, 175n13. *See also* crime news (*nota roja*)

press: censorship as avoided by, 73, 119, 175nn14–15; critique of state authorities' capacity to provide security and justice to citizens, 112; dissonance of discourses and representations by, 119; and dynamics of narration and representation, 12, 119–20, 127nn58–59; readership of, 65–66, 67, 157n4; rumors reported by, as leading to lynching, 94; as source, 119–20, 127n57, 174nn10–11, 175nn13–15. *See also* crime news (*nota roja*)

—REPRESENTATIONS OF LYNCHING: overview, 119–20, 172–73n1; anti-modernization-based lynchings, 66; as carried out in backward, ignorant, and geographically isolated communities, 11, 20–21, 26, 48, 66, 89, 92, 94, 117, 135n94, 148n63; as indigenous "tradition," 11, 126n54; as means to attain justice, 112, 113, 116, 117; mythical-beliefs lynchings, 66, 89, 93, 94, 102; religion-based lynchings as incited by local priests, 49–50; religion-based lynchings as systematic campaign by high rank of the Catholic Church, 48, 62; and terms used to describe lynching, 117. *See also* crime news: representations of mob violence as legitimate form of justice

—REPRESENTATIONS OF VIOLENCE: as obscuring extralegal violence by state actors, 119; as reifying class-based notions about violence, 119; state violence as legitimate and communal forms of violence as illegitimate, 119

PRI. *See* Partido Revolucionario Institucional

Protestantism: and burying of the dead, 154n121; Catholic condemnation of, 57, 58, 143n13, 149n68; Catholic conversions to, and escape from the cargo system, 155–56n141; Catholic fear of missioners of, 154n123, 155n136; definition of, 142n4; and embrace of political ideologies condemned by Catholicism, 58, 155n137; Luis María Martínez's attack on, 41, 57, 144n18; percentage of population, 155n135; as threat to Catholicism, 58, 155–56nn137,140–141; in the United States, and sacrificial ethos, 145n23. *See also* Protestants

Protestants: Comité Nacional de Defensa Evangélica, 59; and context of conservative politics of Manuel Ávila Camacho, 56–57; folk/popular Catholicism and violence against, 154n129; iconoclasm of, 56; local Catholic priests legitimating violence against, 58, 59–60, 112, 156–57n151; nationalist sentiments in violence against, 154n131; as rejecting witches/healers, 169n67; rioting behaviors of, compared to Catholics, 143n11, 150–51n84; riot inside a Catholic church, 155n133; riots against, 56, 154n123; vigilante violence against, 56, 59, 156nn145,147, 174n7; violence against, elsewhere in Latin America, 154n131; violence against, language of higher rank Catholics as inciting, 57

—LYNCHINGS OF: overview, 41, 56; denunciations by Protestants of civil and religious authorities' complicity with, 59–61, 156–57nn145–147,151; despite the détente between state and church, 55, 61, 62; impunity for, 60; intracommunity conflicts and, 59–60; narratives of, 55–56, 57–58, 58–59, 154n120, 155n134, 156n150; as persistent pattern, 11, 61, 157n153; as "sacrificeable" characters, 125–26n46; vigilantes participating in, 174n7

public art: and the aesthetics of nation building, 20, 131n39; in support of socialist teachers, 19–20, 130n31, 131nn37–40
public opinion: as condition of possibility for lynching, 9–10; definition of, 174n11; newspapers as source on, 119, 174n11; support for extralegal violence despite decreasing rates of homicide and crime, 68, 158n10. *See also* community-sanctioned dimension of lynching
Puebla (state): and geography of lynching, 3, 12, 122n7; lynching based on mythical beliefs, 93–94; lynching for crimes against property, 28–29, 34, 85, 86; lynching of anticlericalists/iconoclasts, 40, 41, 60; lynching of criminals, 1–2, 70, 82; lynching of local authorities, 27–28, 29, 31; lynching of Protestants, 41, 55–56, 59–60; lynching of socialist teachers, 18–19, 20, 52, 54–55; lynching of state actors, 21, 22, 23, 26–27, 28–29, 31; popularity of witchcraft beliefs, 170n74; state-sanctioned extralegal violence/staged lynchings, 34–36, 69, 70, 73, 116; state-sanctioned lynchings, 36–37; vigilante attacks on criminals, 70; vigilante attacks on Protestants, 59; vigilante attacks on socialist teachers, 53–54; witchcraft and lynching of witches, 97–98, 100, 101–2, 103, 104–5

Querétaro (state), 19, 89, 96–97, 107, 141nn154,161
Quintana Roo (state), 143n9

Raby, David L., 53, 129n23, 153n114
racism: and lynching in the United States, 6, 10, 124n27, 145n23, 173n3. *See also* United States—lynching in
rape, lynchings of perpetrators of, 28, 82–83, 162nn70,72,74
Rath, Thomas, 133n67, 136n110
Red Shirts (Camisas Rojas, Bloques Juveniles Revolucionarios), 47–48, 147–48nn50,52,56,60
religion: definition of, 41, 143n9; Freemasons, as threat to Catholic religion, 149n68, 155n137; spiritists, as threat to Catholic religion, 40, 149n68, 155n137. *See also* Catholic religion; Protestants
resistance: lynching as, 16–17, 18–27, 38–39, 129n13. *See also* nonviolent resistance; resistance and accommodation, processes of
resistance and accommodation, processes of: overview, 5; anthropology and, 136n98; and consensus among citizens and authorities about the use of extralegal violence, 113; foot-and-mouth disease (cattle) eradication program and, 26, 27; health and sanitation programs and, 27, 135n87, 136n98; language of protest in, 32; military conscription and, 27; in modernization programs, and reduction of lynchings, 10–11, 27, 115; and political and historical processes that are subject to change, 110
Reyes, Aurora, 131n39; *Attack against the Female Rural Teachers (Atentado contra las maestras rurales)*, 20, 131n40
riots: anti-agrarian reform, 132n59; anti-Protestant, 56, 154n123; behaviors of, of Catholics vs. Protestants, 143nn9,11, 150–51n84; as crime, 175n12; and criminals, lynchings of, 72, 74, 75, 76, 82; and economic inequality, 7; and elections, 141n154; and foot-and-mouth (cattle) disease eradication program, 25; methodology and, 174n10; military conscription resistance, 24; moral economy of, 163n80; as part of language of protest, 32; and police, lynching of, 32, 71, 109; pre-revolutionary, 17, 129n13, 174n8; by Protestants in Catholic church, 155n133; in protest of anticlericalism/iconoclasm, 41, 45, 46, 47, 49–50, 146n36, 147n44, 148n64; and soldiers, lynching of, 25, 28
ritualization of lynchings: overview, 3; cruelty as increased with, 118–19; ringing of church bells and, 118, 174n8; time elapse and, 118
Roberts, John M., 99, 167–68n41, 172n93
Rocha, Rogerio, 71
Rodríguez, Enrique (El Tallarín), 53–54, 130–31n36, 132n53, 151n91, 152nn101,108
Rodríguez-Shadow, María, 167n36
Romanucci-Ross, Lola, 170n76
Romero Melgarejo, Osvaldo, 167–68n41
Rueda, José G., 139n135
Ruesga, David Genaro, 59, 156n146
rumors: and Catholic lynchings of impious individuals, 45–46, 147n44; and child theft, 147n41; definition of, 46; elements of reality in, 96–97; and mythical beliefs, lynchings based on, 94–95, 96, 167nn34,38
rural communities: erroneous perception of lynching as limited to, 11, 15–16, 126n53; percentage of population living in, 128n6; violence promoted by mayors and police officers as sign of backwardness of, 18, 129n17. *See also* modernization; urbanization
Rus, Jan, 147n44

"sacrificeable" characters, 125–26n46, 145n25
sacrificial ethos legitimating violence, 43, 145nn23,25
Salinas, Salvador, 129n20, 130n27, 149n65, 152n101
Samper, David, 147n41
Sánchez Aguillón, Felicita, 160n40
Sánchez, Jesús, 167–68n41
sanitation. *See* health and sanitation programs
San Luis Potosí (state), 102–3, 141n161
San Miguel Canoa: Felipe Cazals, *Canoa Memoria de un hecho vergonzoso*, 128n5; lynching of university workers (1968), 116, 141–42n162, 147–48n50, 172n13
Santos, Gonzalo N., 141n161
scapegoating: as global phenomenon, 116; of mythical figures, 91, 108; and "sacrificeable" victims, 145n25; of witches/healers/spiritists, 91, 92, 103, 104, 108
Scott, James C., 94, 125n45
Second Cristiada (La Segunda, 1934–38): overview, 7, 124–25n32; attacks on *agrarista* peasants, 124–25n32; attacks on socialist teachers, 19, 40–41, 52, 124–25n32, 132n53, 151n85,90; attacks on state actors, 132n53; as cohesive armed conflict, 53; as community resistance to socialist policies, 124n32; distancing of church hierarchy from armed resistance/violence during, 144n17, 149n66. *See also* Segunderos
Secretaría de Educación Pública (SEP; Secretariat of Public Education), 19, 129n23, 150n82
secularization: closures of churches and, 44; Cristero War and resistance to, 42; and representations of female fanaticism, 126n54
Segunda, La. *See* Second Cristiada
Segunderos: definition of, 124n32; maiming of opponents by, 151n91; as vigilantes participating in lynch mobs, 142n3, 174n7
self-defense forces, distinguished from lynch mobs, 122–23n13
Senechal de la Roche, Roberta, 173n2
Shadow, Robert, 167n36
Sidar, Pablo, 94
Sinaloa (state), 137–38n122, 170n77
Sinarquistas. *See* Unión Nacional Sinarquista (UNS)
Snodgrass Godoy, Angelina, 160n49
social control: by communities, and lynching as corrective justice, 17; definition of, 129n14; lynching as echoing the use of coercive and extralegal forms by the state, 5; lynching as tool of, 10; status quo, lynching as community defense of, 10, 61, 113, 115, 126n10. *See also* marginalized status of lynching victims; status quo, lynching as community defense of
socialism and socialists: as "sacrificeable" characters, 125–26n46; La Segunda as community resistance to, 124–25n32. *See also* socialist education
socialist education: abandonment of, 56; cultural missions and revolutionary festivals in, 19, 49–50, 51, 149n70; establishment as policy (article 3 of the constitution), 19, 21, 50–51; goal of defanaticization, 19, 21, 51; goal of implementing agrarian reform, 19, 41, 51, 130n27, 150nn76–77; goal of implementing anti-alcohol campaigns, 19, 132n57; goal of implementing health and sanitation programs, 19; goal of undermining the Catholic Church (anticlericalism and iconoclasm), 19, 20–21, 23, 41, 51, 130n30, 150nn79,83; nonviolent resistance to, 130n28; pastoral letter condemning, 144n18; and state formation, 19. *See also* socialist teachers
socialist teachers: ear cropping and other bodily mutilations of, 51–53, 130n34, 150–51nn84,89,91–92; as martyrs, 20, 131n37, 148n59, 151n92; offensive vs. defensive attacks on, 53; parish priests inciting violence against, 49–50, 54–55, 153n113; as "sacrificeable" characters, 125–26n46; La Segunda and attacks on, 19, 40–41, 52, 124–25n32, 132n53, 151n85,90; top-down vs. bottom-up attacks on, 53; vigilante violence against, 20, 51–52, 53–54, 131n42, 150n77, 151nn85,90; vigilante vs. lynch mob violence against, blurred lines between, 53–54, 152nn101,105,108
—LYNCHINGS OF: overview, 40–41; and agrarian reform, 19, 41, 132–33nn60,62; and anticlericalism/iconoclasm, 19, 21, 41; decline of, with abandonment of anticlericalist policy, 23, 55, 153nn114–115; locations of, 19; and the narrative of the state as a civilizing force, 21; narratives of, 18, 20, 52–53, 130–31nn30,34,36,41, 150n83, 153n114; parish priests inciting, 54–55; public art to educate about, 19–20, 130–31nn31,36–40; rejection of ideas as motivation for, 21, 129n15, 132n57; representations of ignorance and fanaticism as cause of, 20–21, 132nn48,50; statistics on, 129n23

INDEX 209

Sodi, Carlos Franco, 148n64
Sonora (state), 23, 132n59, 145n29, 150n79
sources of legitimation: overview, 6–7, 9–10; definition of, 9; and political and historical processes that are subject to change, 110; and E. P. Thompson on defense of traditional rights or customs, 124n31. *See also* Catholic religion—lynchings motivated by; crime news, representations of mob violence as legitimate form of justice; criminals (presumed), lynchings of; justice, lynching viewed as legitimate means to attain; morality of lynching; mythical beliefs—lynchings motivated by; state formation—and lynching
South Africa, 116, 164–65nn6,10
Spain: fat-sucker mythical figures based on colonial practices of, 95, 166nn26,28; folk culture of, and syncretism in Mexico, 165n7; mythical figure arising in, 95
spiritists. *See* witches/healers/spiritists
state actors: documents produced or received by, as source, 12, 120, 127n57, 175n20; the Second Cristiada and attacks on, 132n53. *See also ley fuga* (law of flight); local authorities; military; modernization; socialist teachers; state formation; state-sanctioned extralegal violence; state-sanctioned lynchings
—LYNCHING OF: decline in numbers of, and resistance and accommodation of modernization, 10–11, 27, 115; earliest historical evidence of, 158n13; narratives of, 22, 132nn55,57; by state-sanctioned lynchings, 37; and top-down vs. bottom-up violence, complications of narrative of, 112–13
—THE PEOPLE'S DISTRUST OF: overview, 9; and community-sanctioned dimension of lynching, 2–3, 4, 114, 123n14; and police, lynchings of, 74–75, 110
state formation: overview, 6, 12–13, 38–39; aesthetics of nation building, 20, 131n39; claim of monopolization of legitimate use of violence, 111; definition of, 16; as historical, relational, negotiated, and evolving, 16; and narrative of "revolutionary family," 27, 136n95; narrative of the state as a "civilizing force" meant to incorporate "barbaric" or "uncivilized" communities, 15–16, 17, 18, 35, 38, 111, 129n16, 169n60; socialist education and, 19. *See also* justice system; modernization; state-sanctioned extralegal violence

—AND LYNCHING: overview, 15–16; and encroachment of the state into communal life, 18, 23, 27; and the Latin American "democratic turn," 114; lynching as corrective justice, 16, 17, 27–34, 39, 129nn14–15; lynching as resistance, 16–17, 18–27, 38–39, 129n13; and mob violence as promoted as form of governance and social control, 18; and zones of coercion, 16, 128–29n12; and zones of hegemony, 16, 128–29n12. *See also* state-sanctioned extralegal violence; state-sanctioned lynchings
state-sanctioned extralegal violence: overview, 34, 116, 140n144; assassinations staged as lynchings, 34–35, 72, 140n145; community approval as required for definition as lynching, 35, 118, 173nn3–4; community disapproval of, and lynching of public authorities, 31–32, 71, 138nn124,128; community support for, 113–14; cruelty of, and claim of the state as a "civilizing force," 17, 35, 38, 129n16; "gray zone" and, 173n4; mysterious disappearances and deaths of suspects in police custody, 67, 70, 158n18, 164n93; press coverage as legitimating and obscuring, 119; shift to less overt forms of, 38; torture, 34, 38. *See also ley fuga*; state-sanctioned lynchings
state-sanctioned lynchings: overview, 16, 34–38, 111–12, 116, 129n16; assassinations staged as lynchings, 34–35, 72, 140n145; decline of, 38, 115, 141–42nn162–163,165; definition of, 17; elites and tolerance of, 37–38, 141n161, 142n165; of infamous criminals, 37; narratives of, 34, 140nn140–143; of political opponents, 35–36, 72–73, 140n150, 141n152,154, 159n27
statistics on lynching: deaths resulting from, 123n20; decline of lynching over time in the United States, 6, 124nn27–28; and dynamics of representation, 127n59; socialist teachers killed or injured, 129n23. *See also* crime statistics
status quo: lynching as community defense of, 10, 61, 113, 115, 126n10; pre-revolutionary riots in defense of, 17, 129n13
Steinbeck, John, *The Forgotten Village* (film), 101

Tabasco (state), 47–48, 141n161, 143n9, 145n29, 147n47
Tallarín, El. *See* Rodríguez, Enrique
tax collectors, 10–11, 37, 132n53, 158n13
Taylor, William B., 126n50, 129n13

thefts and robberies: as main offense eliciting contemporary lynchings, 162–63n79; of religious images, 41, 45–46, 55, 146nn35,38, 149n71; soldiers stealing firewood, 28–29; state-sanctioned extralegal violence for, 38. *See also* child snatchers (*robachicos*); criminals (presumed), lynchings of—crimes against property; moral economy of lynching

Thompson, E. P., 124n31, 163n80

Tlaxcala (state): lynching for theft of religious images, 45; and mythical figures, 98; witchcraft and lynching of witches, 99–100, 101, 167–68n41, 168n51, 170n74, 172n93

torture: ear cropping and other bodily mutilations, 51–53, 130n34, 134–35n82, 150–51nn84,89,91–92; past enactments of, as used by vigilantes, 151n91; in state-sanctioned extralegal violence, 34, 38. *See also* cruelty in lynchings

Unión Nacional Sinarquista (UNS): overview, 25, 153n119; accused of Aquiles de la Peña lynching, 139n138; foot-and-mouth disease eradication program opposed by, 25, 134n81; killed at León massacre (1946), 31–32; military conscription opposed by, 134–35nn82–83; national flag flown by, 56, 153n118; Protestants attacked by, 56, 59, 156nn145,147; tensions with higher ranks of the church, 144n16, 149n66, 153n119; as vigilantes participating in lynch mobs, 174n7

United States: Catholic fear of Protestant missioners from, 154n123, 155n136; foot-and-mouth disease (cattle) eradication program of, 24, 26; imperialistic power of, mythical figures expressing anxiety about, 95, 96, 166n26; lynching of American citizens in Mexico, 26; Mexican-American War (1846) and anti-American sentiments, 154n123; newspapers of, as source, 175n13; Texas Rangers as complicit in witchcraft killing, 168n45; witchcraft in colonial New England, 164–65nn6–7

—LYNCHING IN: as "American exception" vs. global phenomenon, 6, 115, 116; community-sanctioned dimension of, 173n3; complicity of authorities in, 111, 168n45; death as expected end of, 122n12; historiography of, 114, 115; of Mexicans, 124n27; modernization and surge of, 8; the noose as tactic of violence in, 4; and perceived threats to white rule, 115; press representation of, as inevitable and suitable response to crimes, 157n5; racism and sacrificial ethos in southern Protestantism, 145n23; racism associated with, 6, 10, 115, 124n27, 173n3; spelling of *"lynchamientos"* and influence of, 117, 172–73n1; statistics on decline over time, 6, 124nn27–28

Universal, El: crime news in, 66; as source, 175n13. *See also* Catholic religion; press

university students, disappearance and massacre of (2014), 172n3

university workers, state-sanctioned lynching of (1968), 116, 141–42n162, 147–48n50, 172n13

urban environments: lynching as occurring in, 11, 126n53; mythical beliefs and, 94; witchcraft beliefs and, 92, 167–68n41

urbanization: lynching as reflection of anxieties of, 8; and newspaper readership, 65–66

vaccination programs: for foot-and-mouth (cattle) disease, 24, 26–27, 135n88; for humans, 26–27, 133n64, 135n94

Vanderwood, Paul, 158n20

Vaughan, Mary Kay, 131n38, 150n79, 166n12

Vázquez, Jenaro, 21

Vega, Odilón, 52

Venezuela, 3

Veracruz (state): among most populated states, 127n56; defanaticization campaigns, 145n29; and geography of lynching, 127n55; lynching of agrarian reform supporters, 23, 35, 150n77; lynching of anticlericalists/iconoclasts/theft of religious images, 41; lynching of criminals, 79; lynching of local authorities, 21, 71, 109–10, 137–38n122; lynching of Protestants, 41, 56; lynching of socialist teachers, 19, 52, 130n34, 131n41; state-sanctioned extralegal violence, 38, 71, 141n152; vigilante attacks on socialist teachers, 52, 151nn85,89; witchcraft and lynching of witches, 104, 106

victims of lynching or attempted lynching: Aguilar, Enrique, 59; Alcántara, Dolores, 74, 159n34; Anguiano Armenta, José, 63, 64, 65, 69, 157n3; Ayala, Alberto, 71–72; Blancas, Leonardo, 160n39; Bobadilla, Pedro, 83; Camacho, Teresa, 103; Castillo Morales, Juan, 28, 70–71, 74, 82, 158, 158n20; Castro, Raúl, 74; Cerezo, Maximino, 82; Cervantes, María Isabel, 168n50; Concha, Fructuoso, 45; Copado Molina, José Abraham and Rey David, 1–2, 122n3; Cruz Martínez, Patricio, 105; Cruz

Rangel, Ruperto, 80; Curiel, Lucero, 99; De la Cruz Carmona, Antonio, 156–57n151; De la Cruz Jimenez, Patricio, 102; De la Peña, Aquiles, 33–34, 38, 139nn132,134–135,136,138, 139nn132,138, 141n161; Domínguez Cruz, Domitila, 79; Durán Andrade, Francisco, 75; Fernández, León, 52; Fierro Gómez, Agustín, 30–31; Flores Hernández, Cleo, 78; Flores, Juana, 79; Flores, Lorenza, 78–79; Flores, Serafin, 85; Fonseca, Carlos, 132–33n60; Fonseca, Clara, 100, 102, 170n69; Fórtiz, Ramón, 70; Fuentes, Hermelinda, 105; Galván, José, 159n33; García, Gregoria, 102–3; García Narvaez, Benito, 81; García, Simón, 36, 37; Garita, Vincente, 58; Gómez, Lorenzo, 162; Gómez Macías, Julián, 24; González, Manuel, 70; Hernández, José, 163n85; Herrera, Alberto and Felix Víctor, 72, 158n25; Hidalgo Ramírez, Catalina, 99, 168n49; Hurtado de Mendoza, Manuel, 18; Jesús, Francisco de, 150n83; Jimenez, Adolfo, 29, 137n117; Jimenez, Pablo, 52, 130n34; Jimenez Romero, Felipe, 83; Juárez Medina, Augusto, 24; Juárez, Moisés, 40, 49; Kullmann, Edgar, 93–95, 97, 166n12; Labastida, Librado, 52, 54; Lara Montes, Humberto, 75; León, Felipe, 35; León, Isabel, 97; Lezama, Melquiades, 59–60; López, Amado, 82; Lopez, Antonio, 137–38n122; López, Fortunato, 86; Malda, Ernesto, 47–48, 49, 57, 147–48nn50,52,56,60; Maldonado, Saúl, 52–53; Mandujano Delgado, Albino, 73; Martínez Cairo, Salvador, 31–32, 38, 138nn123–124,127, 141n161; Martínez Dolores, Arturo, 138n128; Martínez, Pedro, 156n150; Martínez Ramírez, José, 130–31n36; Mendoza González, Porfirio, 22; Moctezuma Ramírez, Vicente, 99, 168n49; Mora, Ramón, 35; Moreno Herrera, David, 18, 52; Moyetón Flores, Valentín, 3; Muste, León J., 43–44; Nájera Guzmán, Rodolfo, 73; Natividad Santín, José, 83, *84*; Nepomuceno, Vicente, 37; Orta del Río, Ramón, 20; Ortega, Micaela, 40, 49, 60, 105–6, 140n143, 149n68; Padilla Maza, Carlos, 82; Palacios, Micaela and Enriqueta, 52, 131n41, 151n92, 152n108; Pastrana, Carlos, 52, 54; Pérez Silva, Guillermo, 23; Pimentel, Miguel, 83; Proctor, Robert L., 26; Ramírez Martínez, José, 53–54; Ramírez, Trinidad, 130n30; Rendón, Hermelinda, 131n41; Rizo Orozco, J. Inés, 162n69; Robles, Trinidad, 137n118; Rodarte Díaz, Antonio, 37; Rodríguez, Aurelio, 171n87; Rodríguez Castillo, Mario, 100; Rodríguez, Guadalupe, 163n85; Saavedra, Rafael, 79–80, *80*, 82, 161n61; Saldaña, Jacinto B., 45–46; Salud Morales, María, 152n105; Sánchez, Alejo and Martiniano, 89, 107; Sánchez, José María, 69; Sayago, Carlos, 52, 54; Sosa Portillo, Arnulfo, 20, 151n90; Suro, Guillermo, 52–53; Tamariz, Leonardo, 59; Toledano, Carlos, 52, 130n34; Topete, Everardo, 137–38n122; Torres, Guadalupe, 82–83; Treviño Martínez, Aliber, 29–30, *30*; Vázquez, Alfaro, 46; Wences, Natividad, 171n87

victims of other violence: Ariza, J. Guadalupe, 138n124; Camacho, María de la Luz, 148n58; Dolores, María Juana, 107; Espinosa, Isabel, 170n77; Fomperosa, Pedro, 71, 141n152; García Pinto, José, 73; Hernández, Delfina, 171n82; Juarez Serrano, Micaela, 104; Mena, Santiago, 156–57n151; Ortega, Pedro, 36; Pita, Agapito and Heliodoro, 38, 142n163; Prieto Mora, Miguel, 38; Rodríguez, Juan, 173n4; Tufiño, Aaron, 35–36, 175n15

vigilantes: Catholic lynch mobs involving the participation of, 142n3, 174n7; death squads, 3–4; distinguished from lynch mobs, 53–54, 122–23n13, 174n7; ear cropping and other bodily mutilations by, 51–53, 130n34, 134–35n82, 150–51nn84,89,91–92; general increase in Latin America of, 3–4; lynch mobs involving the participation of, 41, 118, 142n3, 174n7; militias (*defensas rurales*), 133n63; popular support for, 54, 152n108; Protestants attacked by, 56, 59, 156nn145,147, 174n7; religious motivations of, 53, 152n101; socialist teacher attacks, blurred lines between lynch mob violence and, 53–54, 152nn101,105,108; socialist teachers attacked by, 20, 51–52, 53–54, 131n42, 150n77, 151nn85,90. *See also* paramilitary groups; Unión Nacional Sinarquista (UNS)

vigilantism, as umbrella term, 122–23n13

Villa, Francisco, 151n91

Villanueva, Simón, 131n41, 150n82

violence: lower levels of, in post-revolutionary period, 6, 7. *See also* extralegal violence; lynching; press—representations of violence; violence against women

violence against women: domestic violence, lynchings of perpetrators of, 68, 81–82, 161n65; as normalized, 81; sexual violence, lynchings of perpetrators of, 28, 82–83, 162nn70,72,74

212 INDEX

Viqueira, Carmen, 104
Virgin of Guadalupe, 57, 152n101, 154n129

Webb, Clive, 124n27
witchcraft: deprecation of belief in, 100–102; *The Forgotten Village* (1941), anti-witchcraft film, 101–2, 169nn60,63; and gender, 90–91, 106–7, 108, 164–65n6; not classified as a crime, 90, 168n43; popularity of belief in, 100, 102, 103, 106, 169nn63,67, 170n74; producing both good and evil, vs. solely evil deeds, 165n7; Protestants as rejecting, 169n67. *See also* witches/healers/spiritists (*hierberas/curanderas/espiritistas*)
witches/healers/spiritists (*hierberas/curanderas/espiritistas*): ambiguous position/dual status in communities of, 90, 98–99, 102, 104–5, 165n7; denounced to local authorities, 98, 168n43; embrace of identity as witch, 90, 106–7, 108, 168n49, 171n90; healers as "returned from the dead," 168–69nn52,58; marginalized status of, 91, 97–98, 102, 108, 165n10; modern medicine's cultural mission to, 100–101, 103, 169n58; *nagual* (animal counterpart), 104, 170nn79–80; as "sacrificeable" characters, 125–26n46; and scapegoating, 91, 92, 103, 104, 108; terms for, 90, 100
—LYNCHING OF: overview, 92, 108; bloodsucking witches (*tlahuelpuchi*), 97–98, 99, 167–68n41, 172n93; as community sanctioned, 5, 91–92, 107, 108; cruelty of torments in, 91, 99–100, 105–6, 107, 108, 168nn50–51, 170n77, 171n87; earthly concerns reflected in, 90; economic misfortune and, 90, 92, 165n10; local authorities' complicity in, 98, 99, 100, 103, 106; and modernization, exposure to, 11, 92; narratives of, 89, 97, 98, 99, 100, 102–6, 168n45, 169n55, 170nn76–77; older women, 90, 91, 92, 165n10; personal vendettas and intracommunity conflicts and, 90, 97, 104–5, 170n80, 171n82; political conflicts and, 90, 92, 97, 104, 105–6, 171n89; political conflicts and (Micaela Ortega), 40, 49, 105–6, 140n143, 149n68; press representations of, 102; prosecution/investigation of, 89, 98, 103; sickness and death of family members and, 90, 92, 98, 99, 102–4, 105, 107, 108, 168n49, 169n55, 172n93; status of the accuser and, 102, 103, 170n69; women as overrepresented victims in, 90–91, 92, 164–65nn6,10
women: domestic violence against, lynchings motivated by, 68, 81–82, 161n65; as main perpetrator of lynchings, 82, 83, 86, 126n49, 162n69; sexual violence against, lynchings motivated by, 28, 82–83, 162nn70,72,74. *See also* gender; witchcraft
workers' and peasants' rights: Manuel Ávila Camacho and distancing from, 56; as challenge to private property, 51; Mexican Revolution as driven by, 124n23
World War II: Catholic Church's fear of Protestant missioners and, 155n136; Catholic Church's support for Mexican entry into, 154n126; and Mexico's "economic miracle," 7; and military conscription, 23; and temporary reinstatement of the death penalty in limited circumstances, 158n15

Yucatán (state), 74–75, 145n29

Zacatecas (state), 52–53, 99, 134–35n82
Zapata, Emiliano, 151n91

Founded in 1893,
UNIVERSITY OF CALIFORNIA PRESS
publishes bold, progressive books and journals
on topics in the arts, humanities, social sciences,
and natural sciences—with a focus on social
justice issues—that inspire thought and action
among readers worldwide.

The UC PRESS FOUNDATION
raises funds to uphold the press's vital role
as an independent, nonprofit publisher, and
receives philanthropic support from a wide
range of individuals and institutions—and from
committed readers like you. To learn more, visit
ucpress.edu/supportus.

www.ingramcontent.com/pod-product-compliance
Lightning Source LLC
Chambersburg PA
CBHW030650230426
43665CB00011B/1028